You are going the *wrong way!*

Manga is a *completely* different type of reading experience.

To start at the *BEGINNING,* go to the *END!*

That's right! Authentic manga is read the traditional Japanese way—from right to left, exactly the opposite of how American books are read. It's easy to follow: just go to the other end of the book, and read each page—and each panel—from the right side to the left side, starting at the top right. Now you're experiencing manga as it was meant to be.

A Kodansha Comics Trade Paperback Original
Attack on Titan volume 9 copyright © 2012 Hajime Isayama
English translation copyright © 2013 Hajime Isayama

Published in the United States by Kodansha Comics, an imprint of Kodansha USA Publishing, LLC, New York.

Publication rights for this English edition arranged through Kodansha Ltd, Tokyo.

First published in Japan in 2012 by Kodansha Ltd., Tokyo as *Shingeki no Kyojin*, volume 9.

ISBN 978-1-61262-548-5

Original cover design by Takashi Shimoyama (Red Rooster)

Printed in the United States of America.

www.kodanshacomics.com

9 8 7 6
Translation: Ko Ransom
Lettering: Steve Wands
Editing: Ben Applegate

ATTACK ON TITAN
9
HAJIME ISAYAMA

"Attack on Titan" Character Introductions

104th Corps

Graduated at the top of her training corps, Mikasa is a highly talented soldier. Her parents were murdered before her eyes when she was a child, but Eren saved her life. Since then, she has made it her mission to protect him.

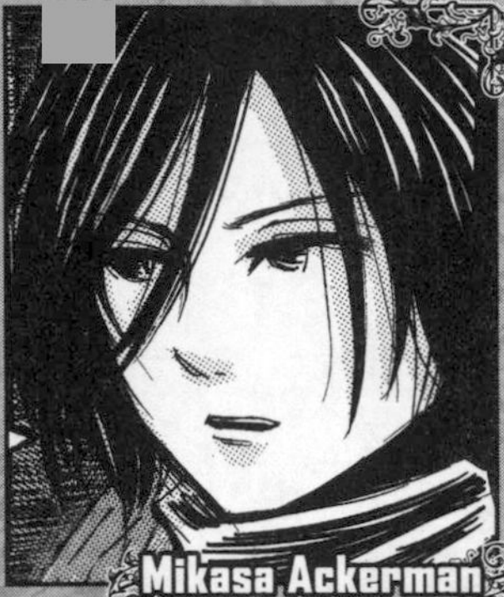
Mikasa Ackerman

Eren joined the Survey Corps out of his longing for the world outside the wall and his hatred of the Titans. He has the power to turn himself into a Titan, but its origins are unknown.

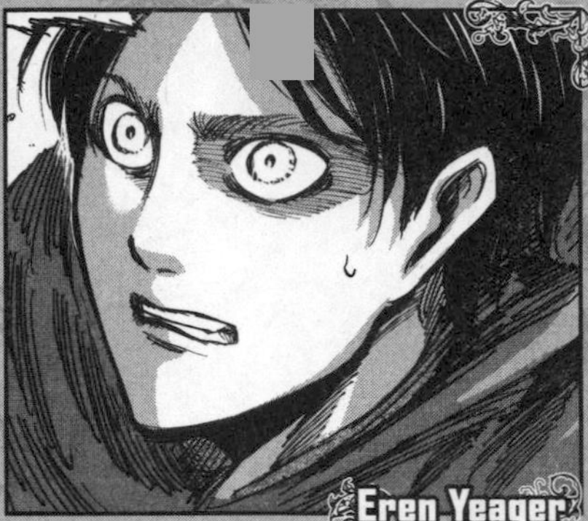
Eren Yeager

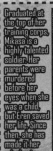

Survey Corps

Soldiers who are prepared to sacrifice themselves as they brave the Titan territory outside the walls.

Eren and Mikasa's childhood friend. Though Armin isn't athletic in the least, he possesses both sharp observational powers and keen insight, and he exhibits an extraordinary ability to develop strategies.

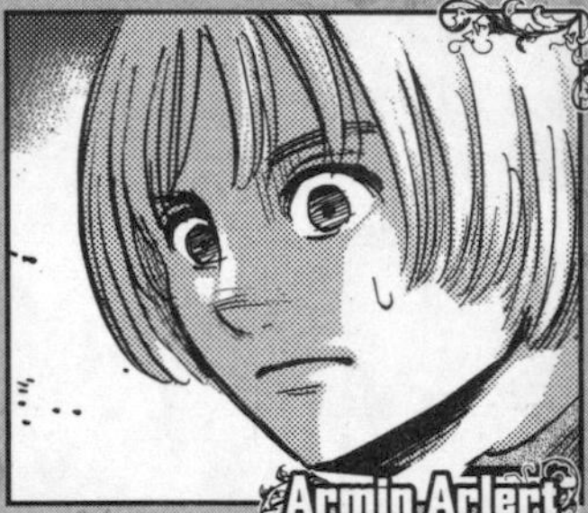
Armin Arlert

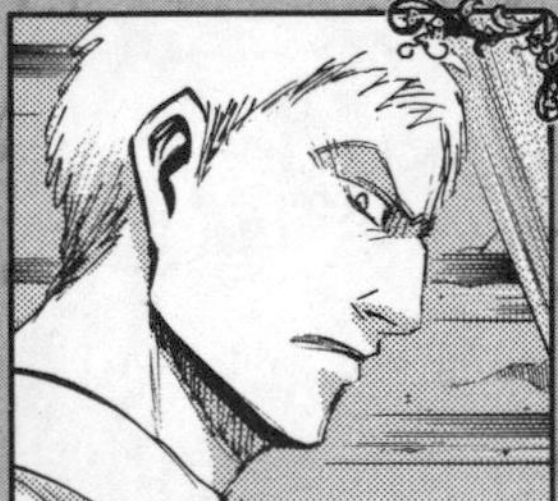
Reiner Braun

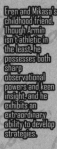

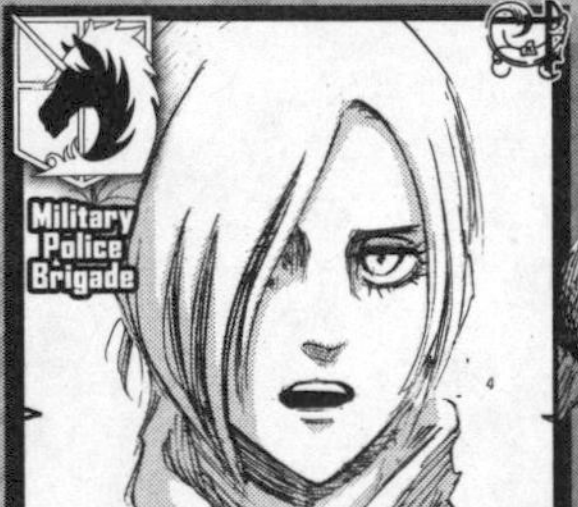
Military Police Brigade
Annie Leonhart

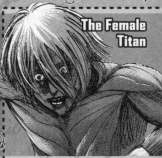

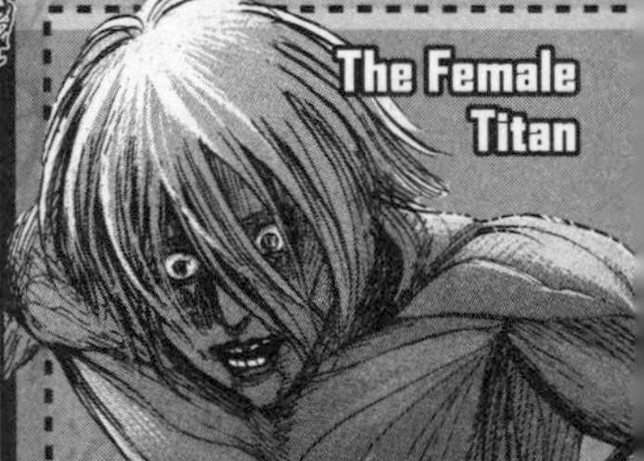
The Female Titan

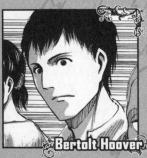

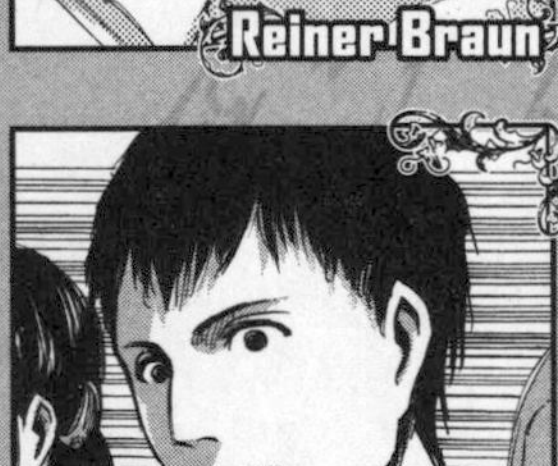
Bertolt Hoover

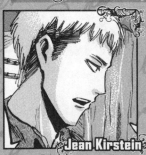

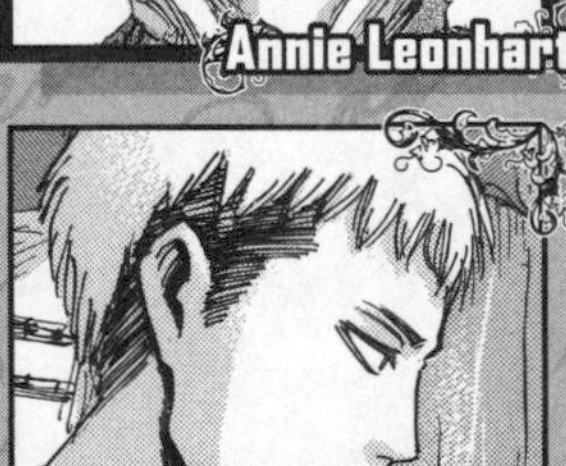
Jean Kirstein

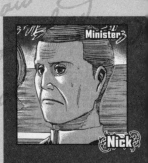

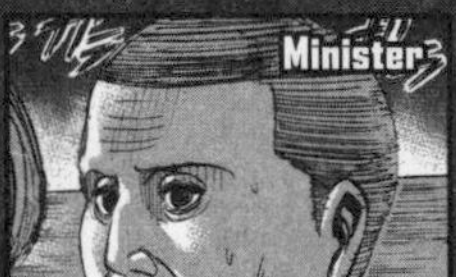
Minister
Nick

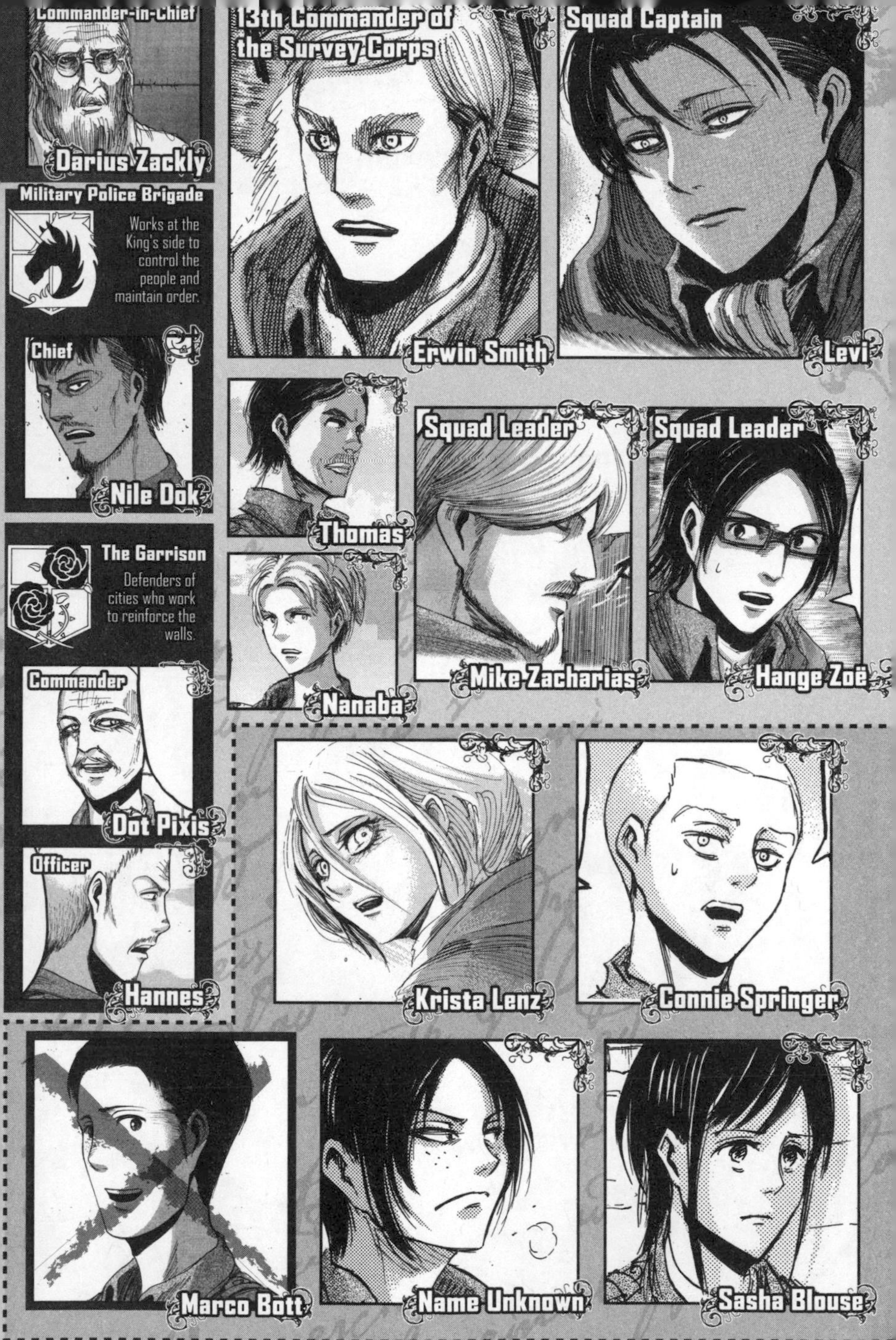

Squad Captain
Levi
13th Commander of the Survey Corps
Erwin Smith
Squad Leader
Hange Zoë
Squad Leader
Mike Zacharias
Thomas
Nanaba
Commander-in-Chief
Darius Zackly
Military Police Brigade
Works at the King's side to control the people and maintain order.
Chief
Nile Dok
The Garrison
Defenders of cities who work to reinforce the walls.
Commander
Dot Pixis
Officer
Hannes
Connie Springer
Krista Lenz
Sasha Blouse
Name Unknown
Marco Bott

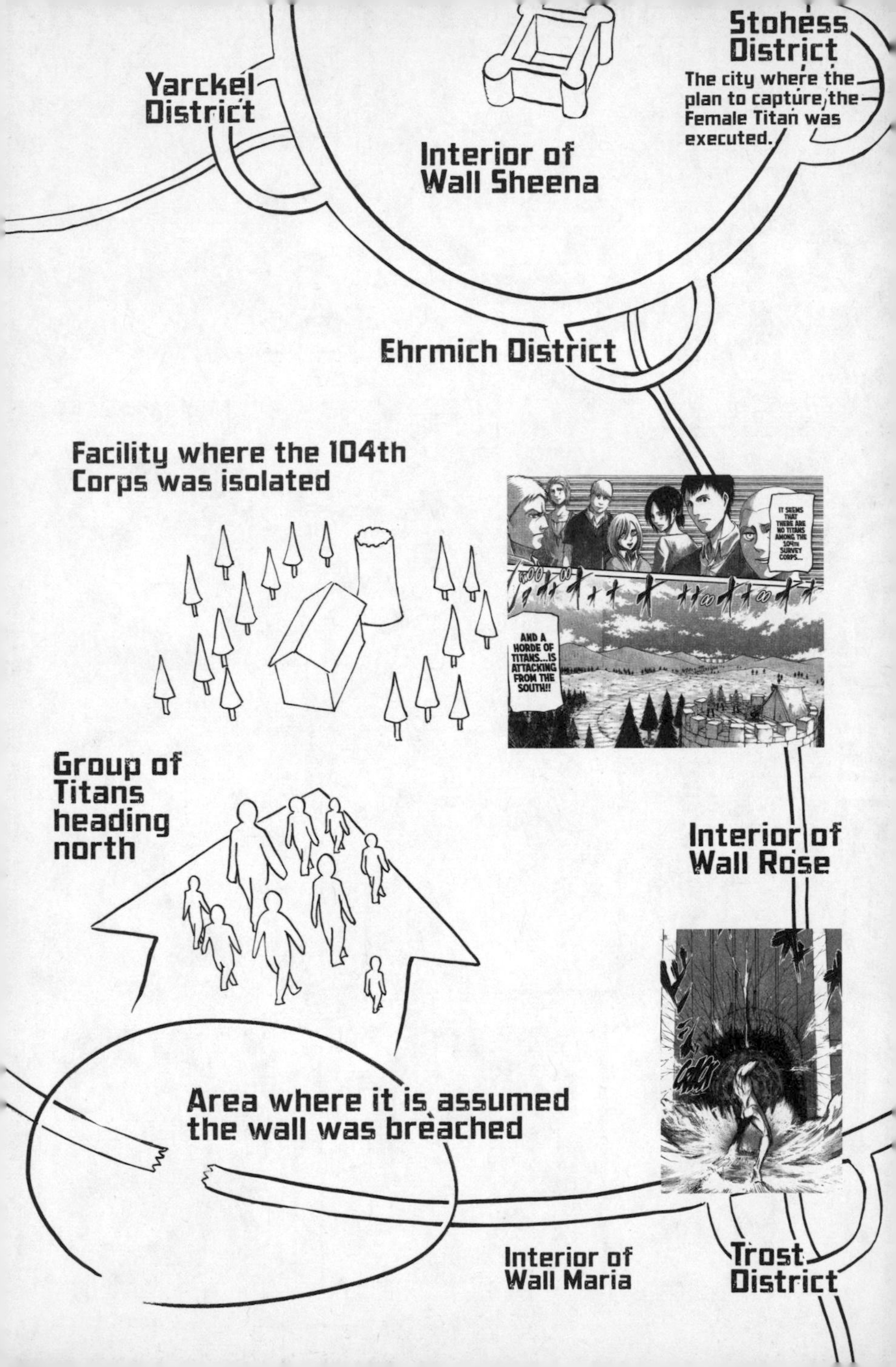
Stohess District
The city where the plan to capture the Female Titan was executed.
Yarckel District
Interior of Wall Sheena
Ehrmich District
Facility where the 104th Corps was isolated
IT SEEMS THAT THERE ARE NO TITANS AMONG THE 104TH SURVEY CORPS...
AND A HORDE OF TITANS...IS ATTACKING FROM THE SOUTH!!
Group of Titans heading north
Interior of Wall Rose
Area where it is assumed the wall was breached
Interior of Wall Maria
Trost District

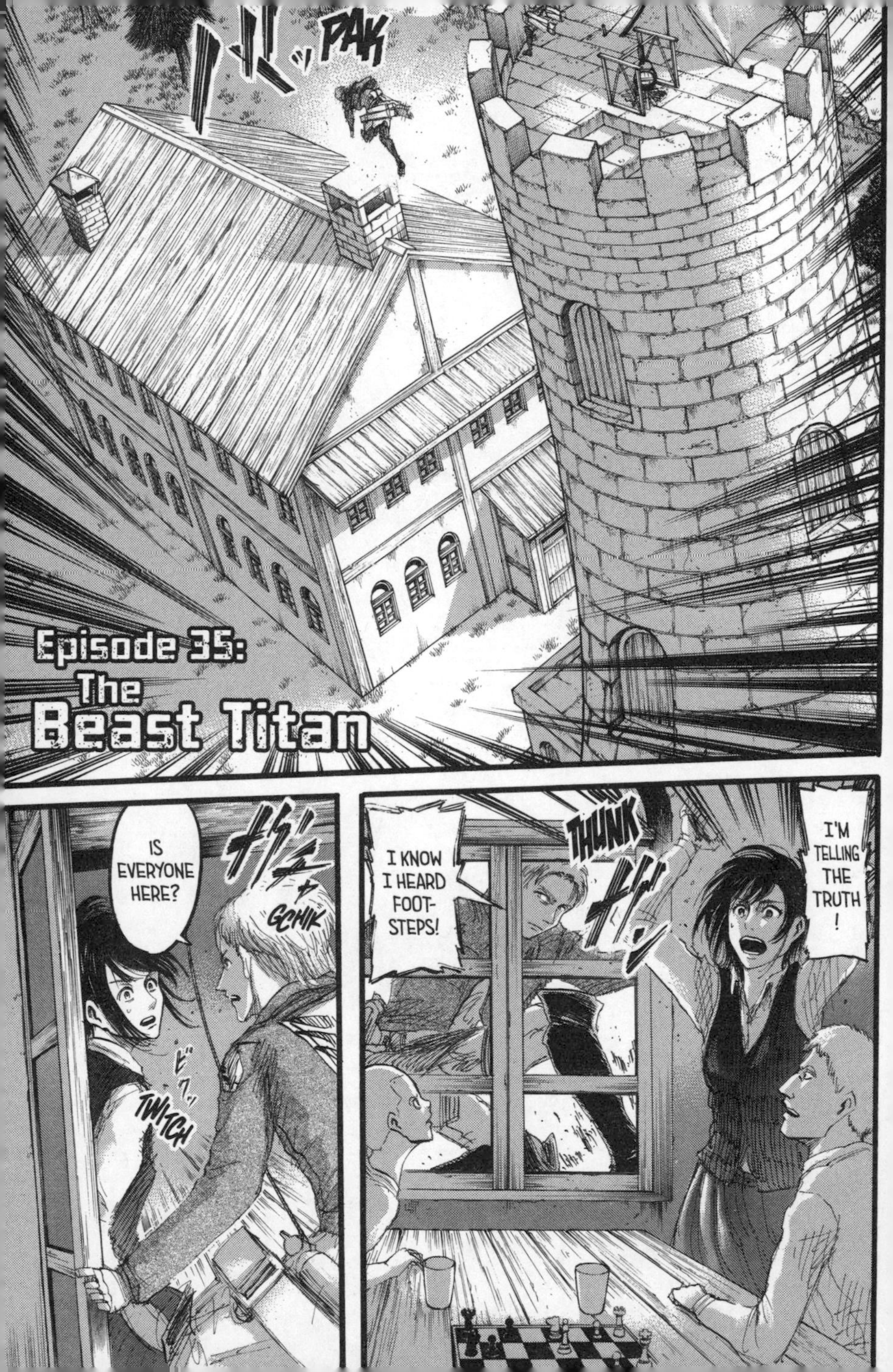
PAK
Episode 35:
The Beast Titan
I'M TELLING THE TRUTH!
THUNK
I KNOW I HEARD FOOT-STEPS!
IS EVERYONE HERE?
GCHIK
TWITCH

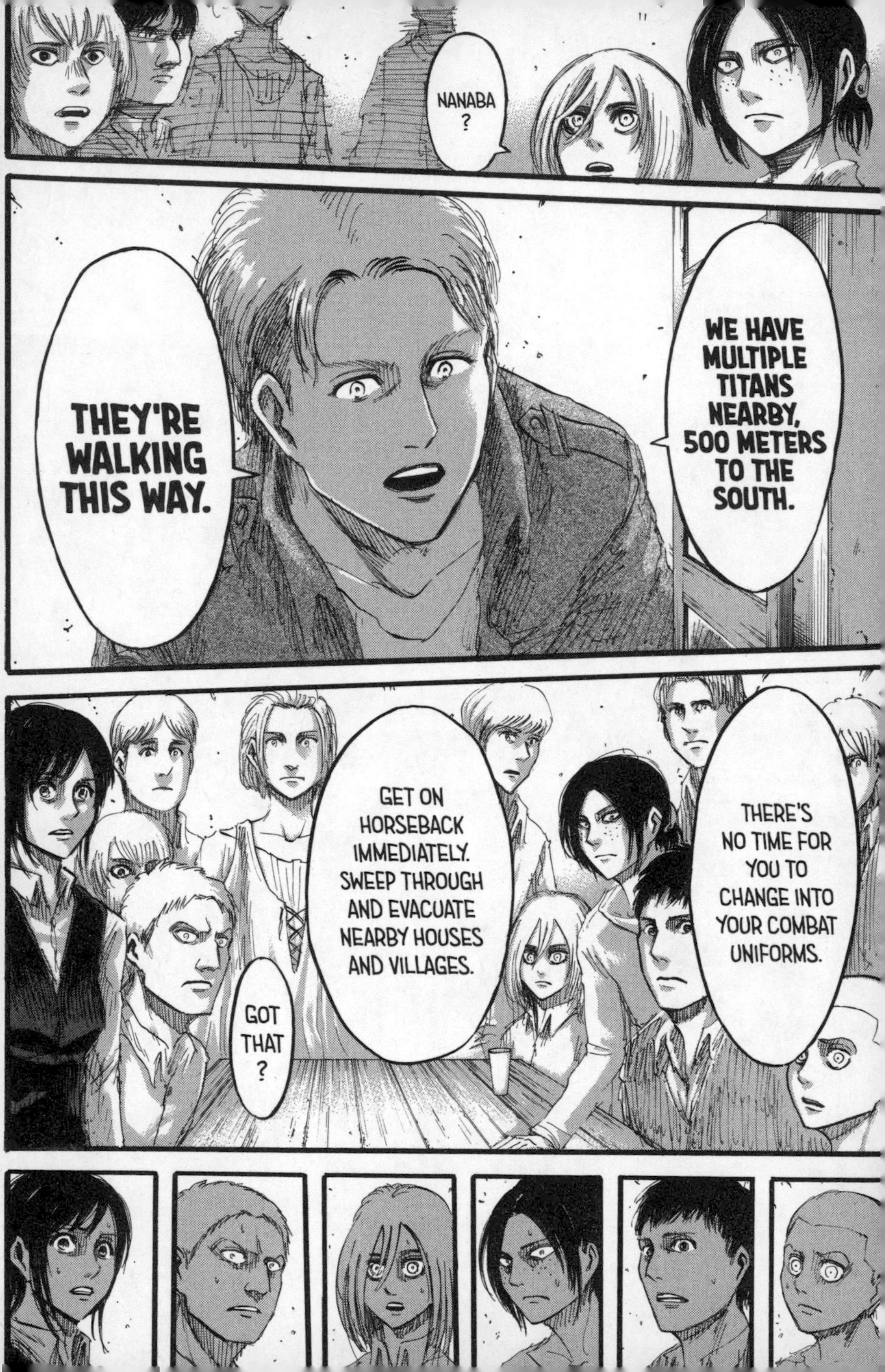
NANABA ?
WE HAVE MULTIPLE TITANS NEARBY, 500 METERS TO THE SOUTH.
THEY'RE WALKING THIS WAY.
THERE'S NO TIME FOR YOU TO CHANGE INTO YOUR COMBAT UNIFORMS.
GET ON HORSEBACK IMMEDIATELY. SWEEP THROUGH AND EVACUATE NEARBY HOUSES AND VILLAGES.
GOT THAT ?

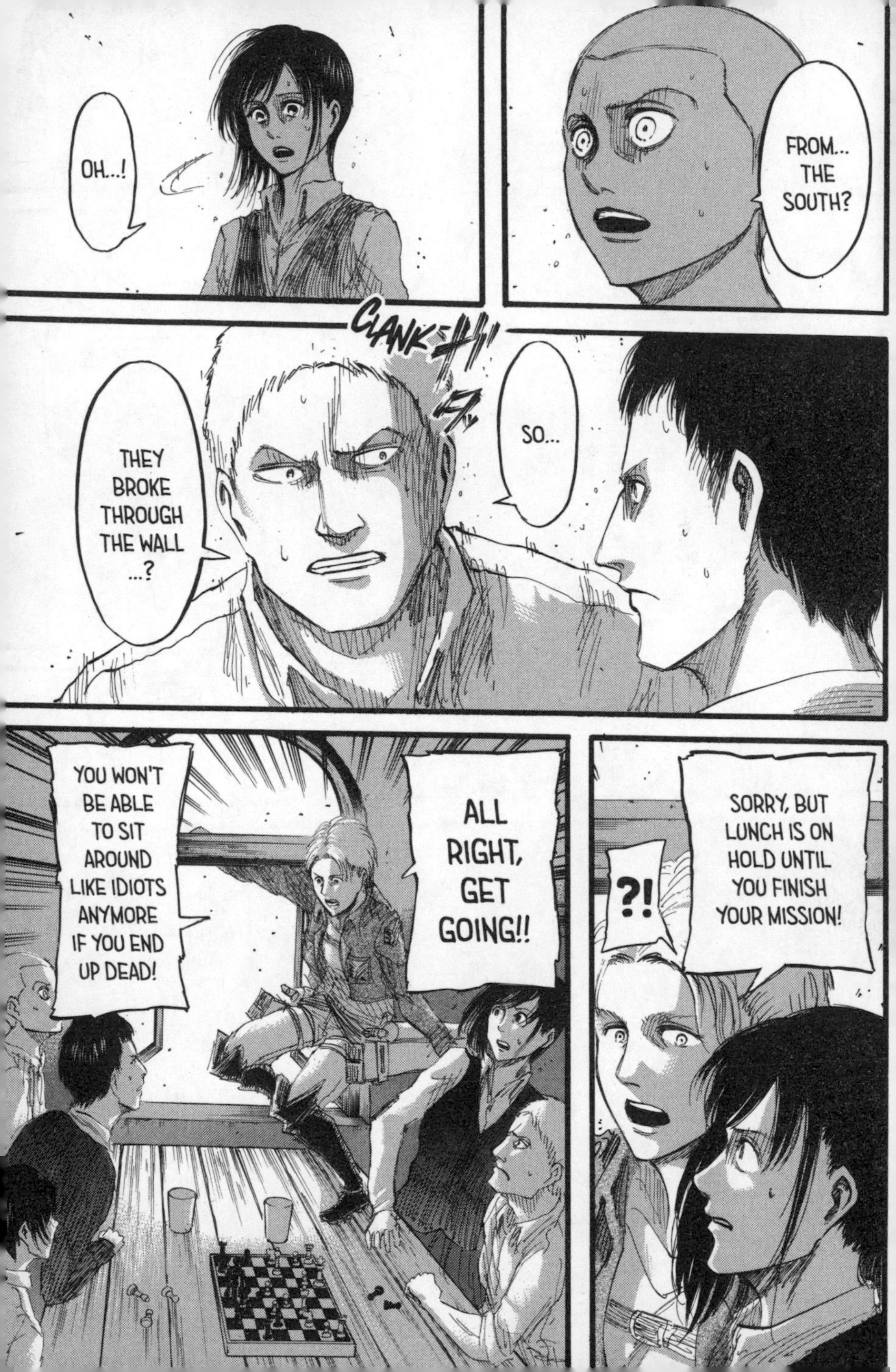
FROM... THE SOUTH?
OH...!
CLANK
SO...
THEY BROKE THROUGH THE WALL ...?
SORRY, BUT LUNCH IS ON HOLD UNTIL YOU FINISH YOUR MISSION!
?!
ALL RIGHT, GET GOING!!
YOU WON'T BE ABLE TO SIT AROUND LIKE IDIOTS ANYMORE IF YOU END UP DEAD!

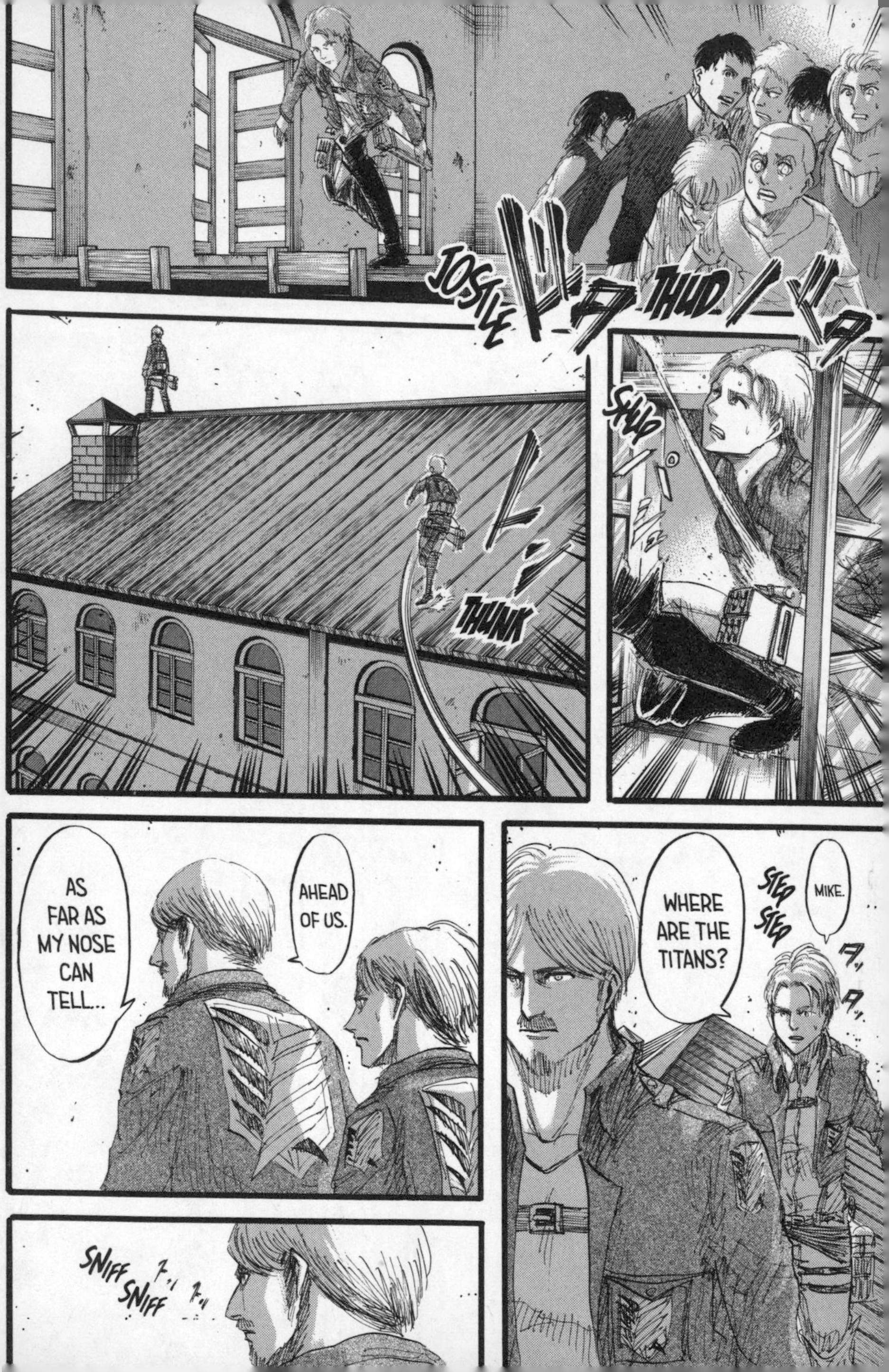
THUD
JOSTLE
THUNK
MIKE.
STEP STEP
WHERE ARE THE TITANS?
AHEAD OF US.
AS FAR AS MY NOSE CAN TELL...
SNIFF SNIFF

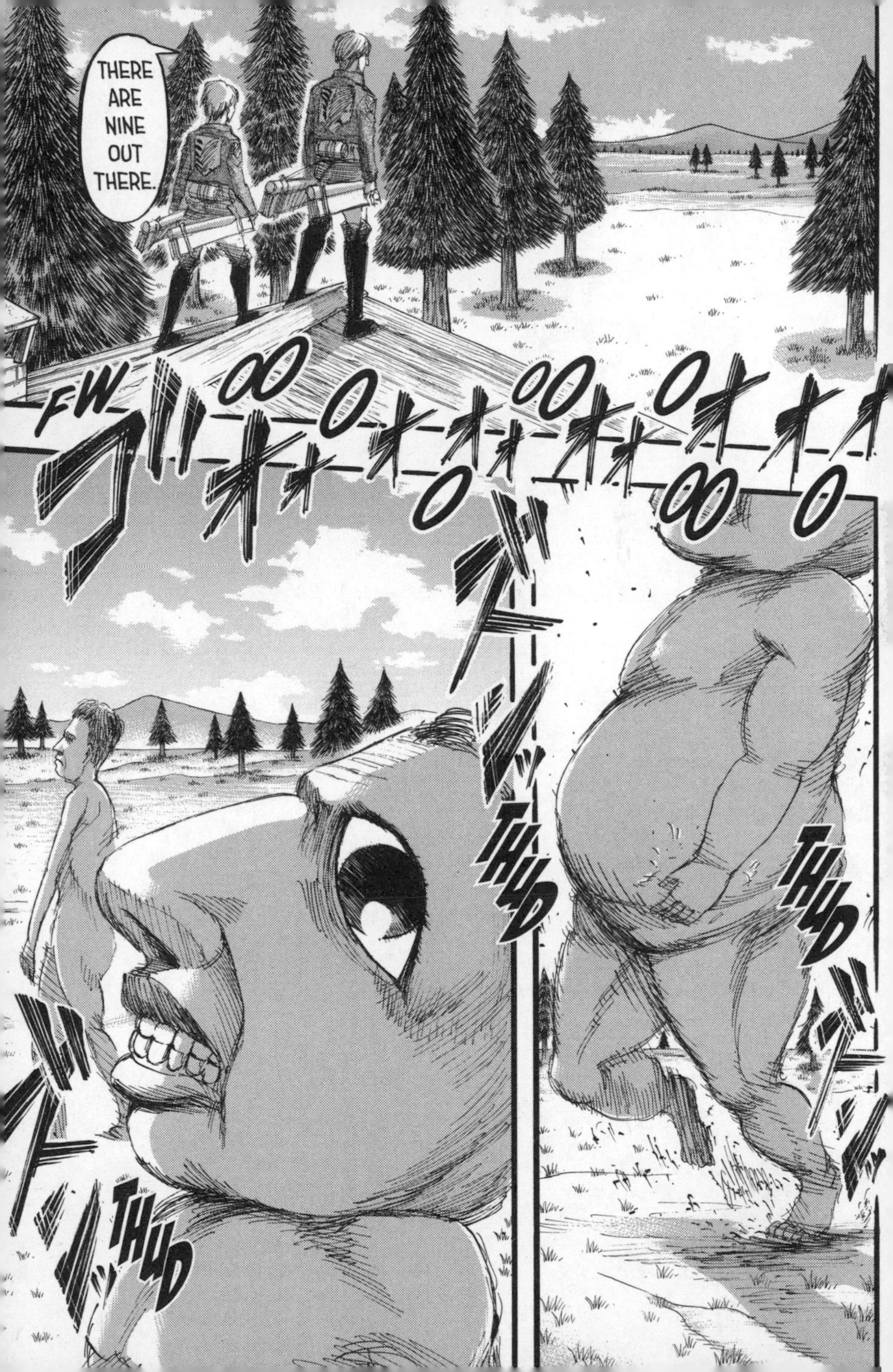
THERE ARE NINE OUT THERE.
FWOOOOOOOOOO
THUD
THUD
THUD

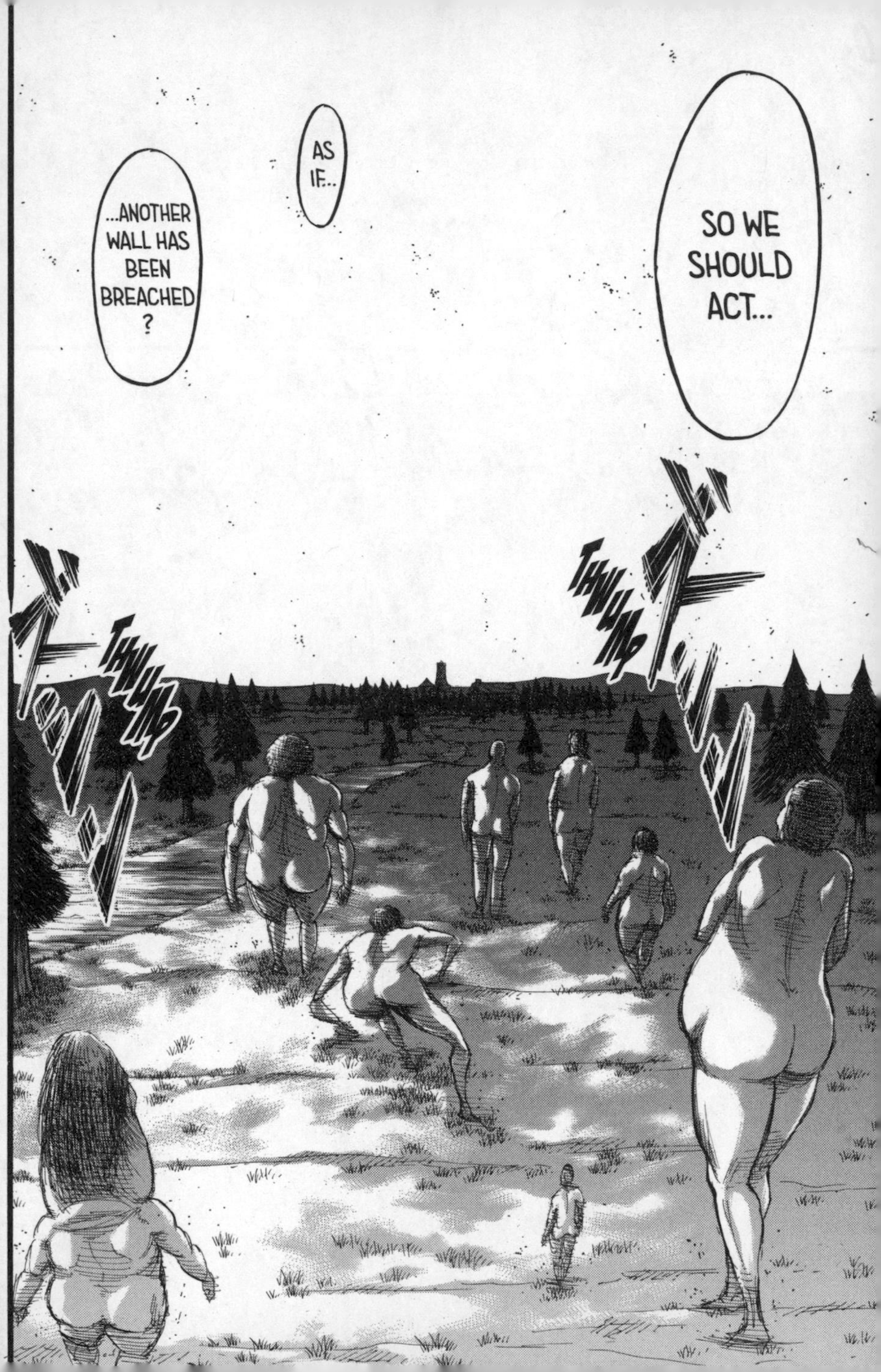
SO WE SHOULD ACT...
AS IF...
...ANOTHER WALL HAS BEEN BREACHED?
THUMP
THUMP

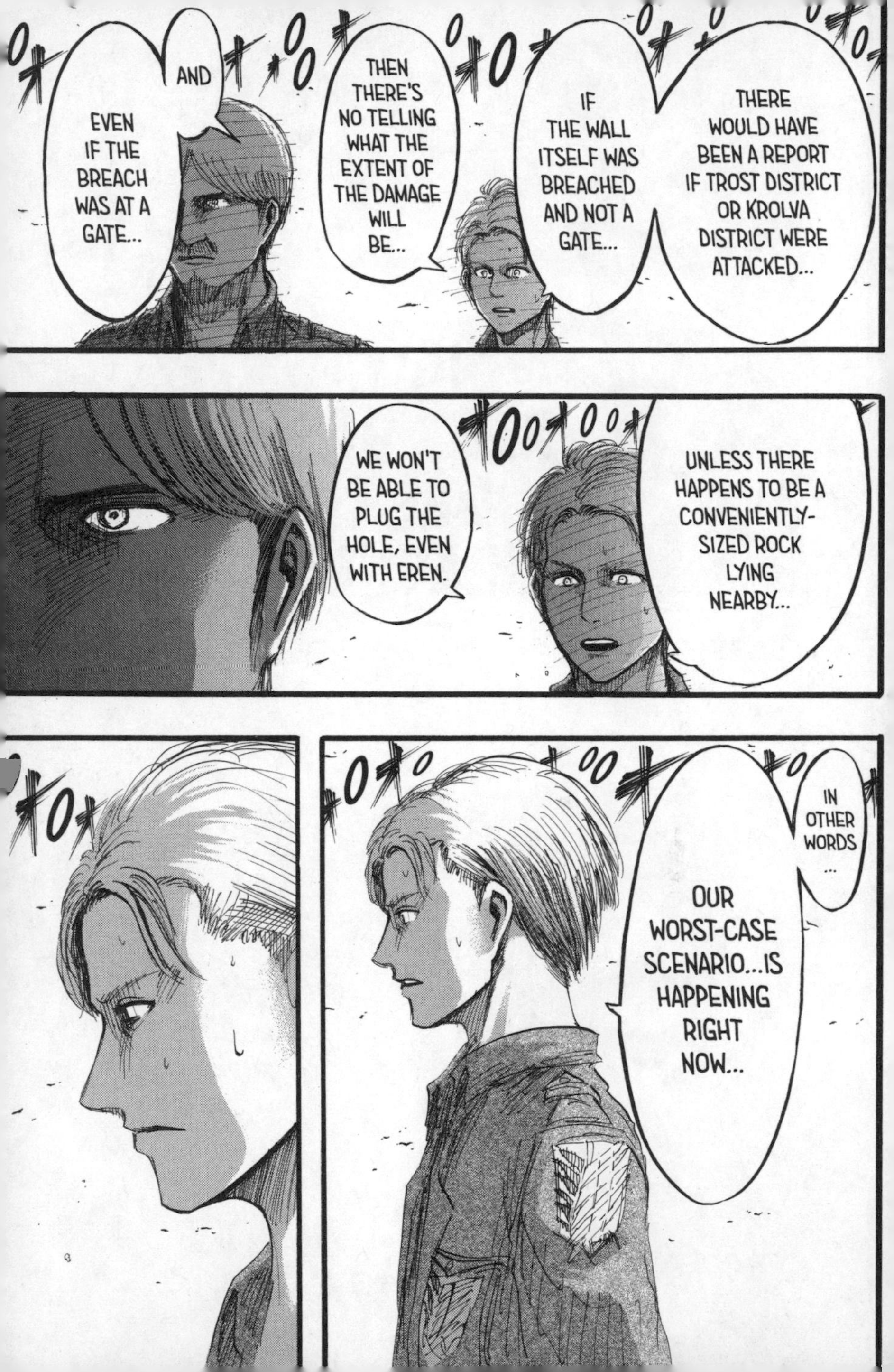
THERE WOULD HAVE BEEN A REPORT IF TROST DISTRICT OR KROLVA DISTRICT WERE ATTACKED...
IF THE WALL ITSELF WAS BREACHED AND NOT A GATE...
THEN THERE'S NO TELLING WHAT THE EXTENT OF THE DAMAGE WILL BE...
AND
EVEN IF THE BREACH WAS AT A GATE...
UNLESS THERE HAPPENS TO BE A CONVENIENTLY-SIZED ROCK LYING NEARBY...
WE WON'T BE ABLE TO PLUG THE HOLE, EVEN WITH EREN.
IN OTHER WORDS...
OUR WORST-CASE SCENARIO...IS HAPPENING RIGHT NOW...

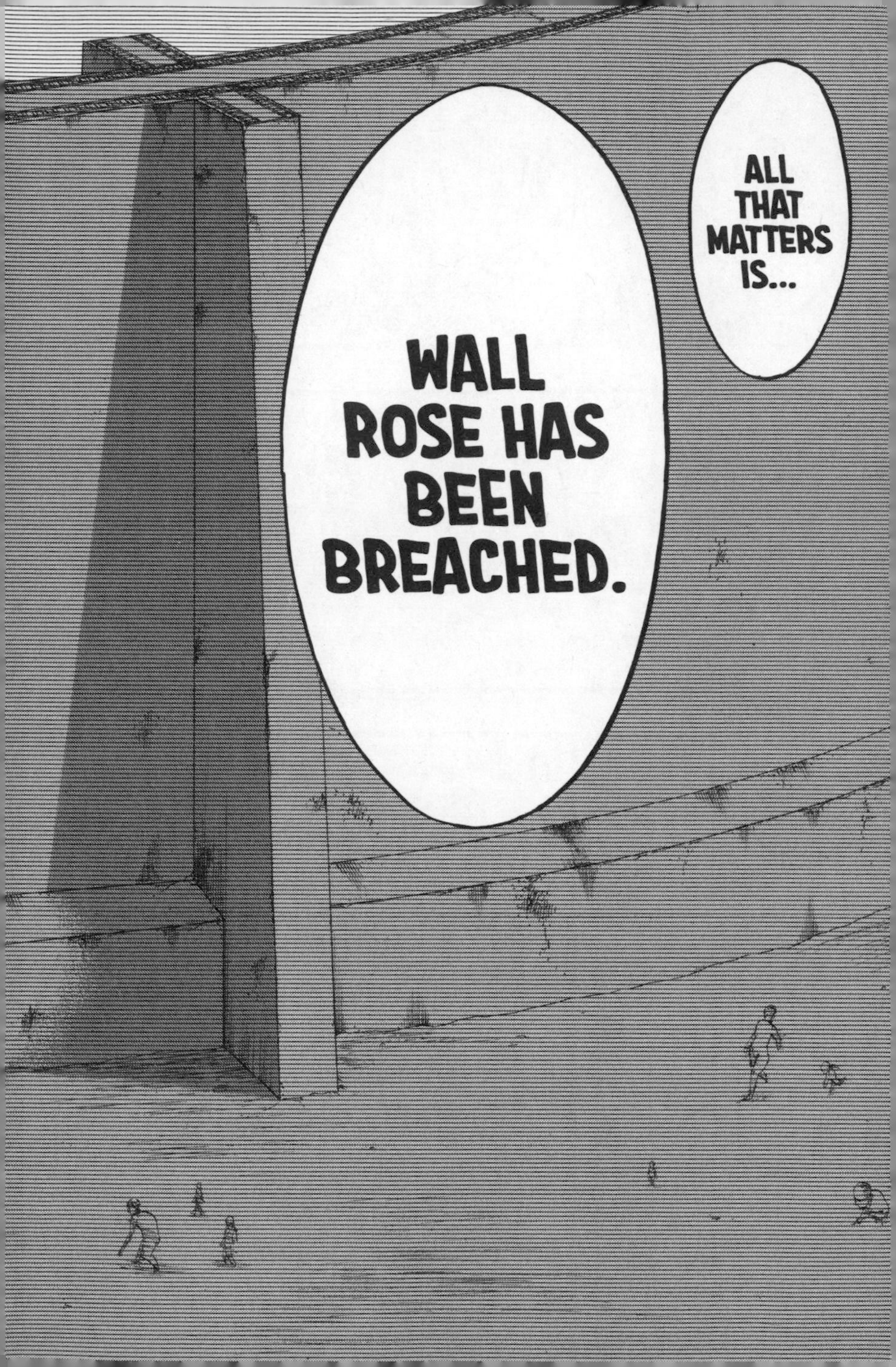
ALL THAT MATTERS IS...
WALL ROSE HAS BEEN BREACHED.

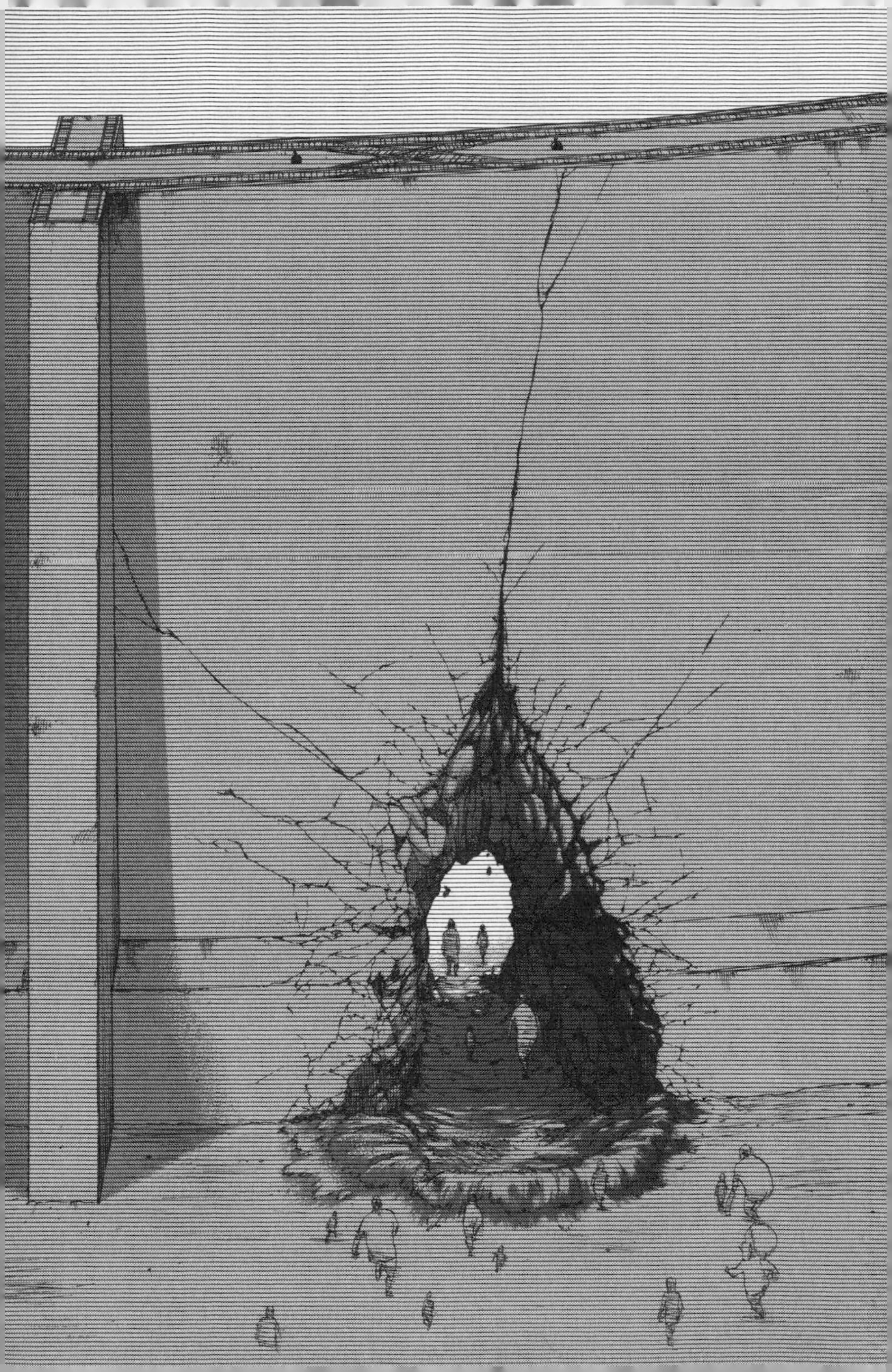

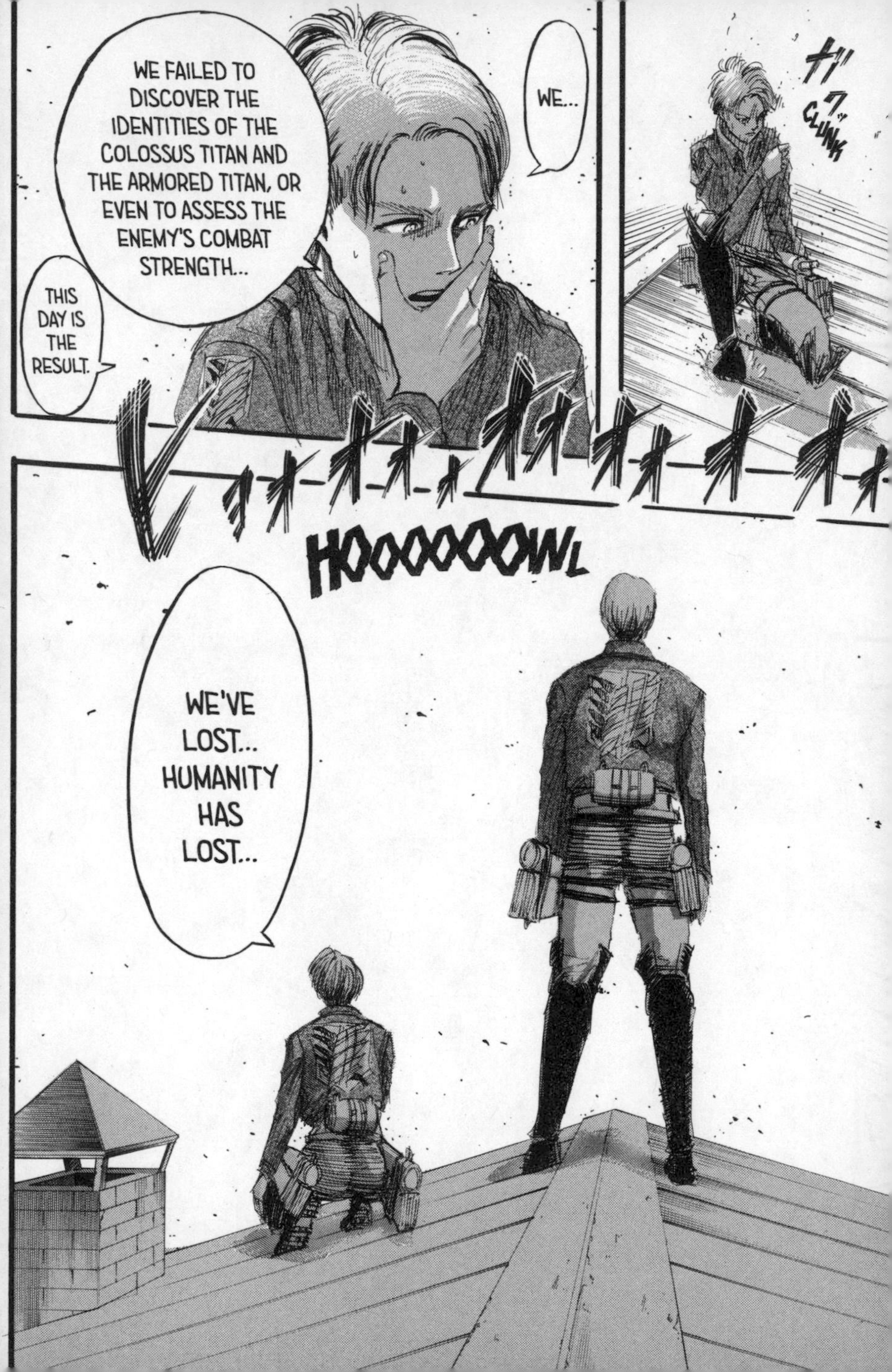
CLUNK
WE...
WE FAILED TO DISCOVER THE IDENTITIES OF THE COLOSSUS TITAN AND THE ARMORED TITAN, OR EVEN TO ASSESS THE ENEMY'S COMBAT STRENGTH...
THIS DAY IS THE RESULT.
HOOOOOOWL
WE'VE LOST... HUMANITY HAS LOST...

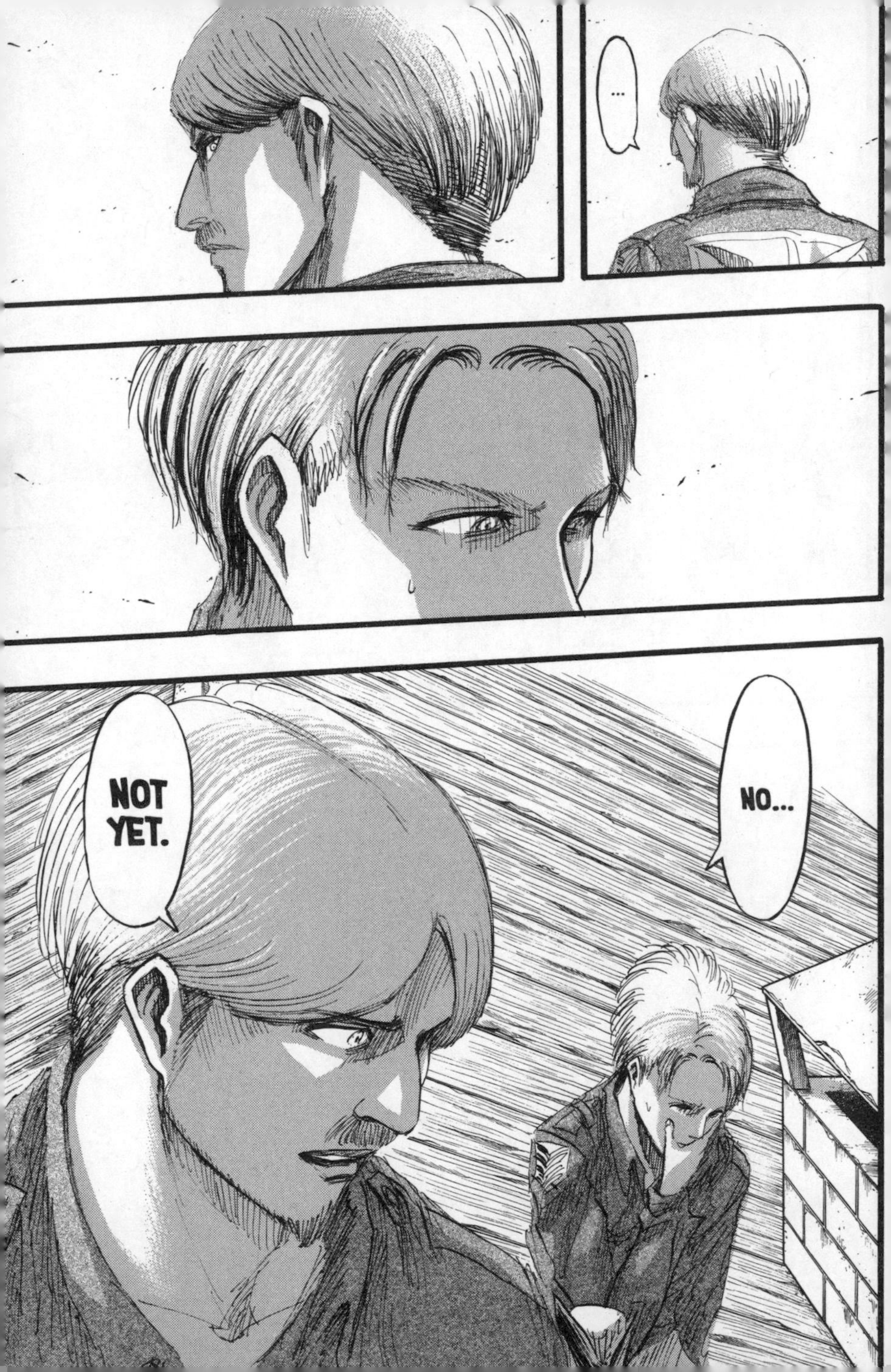
…
NO...
NOT YET.

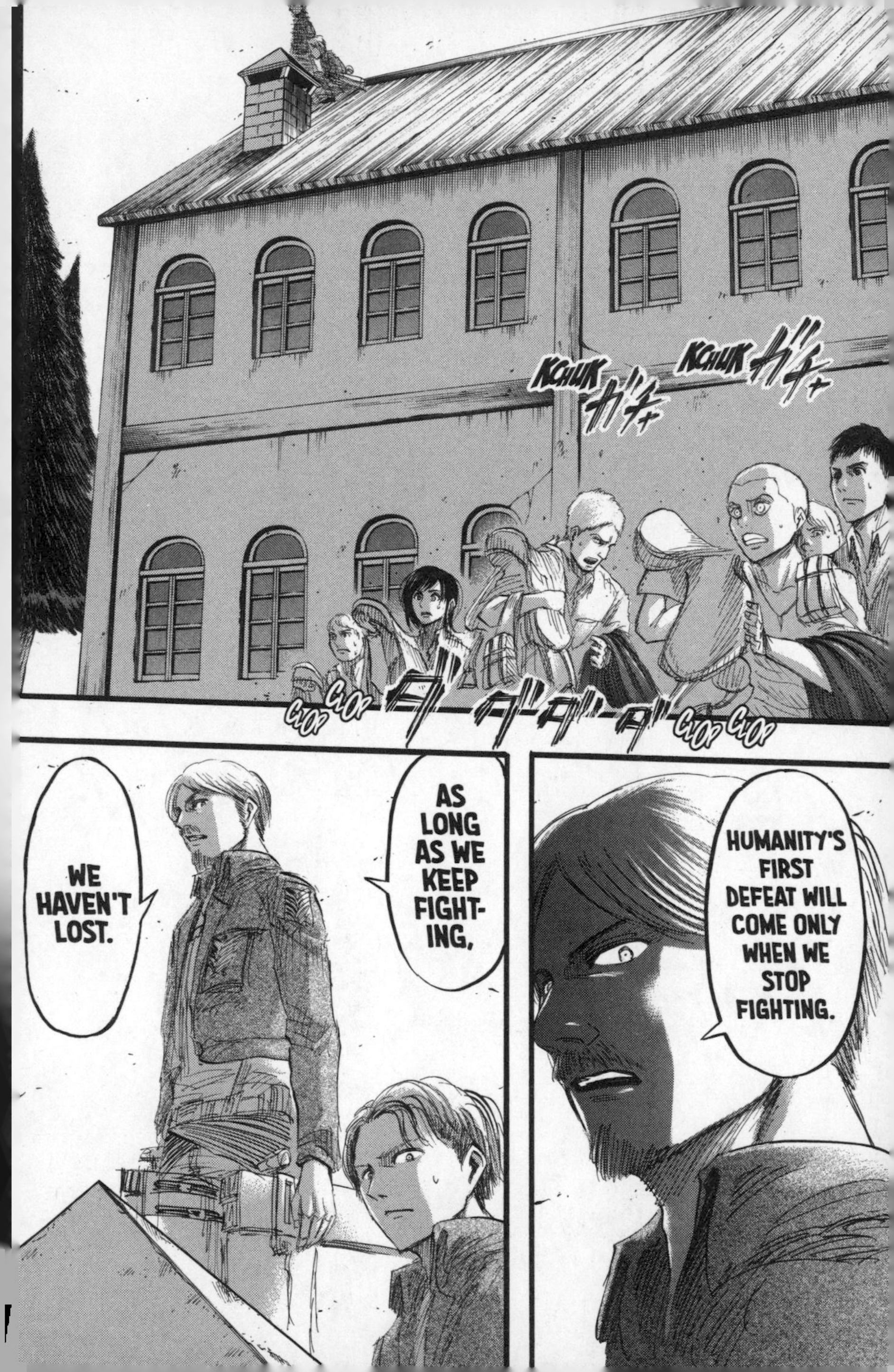
KCHUK
KCHUK
CLOP CLOP
CLOP CLOP
WE HAVEN'T LOST.
AS LONG AS WE KEEP FIGHT-ING,
HUMANITY'S FIRST DEFEAT WILL COME ONLY WHEN WE STOP FIGHTING.

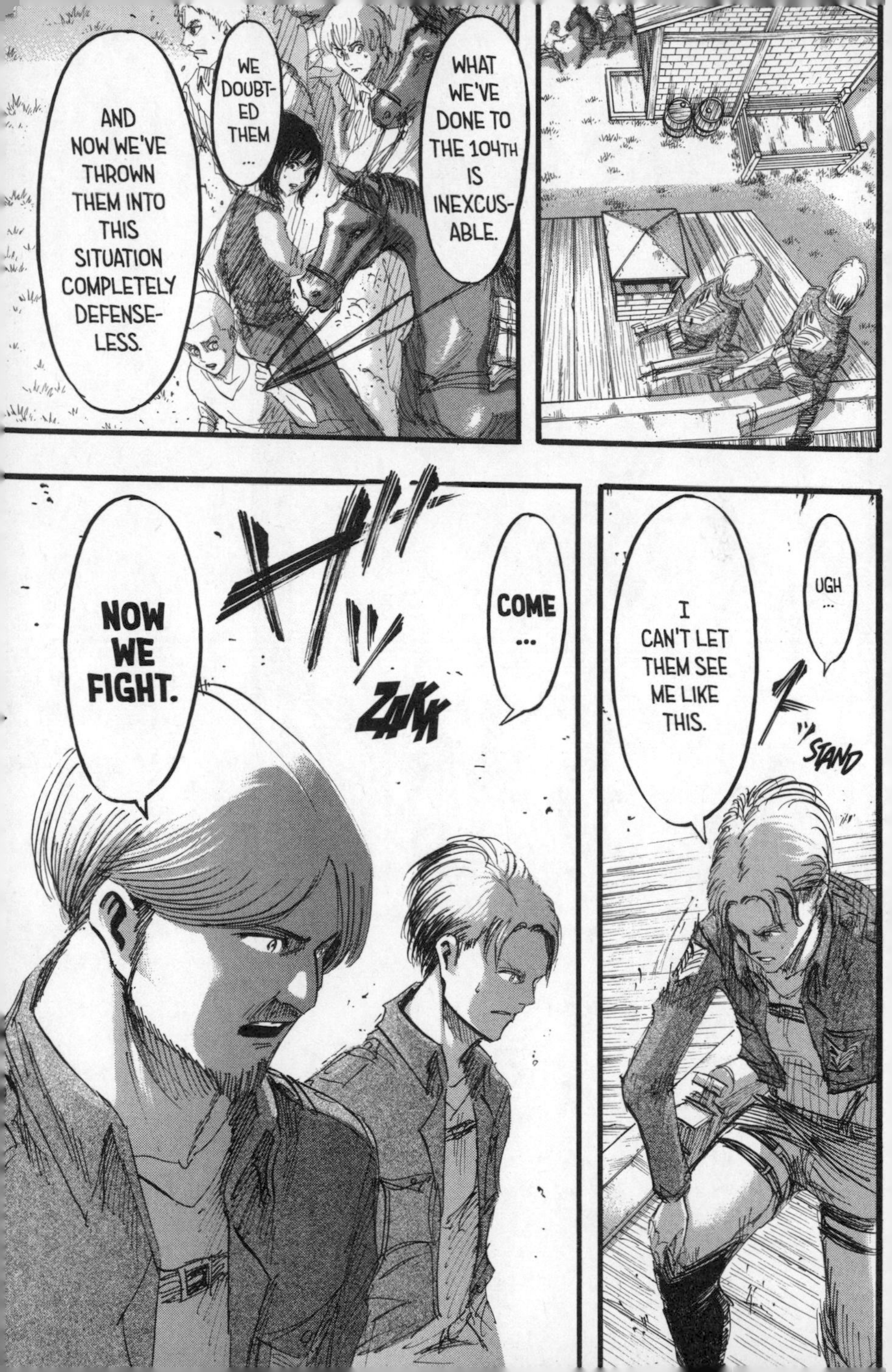
WHAT WE'VE DONE TO THE 104TH IS INEXCUSABLE.
WE DOUBTED THEM ...
AND NOW WE'VE THROWN THEM INTO THIS SITUATION COMPLETELY DEFENSELESS.
UGH ...
I CAN'T LET THEM SEE ME LIKE THIS.
STAND
COME ...
ZAKK
NOW WE FIGHT.

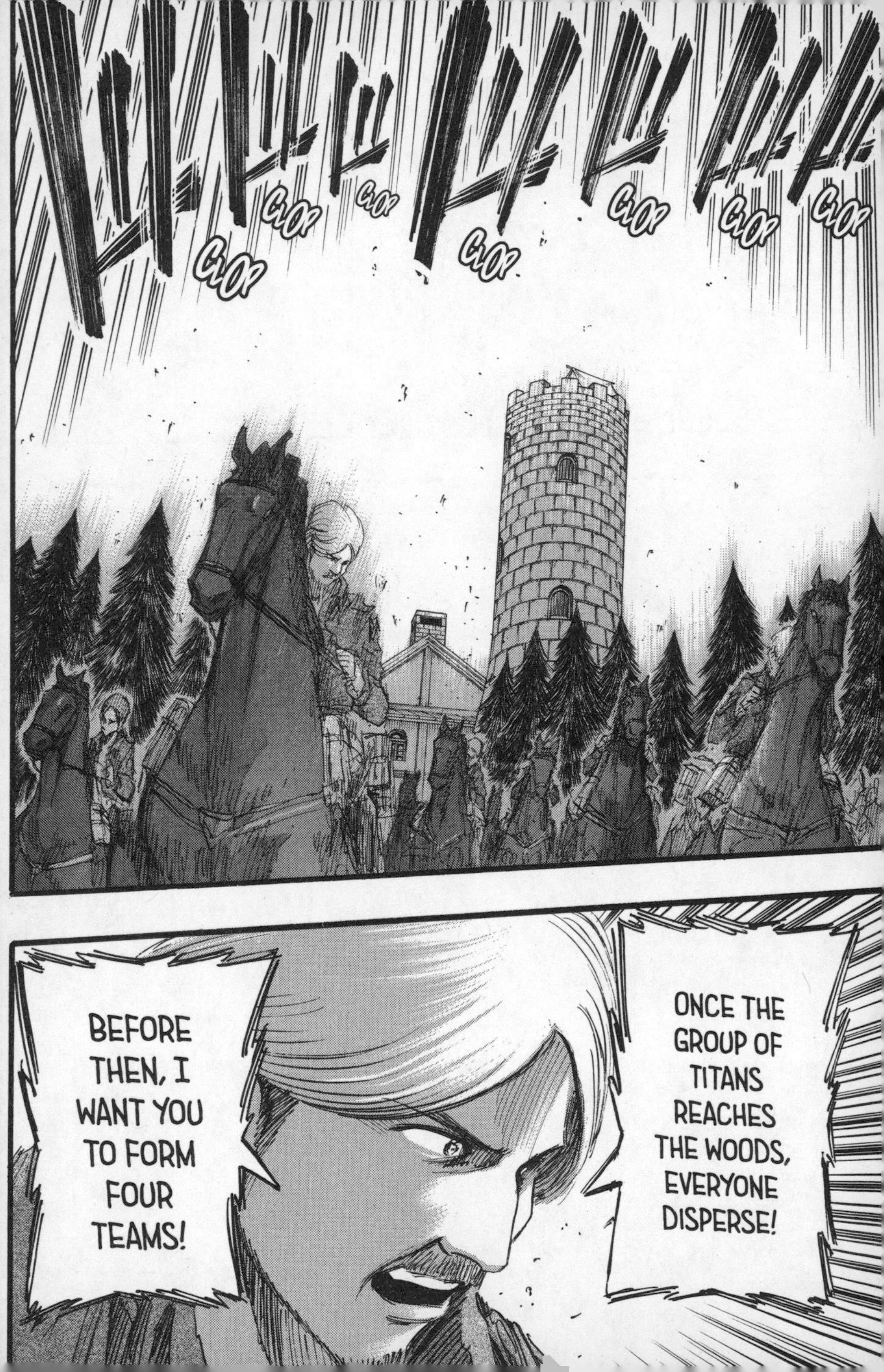
CLOP
CLOP
CLOP
CLOP
CLOP
CLOP
CLOP
ONCE THE GROUP OF TITANS REACHES THE WOODS, EVERYONE DISPERSE!
BEFORE THEN, I WANT YOU TO FORM FOUR TEAMS!

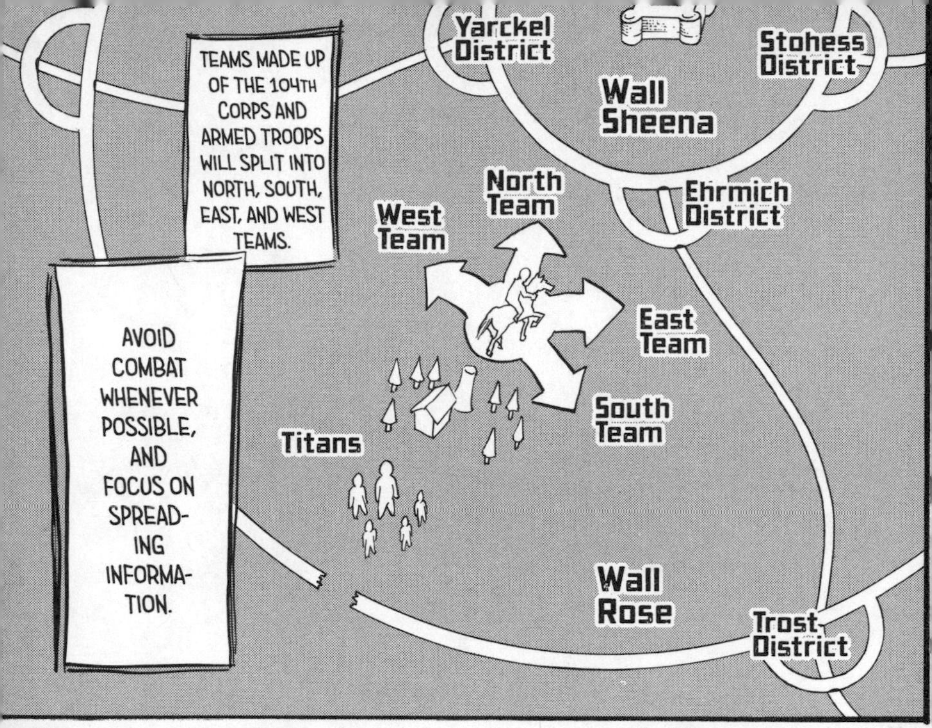

Stohess District
Yarckel District
Wall Sheena
Ehrmich District
North Team
West Team
TEAMS MADE UP OF THE 104TH CORPS AND ARMED TROOPS WILL SPLIT INTO NORTH, SOUTH, EAST, AND WEST TEAMS.
East Team
South Team
AVOID COMBAT WHENEVER POSSIBLE, AND FOCUS ON SPREADING INFORMATION.
Titans
Wall Rose
Trost District

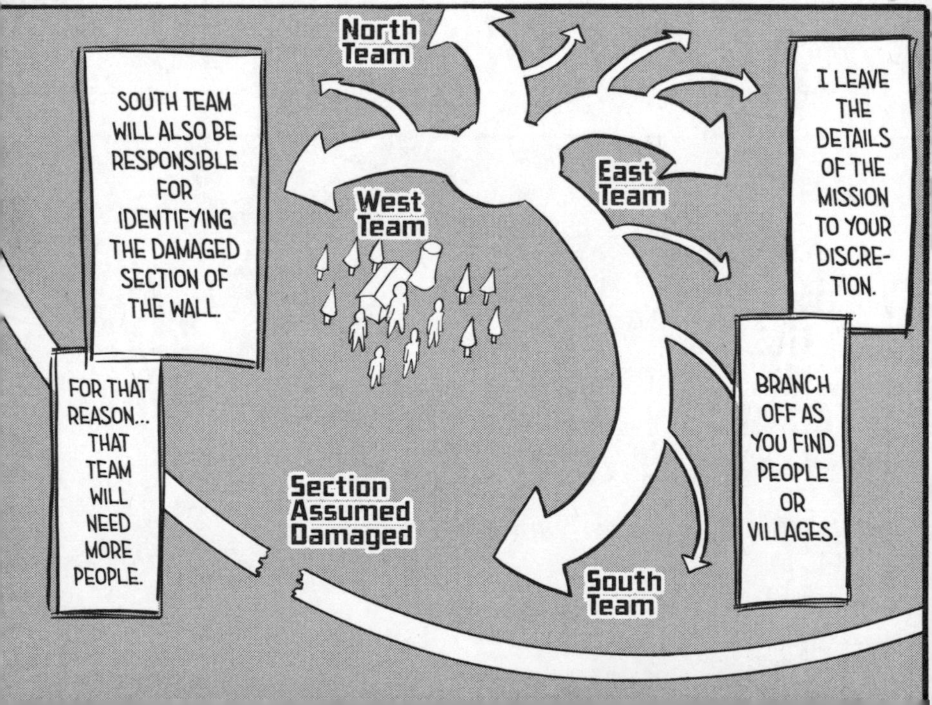

I LEAVE THE DETAILS OF THE MISSION TO YOUR DISCRETION.
North Team
SOUTH TEAM WILL ALSO BE RESPONSIBLE FOR IDENTIFYING THE DAMAGED SECTION OF THE WALL.
East Team
West Team
BRANCH OFF AS YOU FIND PEOPLE OR VILLAGES.
FOR THAT REASON... THAT TEAM WILL NEED MORE PEOPLE.
Section Assumed Damaged
South Team

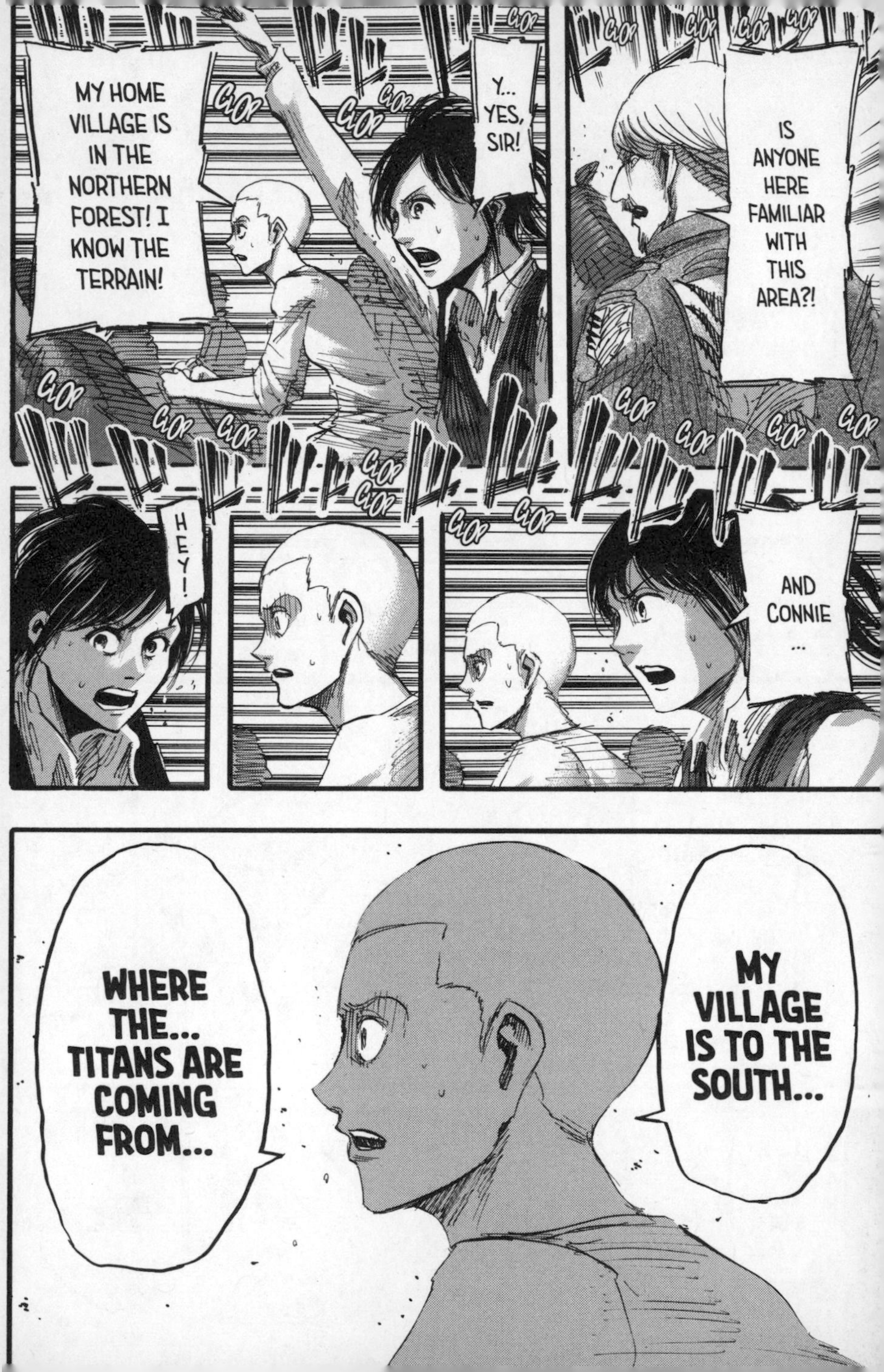

CLOP CLOP CLOP CLOP
IS ANYONE HERE FAMILIAR WITH THIS AREA?!
CLOP CLOP
Y... YES, SIR!
MY HOME VILLAGE IS IN THE NORTHERN FOREST! I KNOW THE TERRAIN!
CLOP CLOP CLOP CLOP CLOP CLOP CLOP CLOP CLOP CLOP
AND CONNIE ...
CLOP CLOP
HEY!
MY VILLAGE IS TO THE SOUTH...
WHERE THE... TITANS ARE COMING FROM...

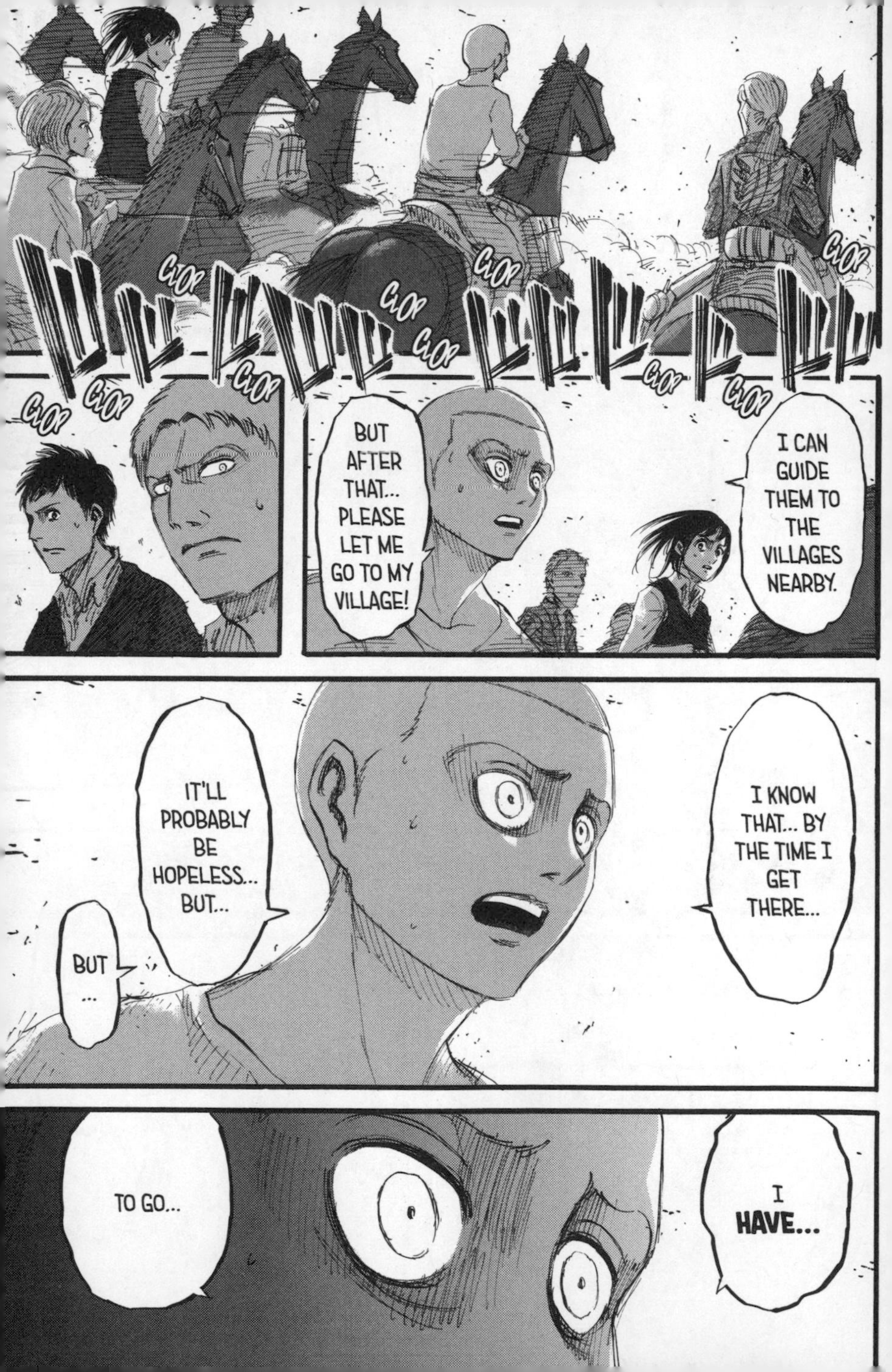
CLOP
CLOP
CLOP
CLOP
CLOP
CLOP
CLOP
CLOP
CLOP
CLOP
CLOP
I CAN GUIDE THEM TO THE VILLAGES NEARBY.
BUT AFTER THAT... PLEASE LET ME GO TO MY VILLAGE!
I KNOW THAT... BY THE TIME I GET THERE...
IT'LL PROBABLY BE HOPELESS... BUT...
BUT ...
I **HAVE...**
TO GO...

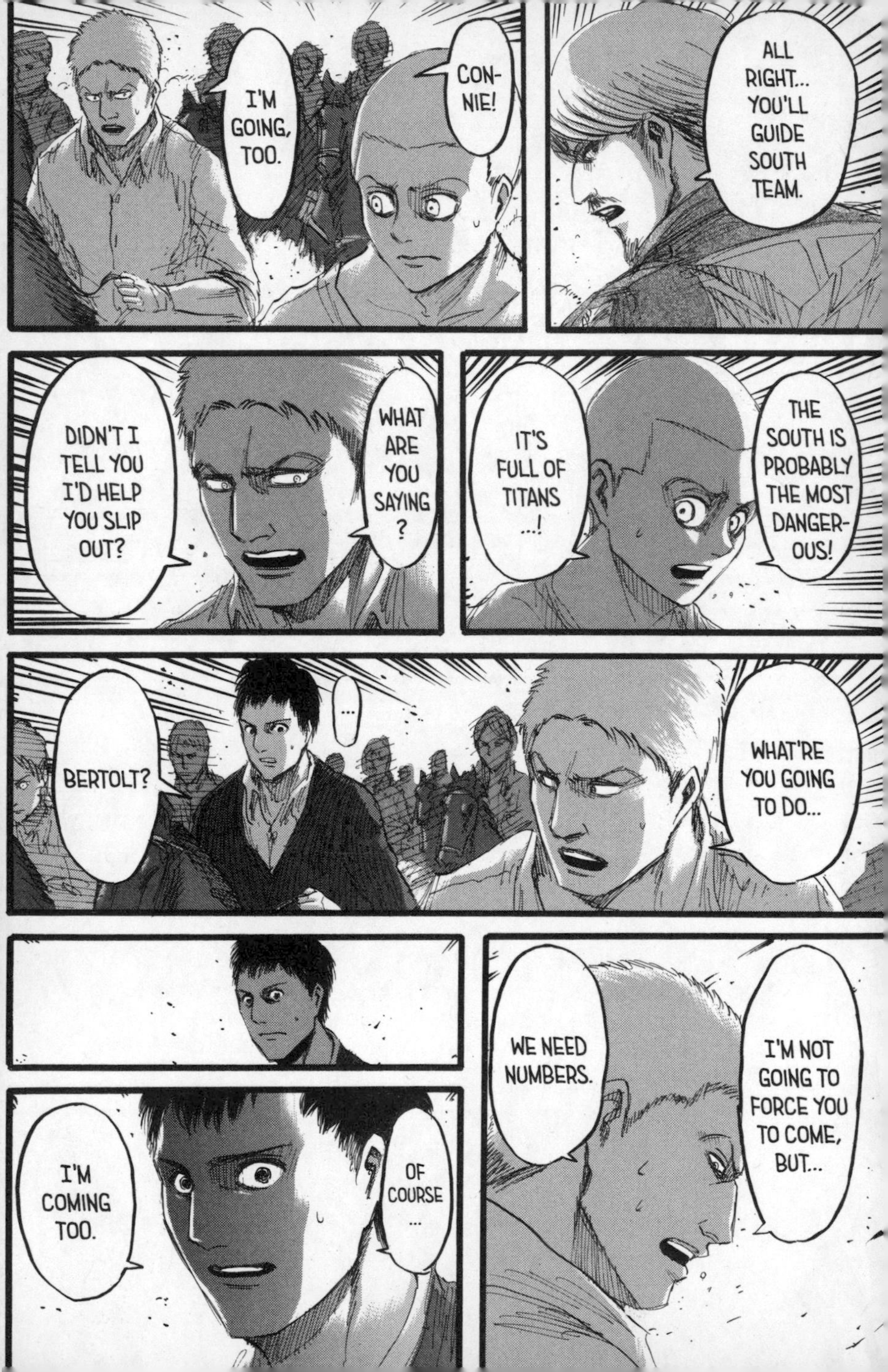
ALL RIGHT... YOU'LL GUIDE SOUTH TEAM.
CON-NIE!
I'M GOING, TOO.
THE SOUTH IS PROBABLY THE MOST DANGER-OUS!
IT'S FULL OF TITANS ...!
WHAT ARE YOU SAYING ?
DIDN'T I TELL YOU I'D HELP YOU SLIP OUT?
WHAT'RE YOU GOING TO DO...
...
BERTOLT?
I'M NOT GOING TO FORCE YOU TO COME, BUT...
WE NEED NUMBERS.
OF COURSE ...
I'M COMING TOO.

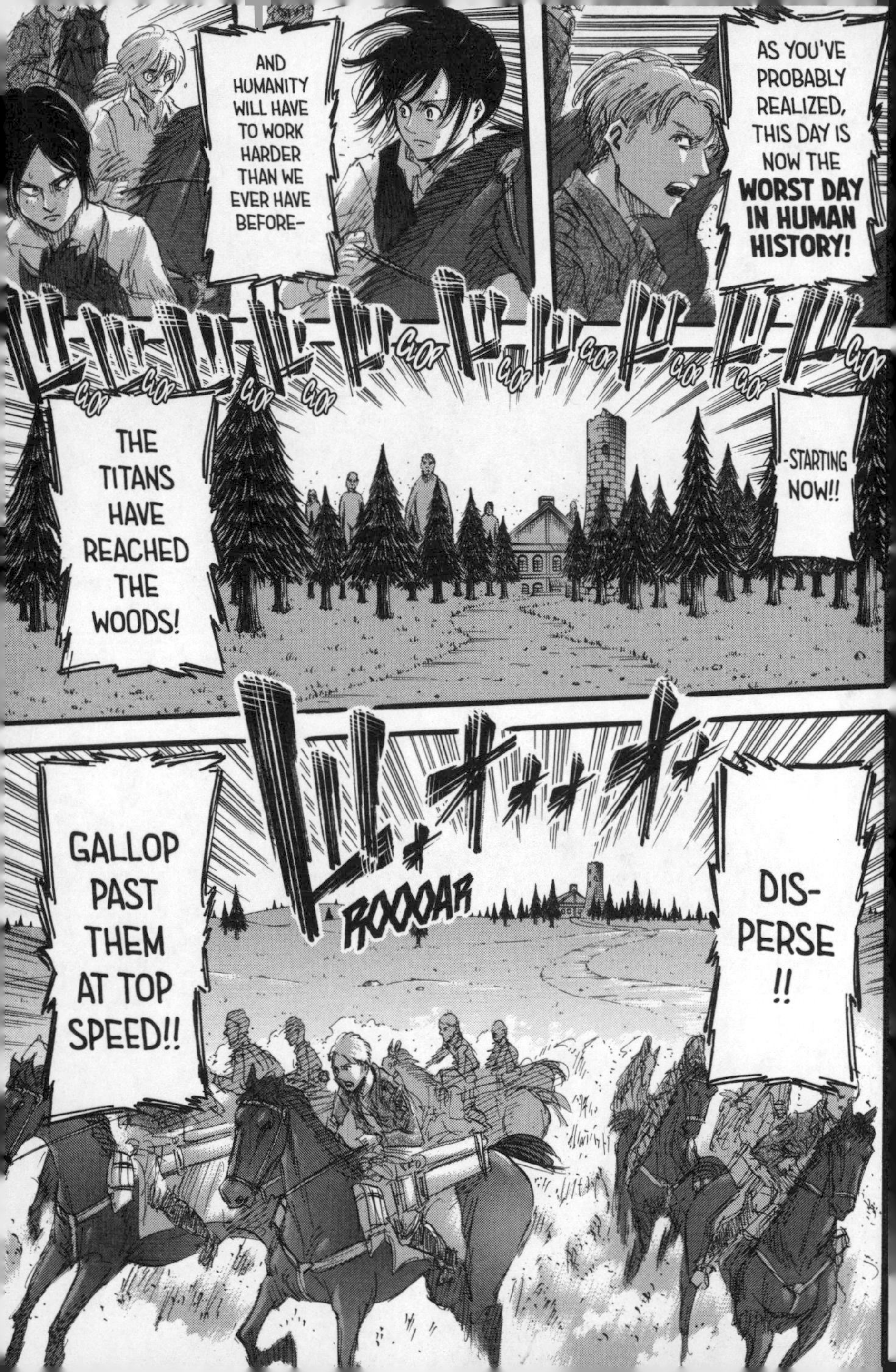
AS YOU'VE PROBABLY REALIZED, THIS DAY IS NOW THE **WORST DAY IN HUMAN HISTORY!**
AND HUMANITY WILL HAVE TO WORK HARDER THAN WE EVER HAVE BEFORE-
CLOP CLOP CLOP CLOP CLOP CLOP CLOP CLOP CLOP CLOP CLOP CLOP
-STARTING NOW!!
THE TITANS HAVE REACHED THE WOODS!
DIS-PERSE!!
ROOOAR
GALLOP PAST THEM AT TOP SPEED!!

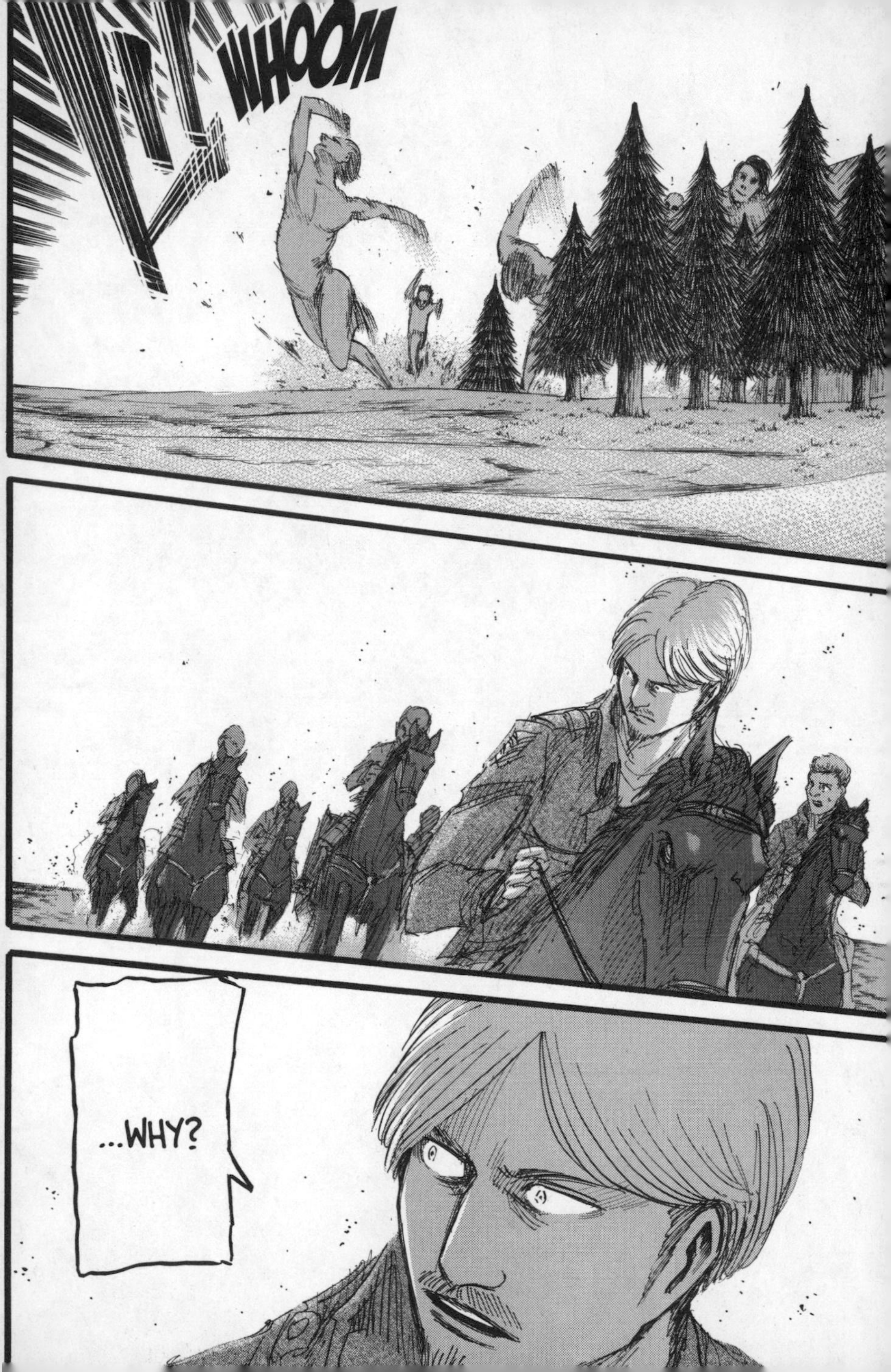
WHOOM
...WHY?

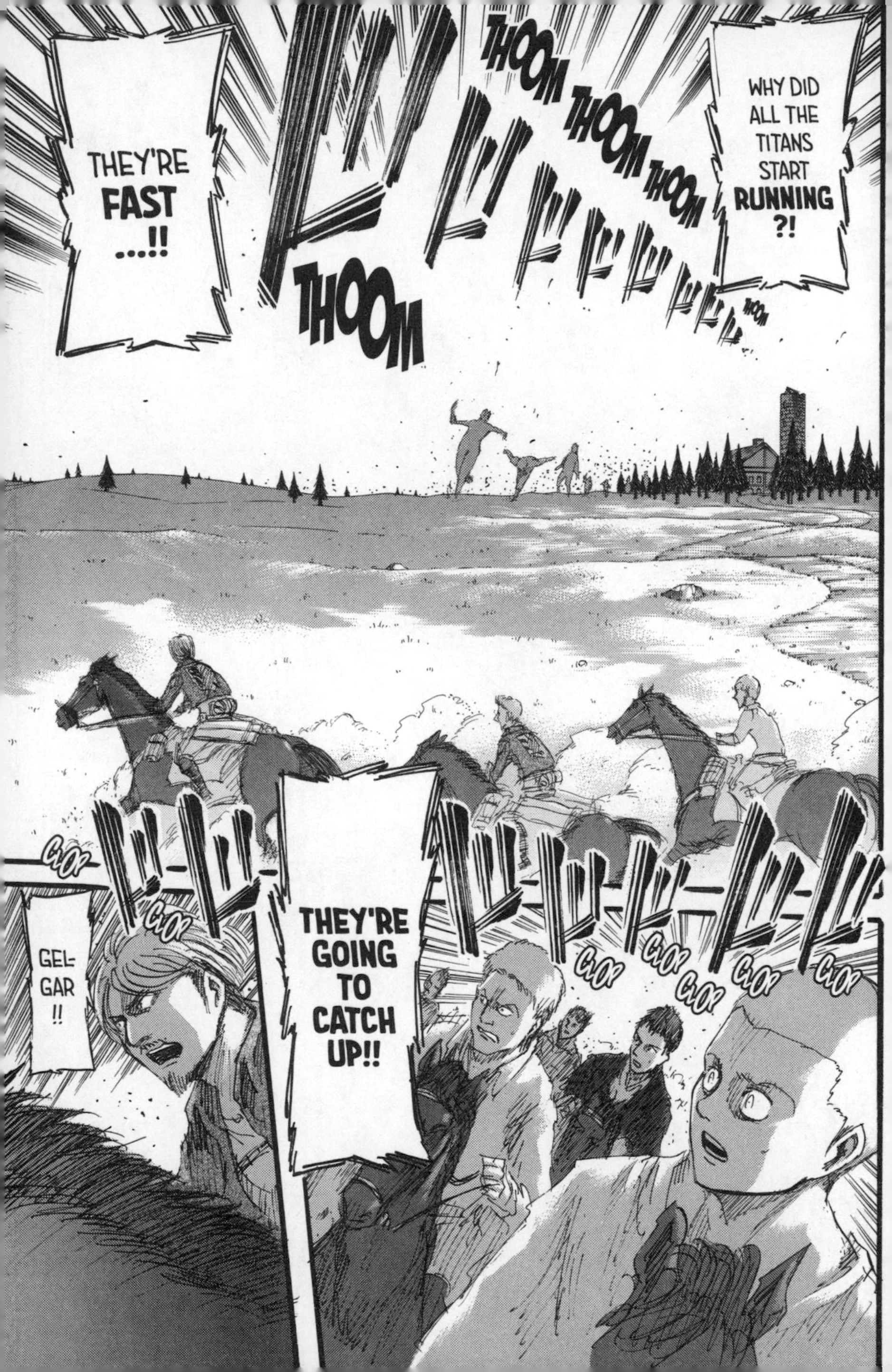
THOOM THOOM THOOM
WHY DID ALL THE TITANS START RUNNING?!
THOOM
THOOM
THEY'RE FAST ...!!
CLOP CLOP CLOP CLOP CLOP CLOP
THEY'RE GOING TO CATCH UP!!
CLOP
CLOP
GEL-GAR!!

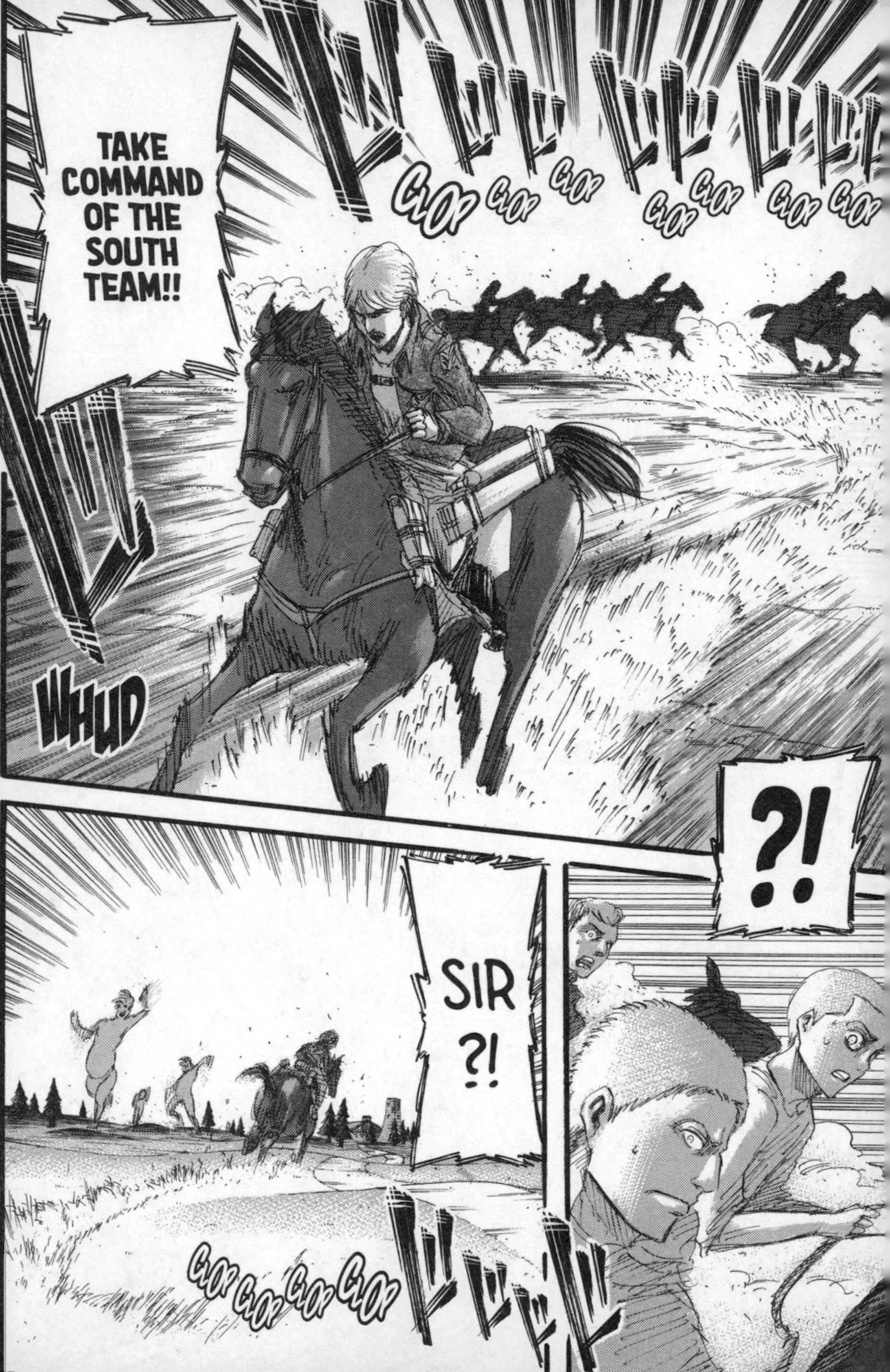

TAKE COMMAND OF THE SOUTH TEAM!!
CLOP CLOP CLOP CLOP CLOP CLOP CLOP
WHUD
?!
SIR ?!
CLOP CLOP CLOP CLOP

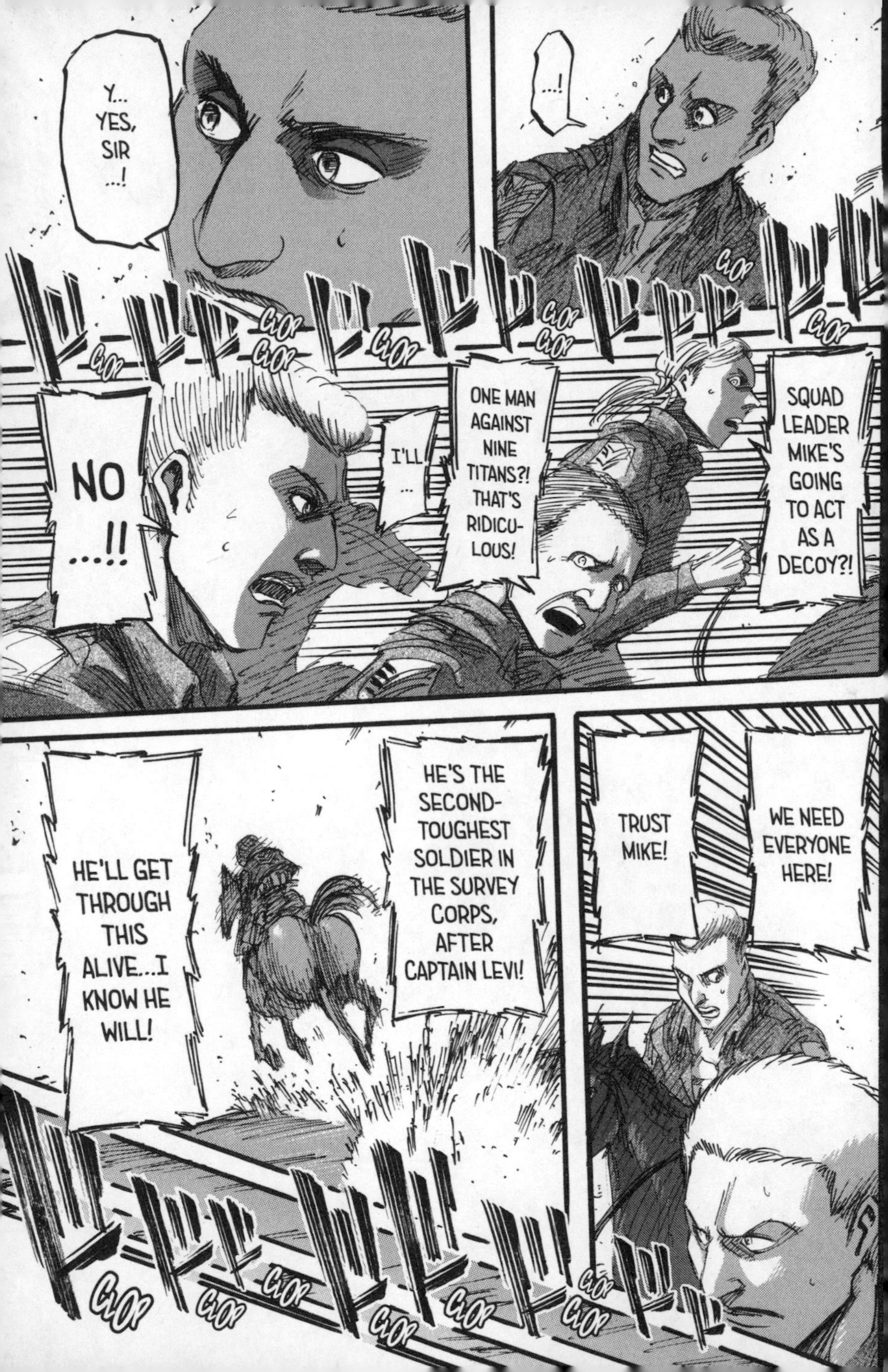
...!
Y... YES, SIR ...!
CLOP CLOP CLOP CLOP CLOP CLOP CLOP
SQUAD LEADER MIKE'S GOING TO ACT AS A DECOY?!
ONE MAN AGAINST NINE TITANS?! THAT'S RIDICULOUS!
I'LL ...
NO ...!!
WE NEED EVERYONE HERE!
TRUST MIKE!
HE'S THE SECOND-TOUGHEST SOLDIER IN THE SURVEY CORPS, AFTER CAPTAIN LEVI!
HE'LL GET THROUGH THIS ALIVE...I KNOW HE WILL!
CLOP CLOP CLOP CLOP CLOP CLOP CLOP

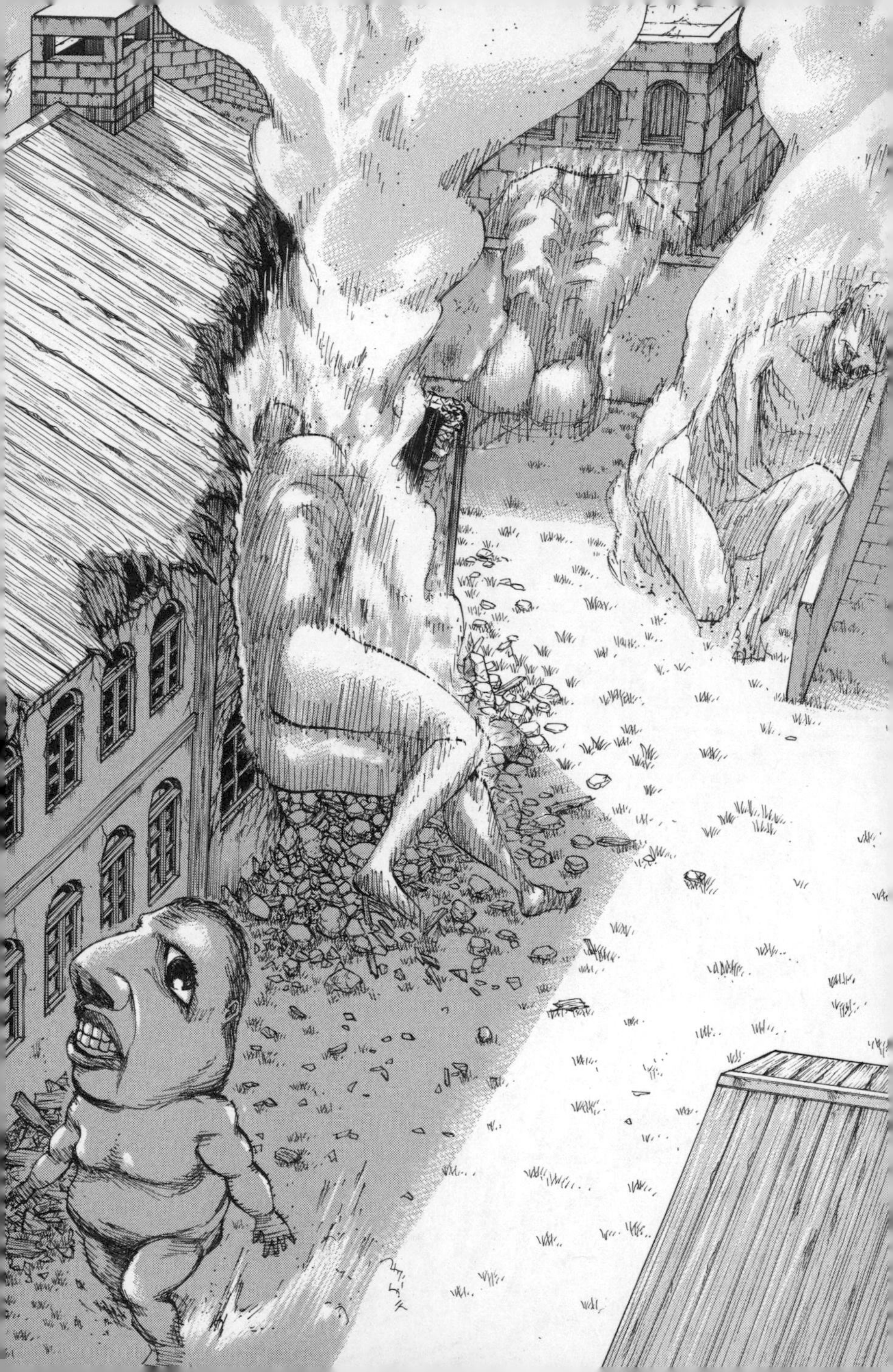

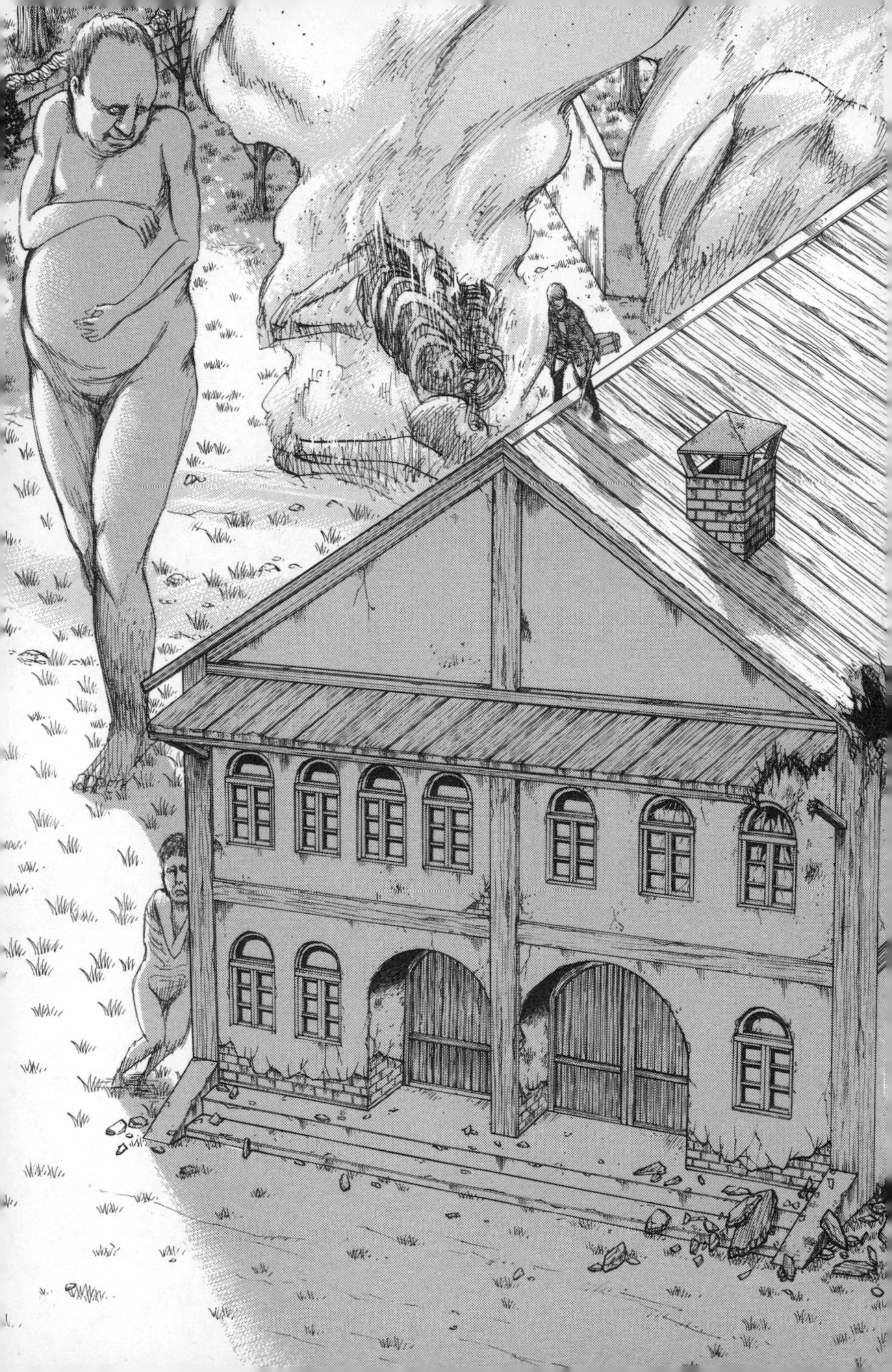

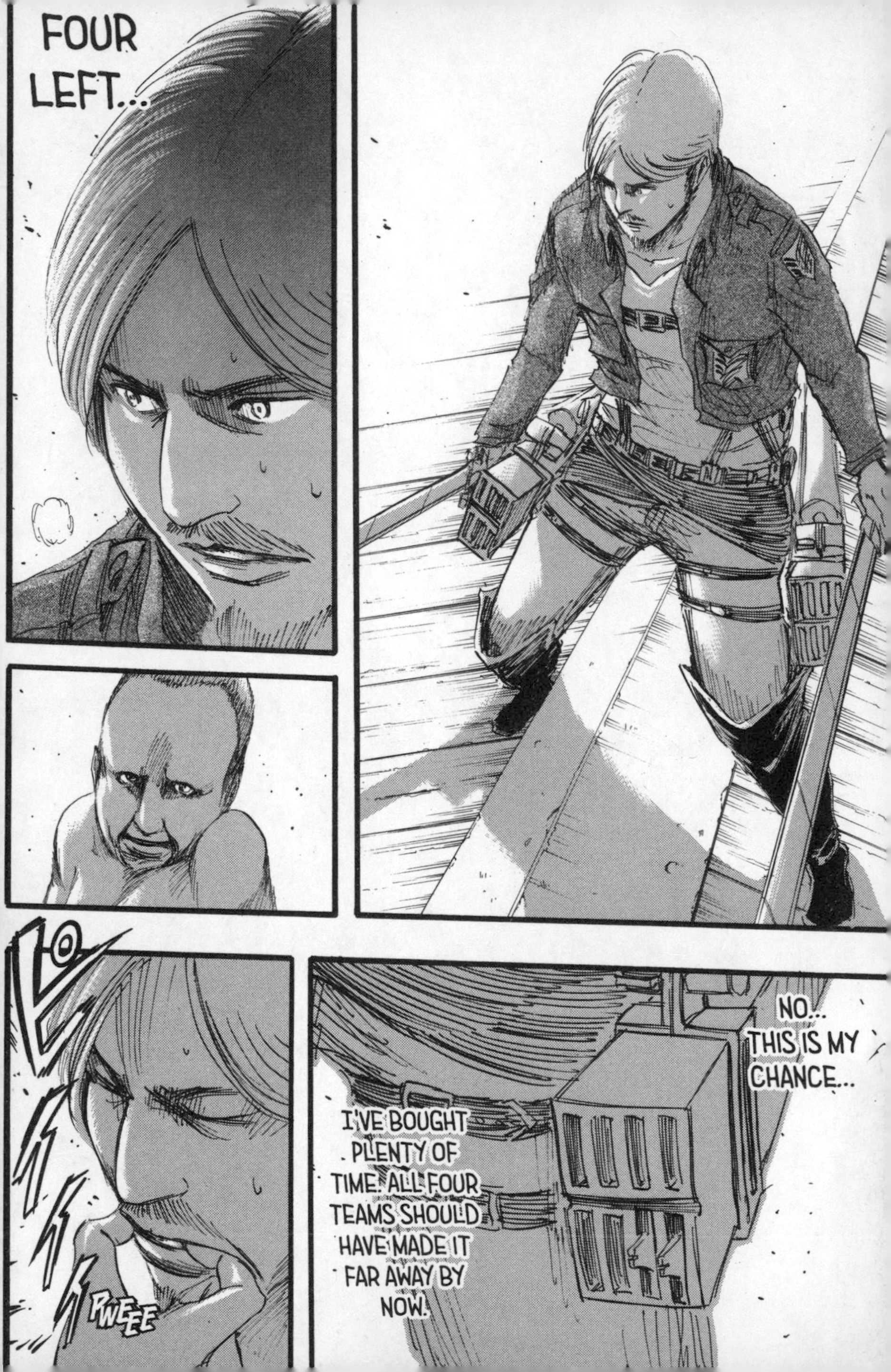
FOUR LEFT...
NO... THIS IS MY CHANCE...
I'VE BOUGHT PLENTY OF TIME. ALL FOUR TEAMS SHOULD HAVE MADE IT FAR AWAY BY NOW.
PWEEE

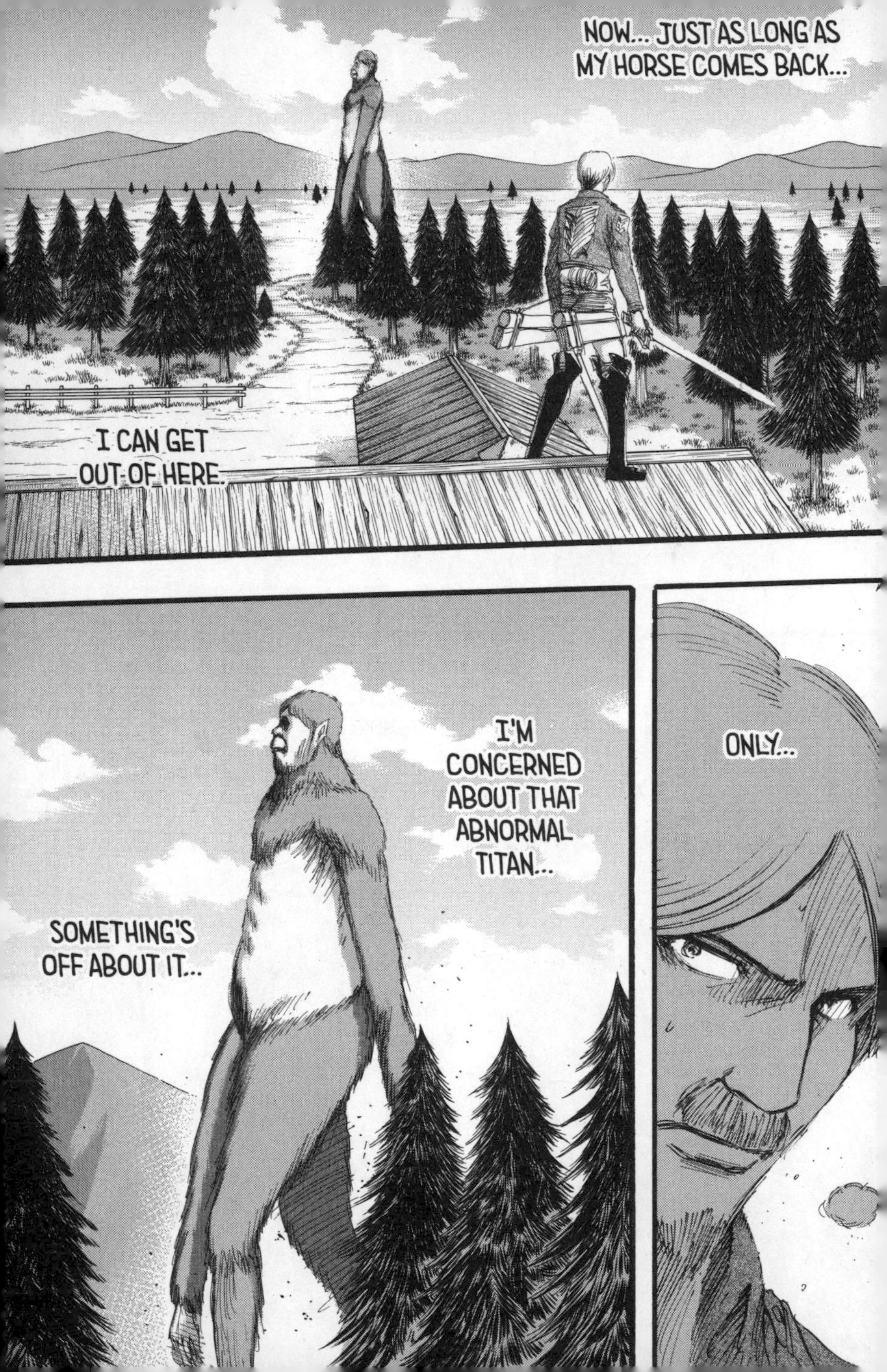
NOW... JUST AS LONG AS MY HORSE COMES BACK...
I CAN GET OUT OF HERE.
ONLY...
I'M CONCERNED ABOUT THAT ABNORMAL TITAN...
SOMETHING'S OFF ABOUT IT...

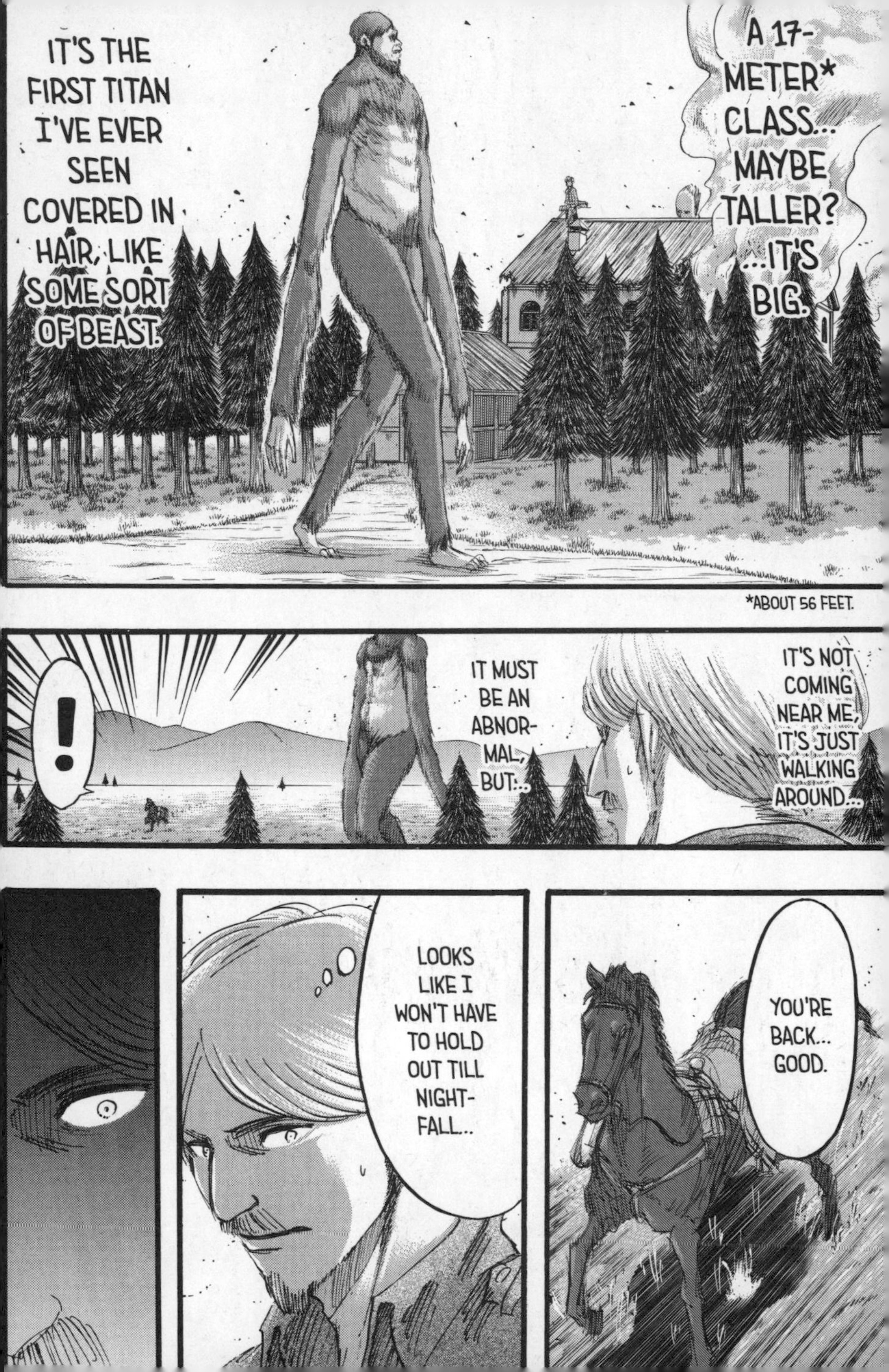
A 17-METER* CLASS... MAYBE TALLER? ...IT'S BIG.
IT'S THE FIRST TITAN I'VE EVER SEEN COVERED IN HAIR, LIKE SOME SORT OF BEAST.
IT'S NOT COMING NEAR ME, IT'S JUST WALKING AROUND...
IT MUST BE AN ABNORMAL, BUT...
!
YOU'RE BACK... GOOD.
LOOKS LIKE I WON'T HAVE TO HOLD OUT TILL NIGHTFALL...

*ABOUT 56 FEET.

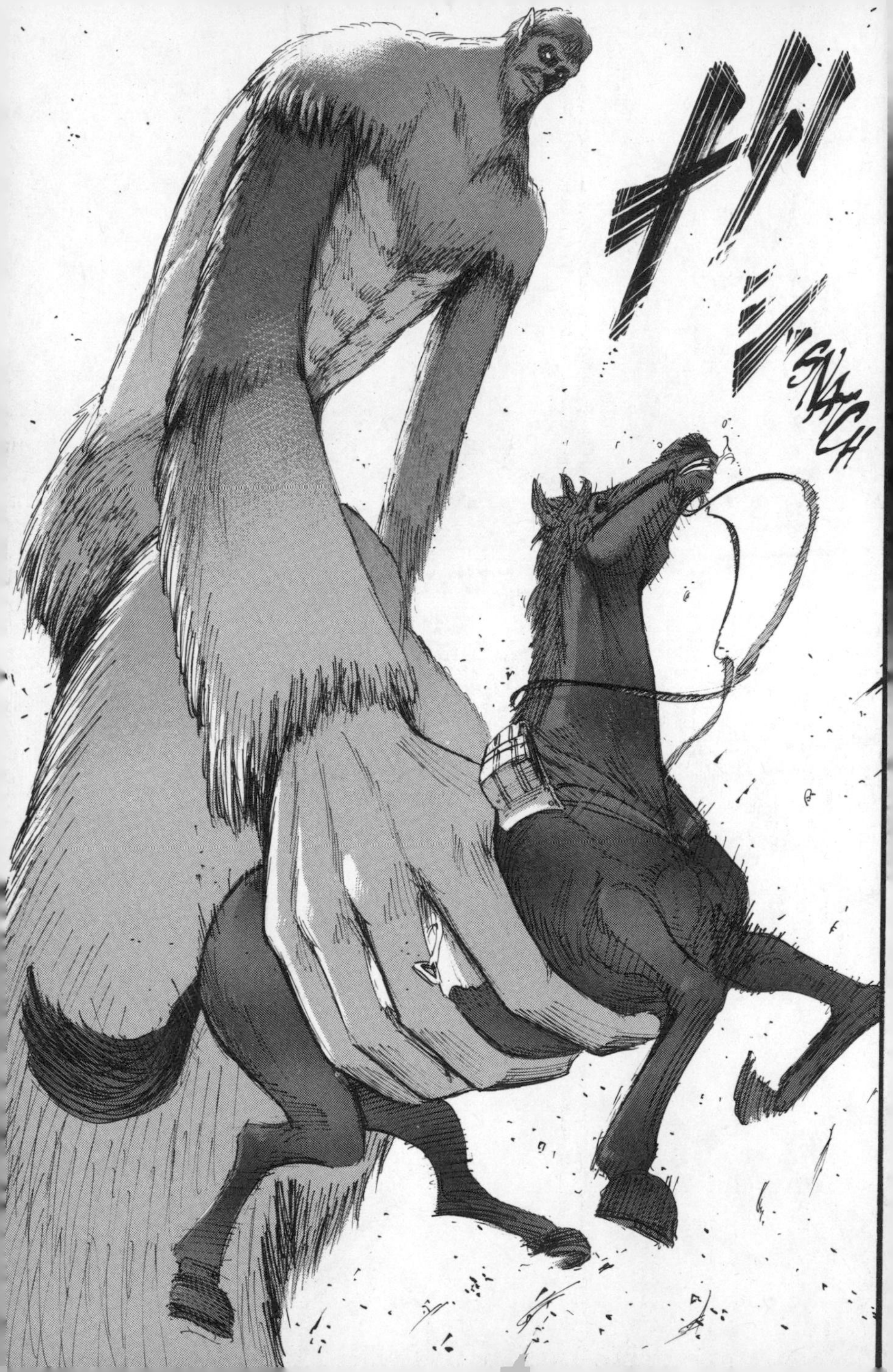
SNATCH

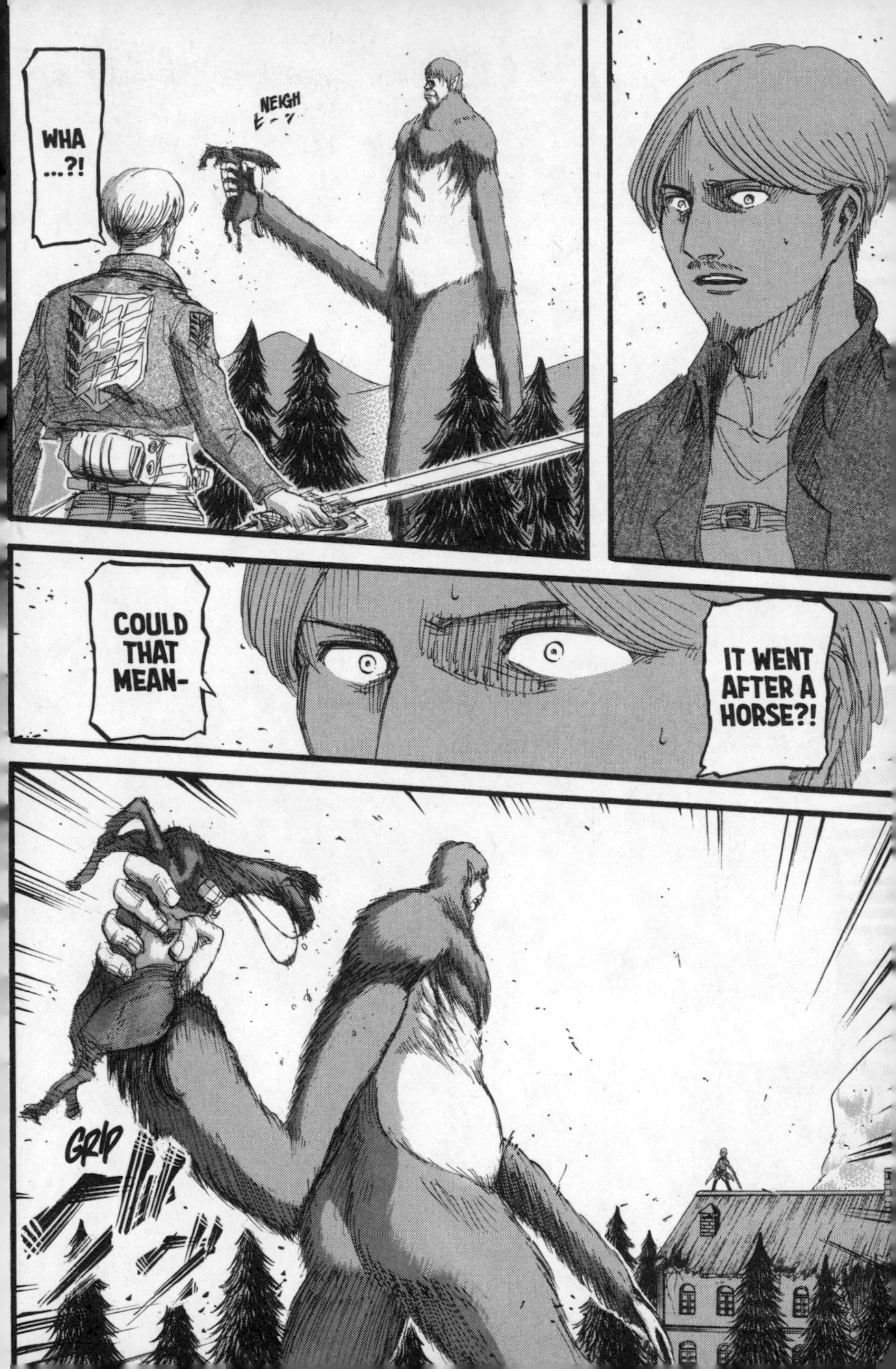
NEIGH
WHA ...?!
IT WENT AFTER A HORSE?!
COULD THAT MEAN-
GRIP

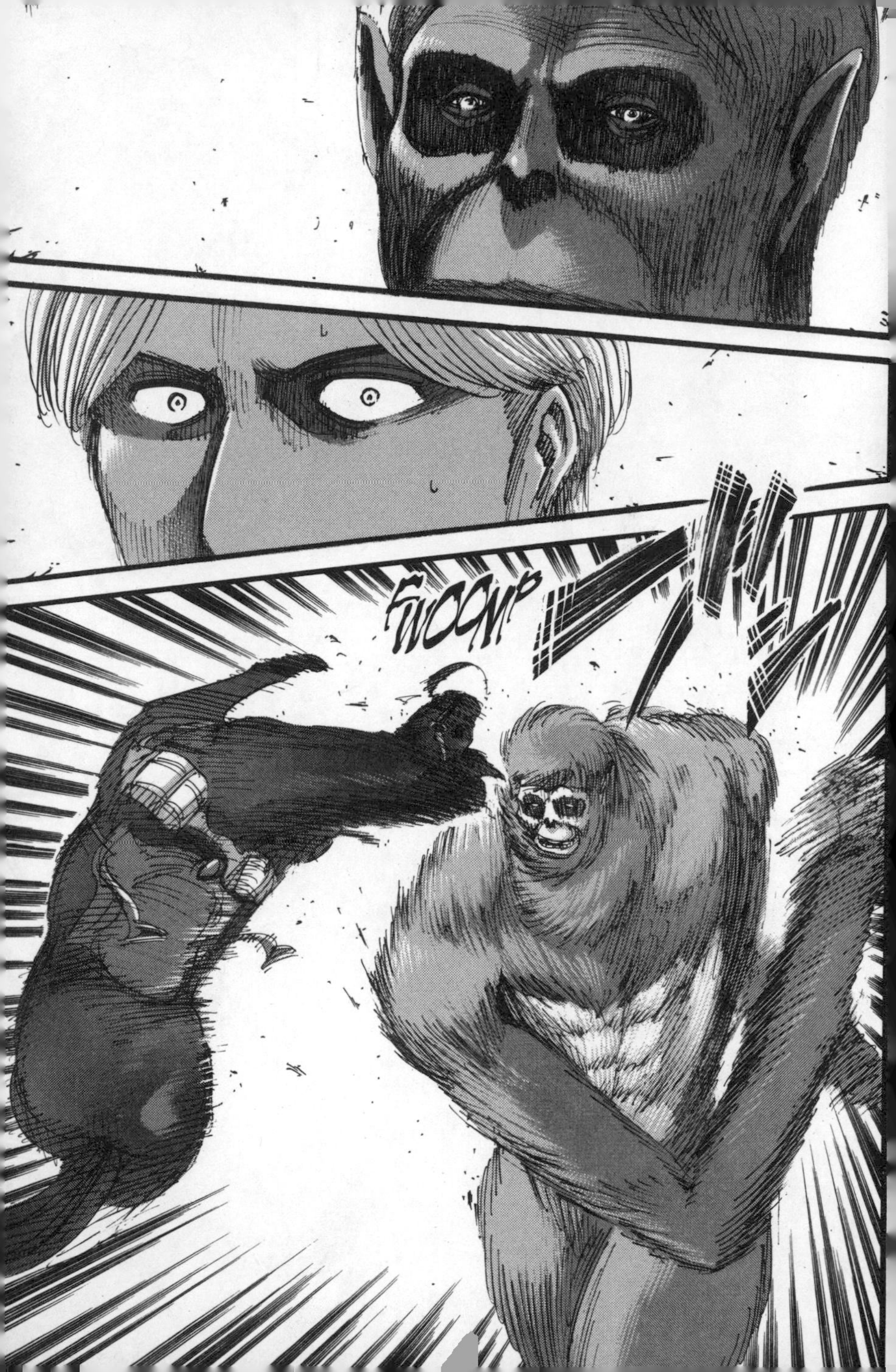
FWOOMP

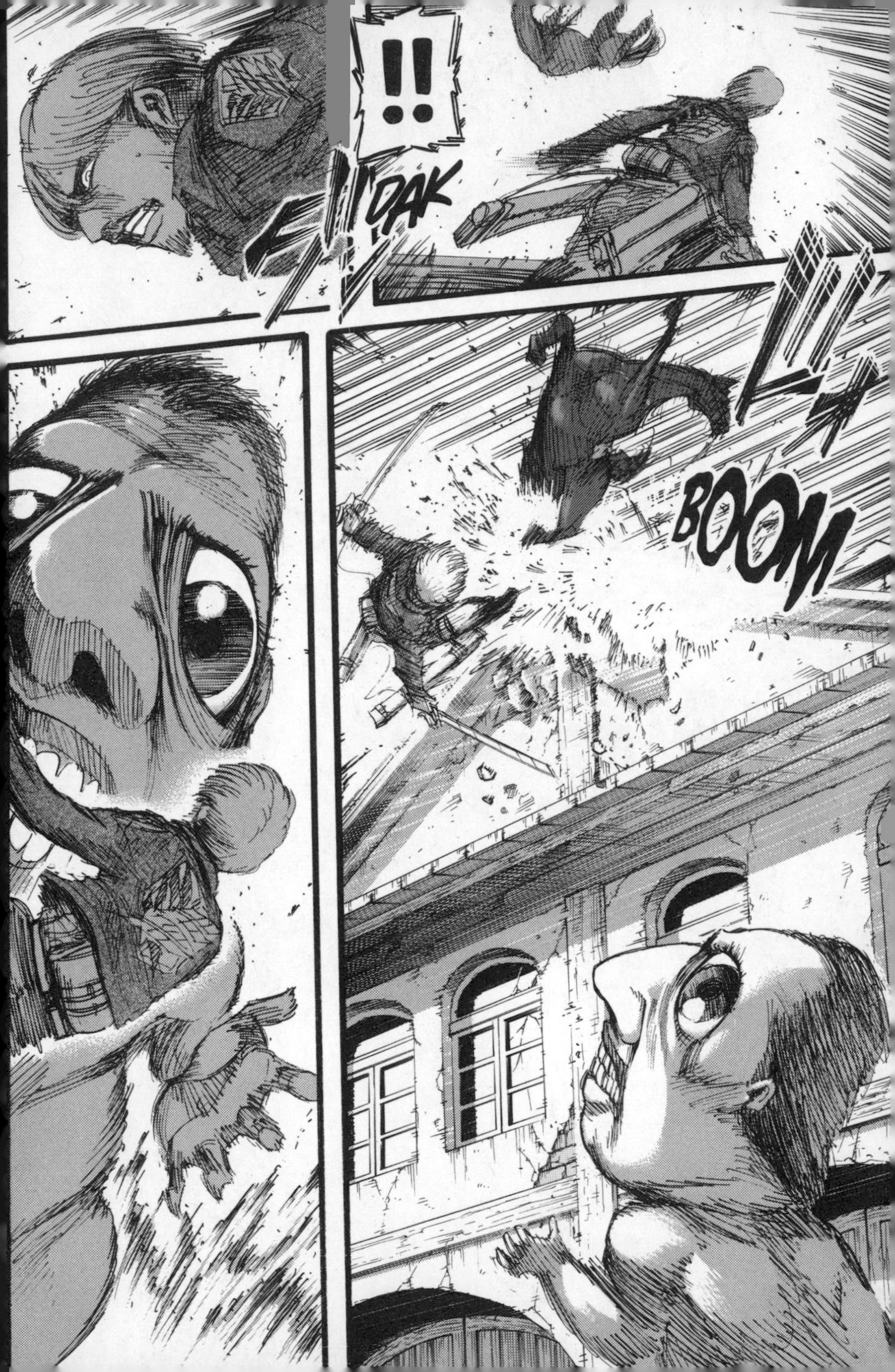
!!
DAK
BOOM

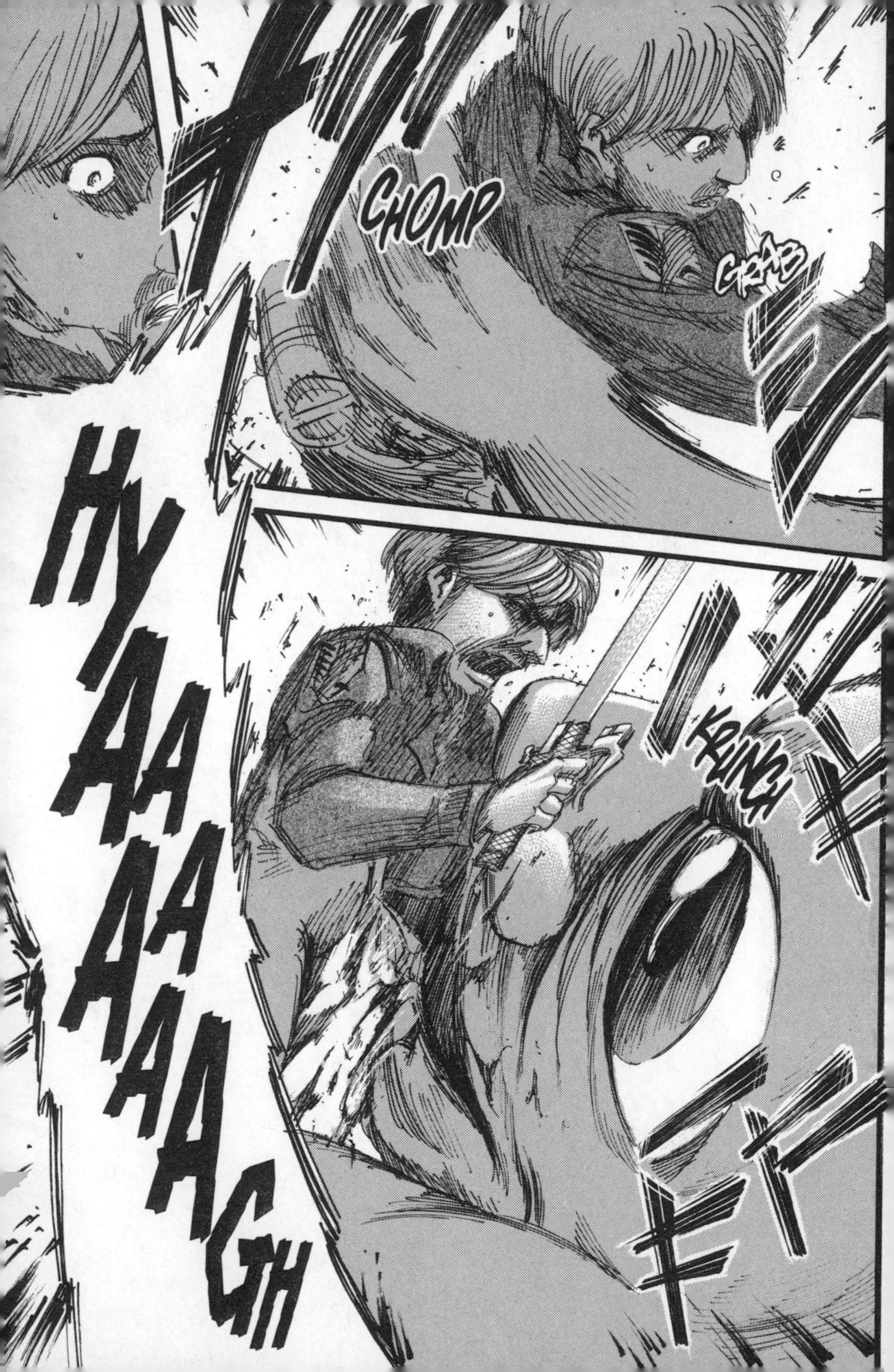
GRAB
CHOMP
KRUNCH
HYAAAAAAAAGH

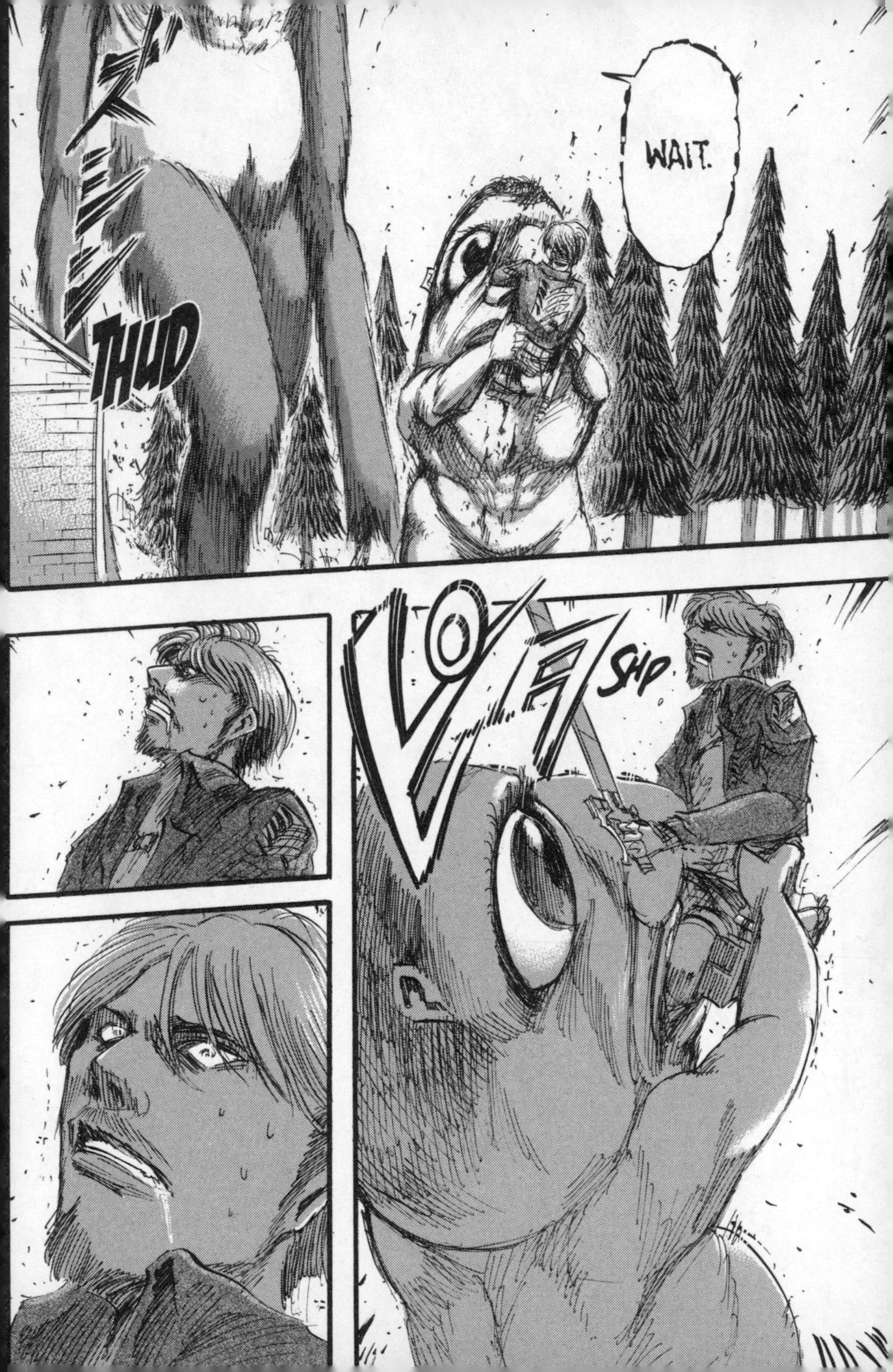
WAIT.
THUD
SHP

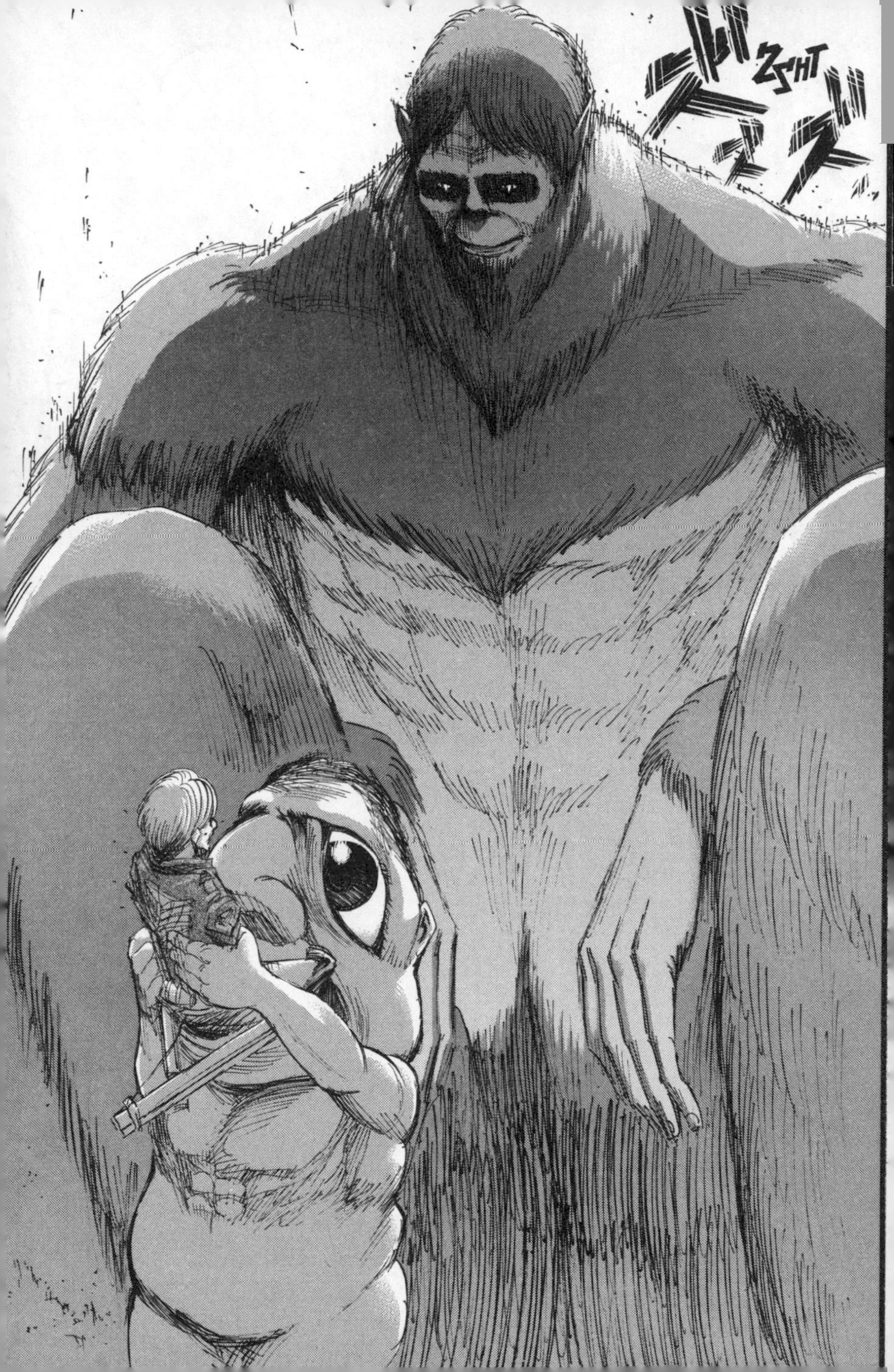
ZSHT

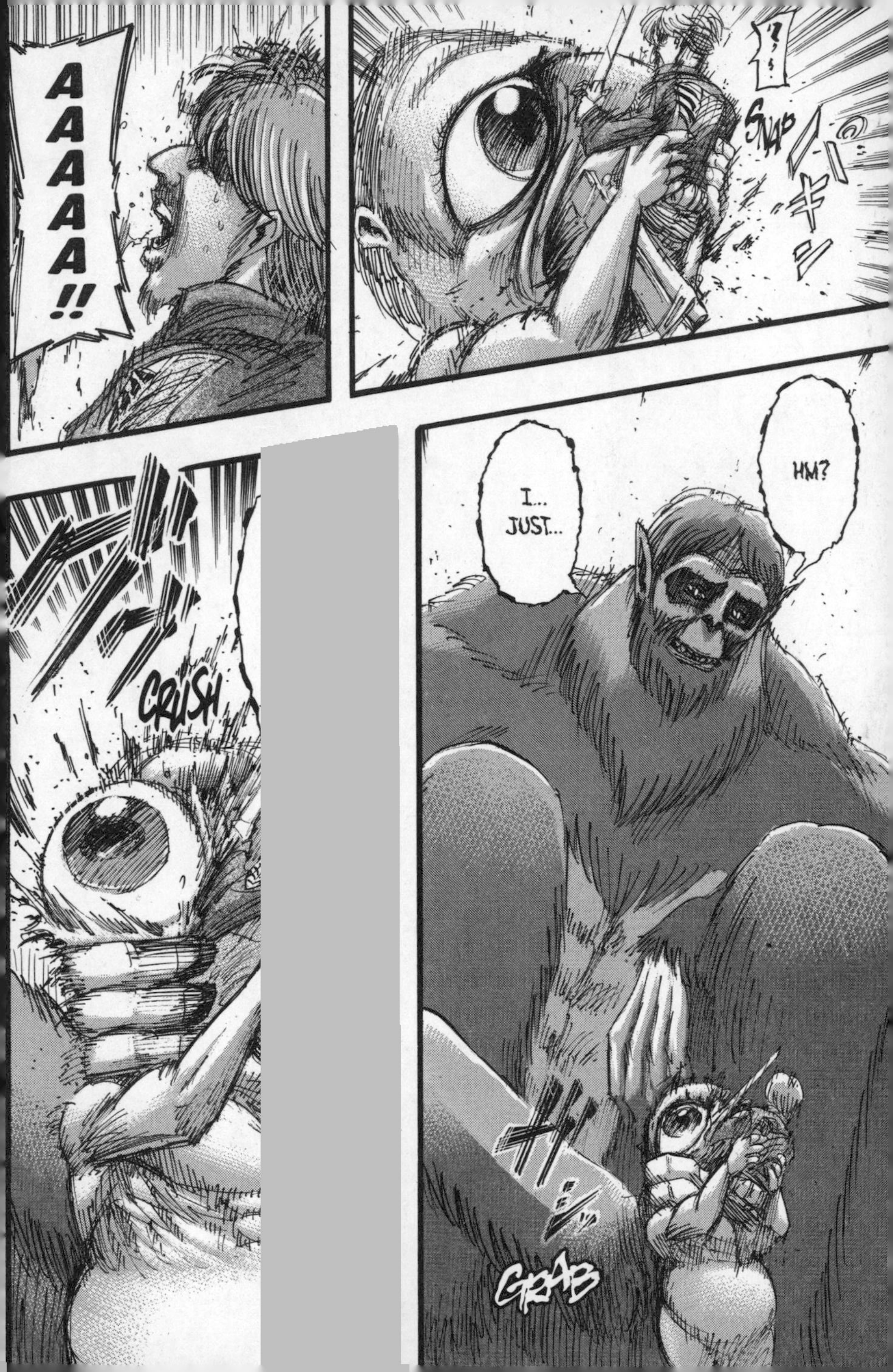
SNAP
AAAAAA!!
HM?
I... JUST...
GRAB
CRUSH

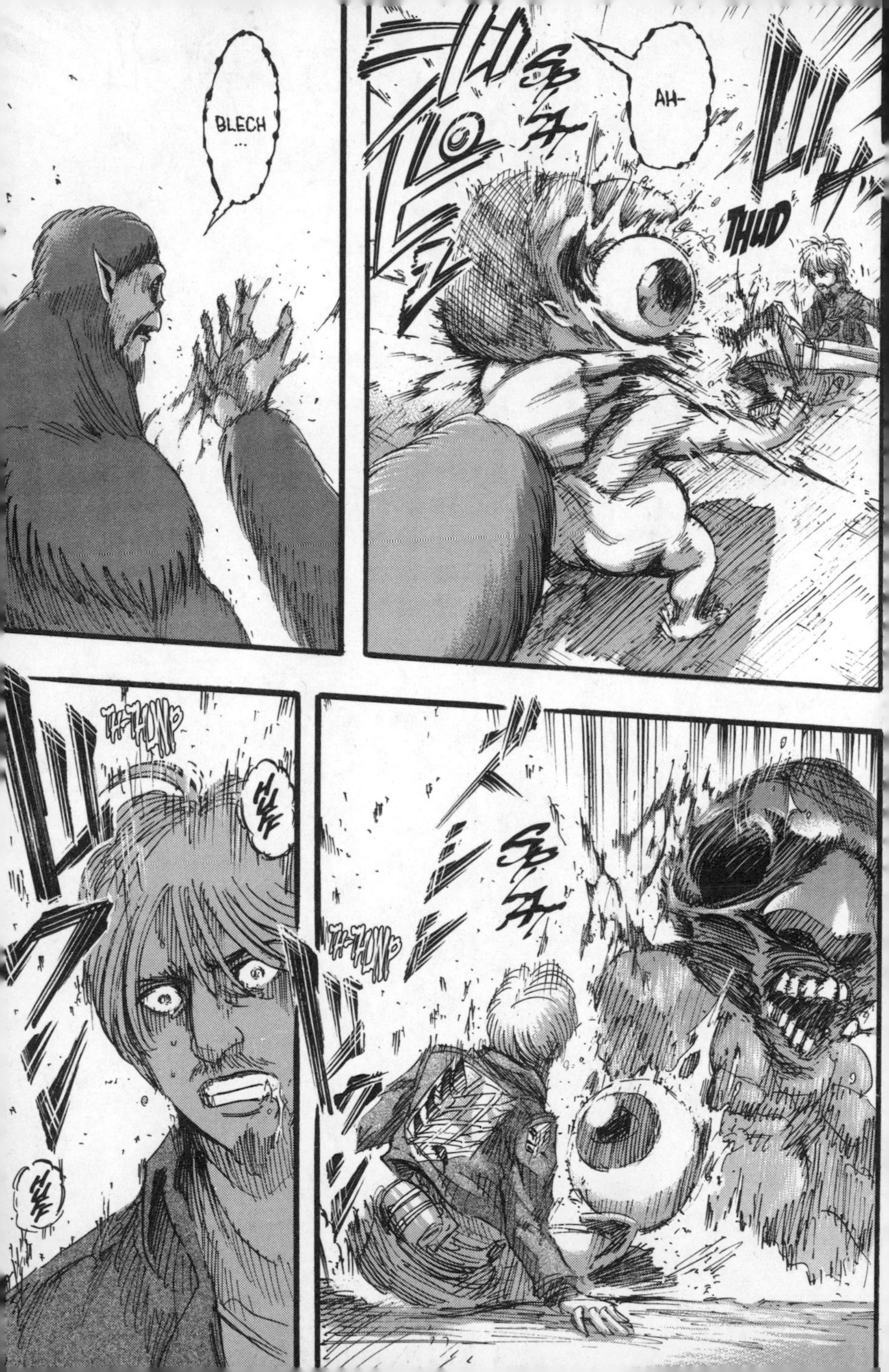
AH-
THUD
BLECH ...
TA-THUMP
TA-THUMP

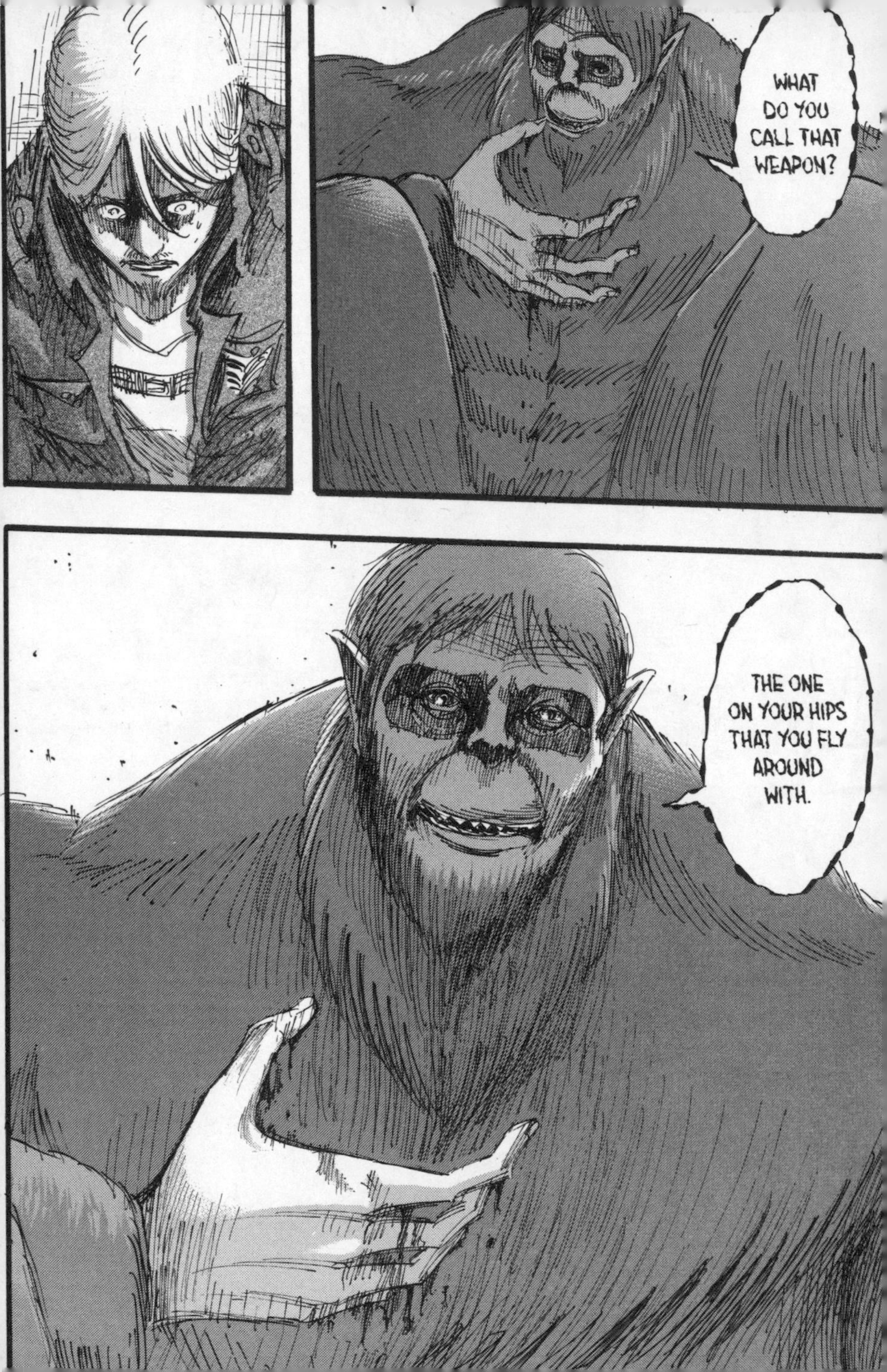
WHAT DO YOU CALL THAT WEAPON?
THE ONE ON YOUR HIPS THAT YOU FLY AROUND WITH.

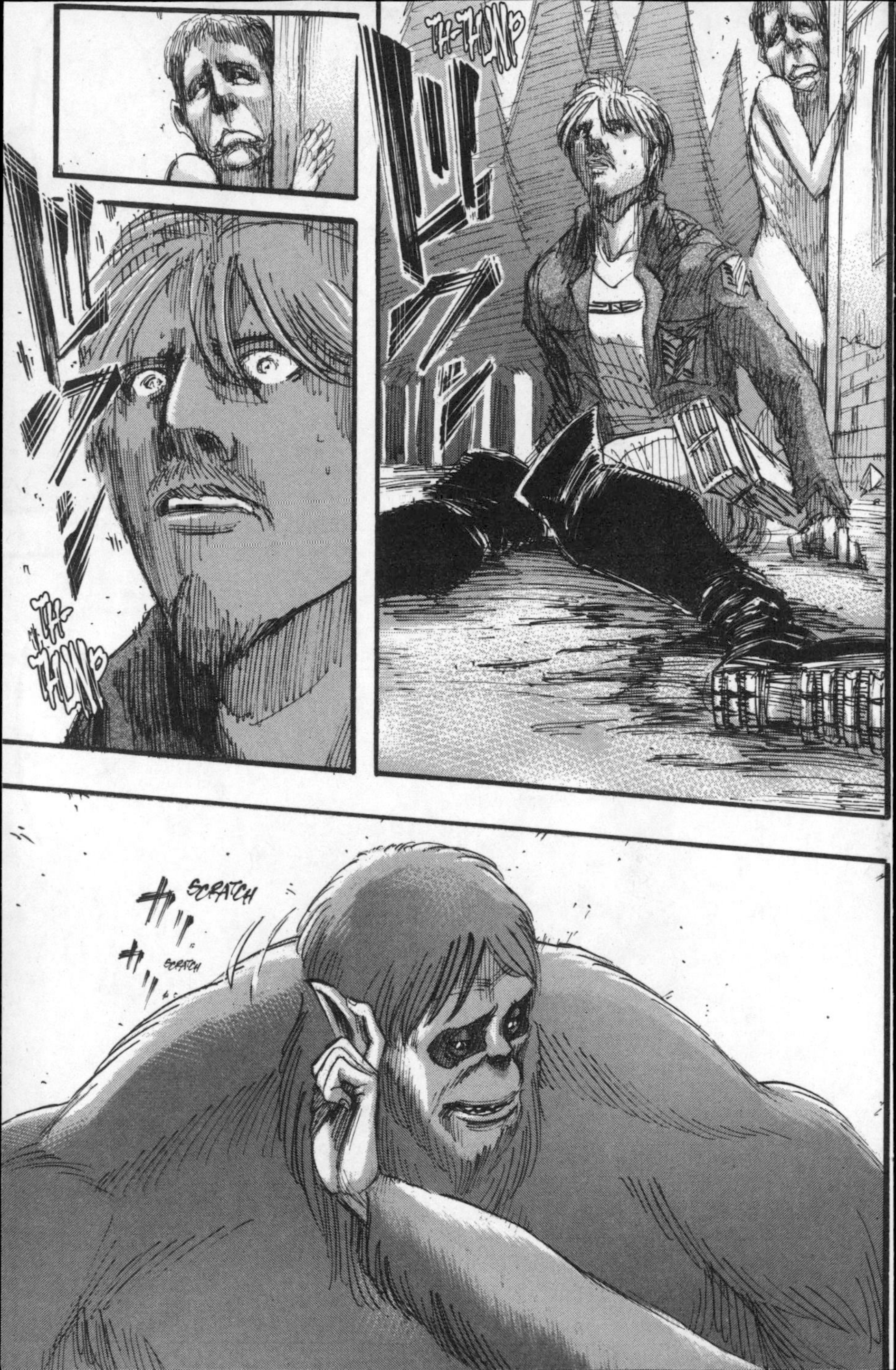
TH-THUMP
TH-THUMP
SCRATCH
SCRATCH

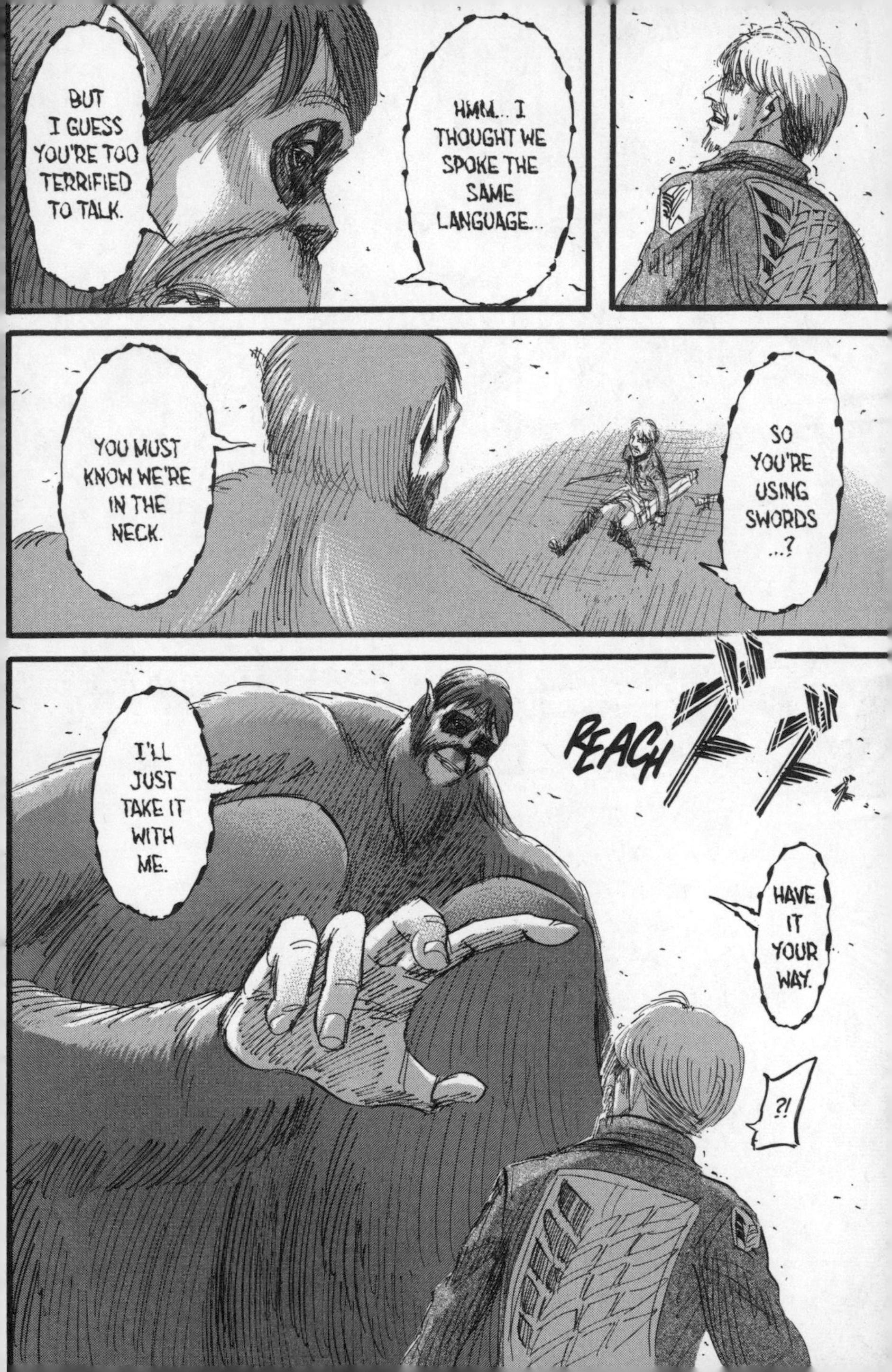
HMM... I THOUGHT WE SPOKE THE SAME LANGUAGE...
BUT I GUESS YOU'RE TOO TERRIFIED TO TALK.
SO YOU'RE USING SWORDS ...?
YOU MUST KNOW WE'RE IN THE NECK.
REACH
I'LL JUST TAKE IT WITH ME.
HAVE IT YOUR WAY.
?!

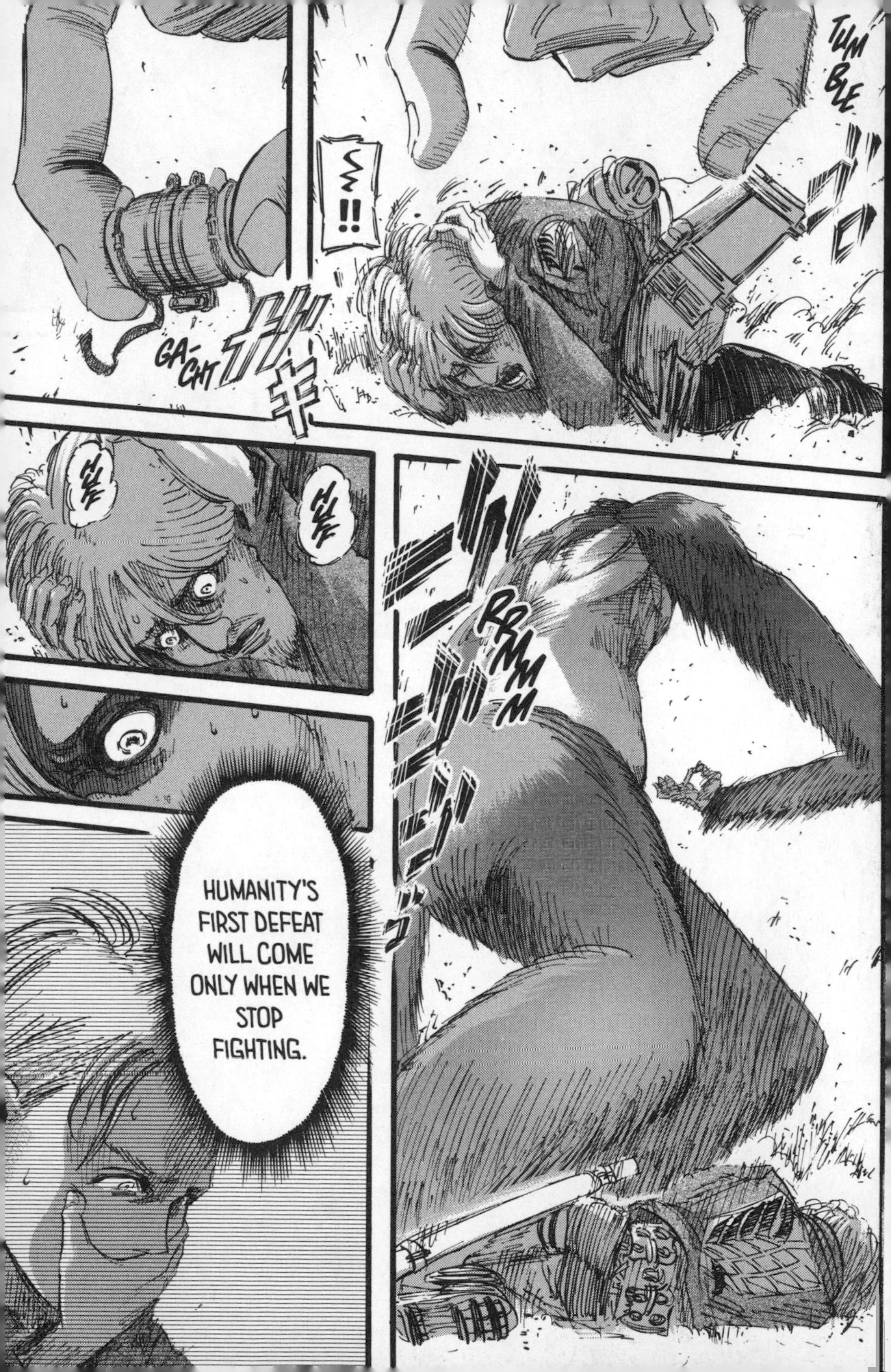
TUMBLE
!!
GA-CHT
RRMMMM
HUMANITY'S FIRST DEFEAT WILL COME ONLY WHEN WE STOP FIGHTING.

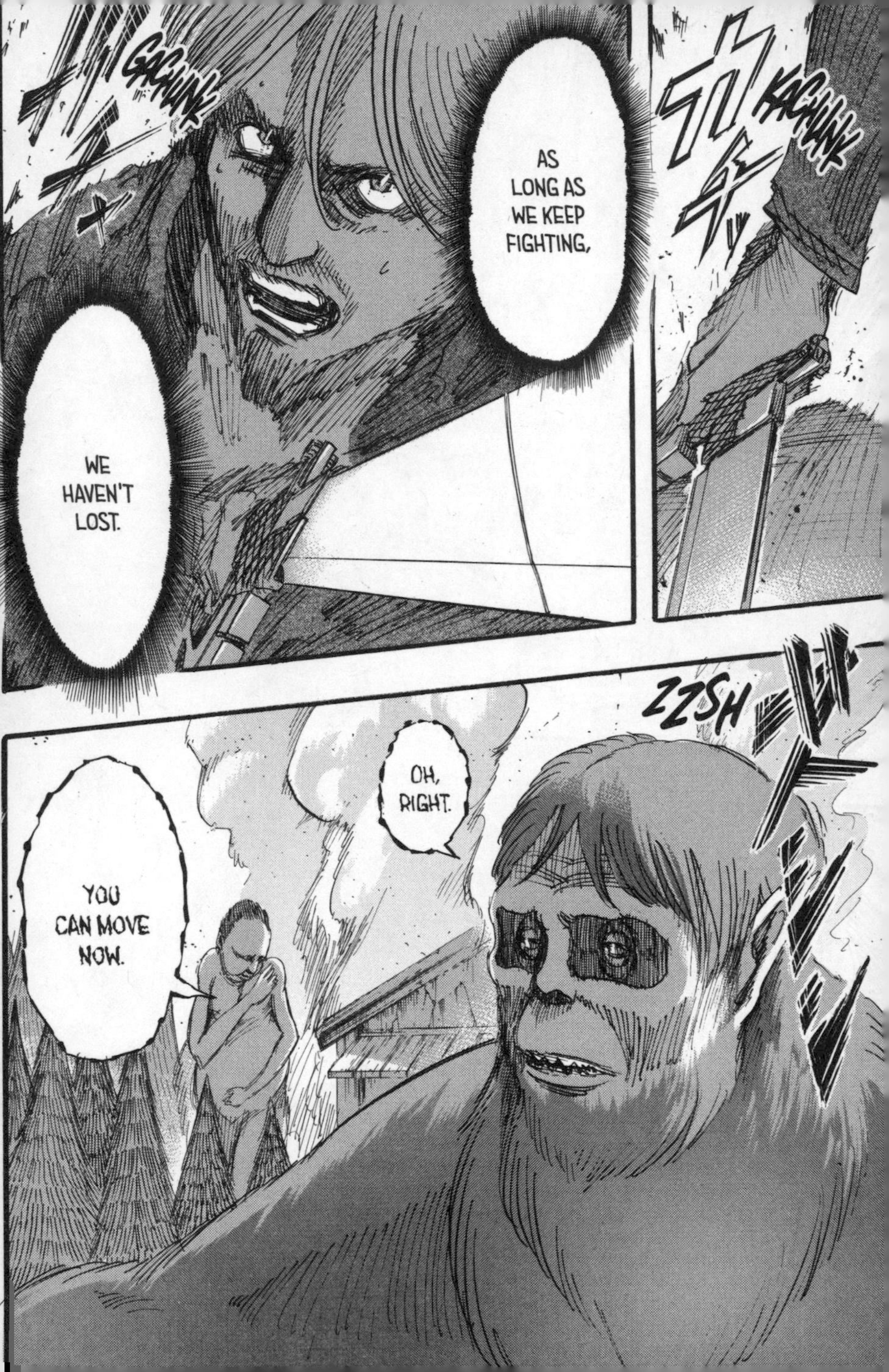
KACHUNK
GACHUNK
AS LONG AS WE KEEP FIGHTING,
WE HAVEN'T LOST.
ZZSH
OH, RIGHT.
YOU CAN MOVE NOW.

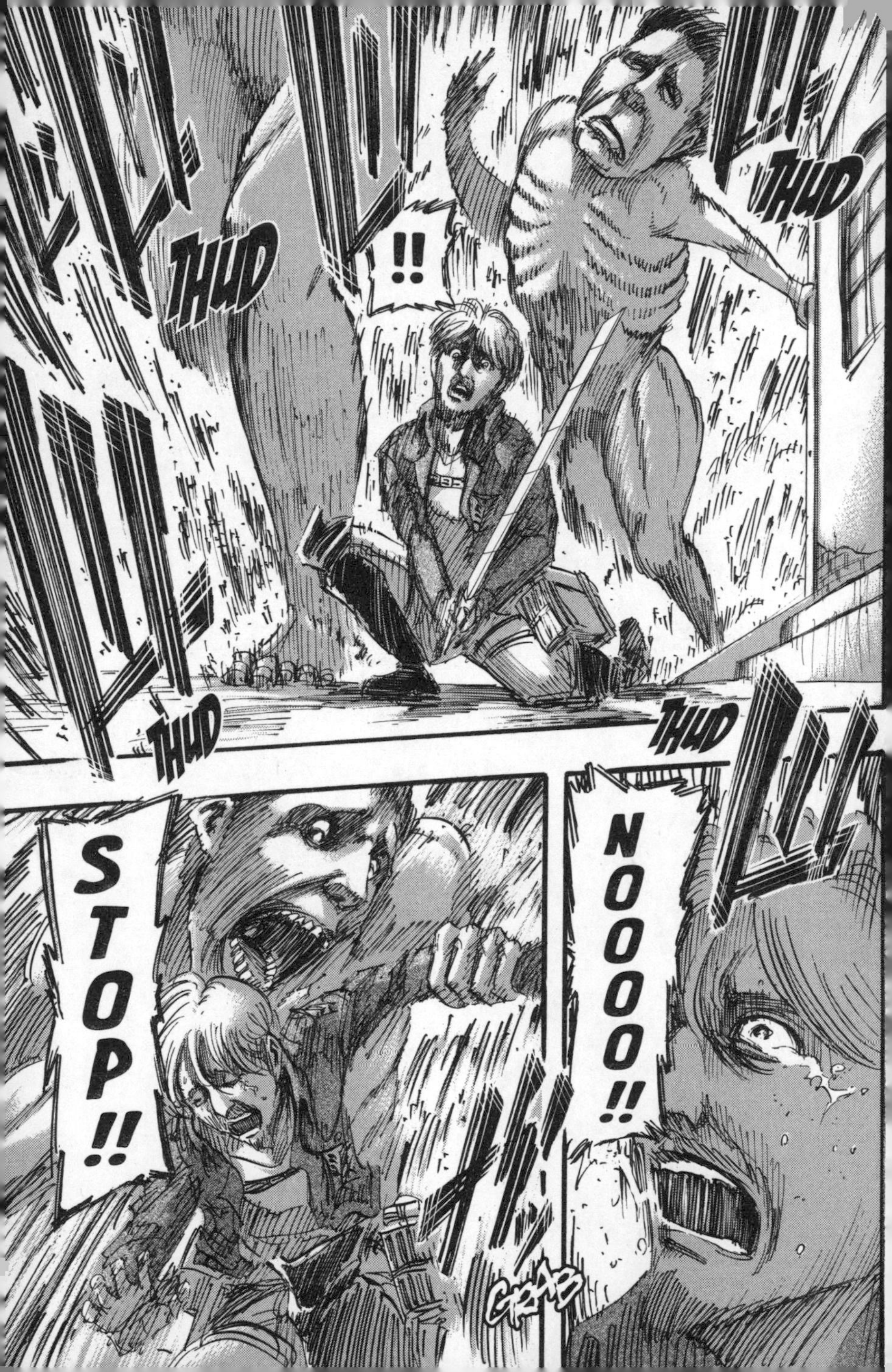
THUD
!!
THUD
THUD
THUD
NOOOOO!!
GRAB
STOP!!

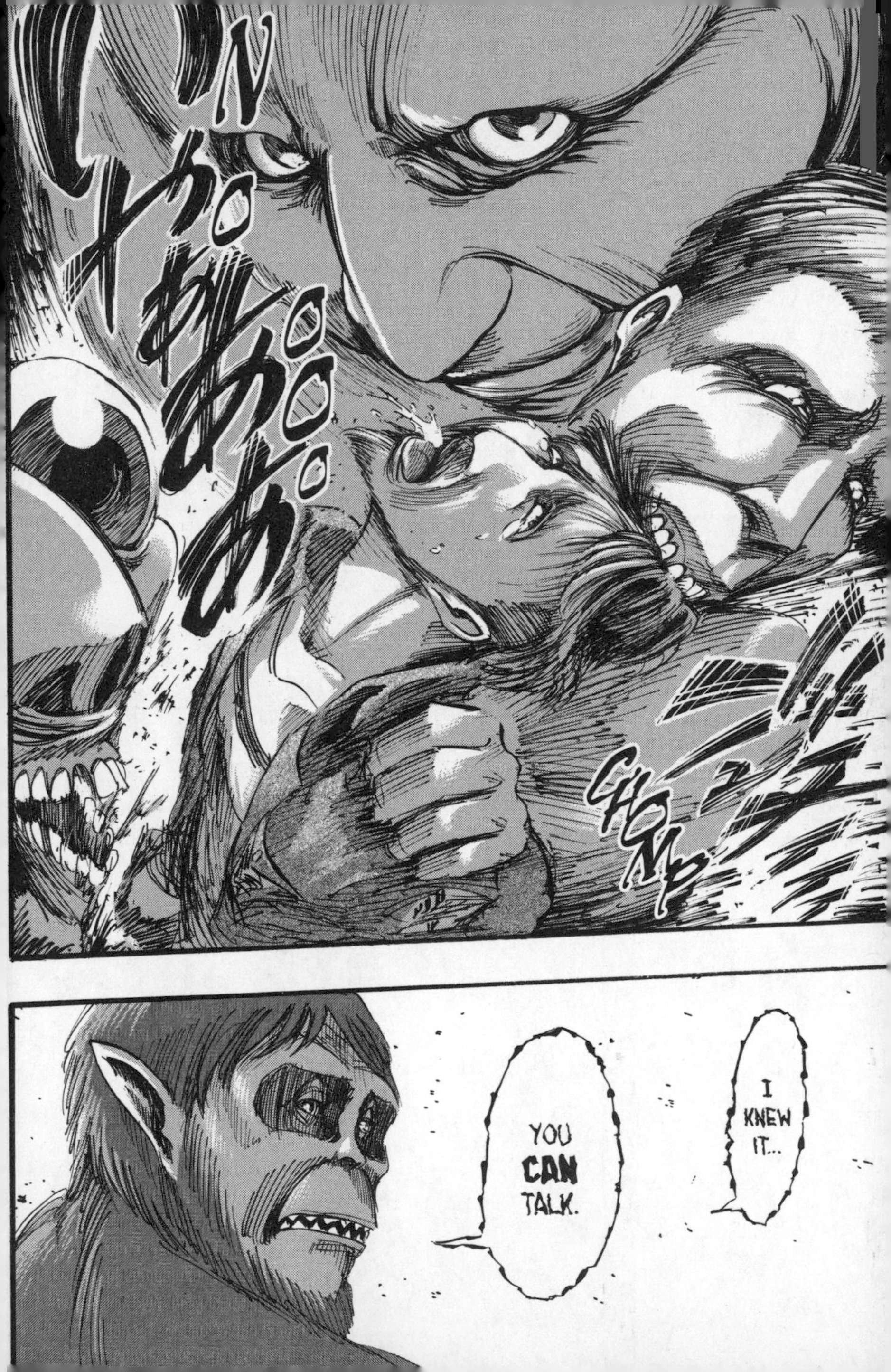
CHOMP
I KNEW IT...
YOU **CAN** TALK.

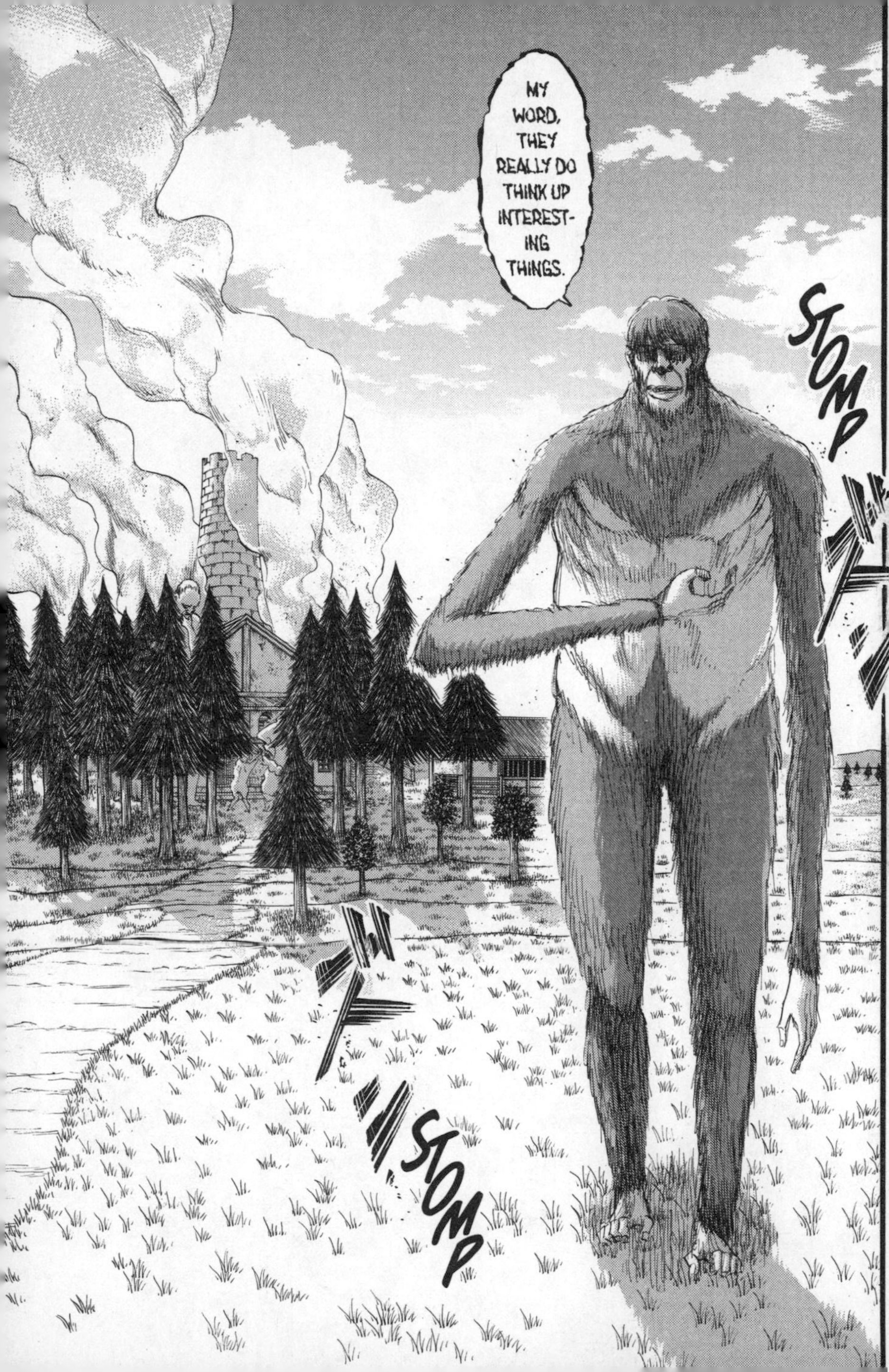
MY WORD, THEY REALLY DO THINK UP INTERESTING THINGS.
STOMP
STOMP

ATTACK on TITAN

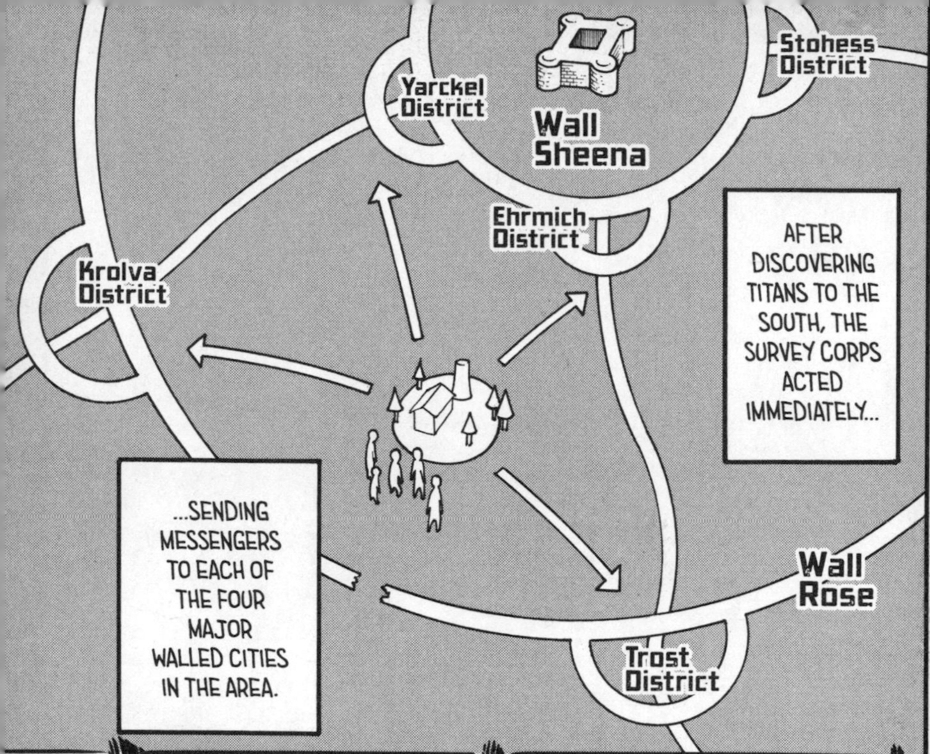
Stohess District
Wall Sheena
Yarckel District
Ehrmich District
Krolva District
AFTER DISCOVERING TITANS TO THE SOUTH, THE SURVEY CORPS ACTED IMMEDIATELY...
...SENDING MESSENGERS TO EACH OF THE FOUR MAJOR WALLED CITIES IN THE AREA.
Wall Rose
Trost District
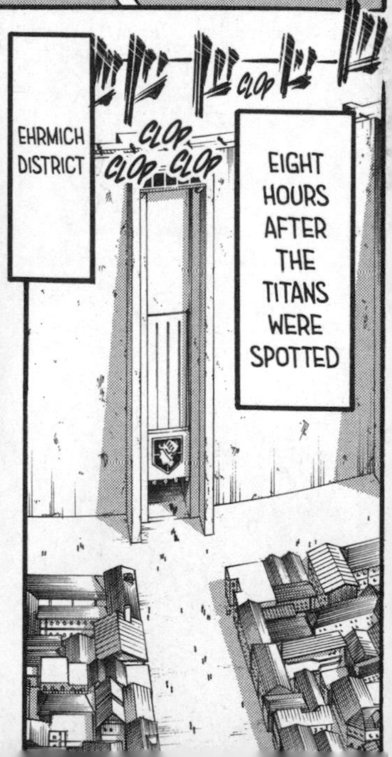
CLOP
EIGHT HOURS AFTER THE TITANS WERE SPOTTED
CLOP CLOP CLOP CLOP
EHRMICH DISTRICT
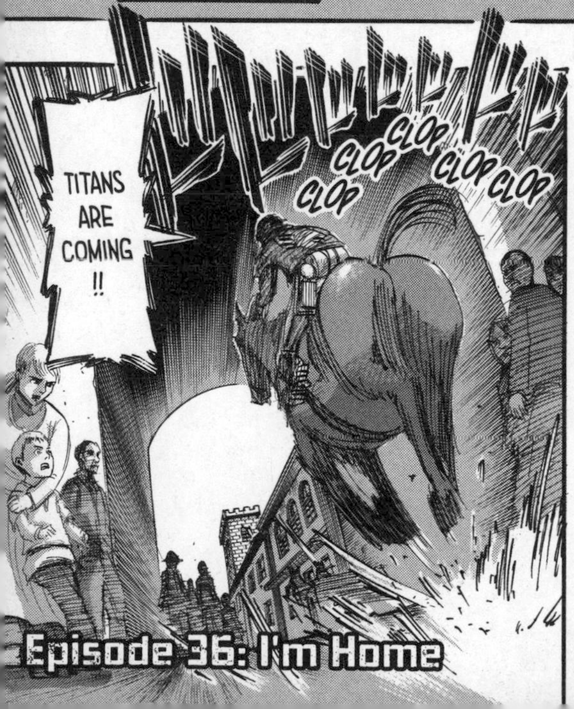
CLOP CLOP CLOP CLOP CLOP
TITANS ARE COMING !!
Episode 36: I'm Home

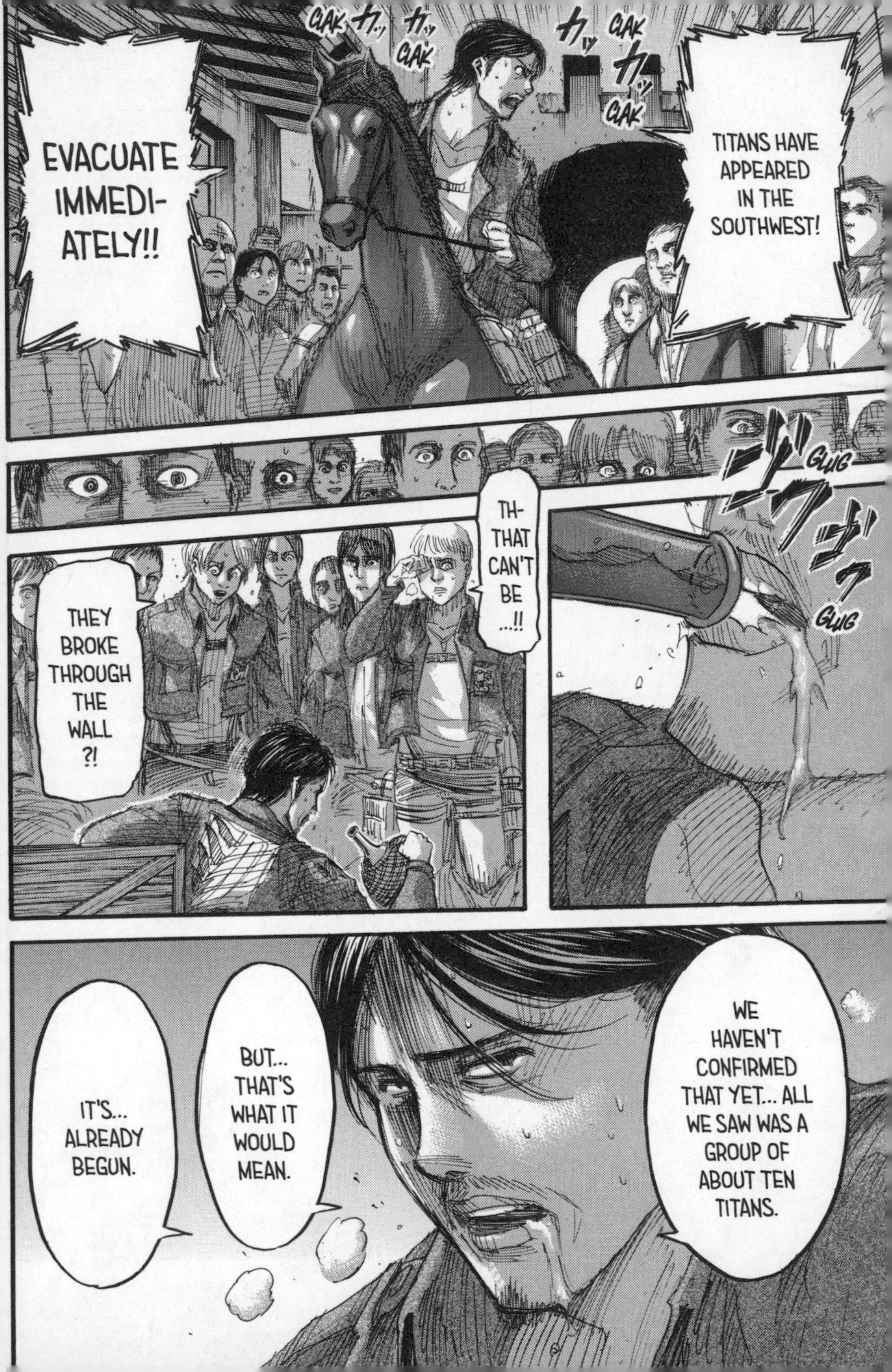
CLAK
CLAK
CLAK
CLAK
TITANS HAVE APPEARED IN THE SOUTHWEST!
EVACUATE IMMEDI-ATELY!!
GLUG
GLUG
TH-THAT CAN'T BE ...!!
THEY BROKE THROUGH THE WALL ?!
WE HAVEN'T CONFIRMED THAT YET... ALL WE SAW WAS A GROUP OF ABOUT TEN TITANS.
BUT... THAT'S WHAT IT WOULD MEAN.
IT'S... ALREADY BEGUN.

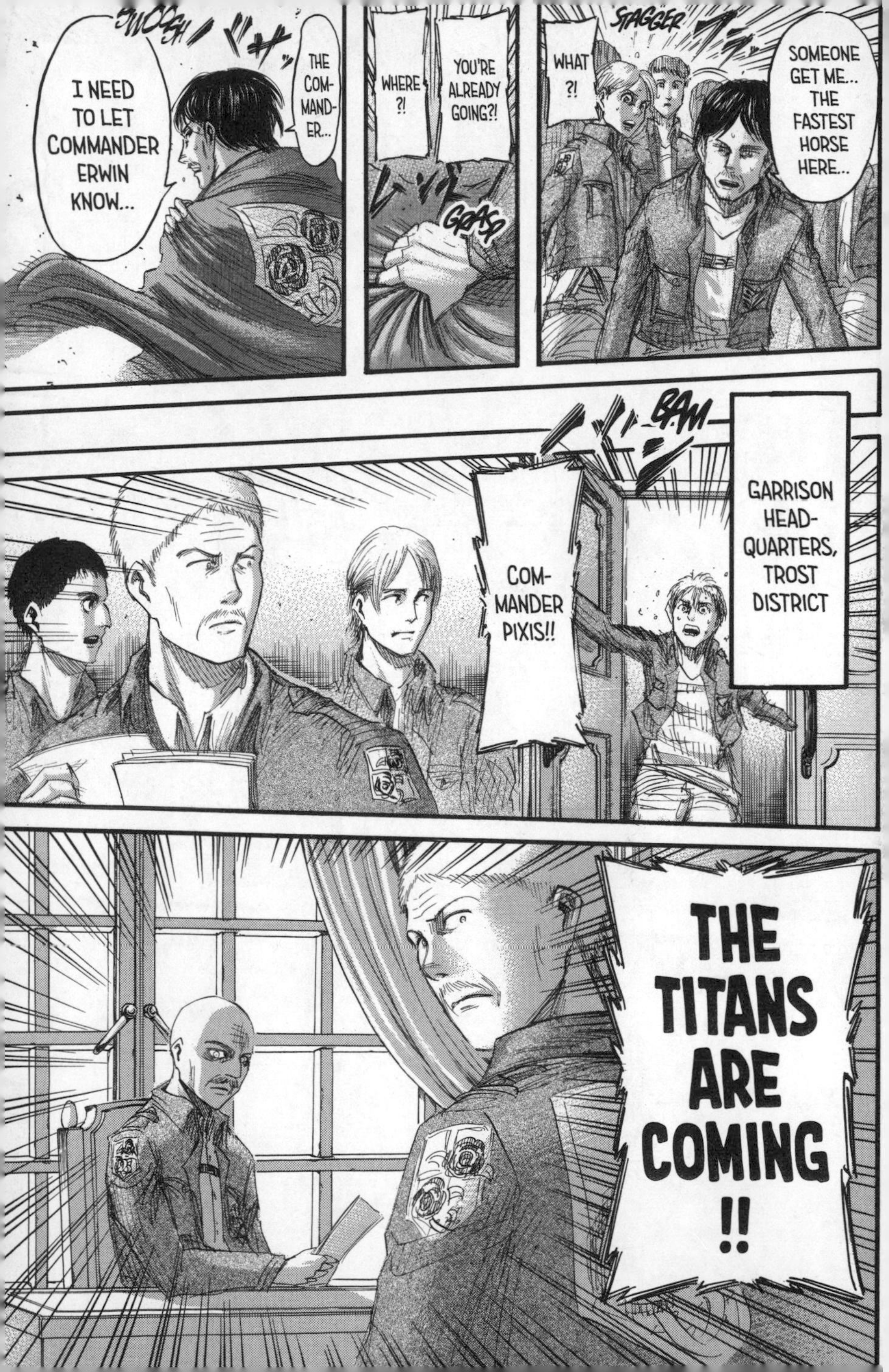
STAGGER
SOMEONE GET ME... THE FASTEST HORSE HERE...
WHAT?!
YOU'RE ALREADY GOING?!
WHERE?!
GRASP
SWOOSH
THE COMMANDER...
I NEED TO LET COMMANDER ERWIN KNOW...
GARRISON HEADQUARTERS, TROST DISTRICT
BAM
COMMANDER PIXIS!!
THE TITANS ARE COMING!!

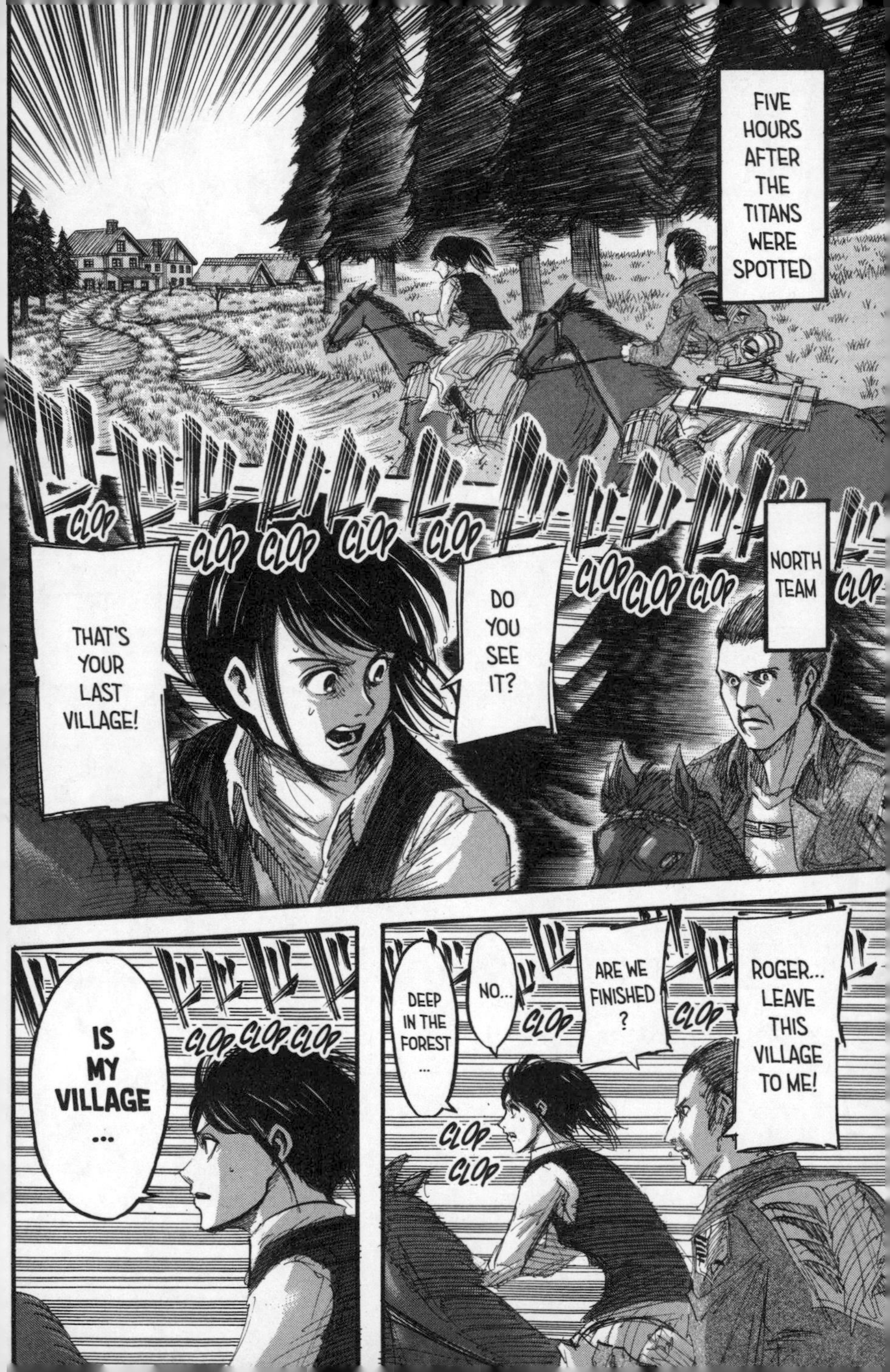
FIVE HOURS AFTER THE TITANS WERE SPOTTED
CLOP CLOP CLOP CLOP CLOP CLOP CLOP CLOP CLOP
NORTH TEAM
DO YOU SEE IT?
THAT'S YOUR LAST VILLAGE!
ROGER... LEAVE THIS VILLAGE TO ME!
CLOP
ARE WE FINISHED ?
CLOP
NO...
DEEP IN THE FOREST ...
CLOP CLOP
CLOP CLOP CLOP
IS MY VILLAGE ...

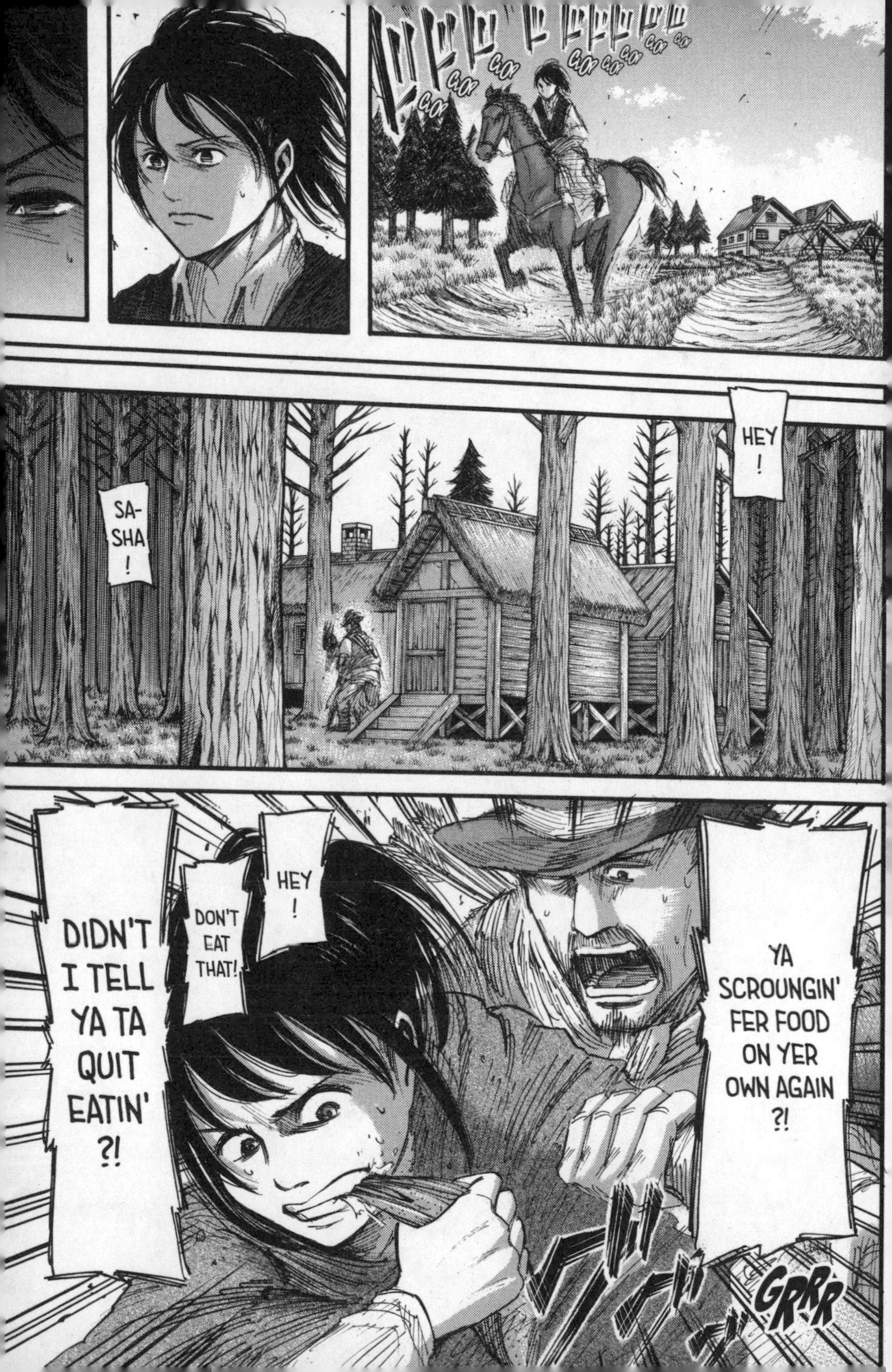
HEY!
SA-SHA!
YA SCROUNGIN' FER FOOD ON YER OWN AGAIN ?!
HEY!
DON'T EAT THAT!
DIDN'T I TELL YA TA QUIT EATIN' ?!
GRRR

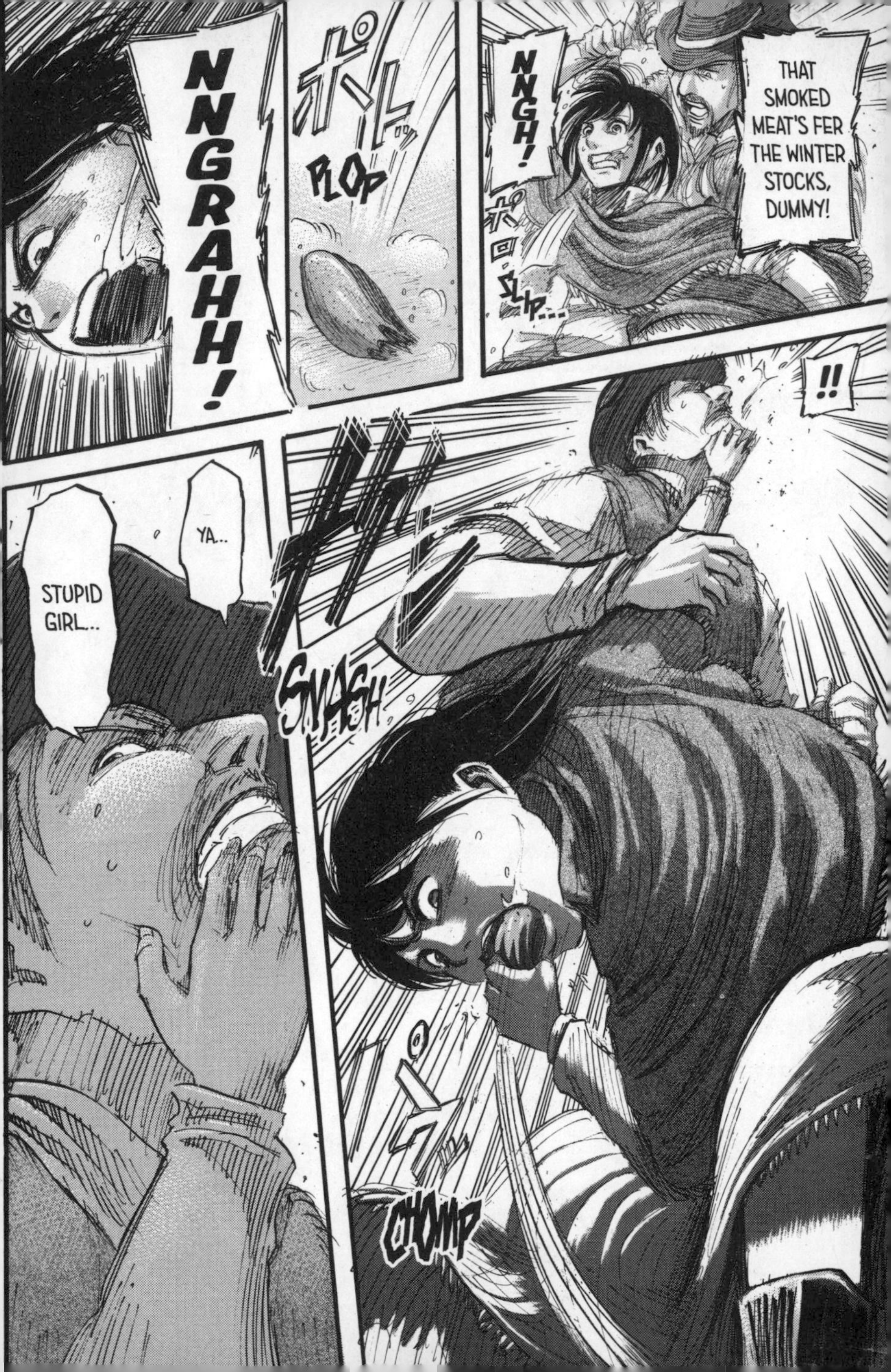
THAT SMOKED MEAT'S FER THE WINTER STOCKS, DUMMY!
NNGH!
SLIP...
PLOP
NNGRAHH!
!!
SMASH!
CHOMP
YA...
STUPID GIRL...

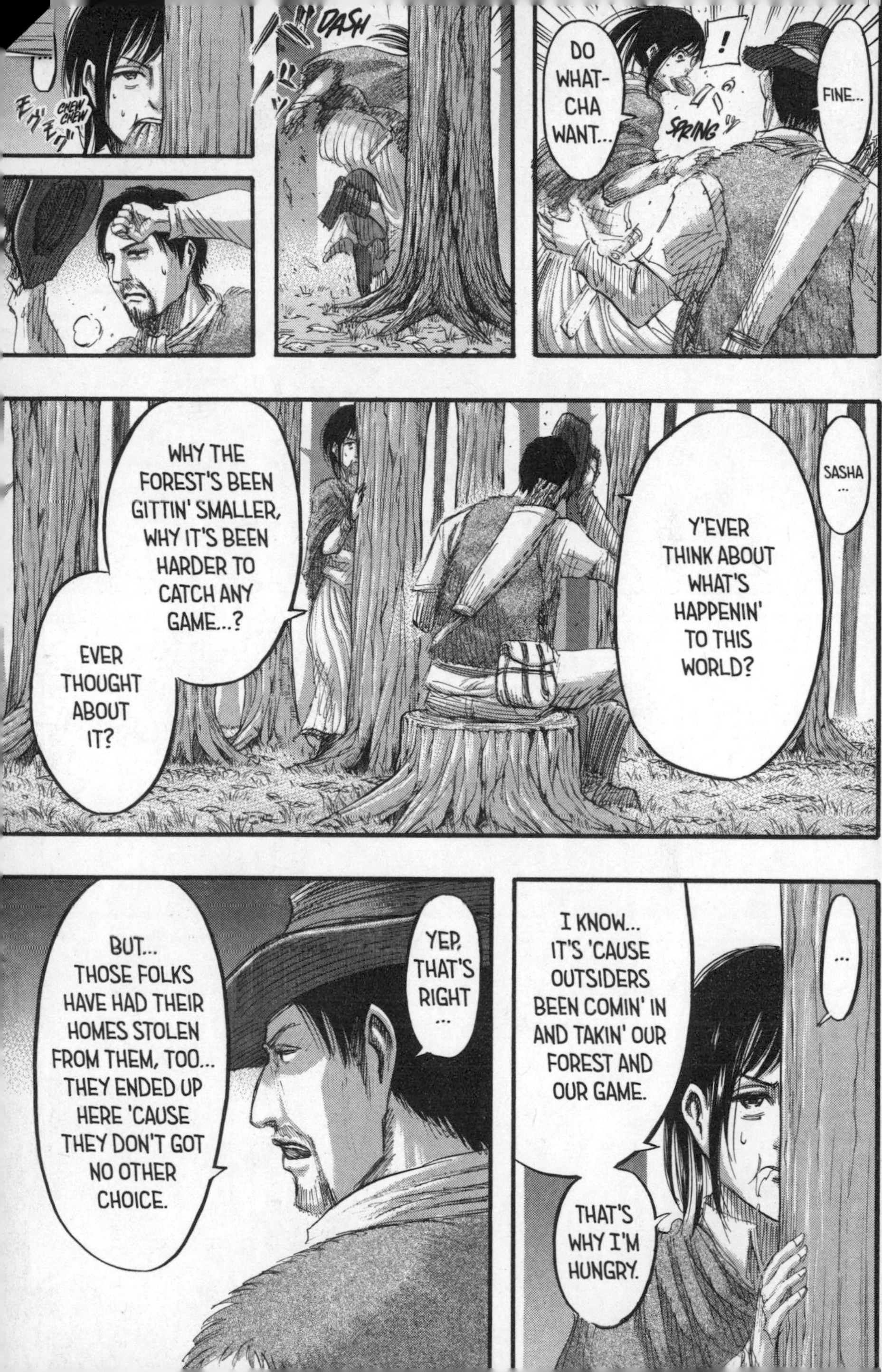
FINE...
!
SPRING
DO WHAT-CHA WANT...
DASH
...
モグモグ
CHEW CHEW
SASHA...
Y'EVER THINK ABOUT WHAT'S HAPPENIN' TO THIS WORLD?
WHY THE FOREST'S BEEN GITTIN' SMALLER, WHY IT'S BEEN HARDER TO CATCH ANY GAME...?
EVER THOUGHT ABOUT IT?
...
I KNOW... IT'S 'CAUSE OUTSIDERS BEEN COMIN' IN AND TAKIN' OUR FOREST AND OUR GAME.
THAT'S WHY I'M HUNGRY.
YEP, THAT'S RIGHT...
BUT... THOSE FOLKS HAVE HAD THEIR HOMES STOLEN FROM THEM, TOO... THEY ENDED UP HERE 'CAUSE THEY DON'T GOT NO OTHER CHOICE.

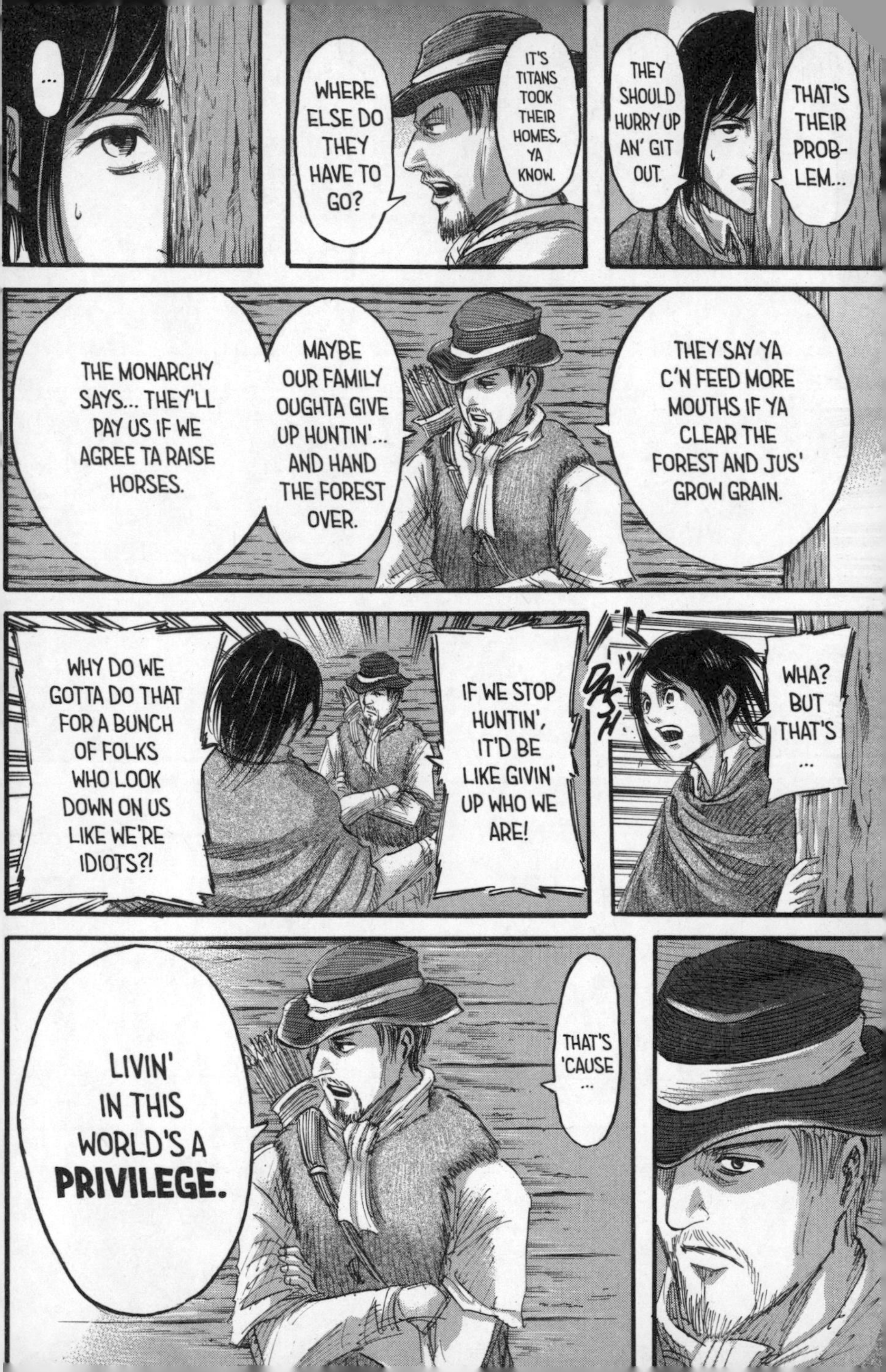
THAT'S THEIR PROBLEM...
THEY SHOULD HURRY UP AN' GIT OUT.
IT'S TITANS TOOK THEIR HOMES, YA KNOW.
WHERE ELSE DO THEY HAVE TO GO?
...
THEY SAY YA C'N FEED MORE MOUTHS IF YA CLEAR THE FOREST AND JUS' GROW GRAIN.
MAYBE OUR FAMILY OUGHTA GIVE UP HUNTIN'... AND HAND THE FOREST OVER.
THE MONARCHY SAYS... THEY'LL PAY US IF WE AGREE TA RAISE HORSES.
WHA? BUT THAT'S ...
DASH
IF WE STOP HUNTIN', IT'D BE LIKE GIVIN' UP WHO WE ARE!
WHY DO WE GOTTA DO THAT FOR A BUNCH OF FOLKS WHO LOOK DOWN ON US LIKE WE'RE IDIOTS?!
THAT'S 'CAUSE ...
LIVIN' IN THIS WORLD'S A PRIVILEGE.

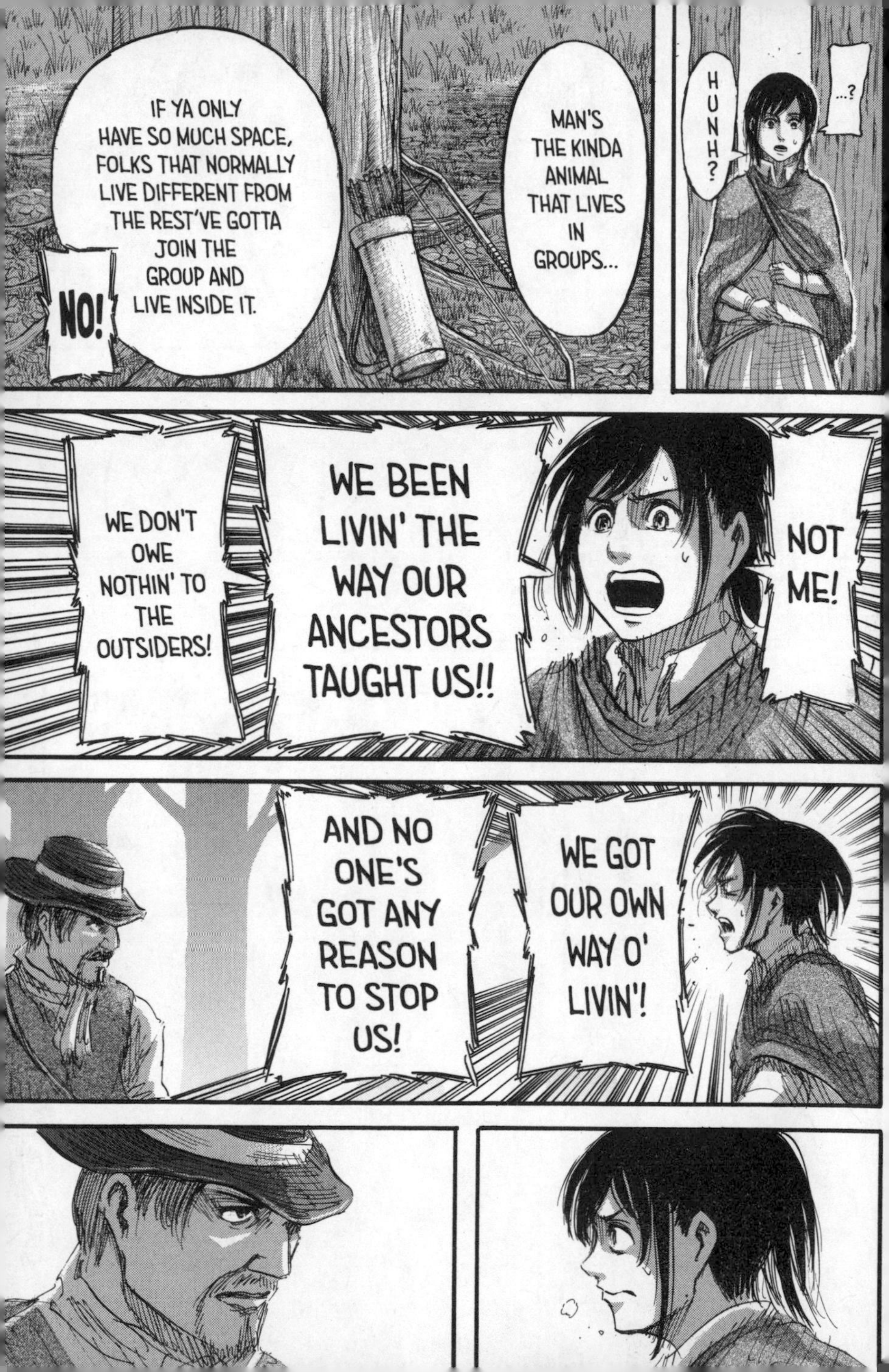

...?
HUNH?
MAN'S THE KINDA ANIMAL THAT LIVES IN GROUPS...
IF YA ONLY HAVE SO MUCH SPACE, FOLKS THAT NORMALLY LIVE DIFFERENT FROM THE REST'VE GOTTA JOIN THE GROUP AND LIVE INSIDE IT.
NO!
NOT ME!
WE BEEN LIVIN' THE WAY OUR ANCESTORS TAUGHT US!!
WE DON'T OWE NOTHIN' TO THE OUTSIDERS!
WE GOT OUR OWN WAY O' LIVIN'!
AND NO ONE'S GOT ANY REASON TO STOP US!

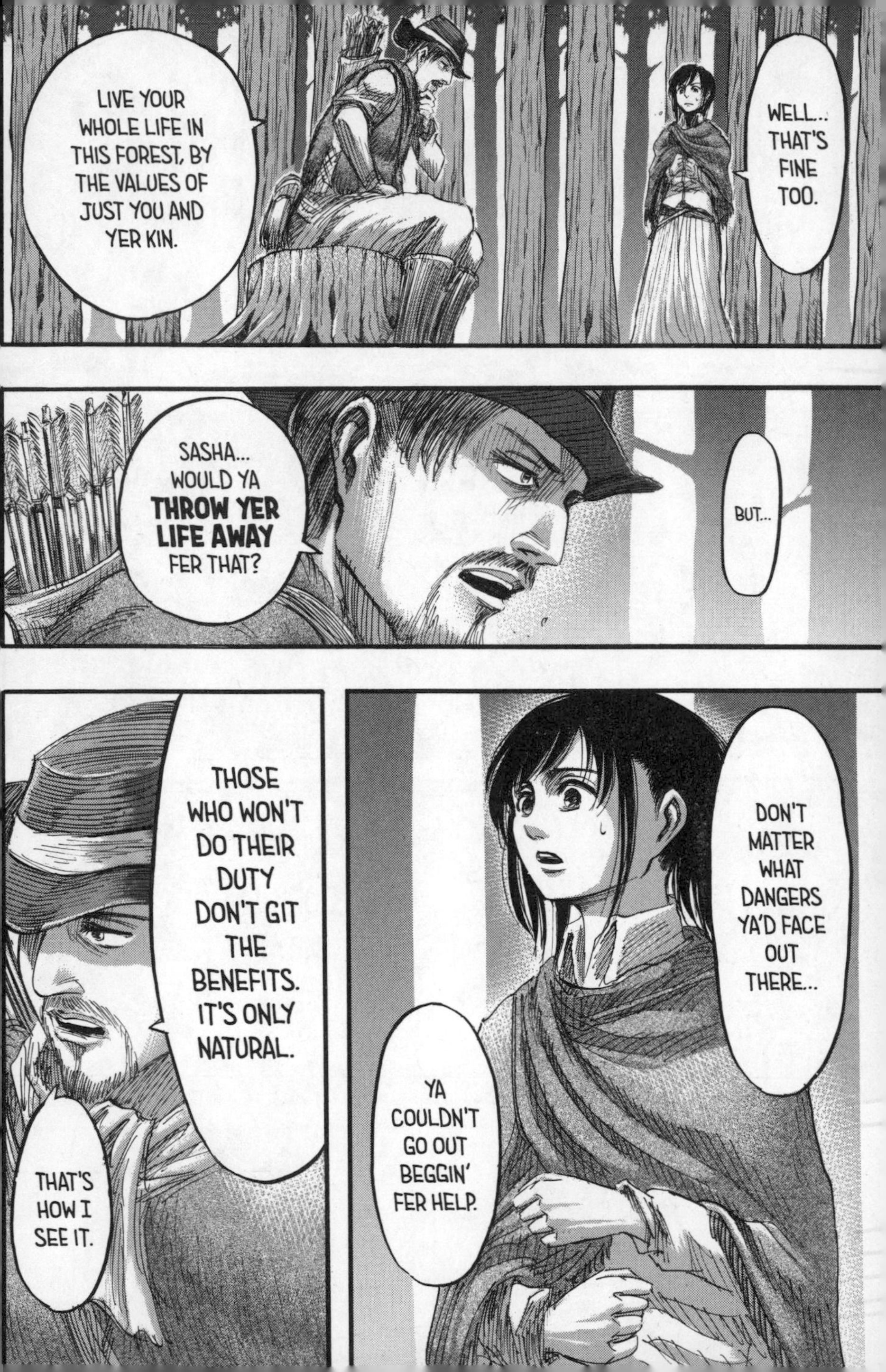
WELL... THAT'S FINE TOO.
LIVE YOUR WHOLE LIFE IN THIS FOREST, BY THE VALUES OF JUST YOU AND YER KIN.
BUT...
SASHA... WOULD YA **THROW YER LIFE AWAY** FER THAT?
DON'T MATTER WHAT DANGERS YA'D FACE OUT THERE...
YA COULDN'T GO OUT BEGGIN' FER HELP.
THOSE WHO WON'T DO THEIR DUTY DON'T GIT THE BENEFITS. IT'S ONLY NATURAL.
THAT'S HOW I SEE IT.

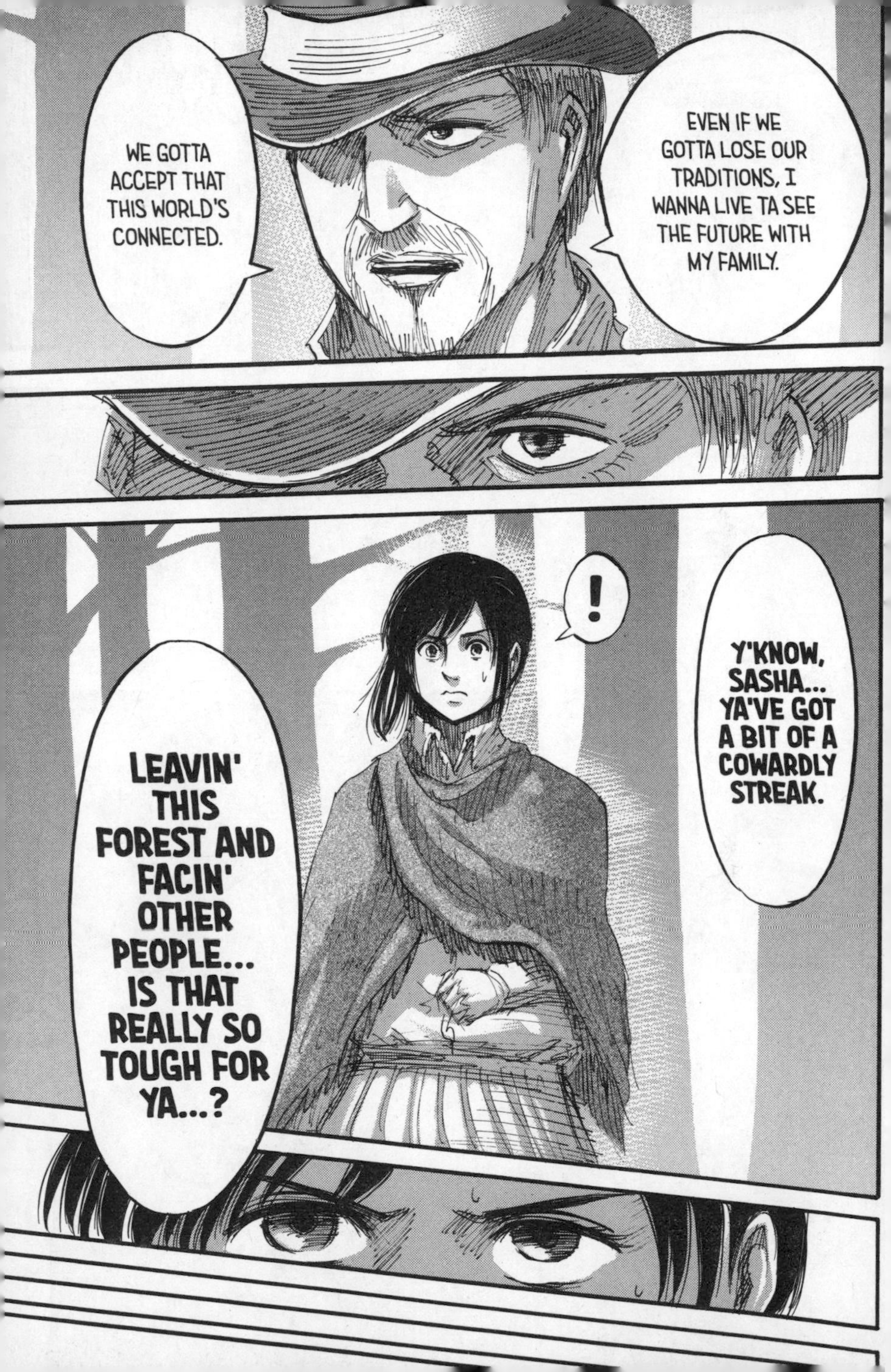

EVEN IF WE GOTTA LOSE OUR TRADITIONS, I WANNA LIVE TA SEE THE FUTURE WITH MY FAMILY.
WE GOTTA ACCEPT THAT THIS WORLD'S CONNECTED.
Y'KNOW, SASHA... YA'VE GOT A BIT OF A COWARDLY STREAK.
!
LEAVIN' THIS FOREST AND FACIN' OTHER PEOPLE... IS THAT REALLY SO TOUGH FOR YA...?

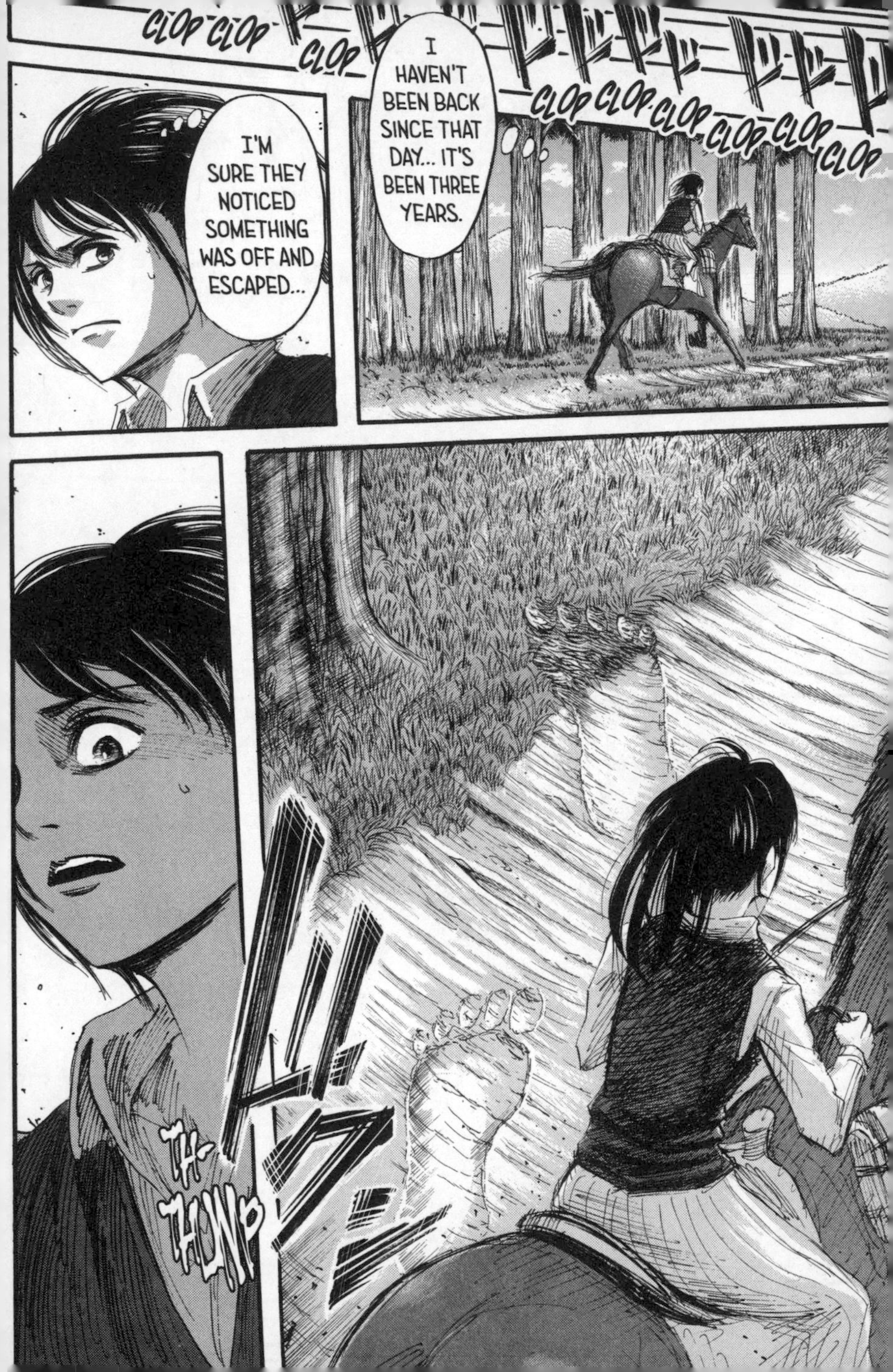
CLOP CLOP CLOP CLOP CLOP CLOP
CLOP CLOP CLOP
I HAVEN'T BEEN BACK SINCE THAT DAY... IT'S BEEN THREE YEARS.
I'M SURE THEY NOTICED SOMETHING WAS OFF AND ESCAPED...
TH-THUMP

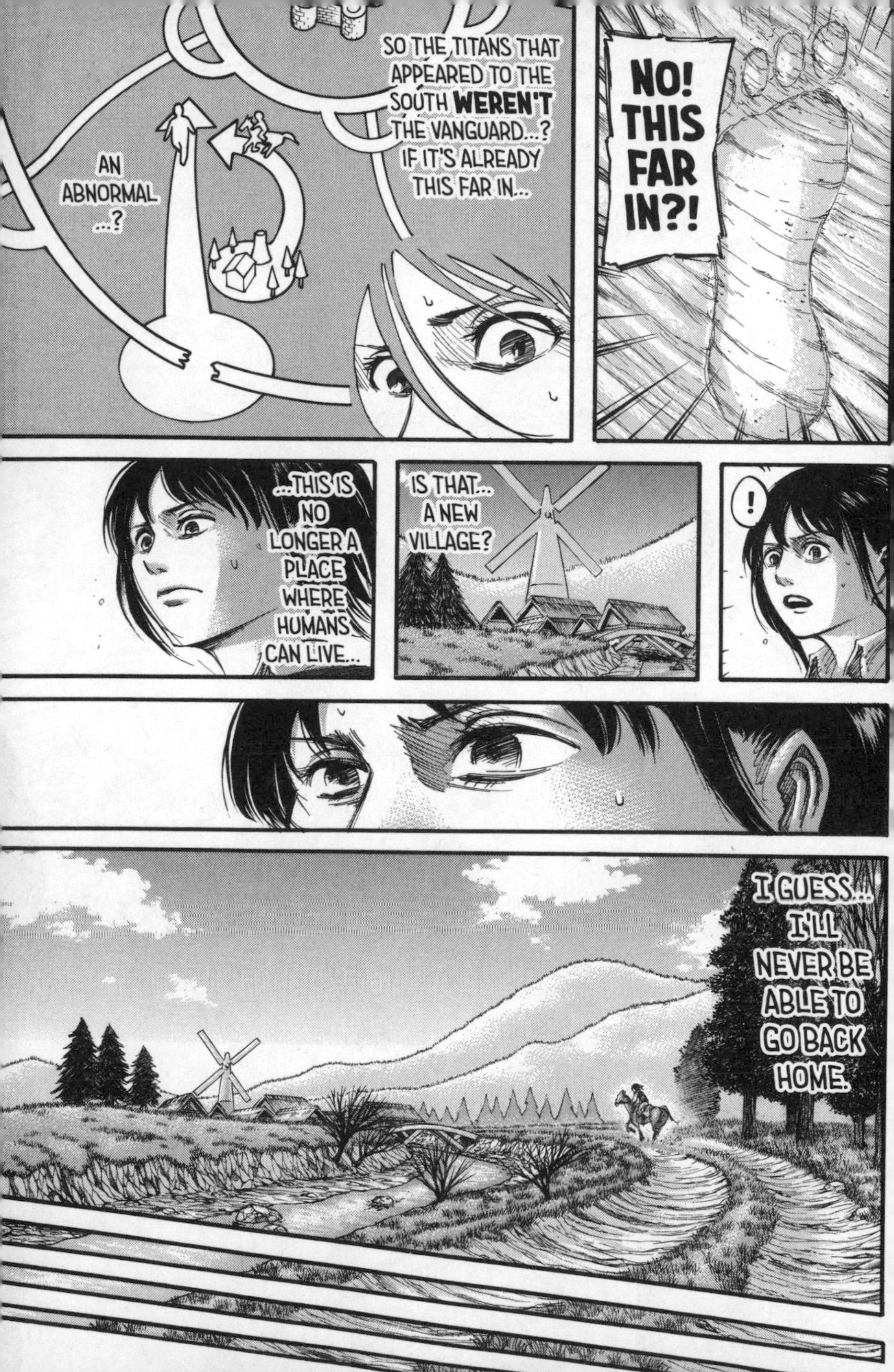
NO! THIS FAR IN?!
SO THE TITANS THAT APPEARED TO THE SOUTH **WEREN'T** THE VANGUARD...? IF IT'S ALREADY THIS FAR IN...
AN ABNORMAL ...?
!
IS THAT... A NEW VILLAGE?
...THIS IS NO LONGER A PLACE WHERE HUMANS CAN LIVE...
I GUESS... I'LL NEVER BE ABLE TO GO BACK HOME.

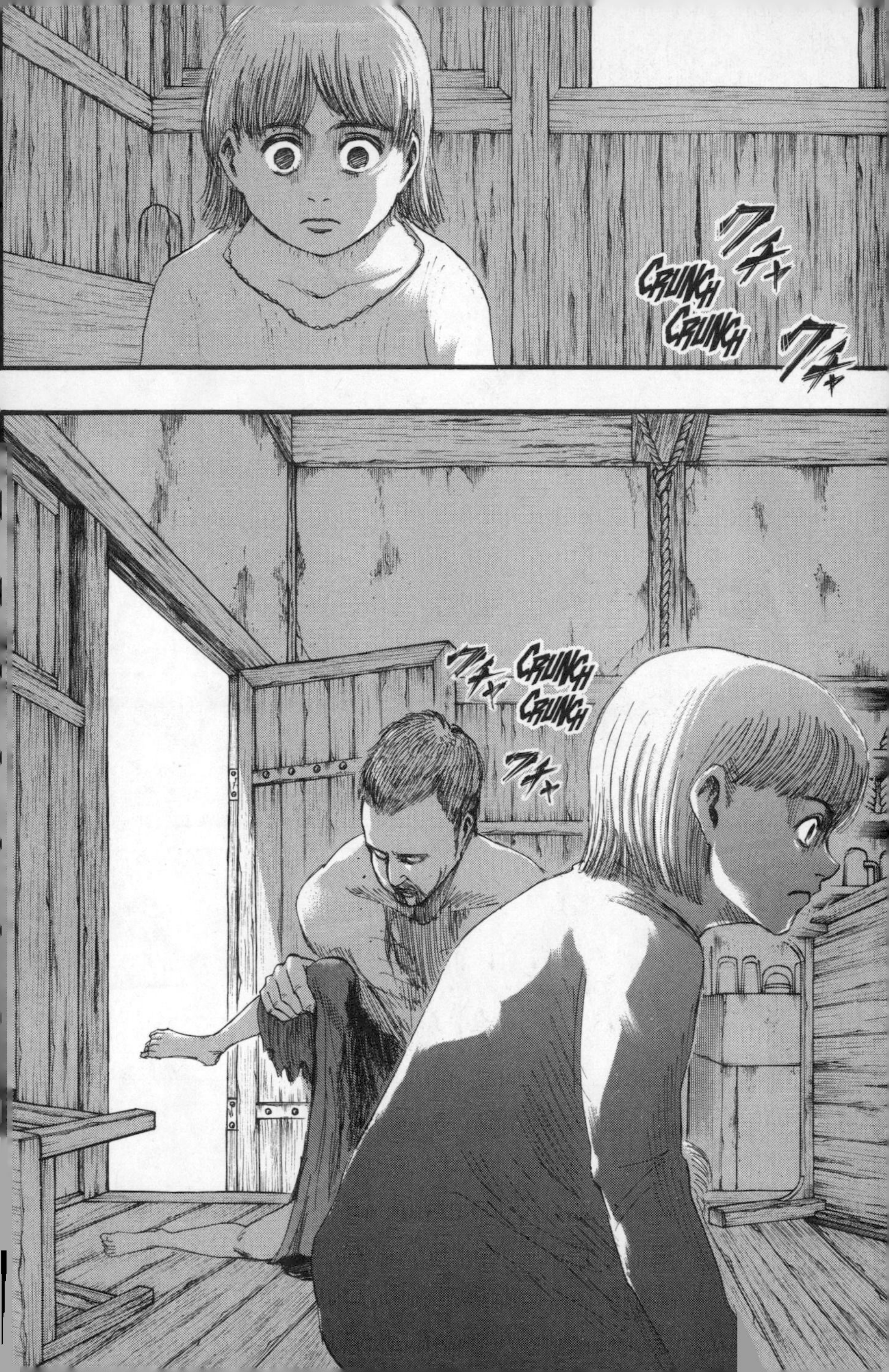
クチャ
CRUNCH
CRUNCH
クチャ
クチャ
CRUNCH
CRUNCH
クチャ

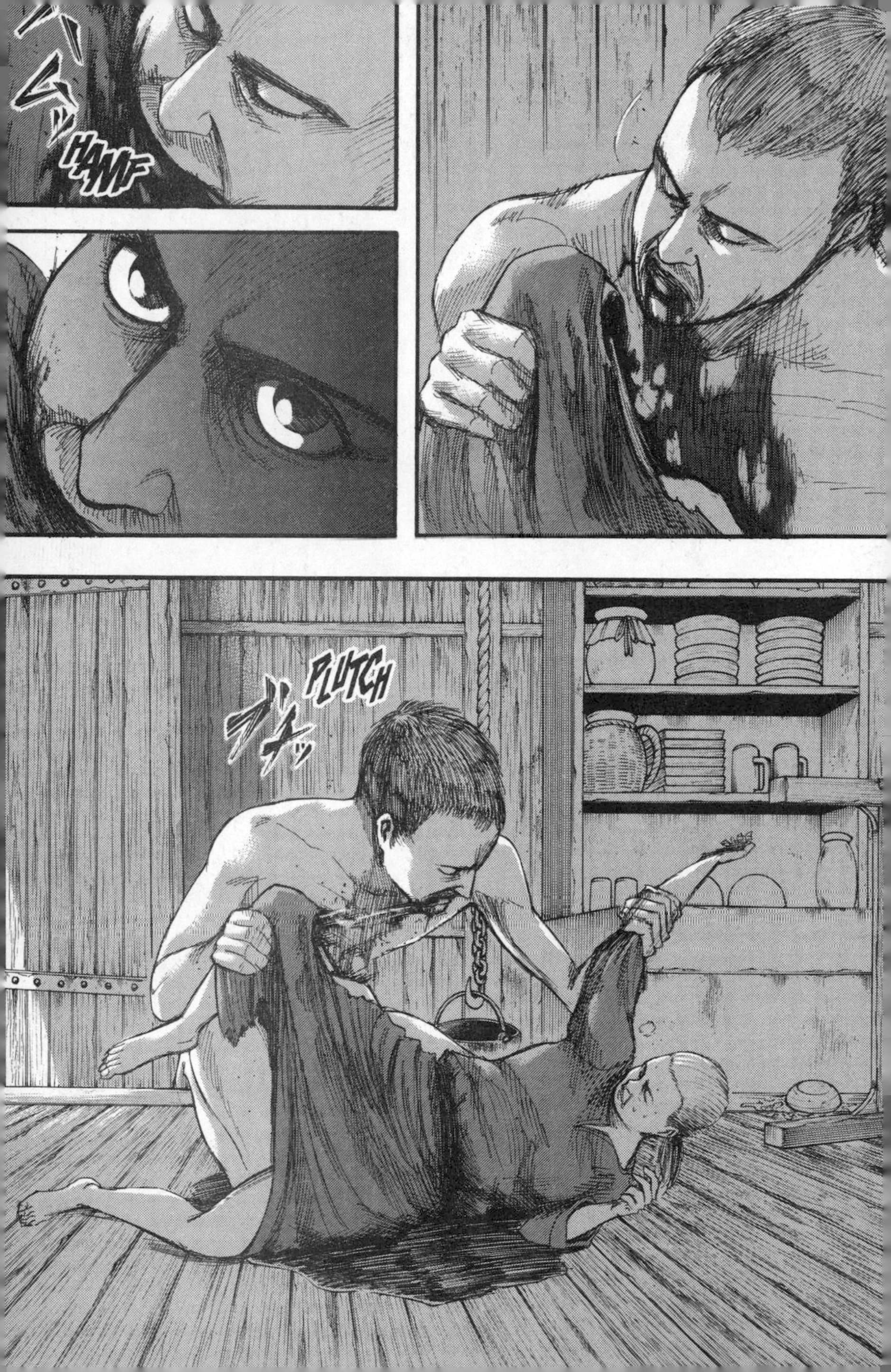
ハムッ
HAMF
ブチッ
PLUTCH

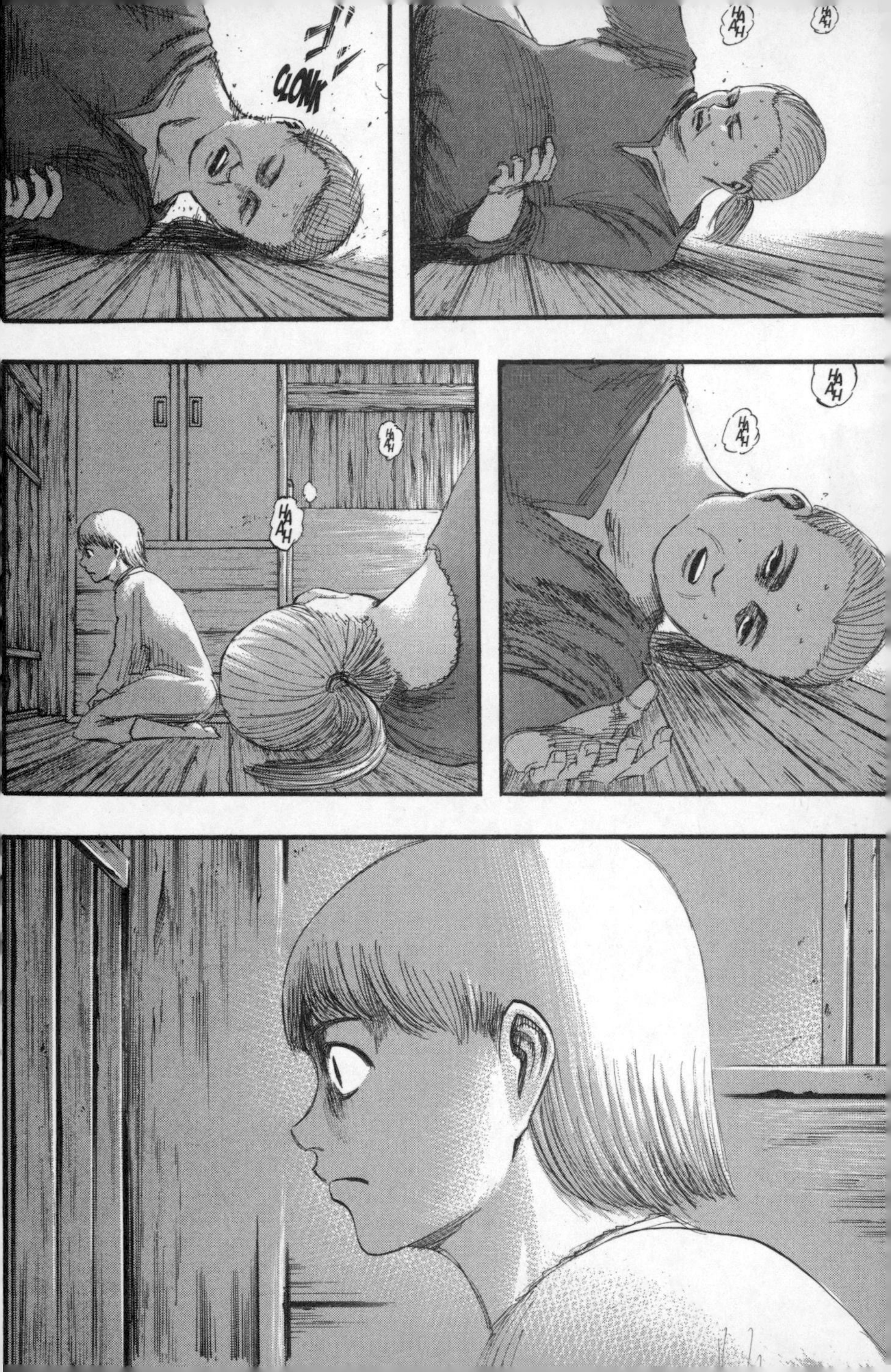
HAAH
HAAH
CLONK
HAAH
HAAH
HAAH
HAAH

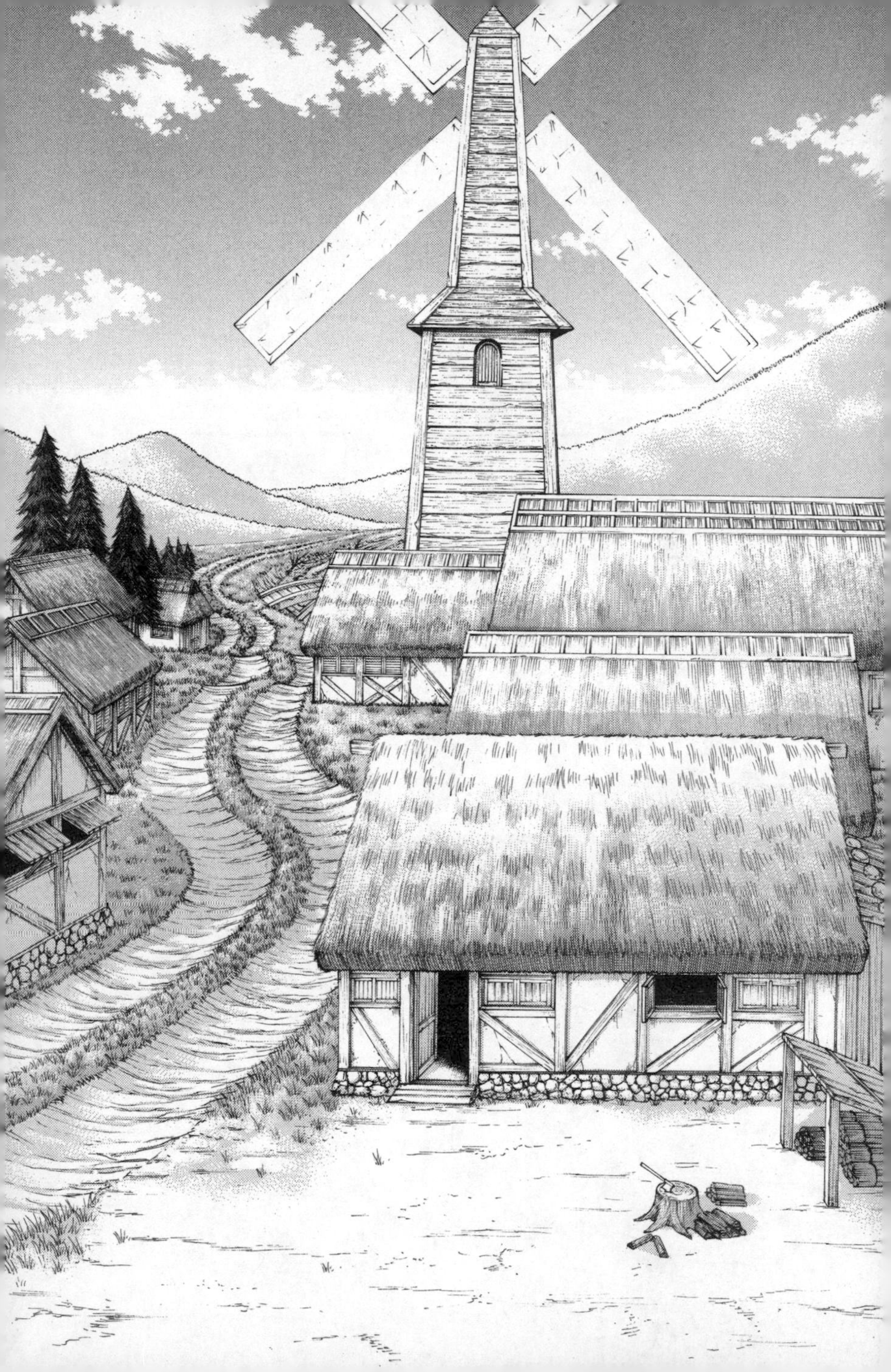

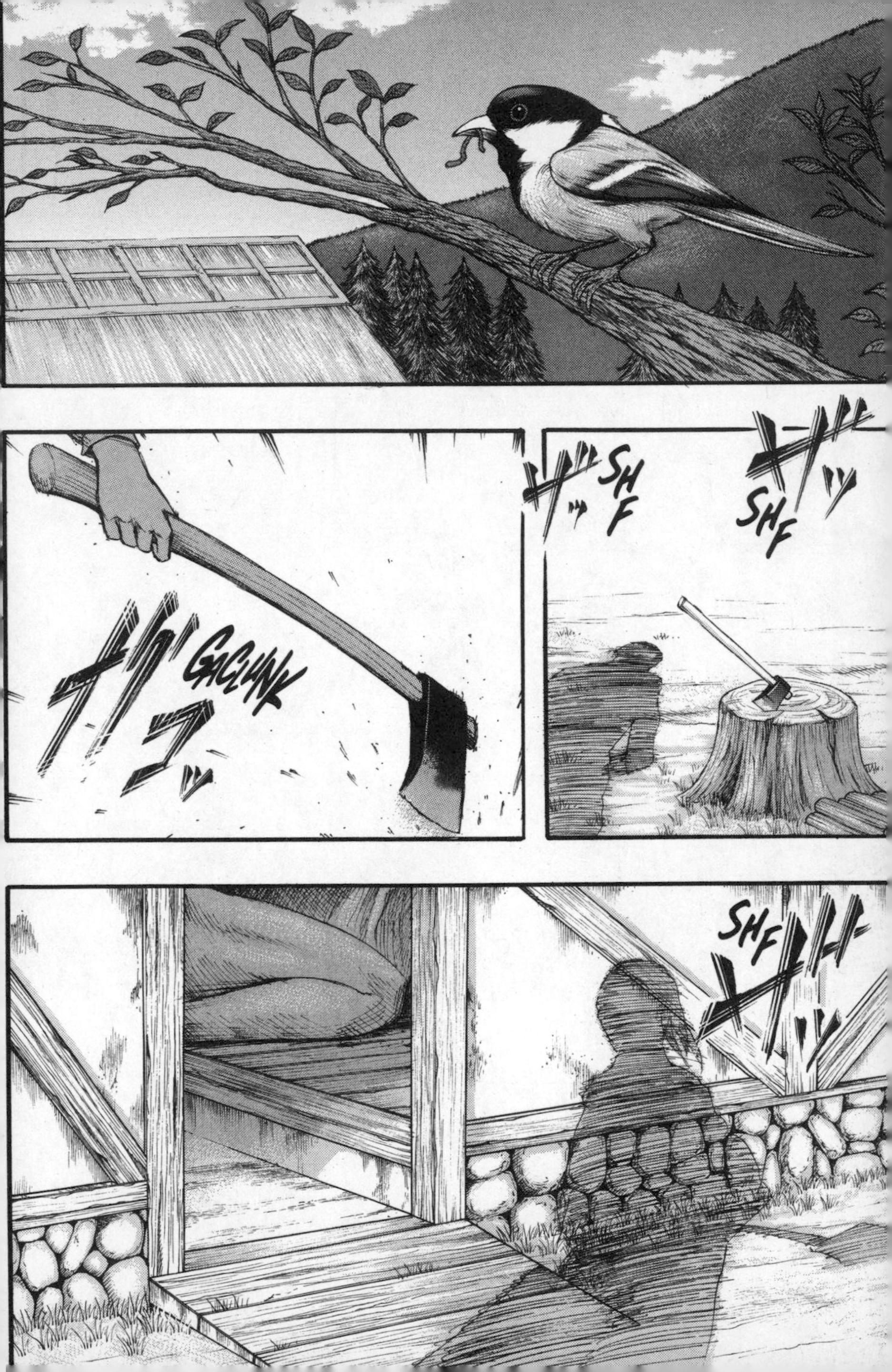
SHF
SHF
GACLUNK
SHF

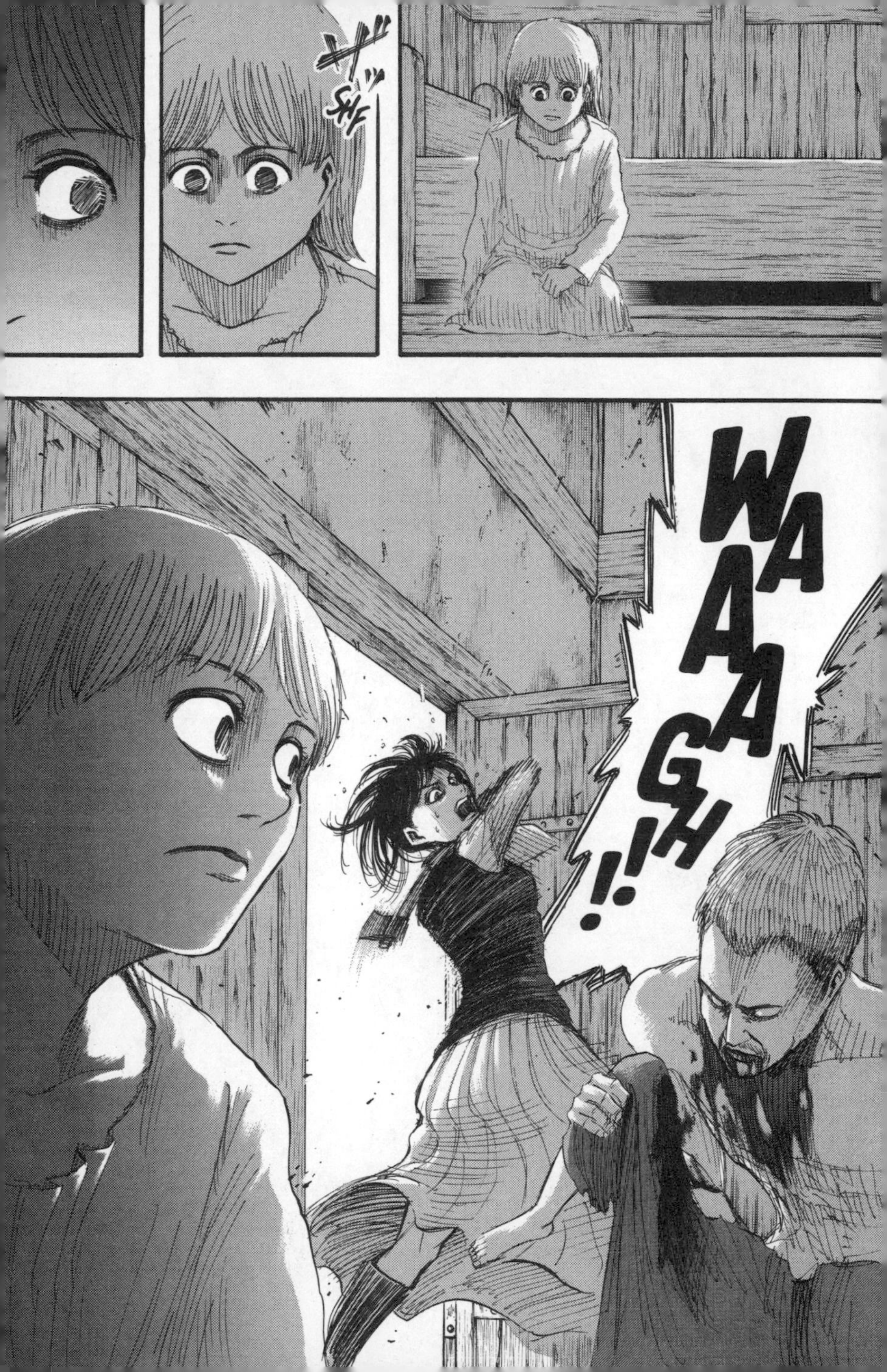
SHF
WAAAAGH!!

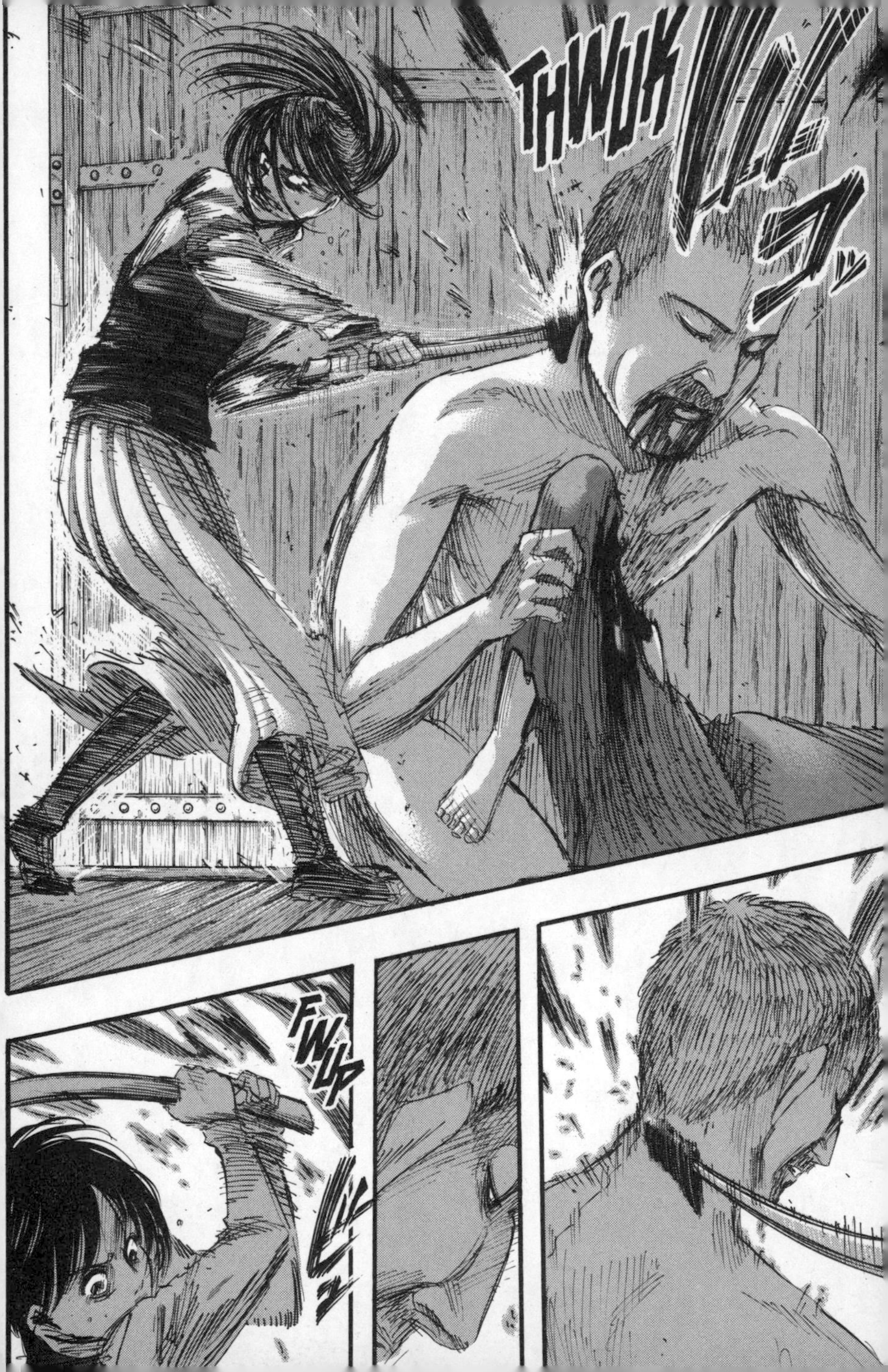
THWUK
FWUP

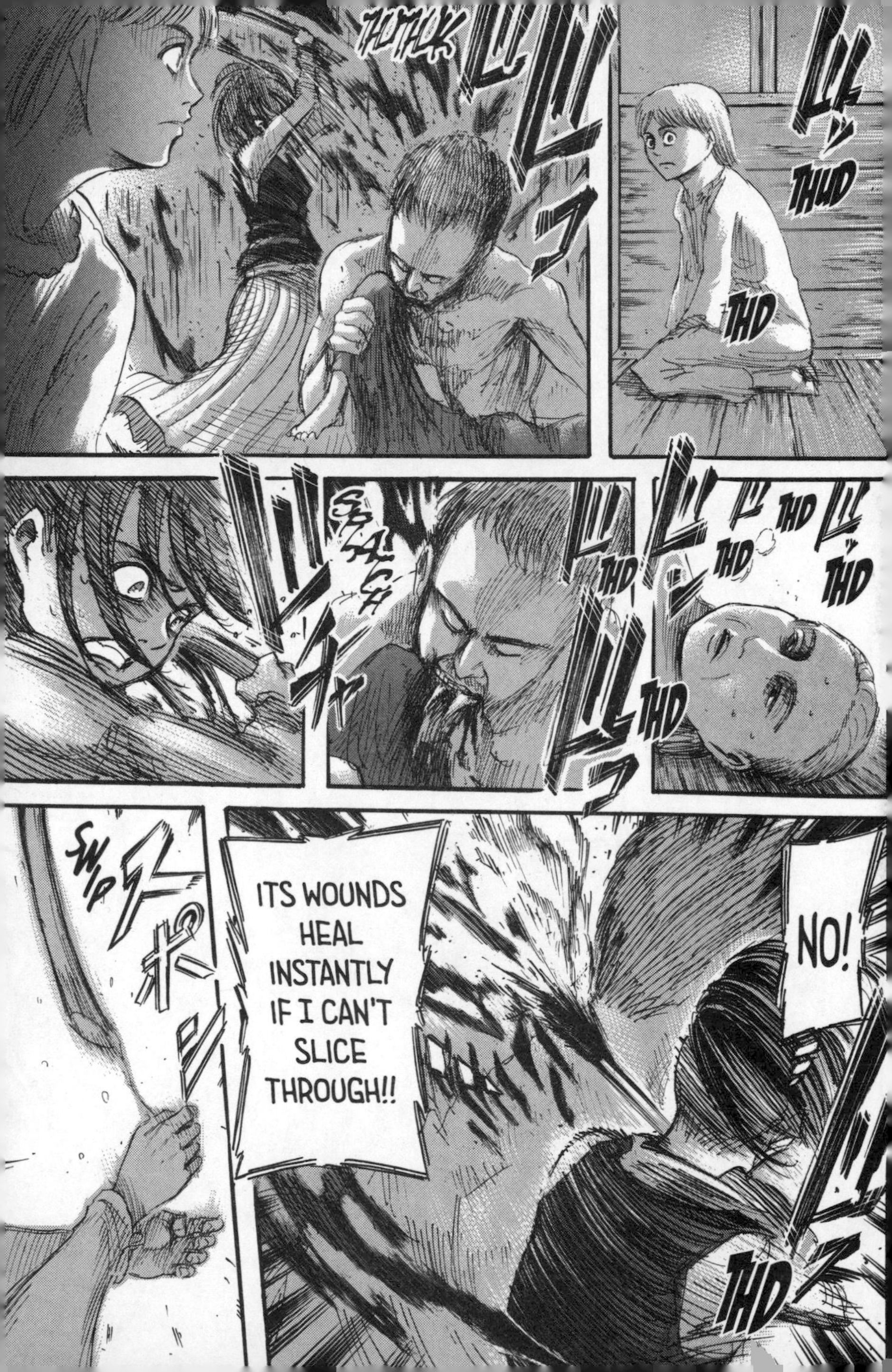
THUD
THD
THOTHOK
THD
THD
THD
THD
THD
NO!
ITS WOUNDS HEAL INSTANTLY IF I CAN'T SLICE THROUGH!!
THD
SNIP

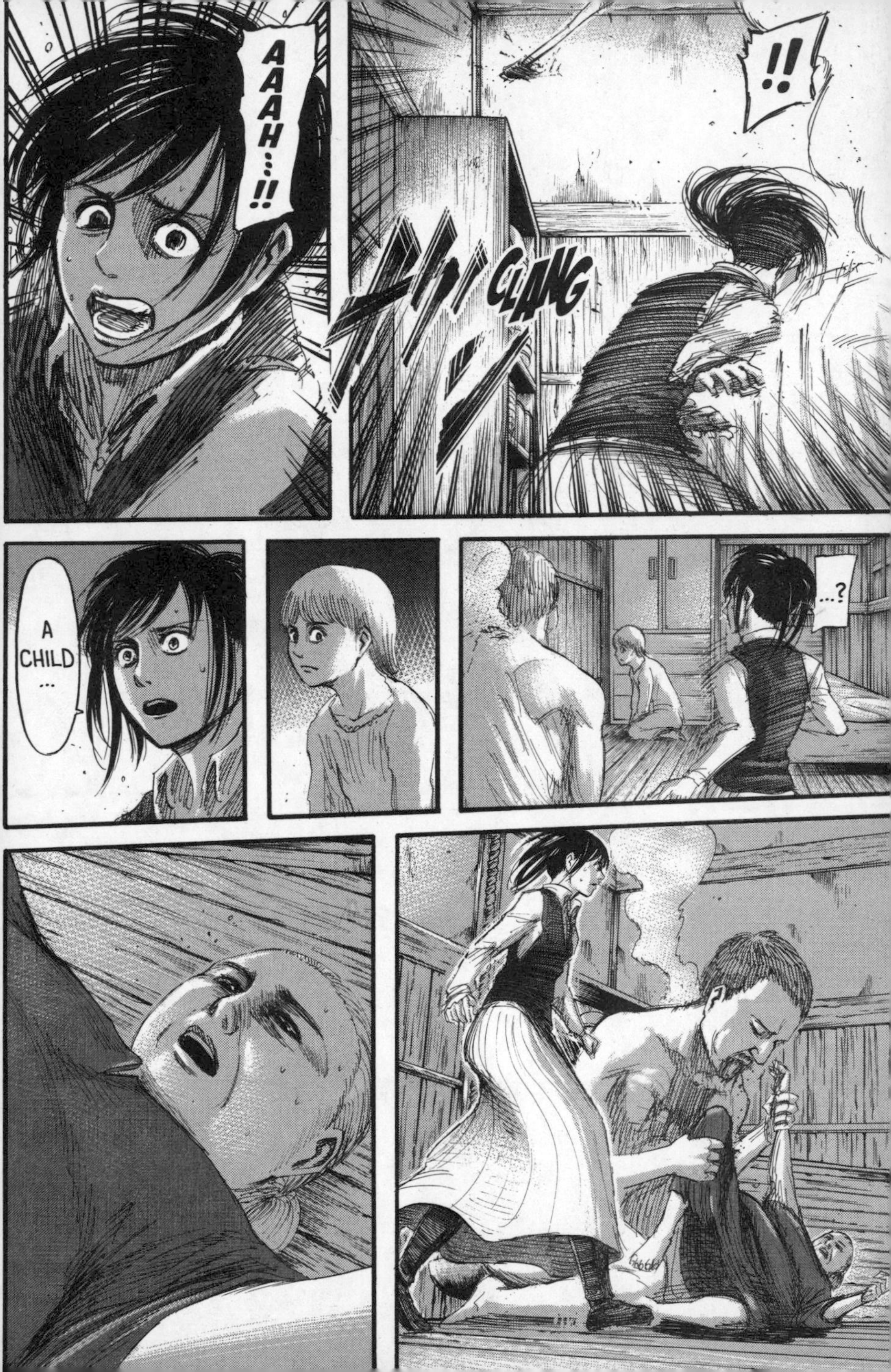
!!
CLANG
AAAH...!!
...?
A CHILD ...

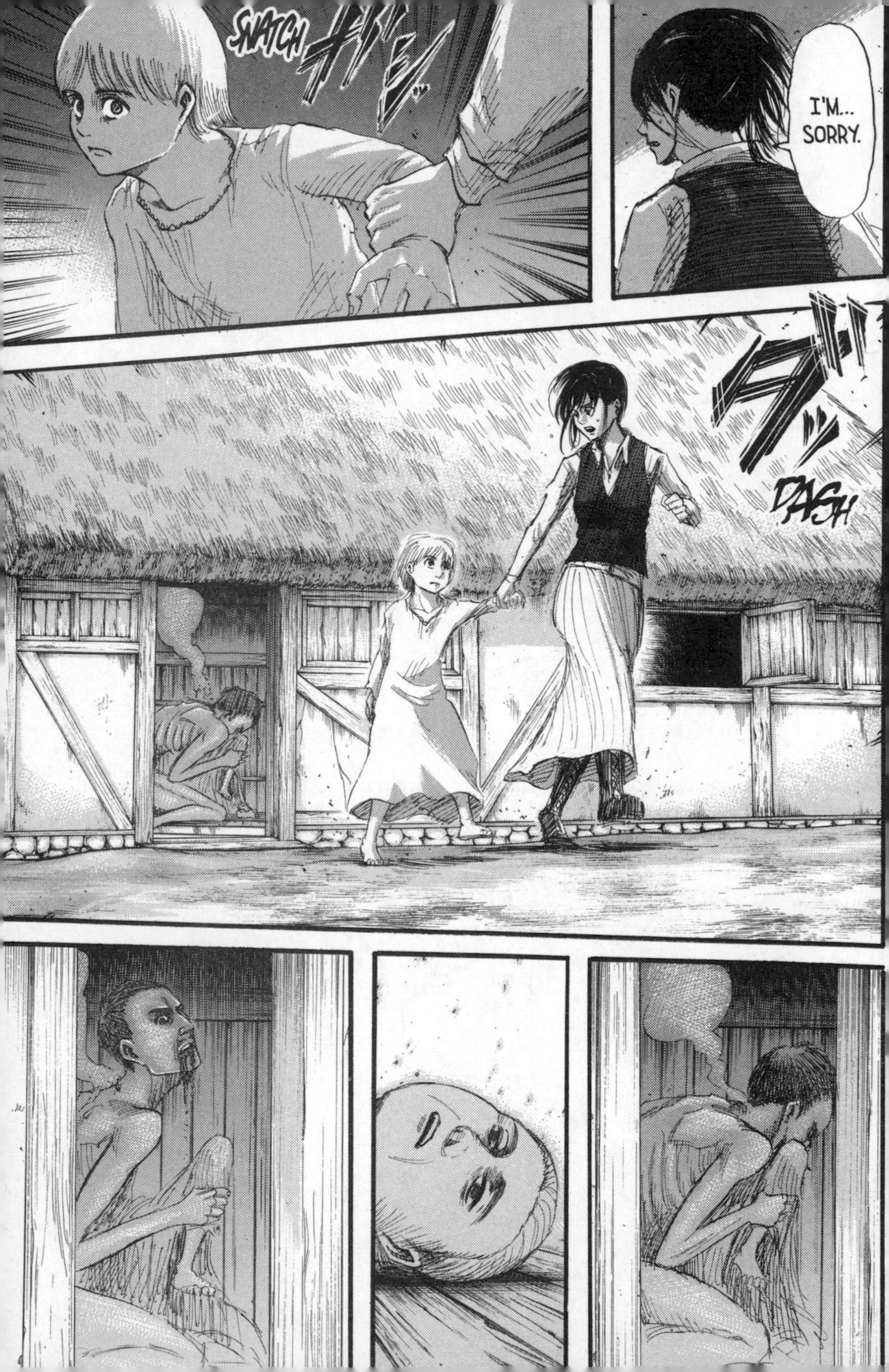
I'M... SORRY.
SNATCH
DASH

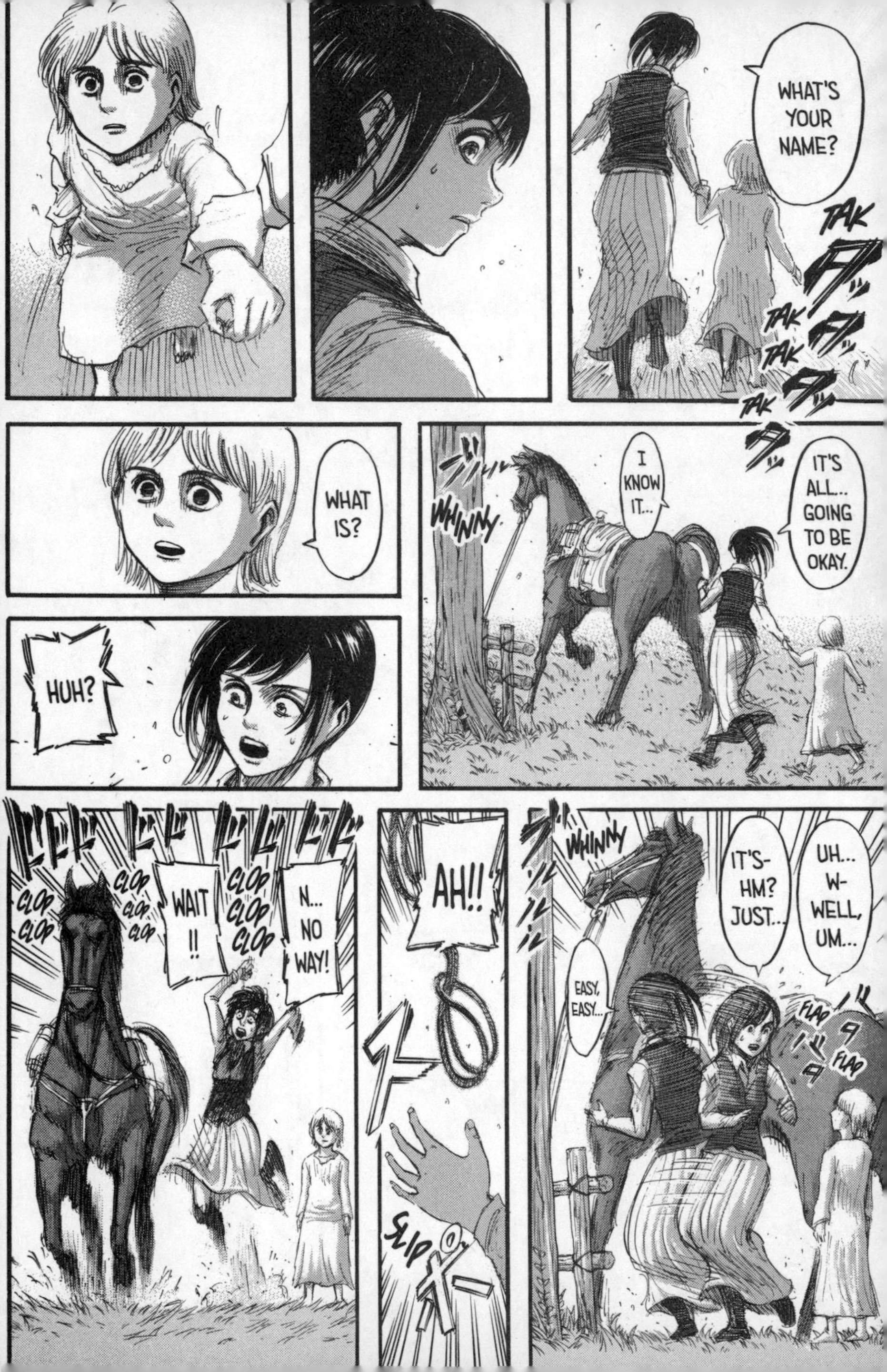

WHAT'S YOUR NAME?
TAK
TAK
TAK
TAK
IT'S ALL... GOING TO BE OKAY.
I KNOW IT...
WHINNY
WHAT IS?
HUH?
UH... W-WELL, UM...
IT'S-HM? JUST...
WHINNY
FLAP
FLAP
EASY, EASY...
AH!!
SLIP
N... NO WAY!
CLOP CLOP CLOP
WAIT!!
CLOP CLOP CLOP
CLOP CLOP

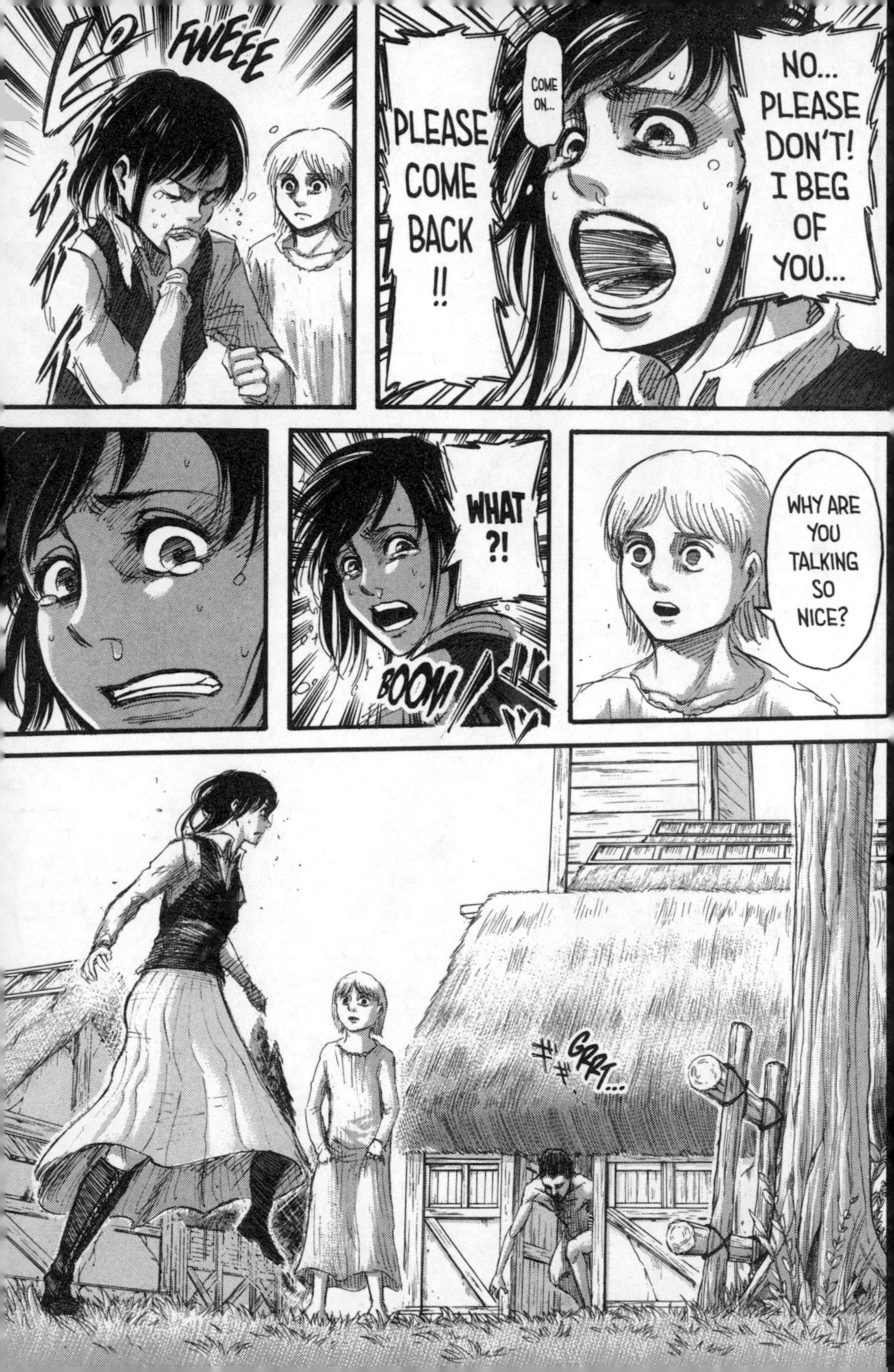
NO... PLEASE DON'T! I BEG OF YOU...
COME ON...
PLEASE COME BACK !!
FWEEE
WHY ARE YOU TALKING SO NICE?
WHAT ?!
BOOM
GRRT...

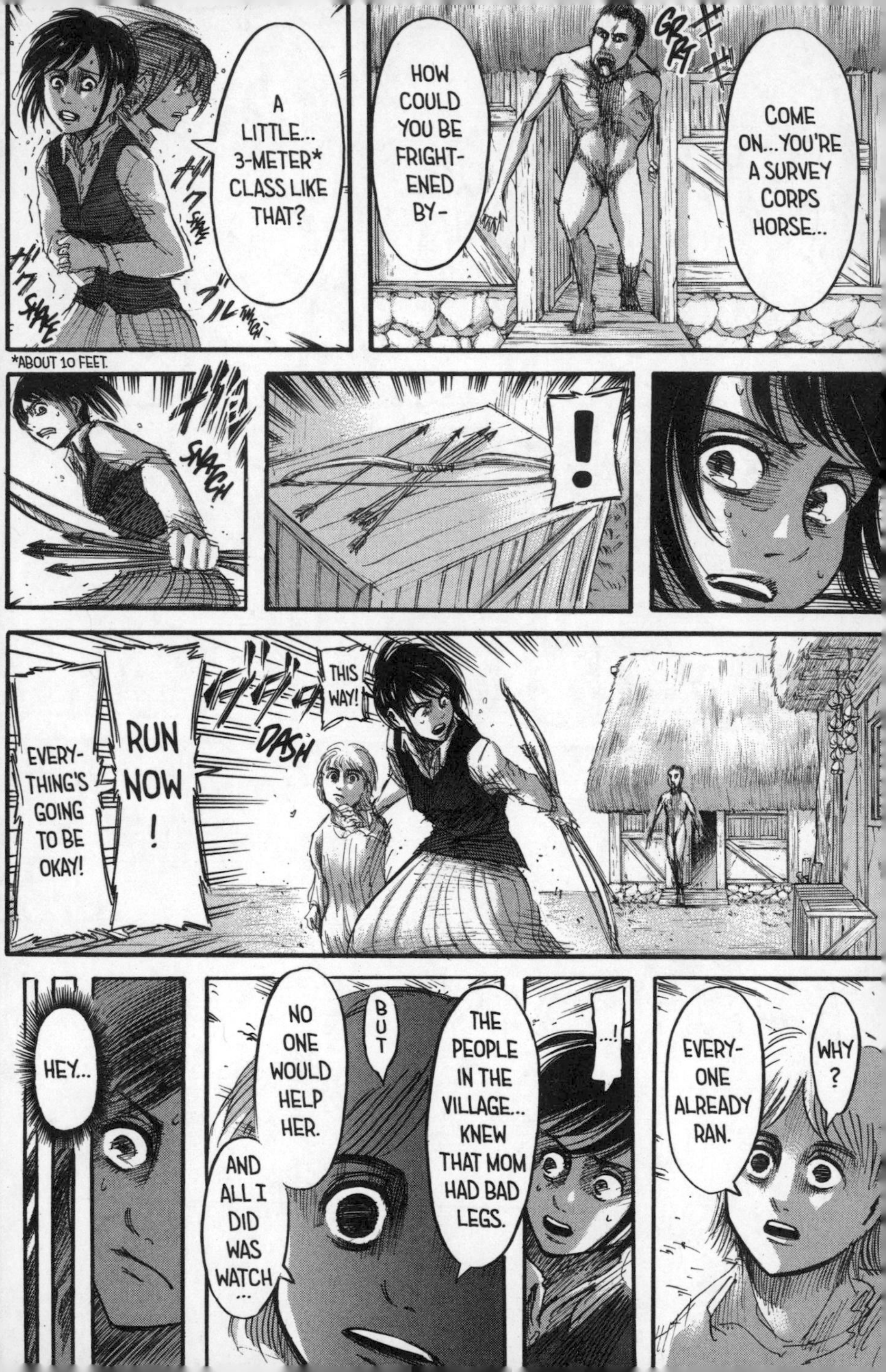
GRR
COME ON... YOU'RE A SURVEY CORPS HORSE...
HOW COULD YOU BE FRIGHT-ENED BY-
A LITTLE... 3-METER* CLASS LIKE THAT?
SHAKE
SHAKE
TWITCH
!
SNATCH
THIS WAY!
DASH
RUN NOW!
EVERY-THING'S GOING TO BE OKAY!
WHY?
EVERY-ONE ALREADY RAN.
...!
THE PEOPLE IN THE VILLAGE... KNEW THAT MOM HAD BAD LEGS.
BUT
NO ONE WOULD HELP HER.
AND ALL I DID WAS WATCH...
HEY...

*ABOUT 10 FEET.

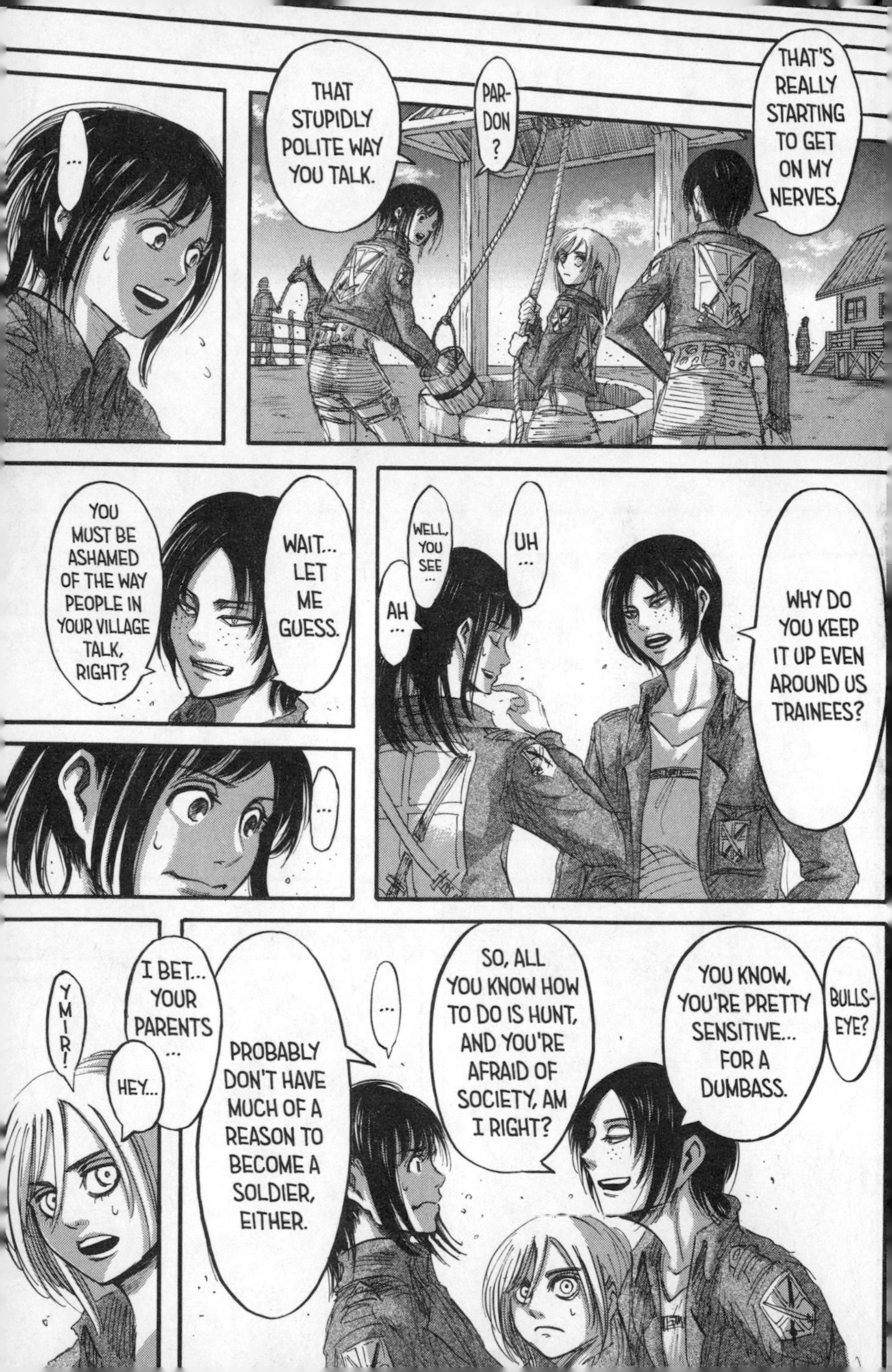

THAT'S REALLY STARTING TO GET ON MY NERVES.
PAR-DON?
THAT STUPIDLY POLITE WAY YOU TALK.
...
WHY DO YOU KEEP IT UP EVEN AROUND US TRAINEES?
UH...
WELL, YOU SEE...
AH...
WAIT... LET ME GUESS.
YOU MUST BE ASHAMED OF THE WAY PEOPLE IN YOUR VILLAGE TALK, RIGHT?
...
BULLS-EYE?
YOU KNOW, YOU'RE PRETTY SENSITIVE... FOR A DUMBASS.
SO, ALL YOU KNOW HOW TO DO IS HUNT, AND YOU'RE AFRAID OF SOCIETY, AM I RIGHT?
...
I BET... YOUR PARENTS...
PROBABLY DON'T HAVE MUCH OF A REASON TO BECOME A SOLDIER, EITHER.
YMIR!
HEY...

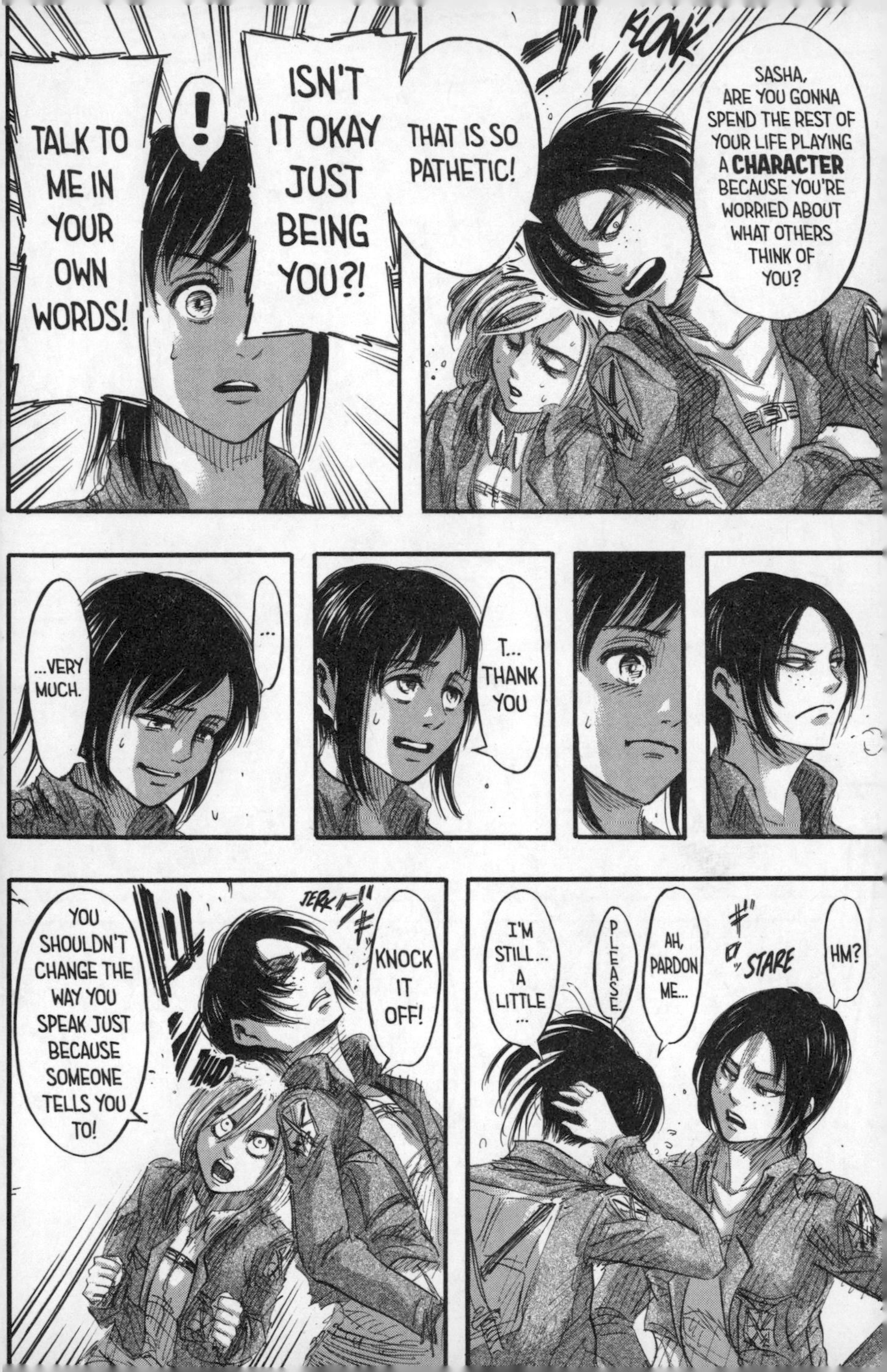
KLONK
SASHA, ARE YOU GONNA SPEND THE REST OF YOUR LIFE PLAYING A **CHARACTER** BECAUSE YOU'RE WORRIED ABOUT WHAT OTHERS THINK OF YOU?
THAT IS SO PATHETIC!
ISN'T IT OKAY JUST BEING YOU?!
!
TALK TO ME IN YOUR OWN WORDS!
T... THANK YOU
...
...VERY MUCH.
HM?
STARE
AH, PARDON ME...
PLEASE.
I'M STILL... A LITTLE ...
KNOCK IT OFF!
JERK
YOU SHOULDN'T CHANGE THE WAY YOU SPEAK JUST BECAUSE SOMEONE TELLS YOU TO!
THUD

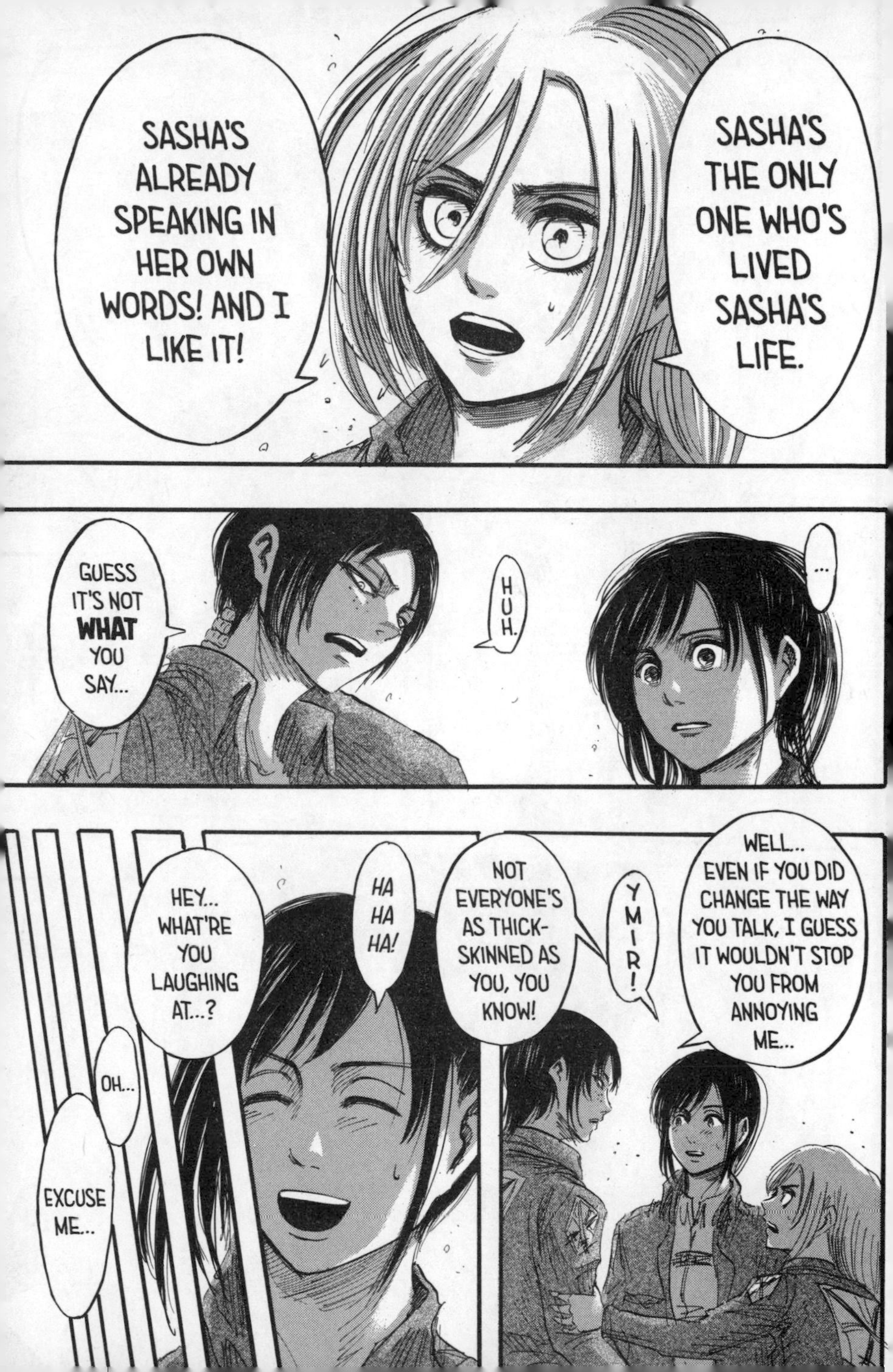
SASHA'S THE ONLY ONE WHO'S LIVED SASHA'S LIFE.
SASHA'S ALREADY SPEAKING IN HER OWN WORDS! AND I LIKE IT!
...
HUH.
GUESS IT'S NOT **WHAT** YOU SAY...
WELL... EVEN IF YOU DID CHANGE THE WAY YOU TALK, I GUESS IT WOULDN'T STOP YOU FROM ANNOYING ME...
YMIR!
NOT EVERYONE'S AS THICK-SKINNED AS YOU, YOU KNOW!
HA HA HA!
HEY... WHAT'RE YOU LAUGHING AT...?
OH...
EXCUSE ME...

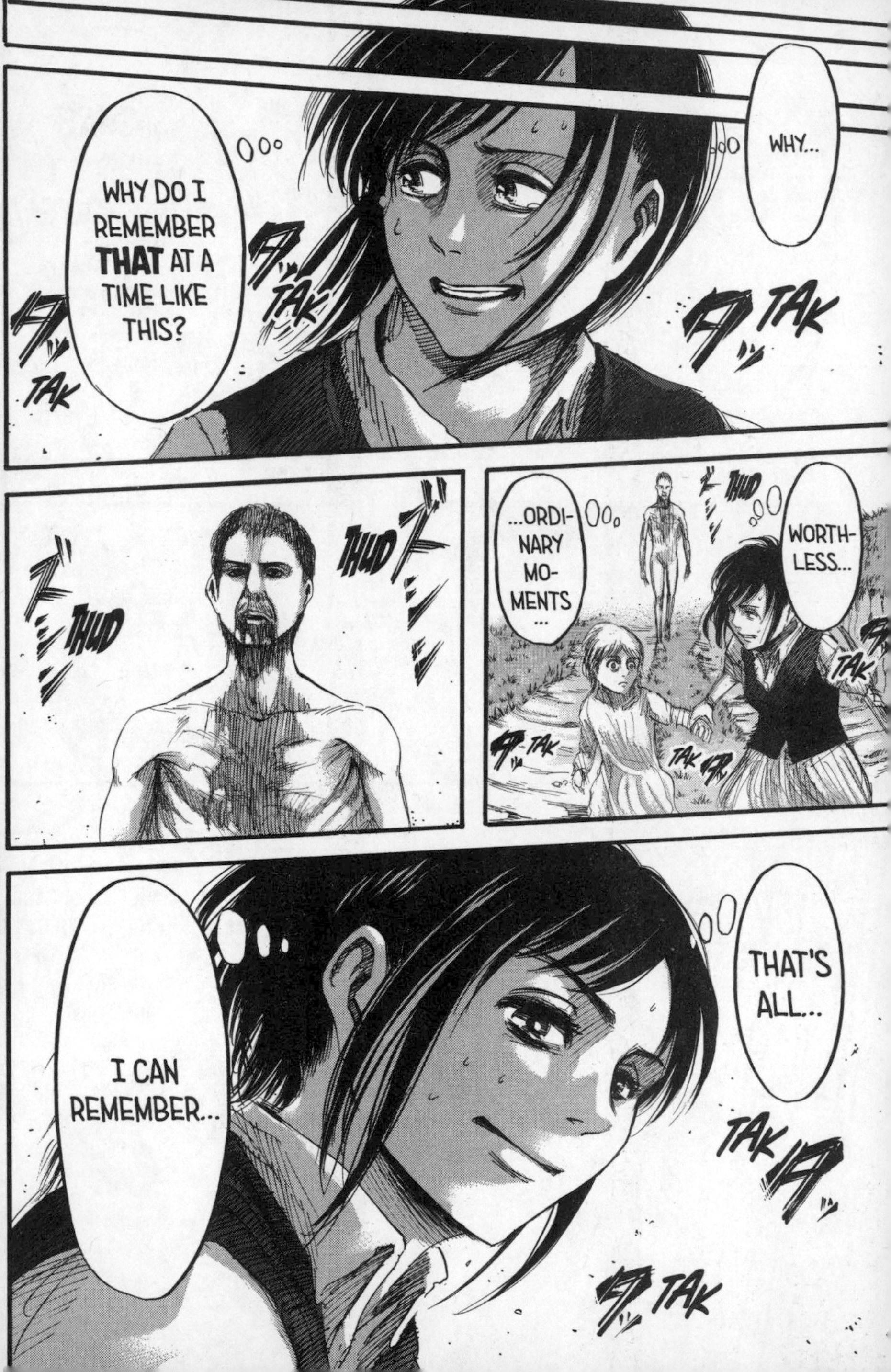
WHY...
TAK
WHY DO I REMEMBER **THAT** AT A TIME LIKE THIS?
TAK
TAK
WORTHLESS...
TAK
THUD
...ORDINARY MOMENTS...
TAK
TAK
THUD
THUD
THAT'S ALL...
TAK
I CAN REMEMBER...
TAK

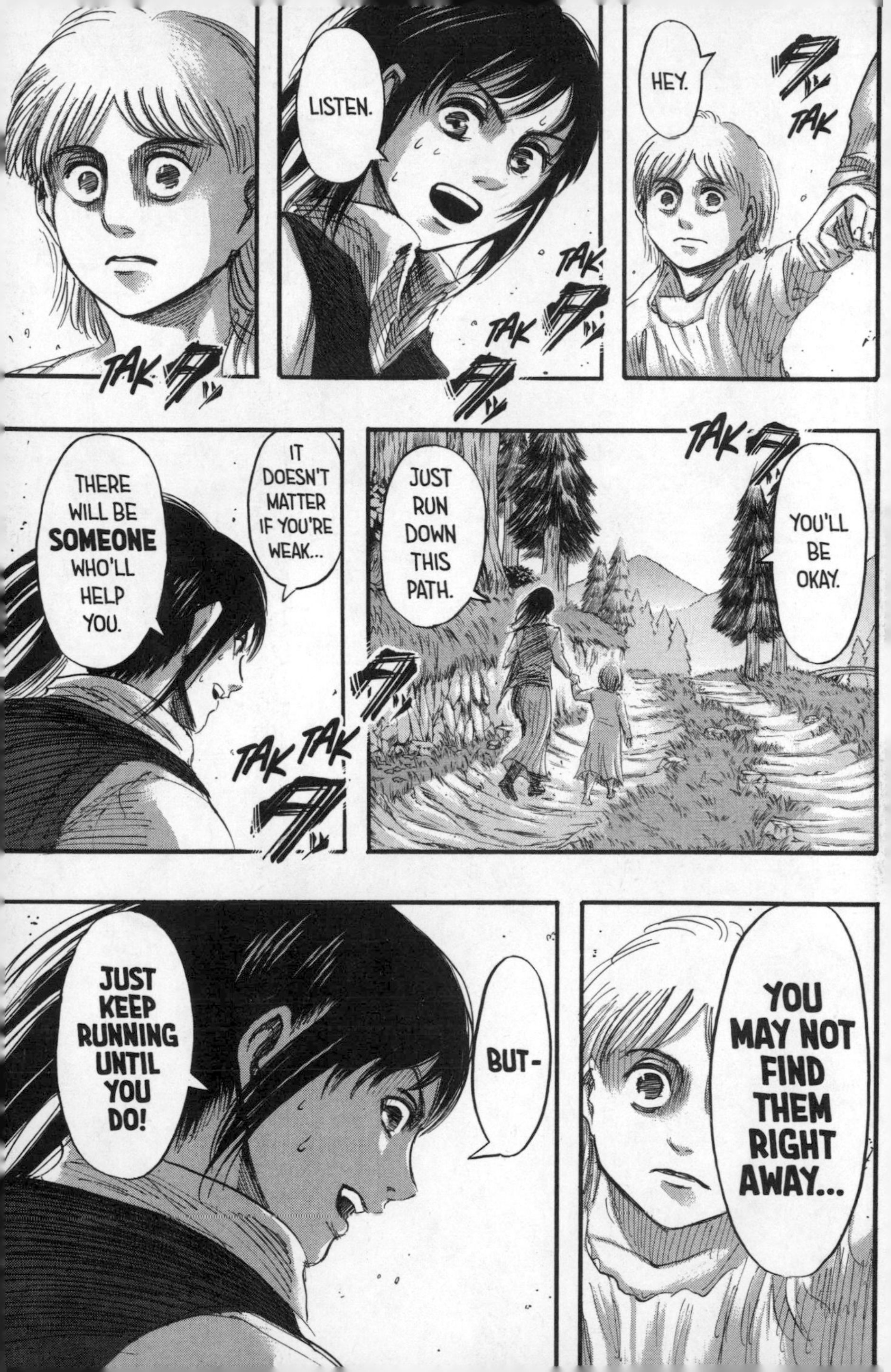
HEY.
TAK
TAK
LISTEN.
TAK
TAK
TAK
TAK
YOU'LL BE OKAY.
JUST RUN DOWN THIS PATH.
IT DOESN'T MATTER IF YOU'RE WEAK...
THERE WILL BE **SOMEONE** WHO'LL HELP YOU.
TAK TAK
YOU MAY NOT FIND THEM RIGHT AWAY...
BUT-
JUST KEEP RUNNING UNTIL YOU DO!

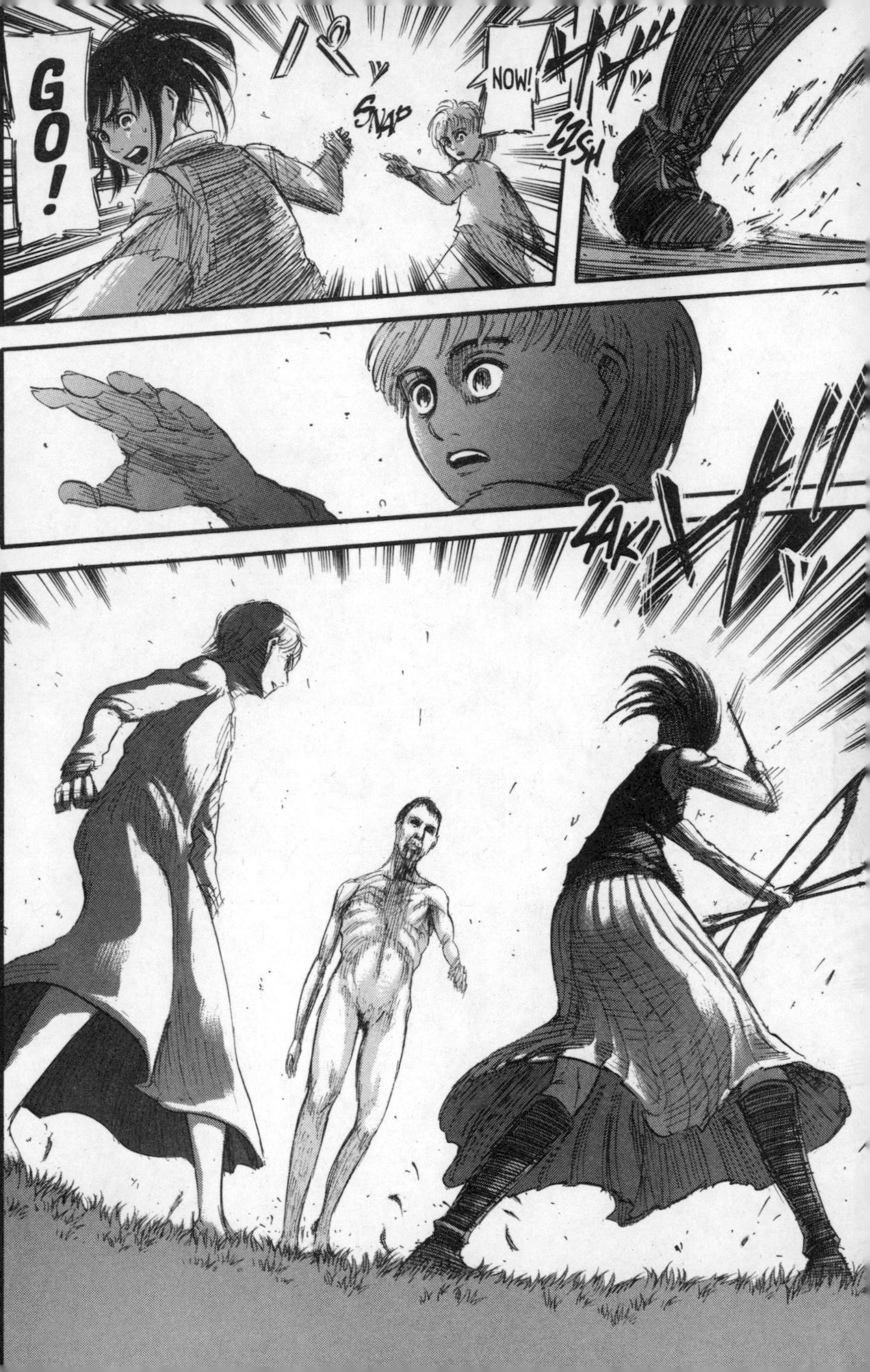
ZZSH
NOW!
SNAP
GO!
ZAK

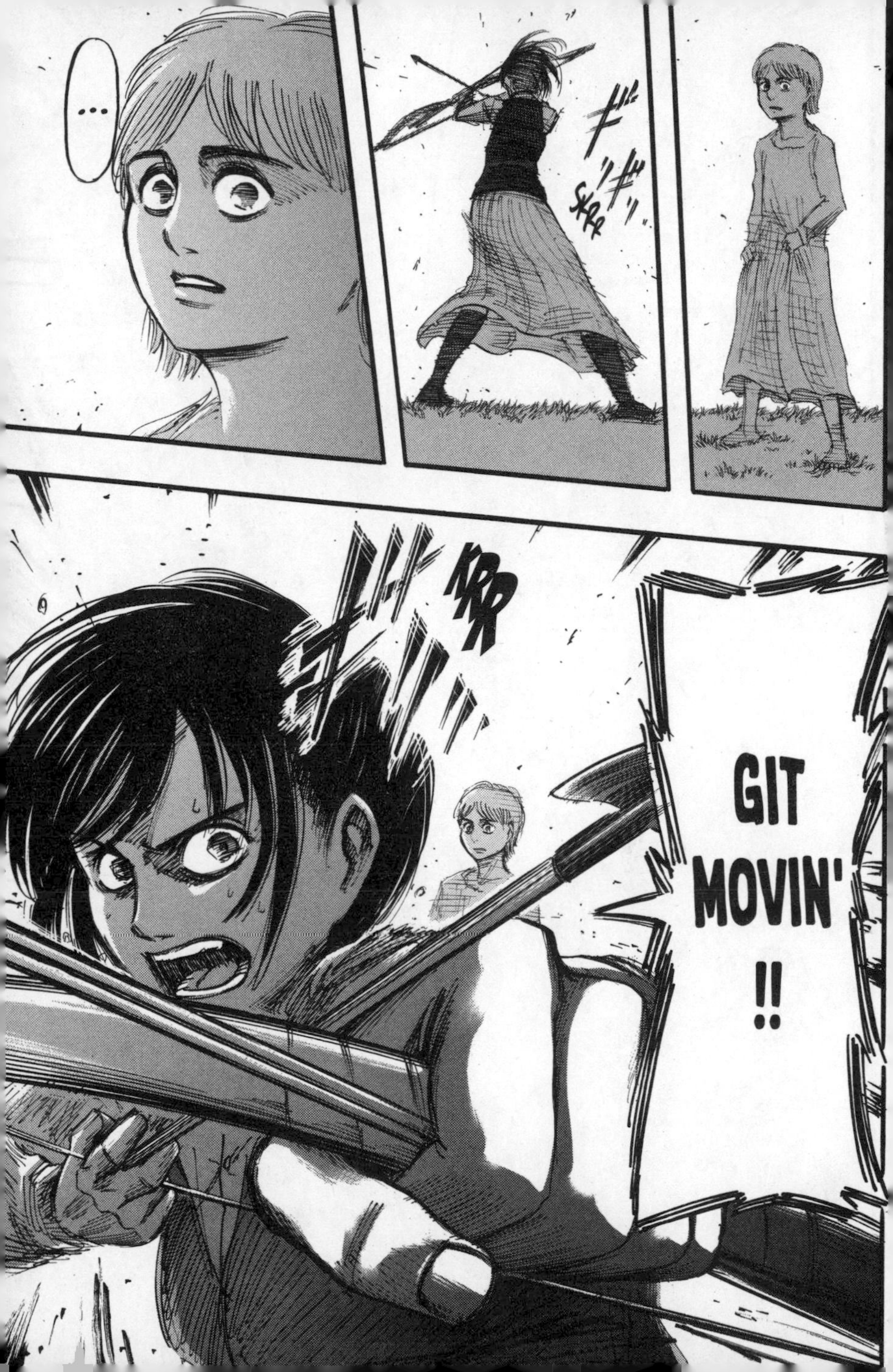
SKRR
...
KRR
GIT MOVIN' !!

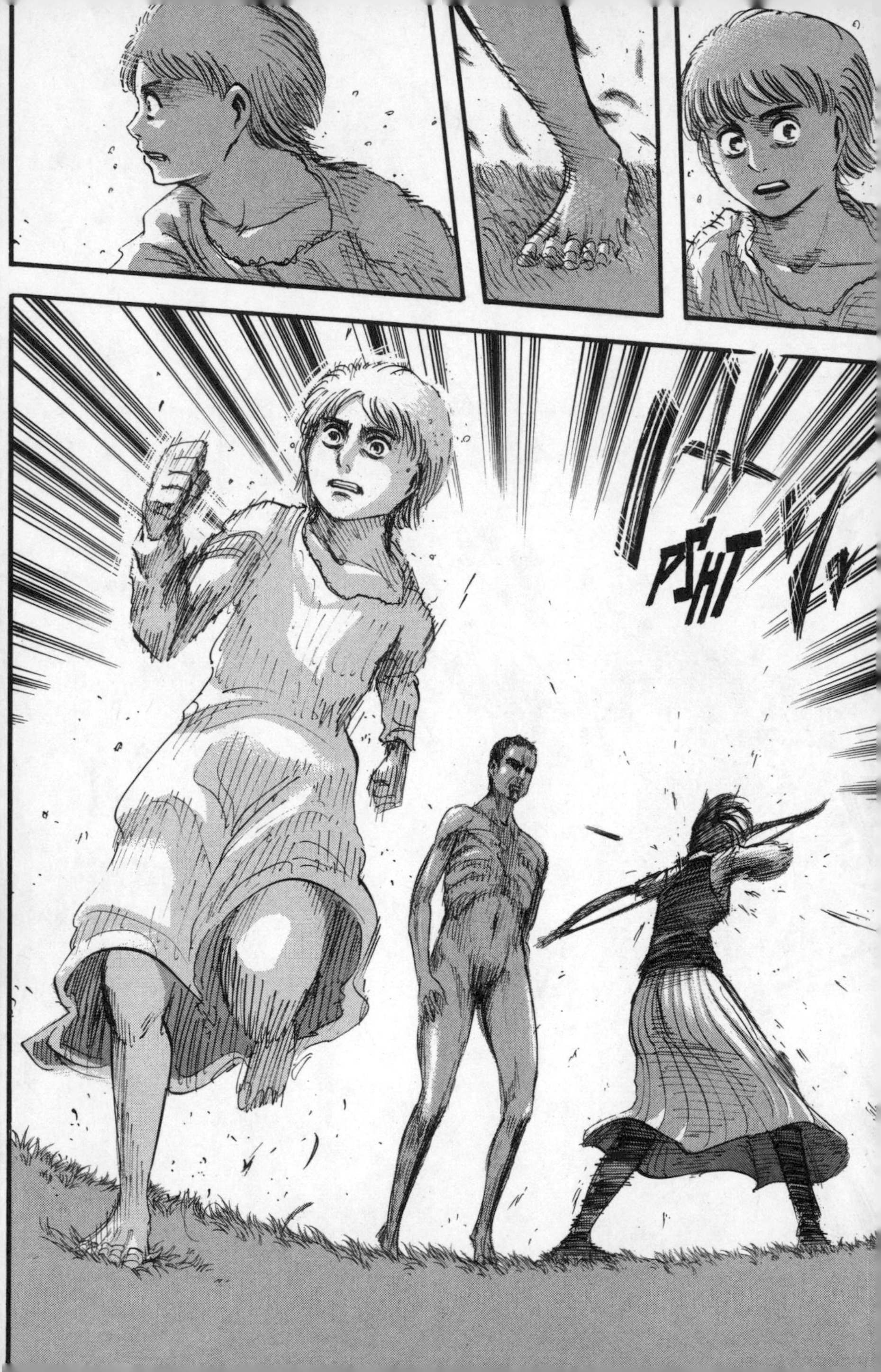
PSHT

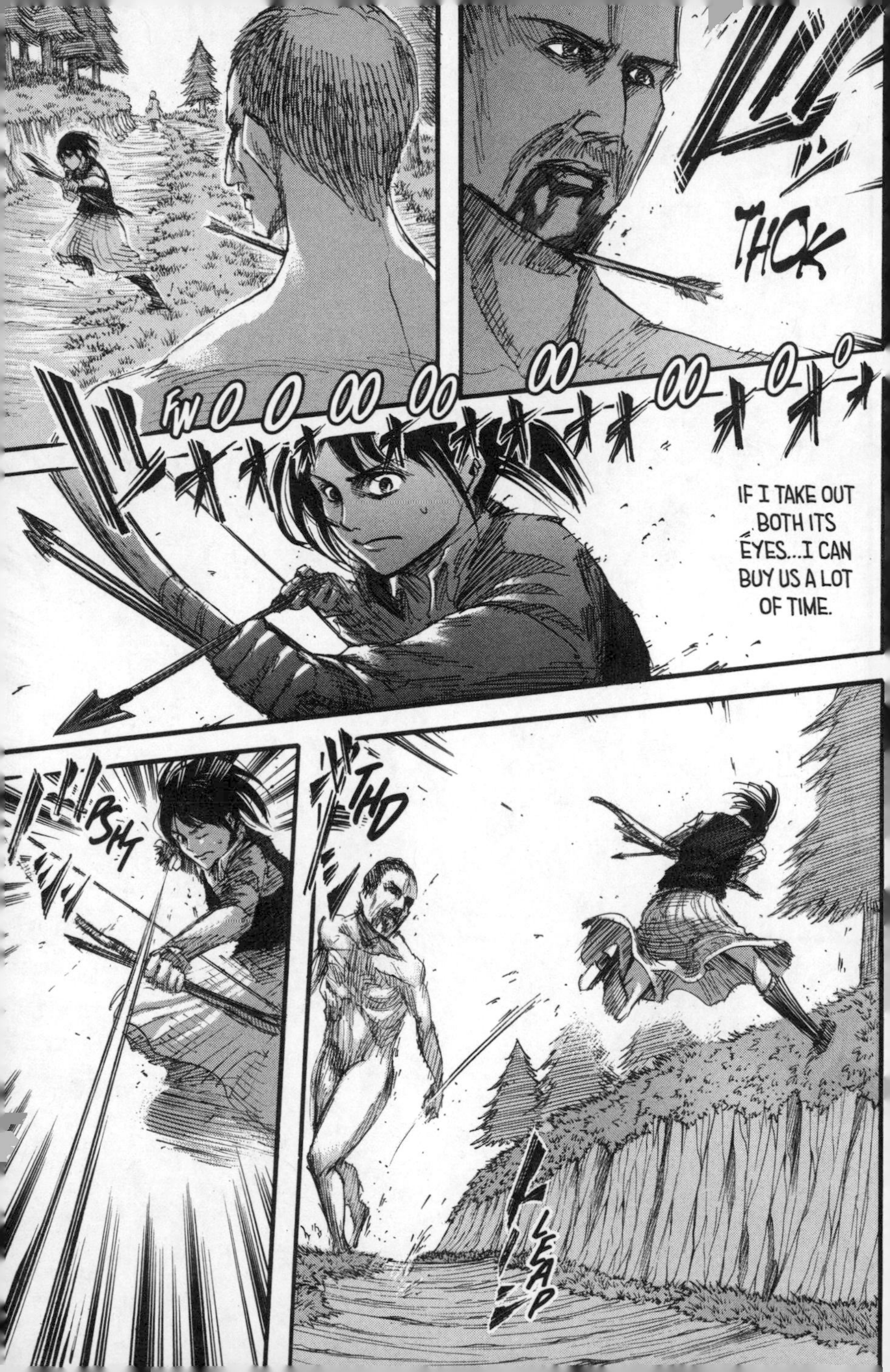
THOK
FWOOOOOOOOOOOO
IF I TAKE OUT BOTH ITS EYES...I CAN BUY US A LOT OF TIME.
THD
LEAP
PSHH

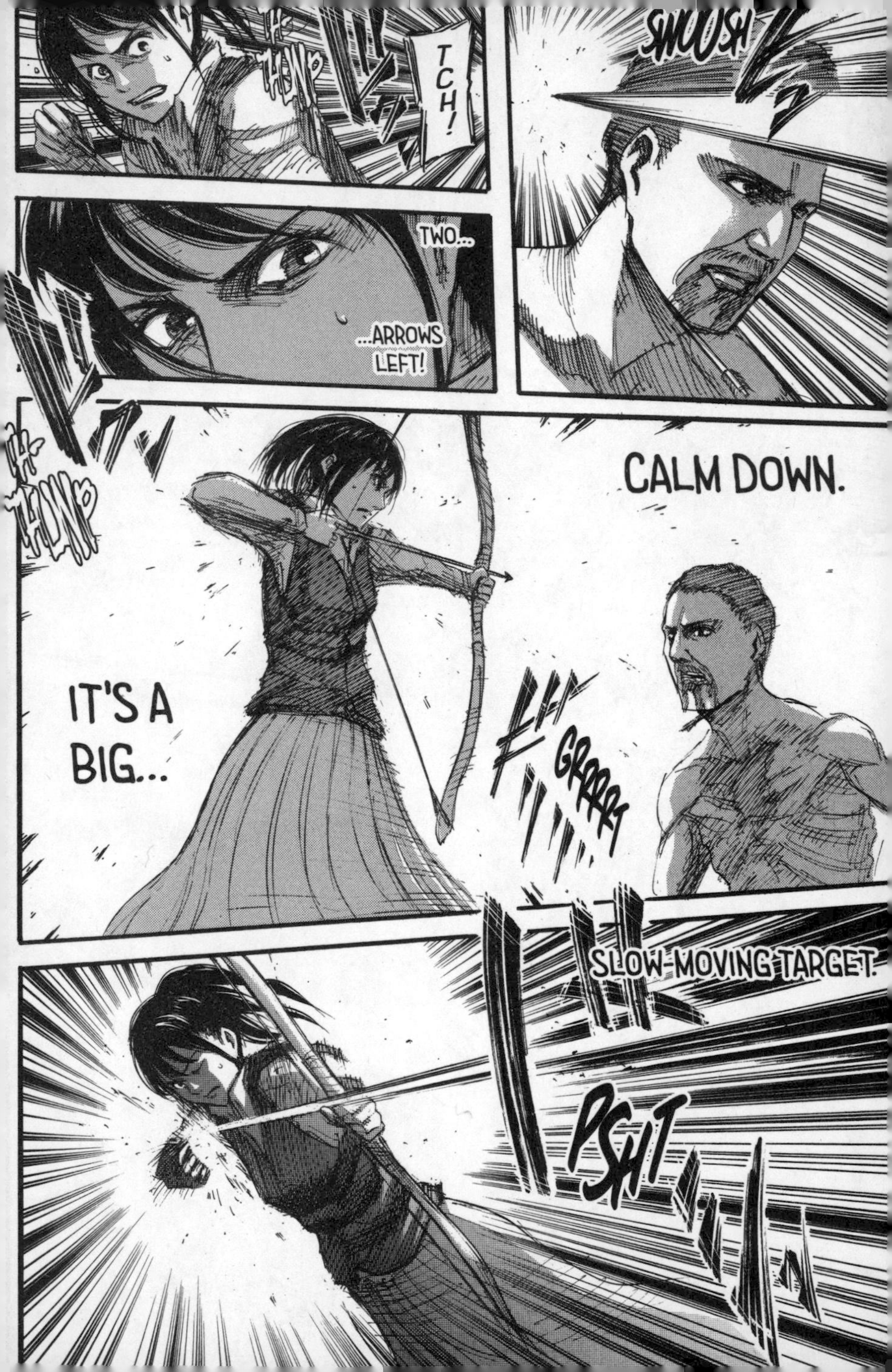

SWOOSH
TCH!
THUNK
TWO...
...ARROWS LEFT!
CALM DOWN.
THUNK
GRRRR
IT'S A BIG...
SLOW-MOVING TARGET.
PSHT

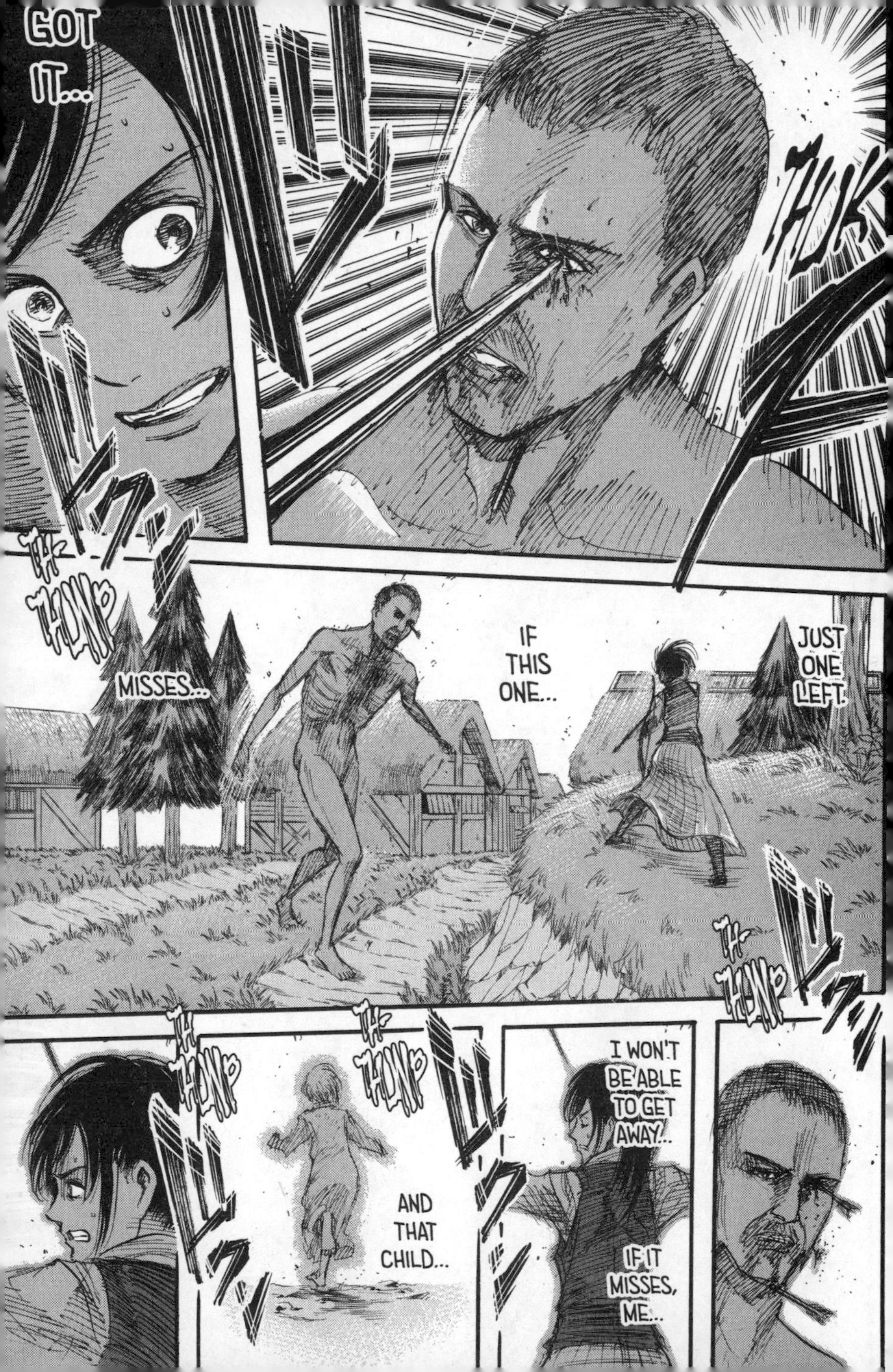
THUK
GOT IT...
THA-THUMP
JUST ONE LEFT.
IF THIS ONE...
MISSES...
THA-THUMP
I WON'T BE ABLE TO GET AWAY...
IF IT MISSES, ME...
THA-THUMP
AND THAT CHILD...
THA-THUMP

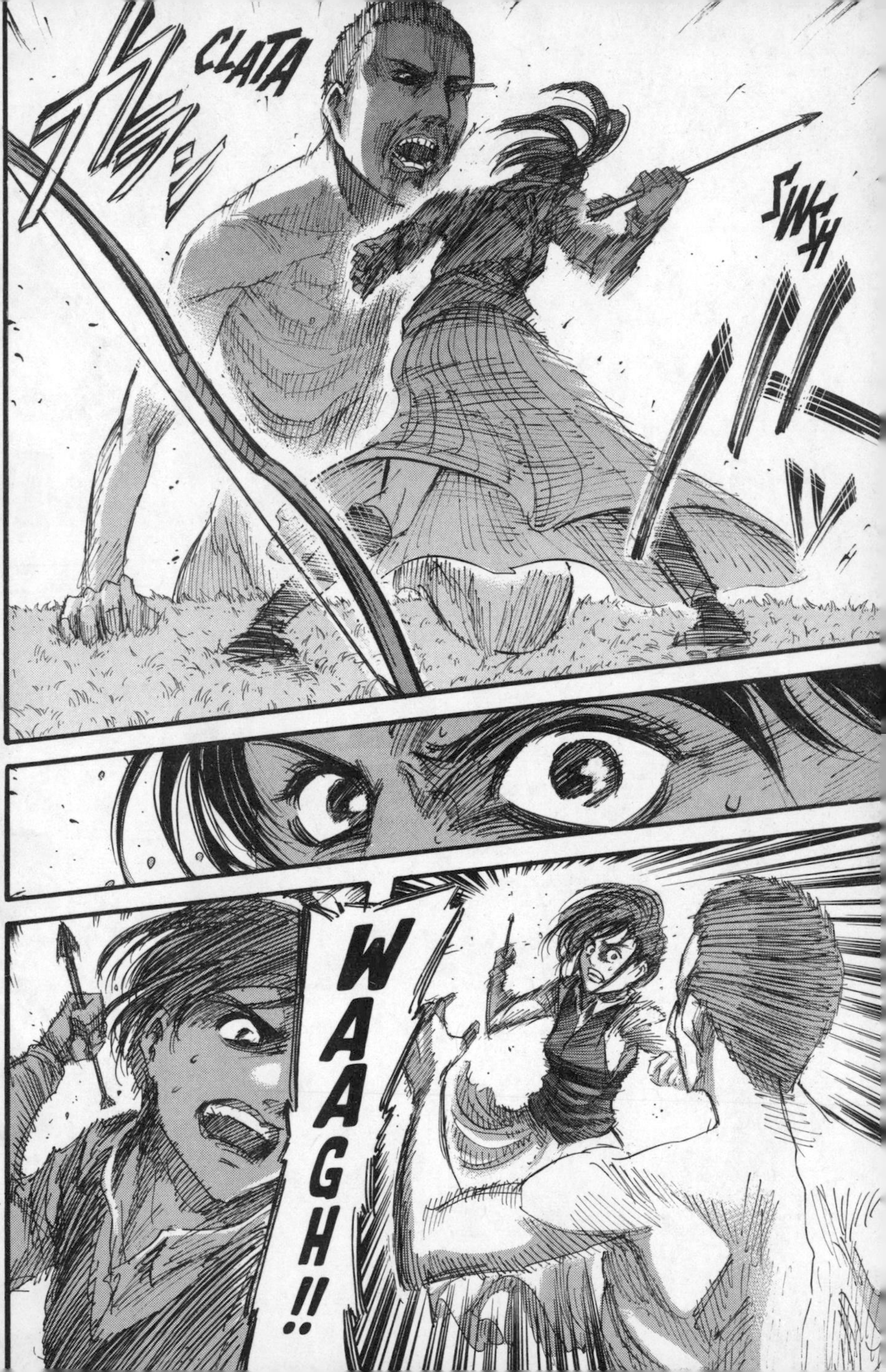
SWSH
CLATA
WAAAGH!!

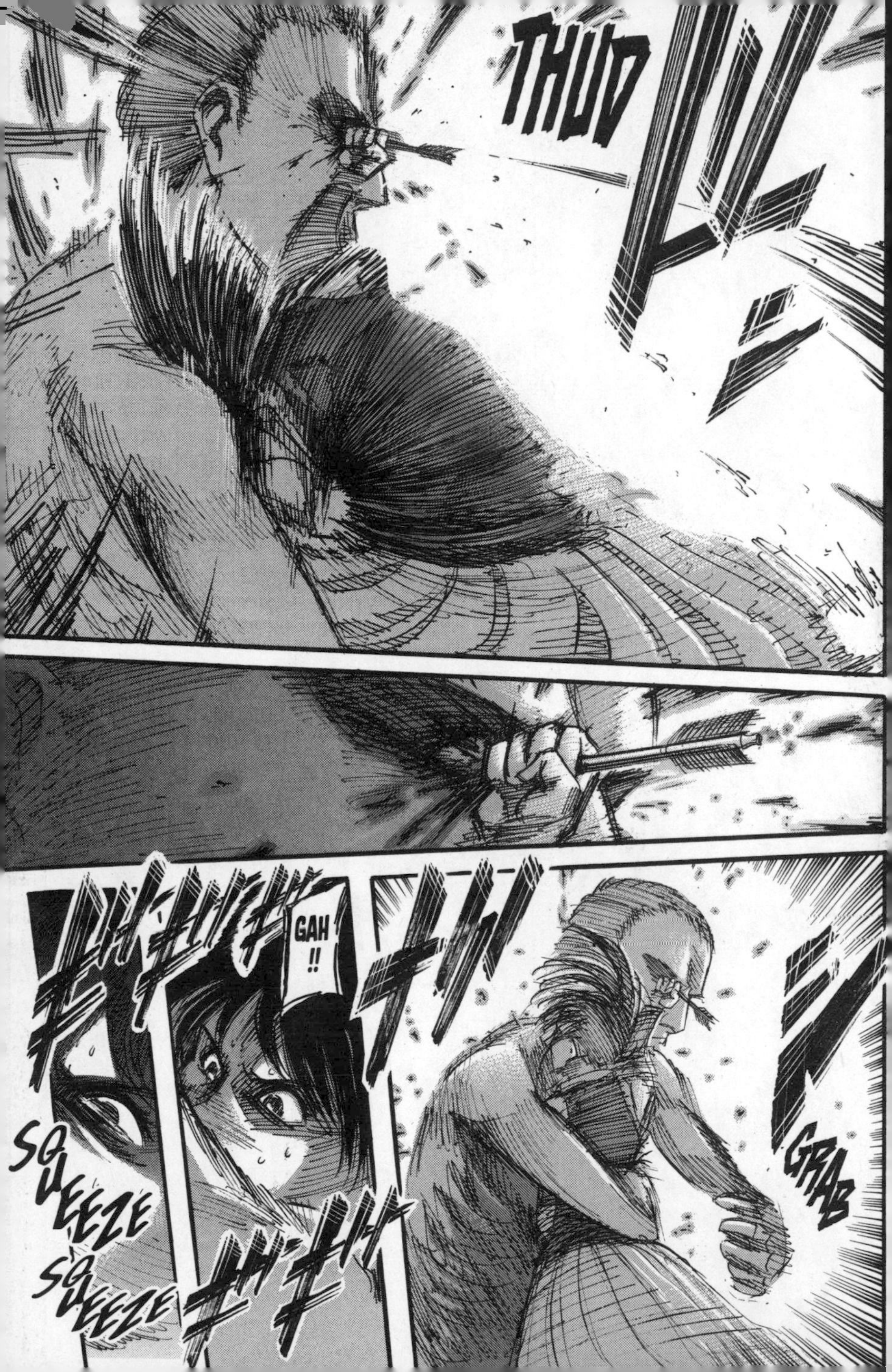
THUD
GAH !!
GRAB
SQUEEZE
SQUEEZE

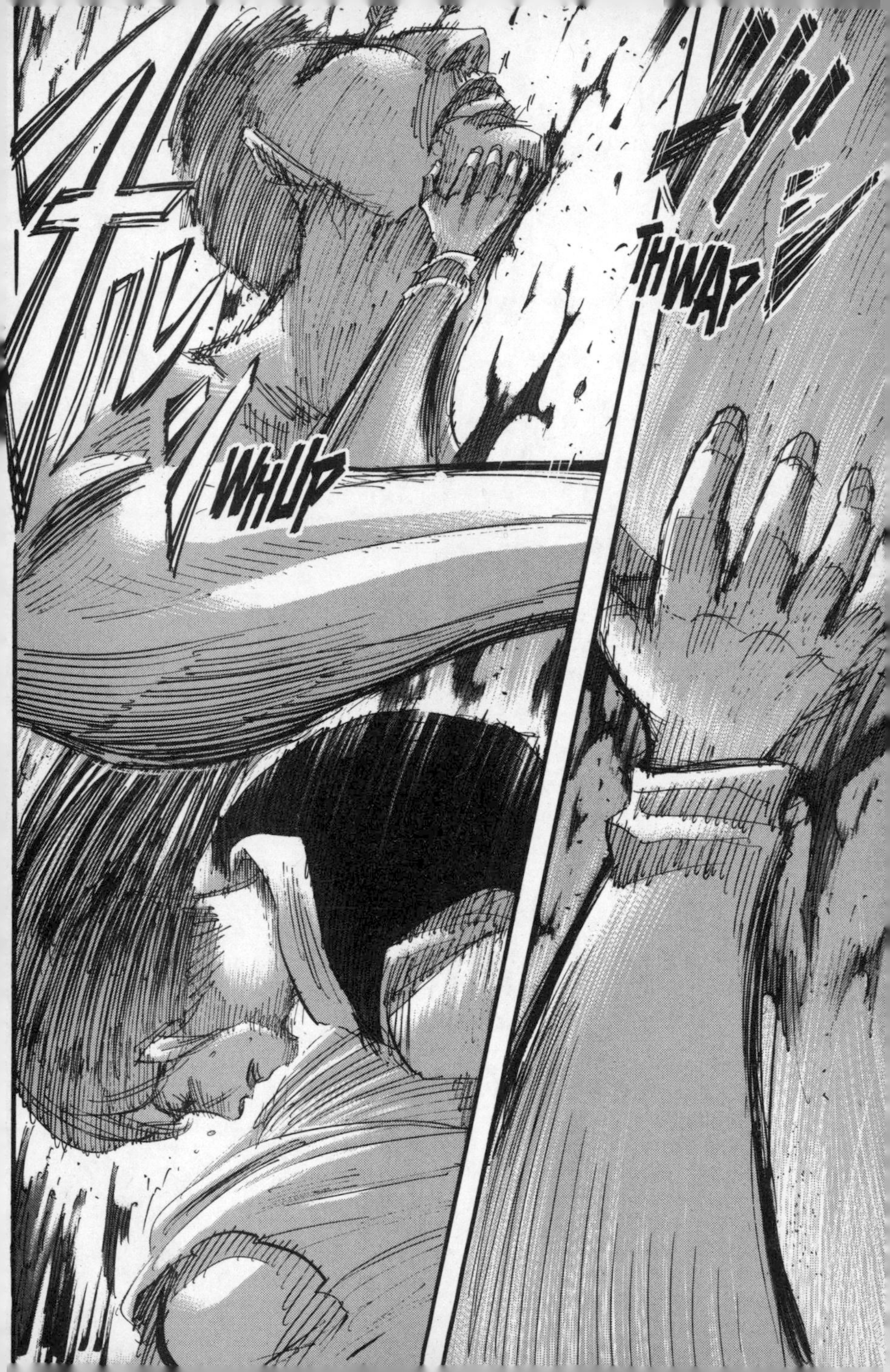
THWAP
WHUP

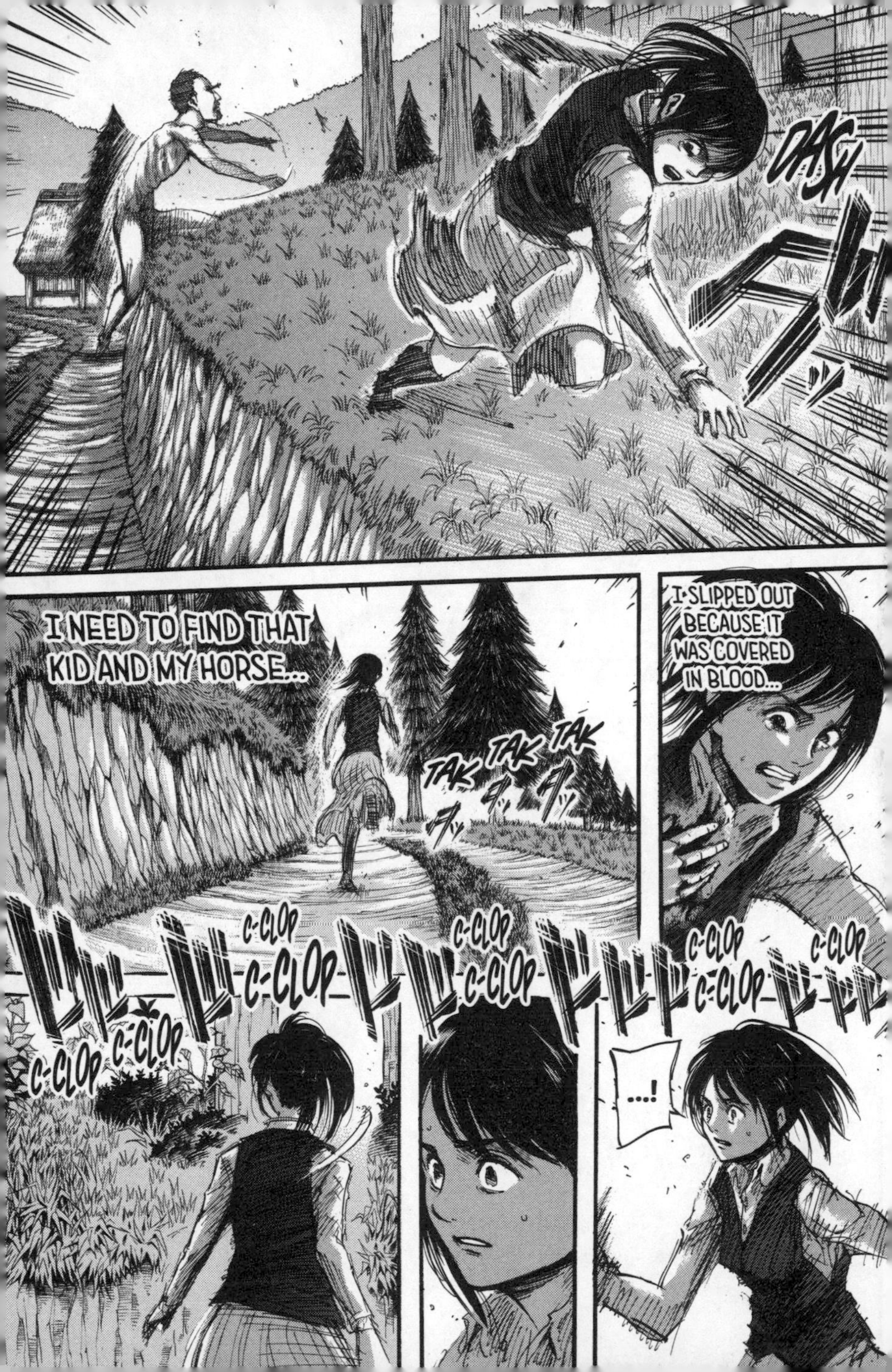
DASH
I SLIPPED OUT BECAUSE IT WAS COVERED IN BLOOD...
I NEED TO FIND THAT KID AND MY HORSE...
TAK TAK TAK
C-CLOP C-CLOP
C-CLOP C-CLOP
C-CLOP C-CLOP
C-CLOP C-CLOP
...!
C-CLOP C-CLOP

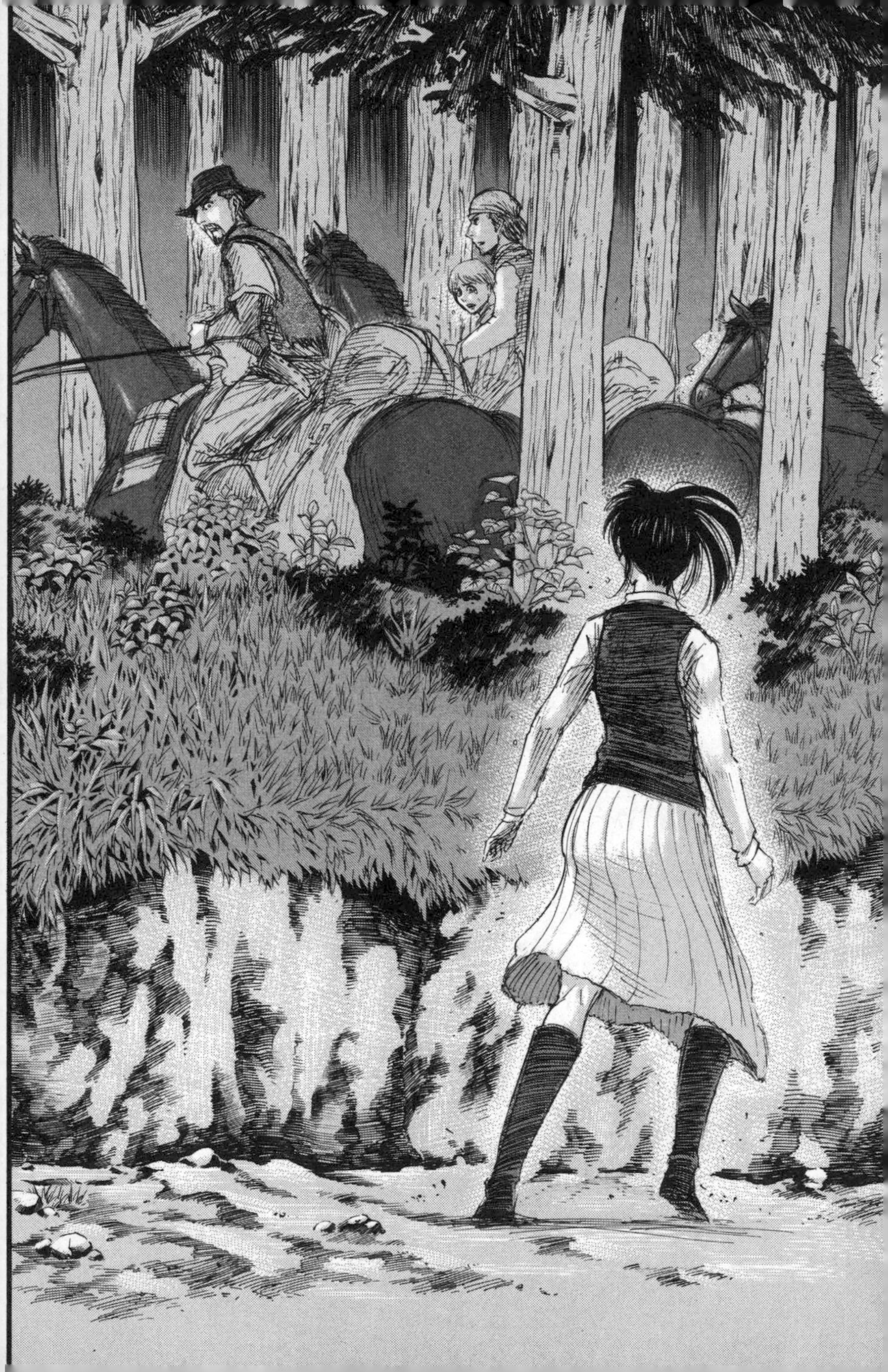

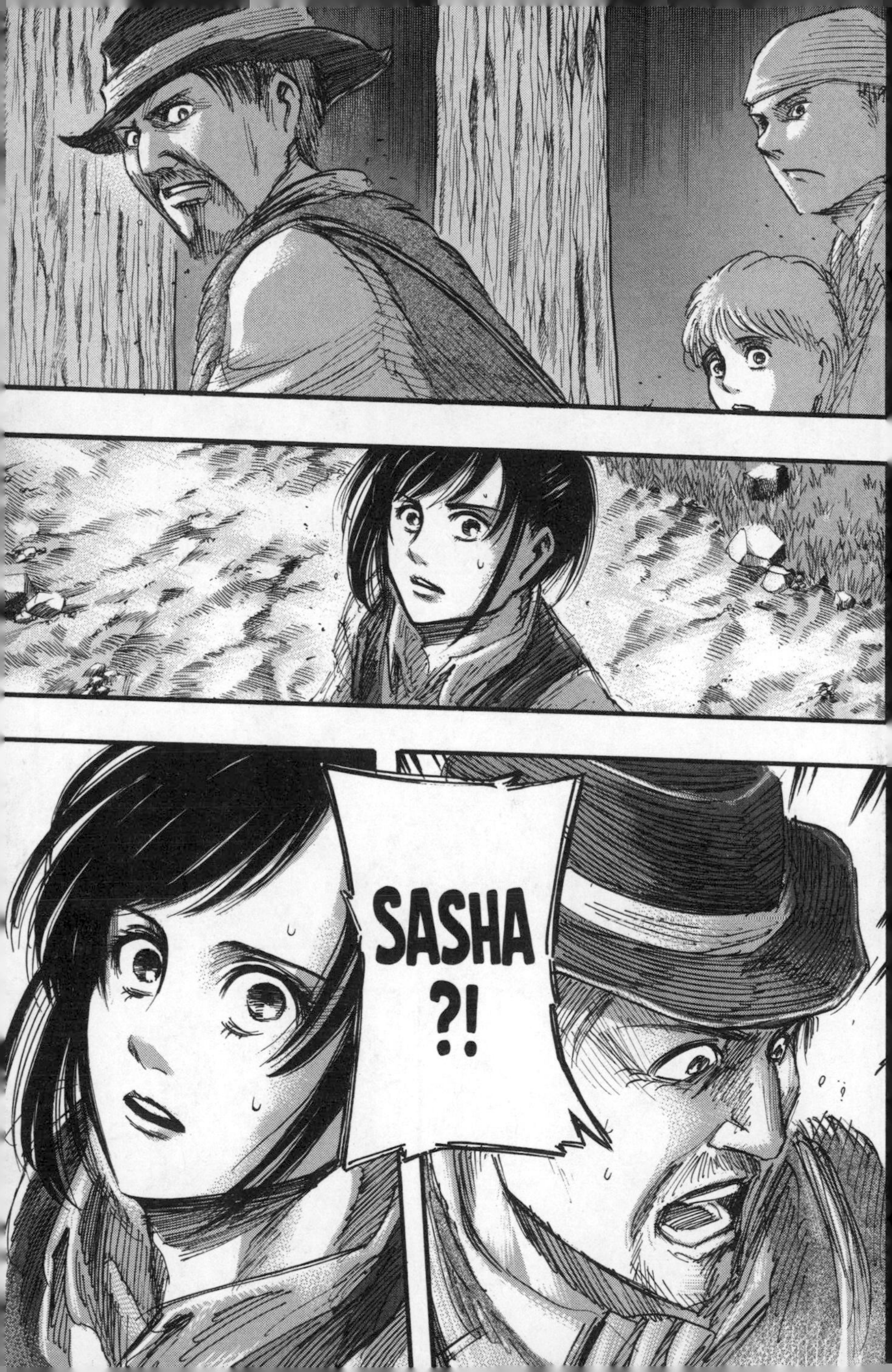
SASHA ?!

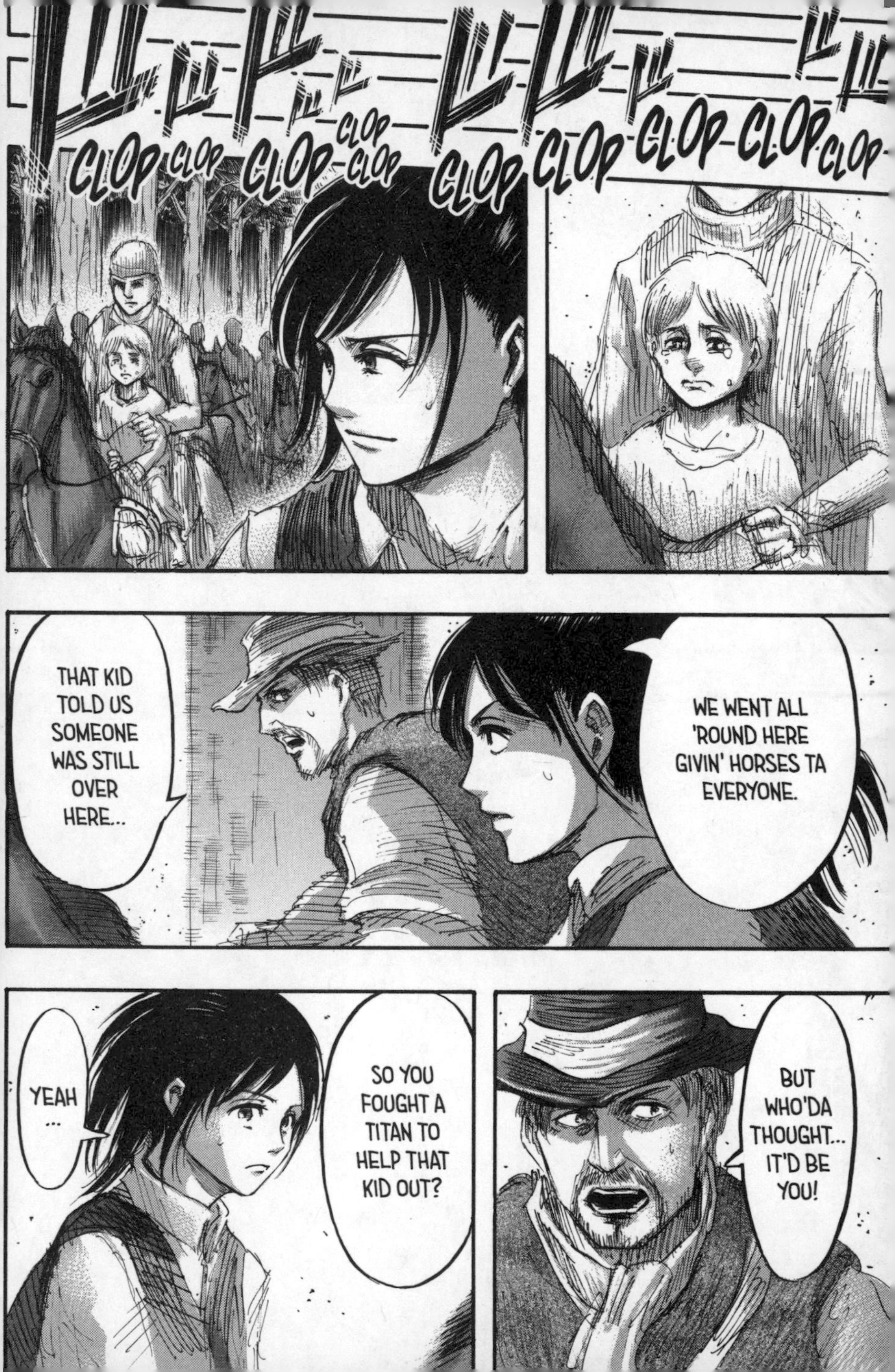
CLOP CLOP CLOP CLOP CLOP CLOP CLOP CLOP CLOP CLOP
WE WENT ALL 'ROUND HERE GIVIN' HORSES TA EVERYONE.
THAT KID TOLD US SOMEONE WAS STILL OVER HERE...
BUT WHO'DA THOUGHT... IT'D BE YOU!
SO YOU FOUGHT A TITAN TO HELP THAT KID OUT?
YEAH ...

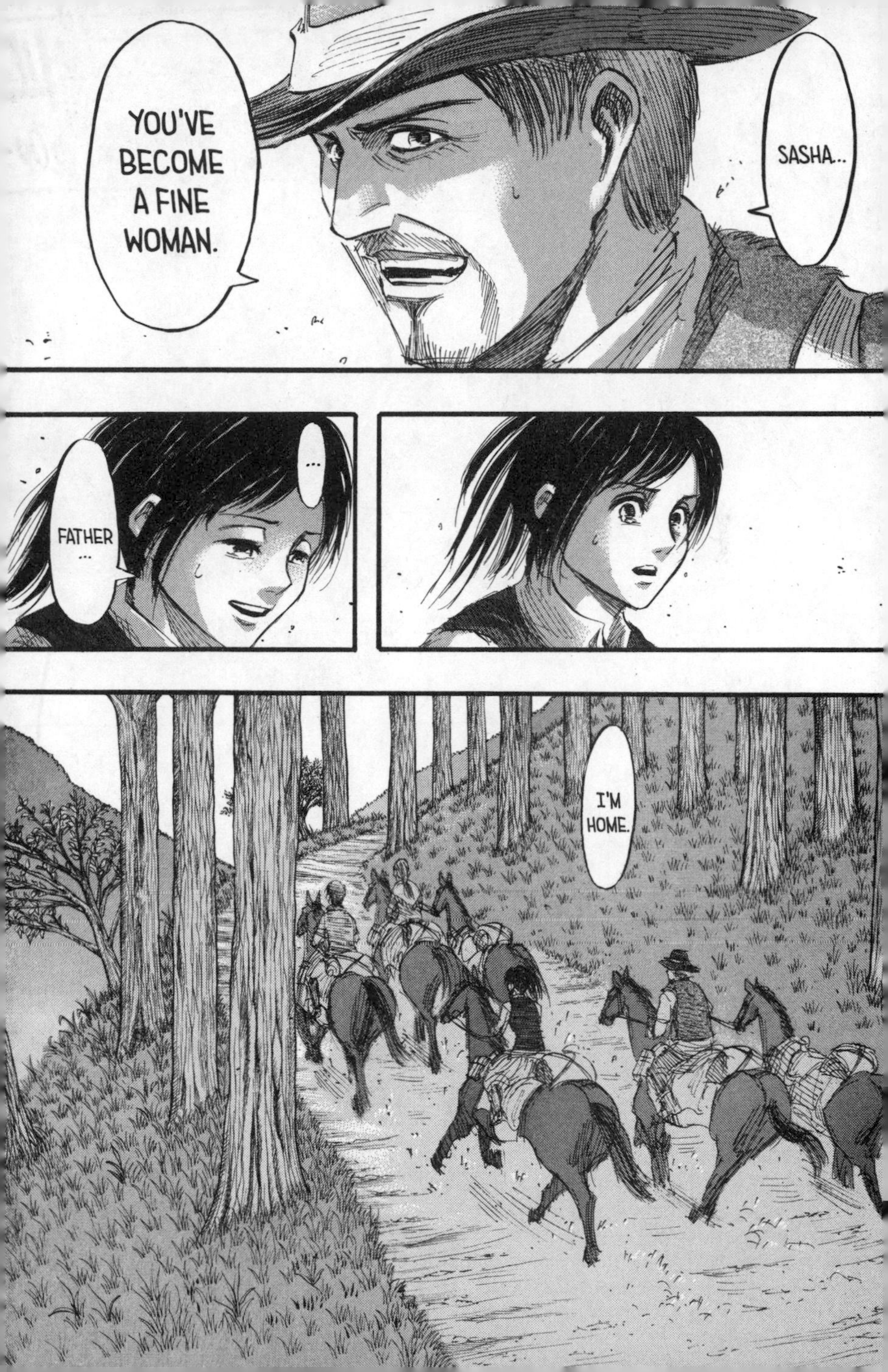
SASHA...
YOU'VE BECOME A FINE WOMAN.
...
FATHER ...
I'M HOME.

ATTACK on TITAN

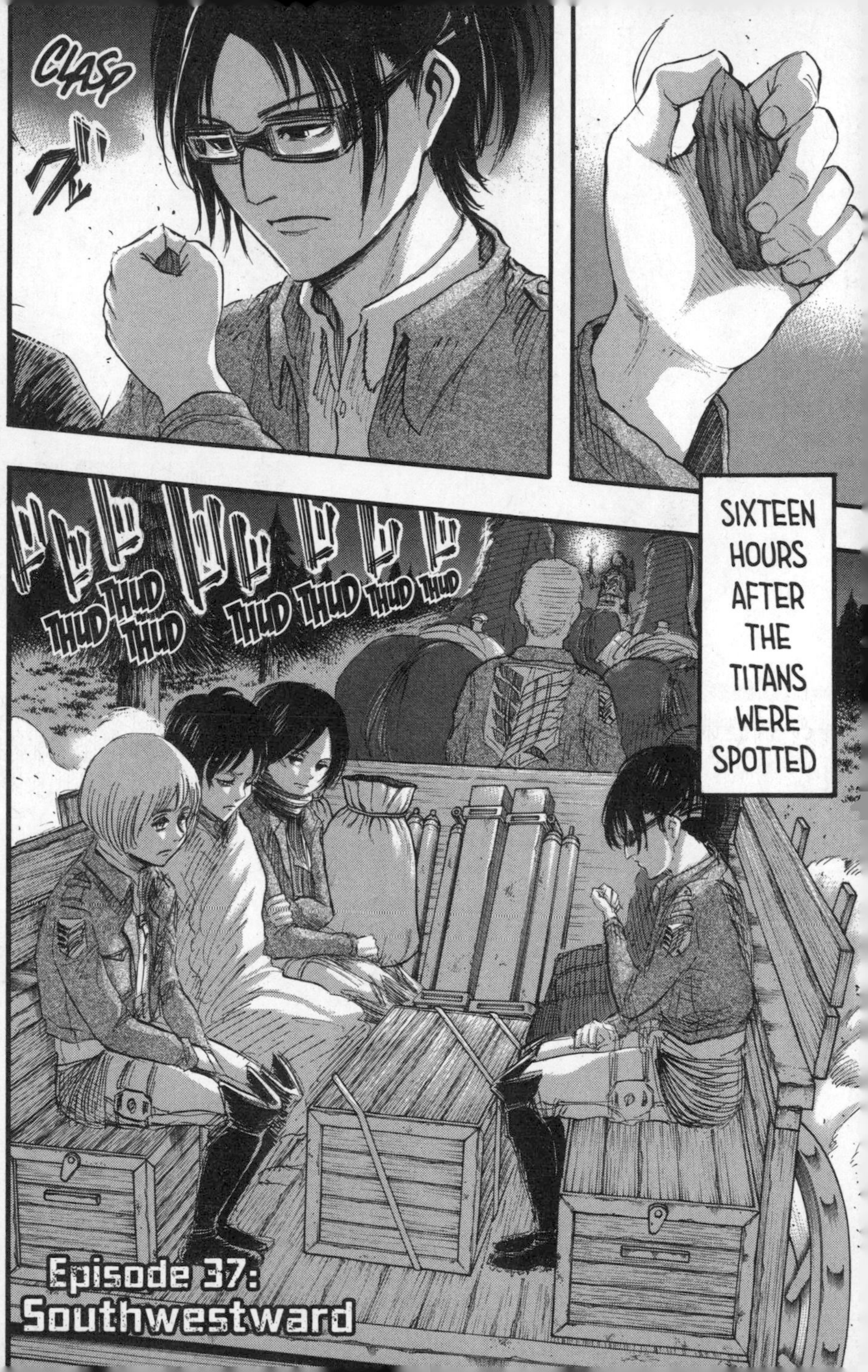
CLASP
SIXTEEN HOURS AFTER THE TITANS WERE SPOTTED
THUD THUD THUD THUD THUD THUD THUD
Episode 37: Southwestward

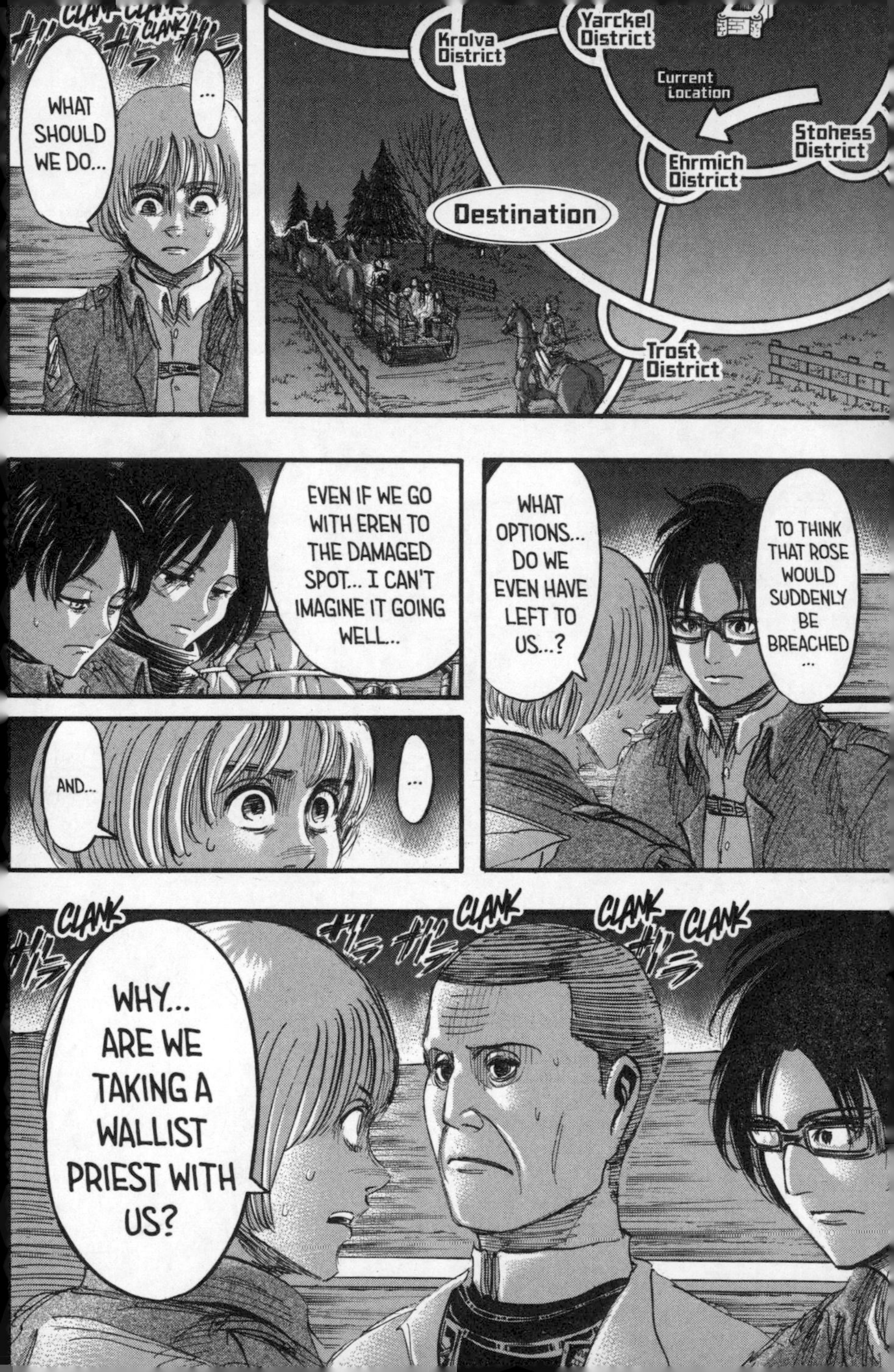
Yarckel District
Krolva District
Current Location
Stohess District
Ehrmich District
Destination
Trost District
CLANK CLANK CLANK
...
WHAT SHOULD WE DO...
TO THINK THAT ROSE WOULD SUDDENLY BE BREACHED ...
WHAT OPTIONS... DO WE EVEN HAVE LEFT TO US...?
EVEN IF WE GO WITH EREN TO THE DAMAGED SPOT... I CAN'T IMAGINE IT GOING WELL...
...
AND...
CLANK
CLANK
CLANK
CLANK
WHY... ARE WE TAKING A WALLIST PRIEST WITH US?

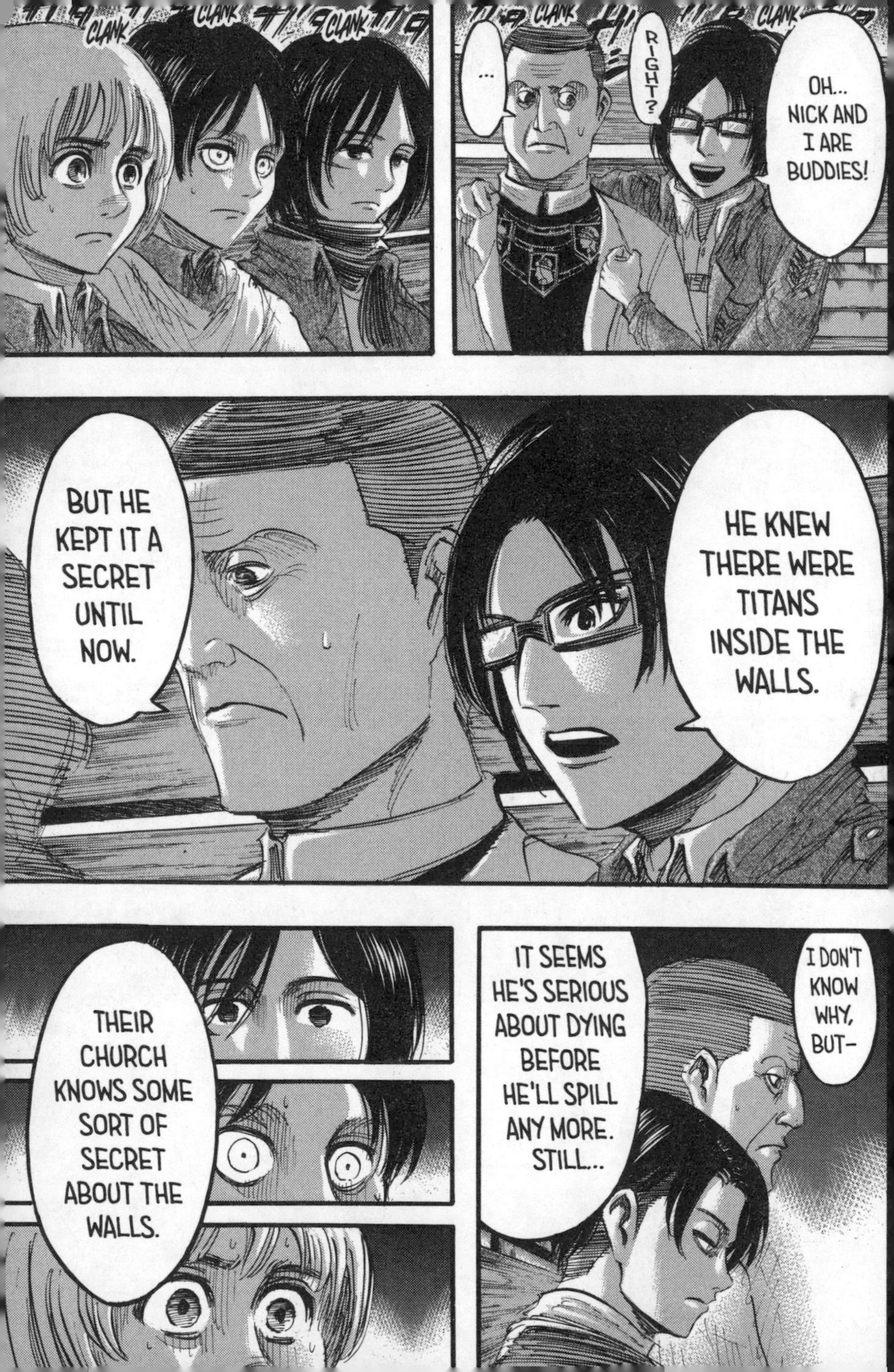
CLANK
CLANK
OH... NICK AND I ARE BUDDIES!
RIGHT?
...
CLANK
CLANK
CLANK
HE KNEW THERE WERE TITANS INSIDE THE WALLS.
BUT HE KEPT IT A SECRET UNTIL NOW.
I DON'T KNOW WHY, BUT-
IT SEEMS HE'S SERIOUS ABOUT DYING BEFORE HE'LL SPILL ANY MORE. STILL...
THEIR CHURCH KNOWS SOME SORT OF SECRET ABOUT THE WALLS.

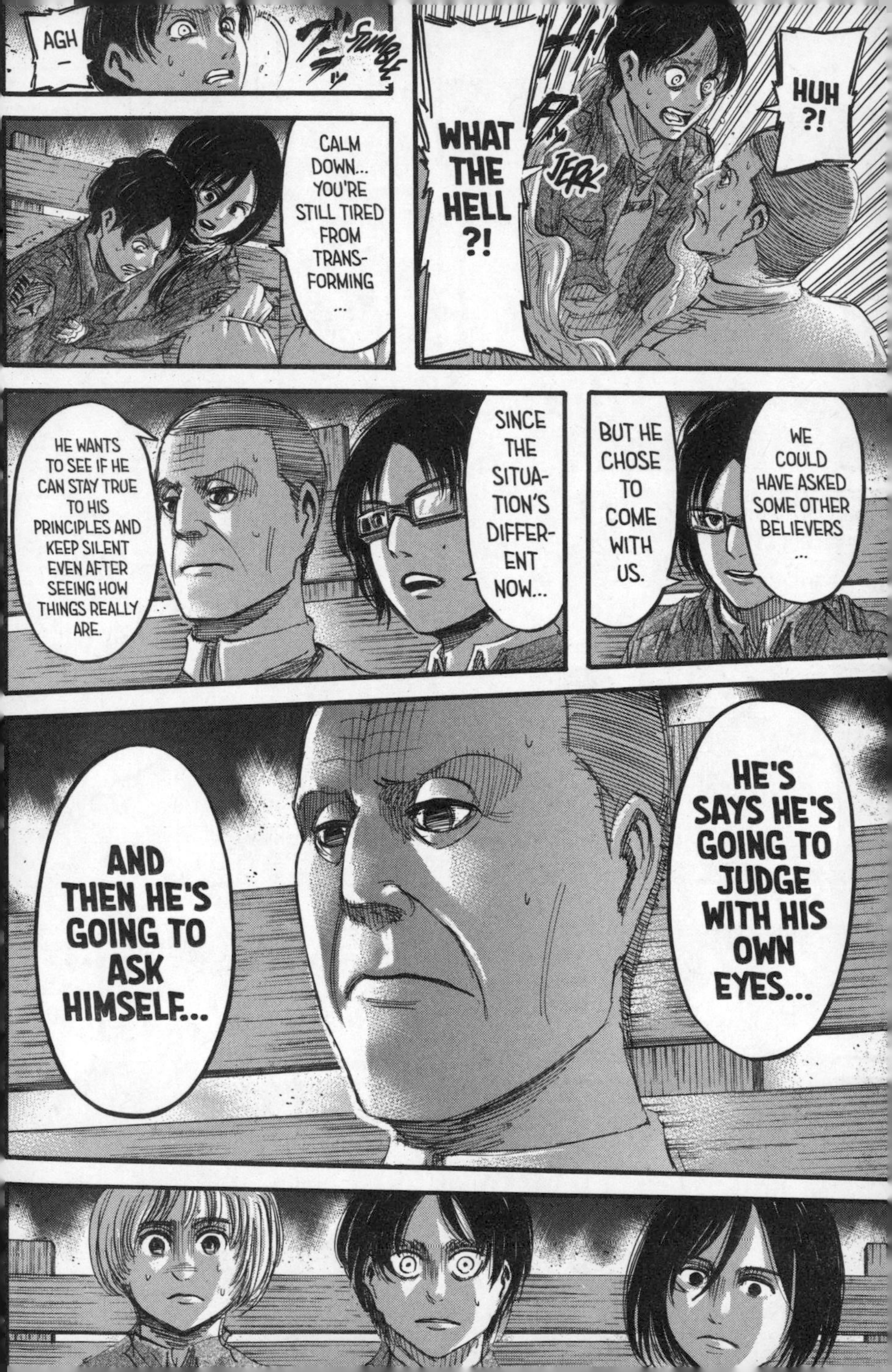

WHAT THE HELL ?!
JERK
HUH ?!
AGH —
STUMBLE
CALM DOWN... YOU'RE STILL TIRED FROM TRANS-FORMING ...
WE COULD HAVE ASKED SOME OTHER BELIEVERS ...
BUT HE CHOSE TO COME WITH US.
SINCE THE SITUA-TION'S DIFFER-ENT NOW...
HE WANTS TO SEE IF HE CAN STAY TRUE TO HIS PRINCIPLES AND KEEP SILENT EVEN AFTER SEEING HOW THINGS REALLY ARE.
HE'S SAYS HE'S GOING TO JUDGE WITH HIS OWN EYES...
AND THEN HE'S GOING TO ASK HIMSELF...

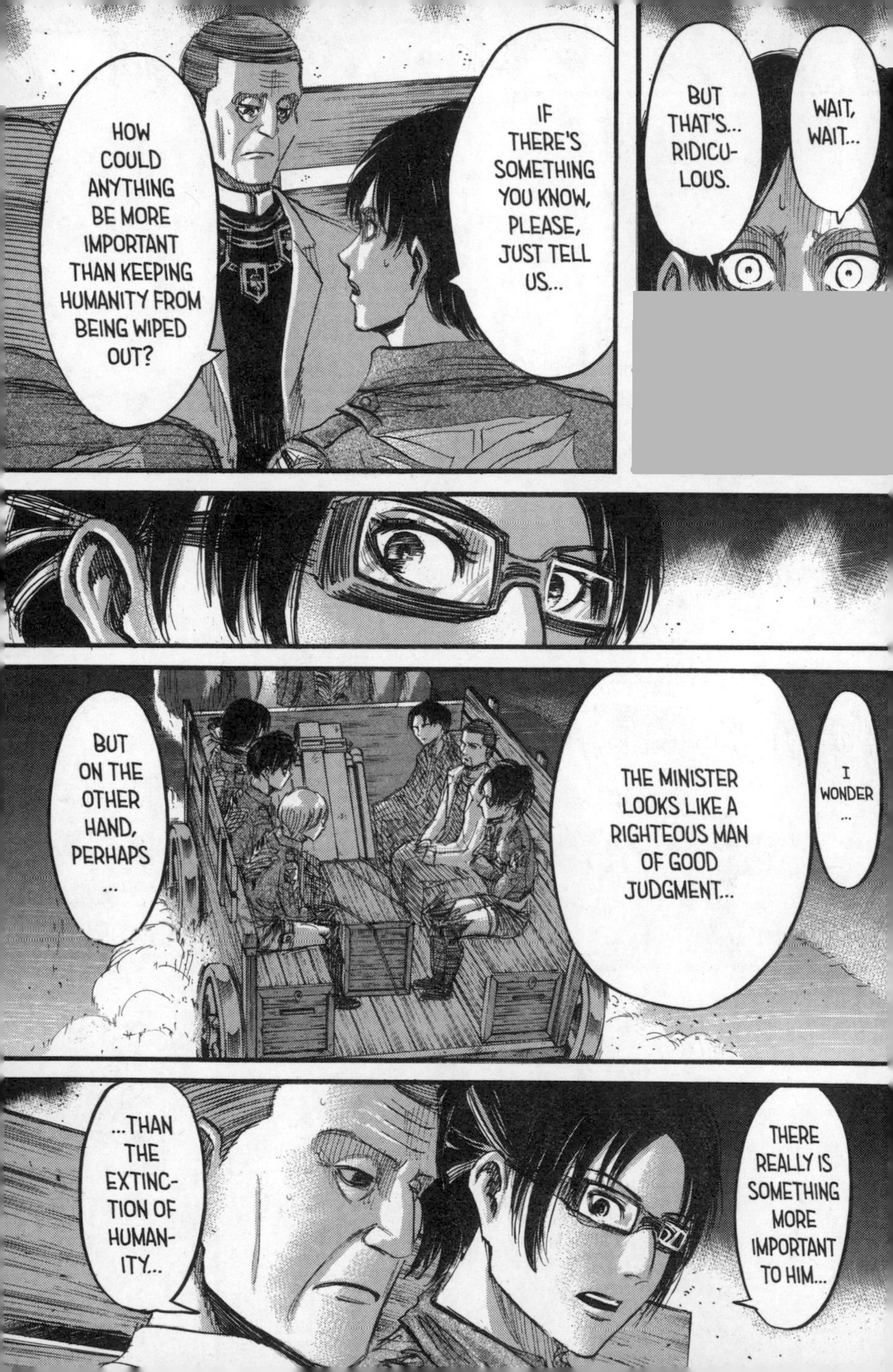
WAIT, WAIT...
BUT THAT'S... RIDICULOUS.
IF THERE'S SOMETHING YOU KNOW, PLEASE, JUST TELL US...
HOW COULD ANYTHING BE MORE IMPORTANT THAN KEEPING HUMANITY FROM BEING WIPED OUT?
I WONDER...
THE MINISTER LOOKS LIKE A RIGHTEOUS MAN OF GOOD JUDGMENT...
BUT ON THE OTHER HAND, PERHAPS...
THERE REALLY IS SOMETHING MORE IMPORTANT TO HIM...
...THAN THE EXTINCTION OF HUMANITY...

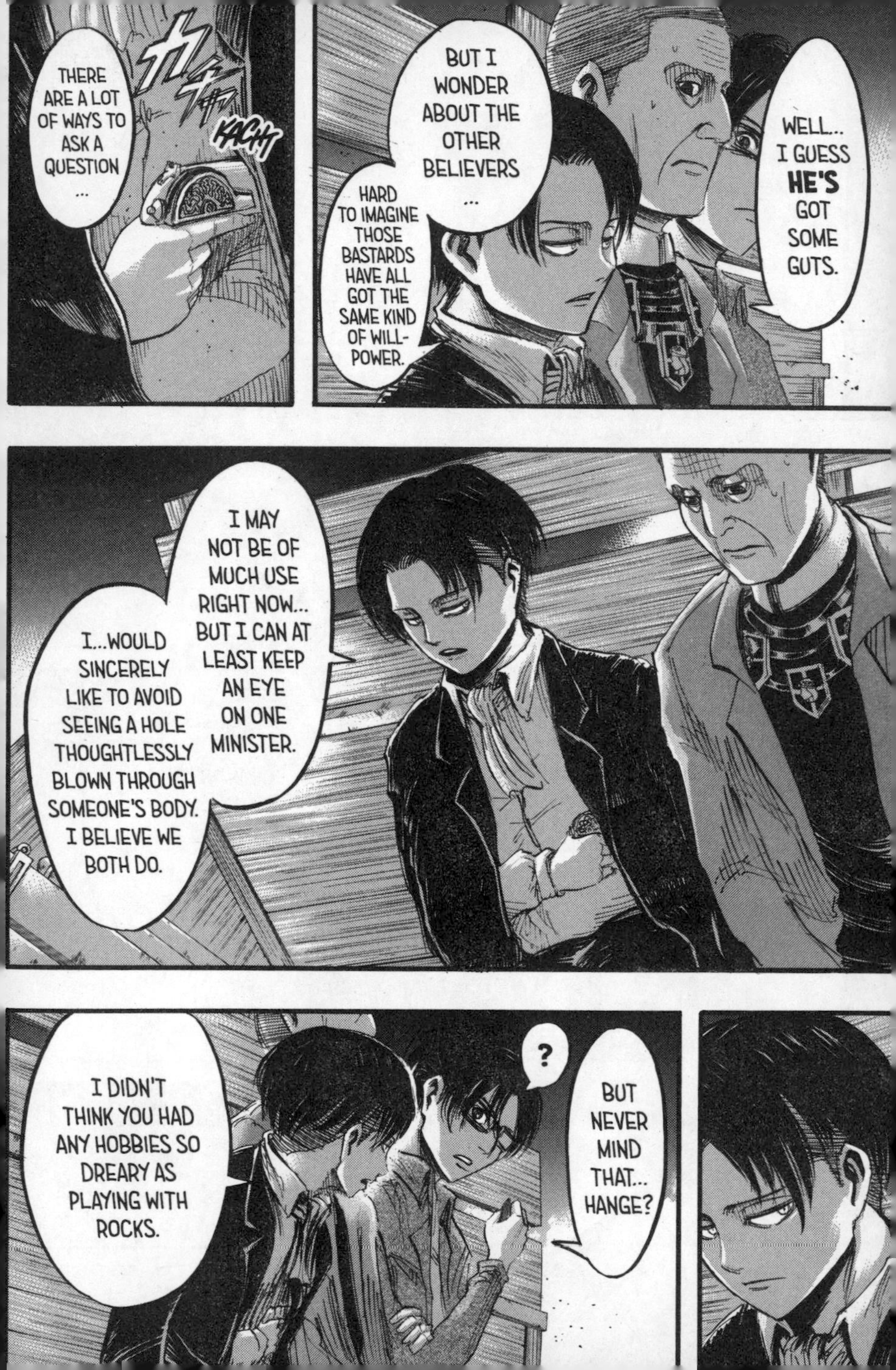

WELL... I GUESS **HE'S** GOT SOME GUTS.
BUT I WONDER ABOUT THE OTHER BELIEVERS ...
HARD TO IMAGINE THOSE BASTARDS HAVE ALL GOT THE SAME KIND OF WILL-POWER.
KACHI
THERE ARE A LOT OF WAYS TO ASK A QUESTION ...
I MAY NOT BE OF MUCH USE RIGHT NOW... BUT I CAN AT LEAST KEEP AN EYE ON ONE MINISTER.
I...WOULD SINCERELY LIKE TO AVOID SEEING A HOLE THOUGHTLESSLY BLOWN THROUGH SOMEONE'S BODY. I BELIEVE WE BOTH DO.
BUT NEVER MIND THAT... HANGE?
?
I DIDN'T THINK YOU HAD ANY HOBBIES SO DREARY AS PLAYING WITH ROCKS.

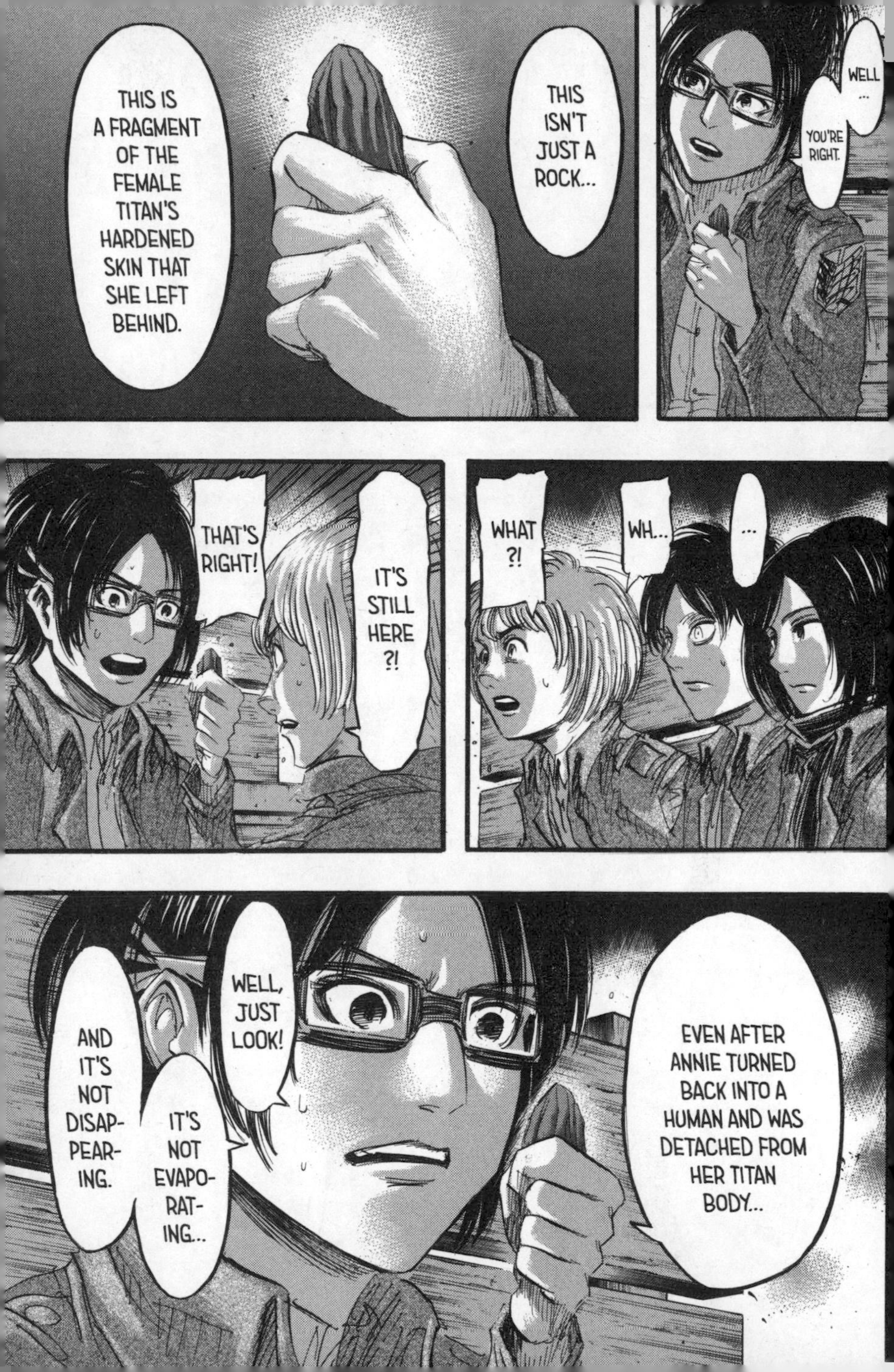
WELL ...
YOU'RE RIGHT.
THIS ISN'T JUST A ROCK...
THIS IS A FRAGMENT OF THE FEMALE TITAN'S HARDENED SKIN THAT SHE LEFT BEHIND.
...
WH...
WHAT ?!
IT'S STILL HERE ?!
THAT'S RIGHT!
EVEN AFTER ANNIE TURNED BACK INTO A HUMAN AND WAS DETACHED FROM HER TITAN BODY...
WELL, JUST LOOK!
IT'S NOT EVAPO-RAT-ING...
AND IT'S NOT DISAP-PEAR-ING.

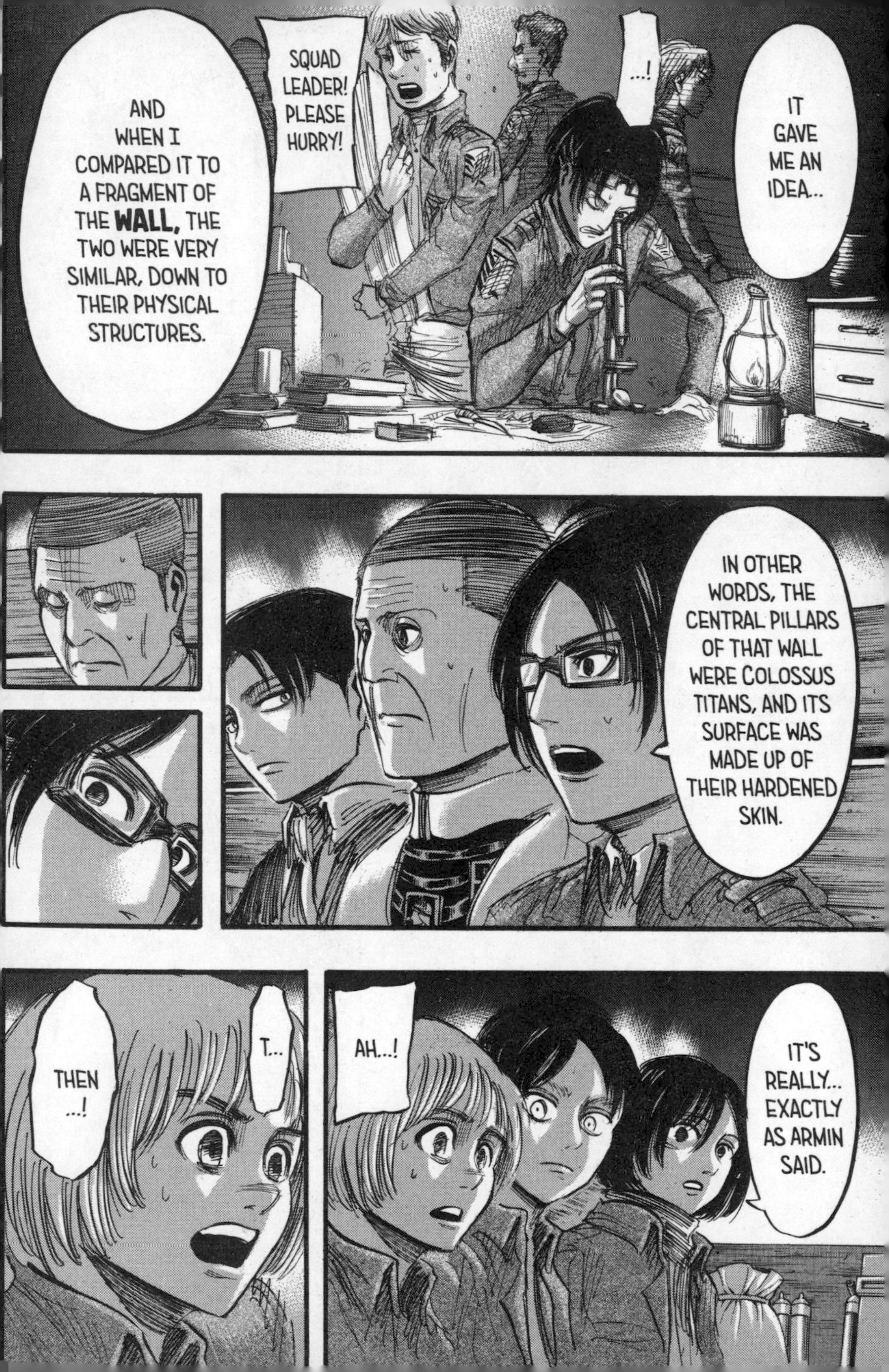
IT GAVE ME AN IDEA...
...!
SQUAD LEADER! PLEASE HURRY!
AND WHEN I COMPARED IT TO A FRAGMENT OF THE WALL, THE TWO WERE VERY SIMILAR, DOWN TO THEIR PHYSICAL STRUCTURES.
IN OTHER WORDS, THE CENTRAL PILLARS OF THAT WALL WERE COLOSSUS TITANS, AND ITS SURFACE WAS MADE UP OF THEIR HARDENED SKIN.
IT'S REALLY... EXACTLY AS ARMIN SAID.
AH...!
T...
THEN ...!

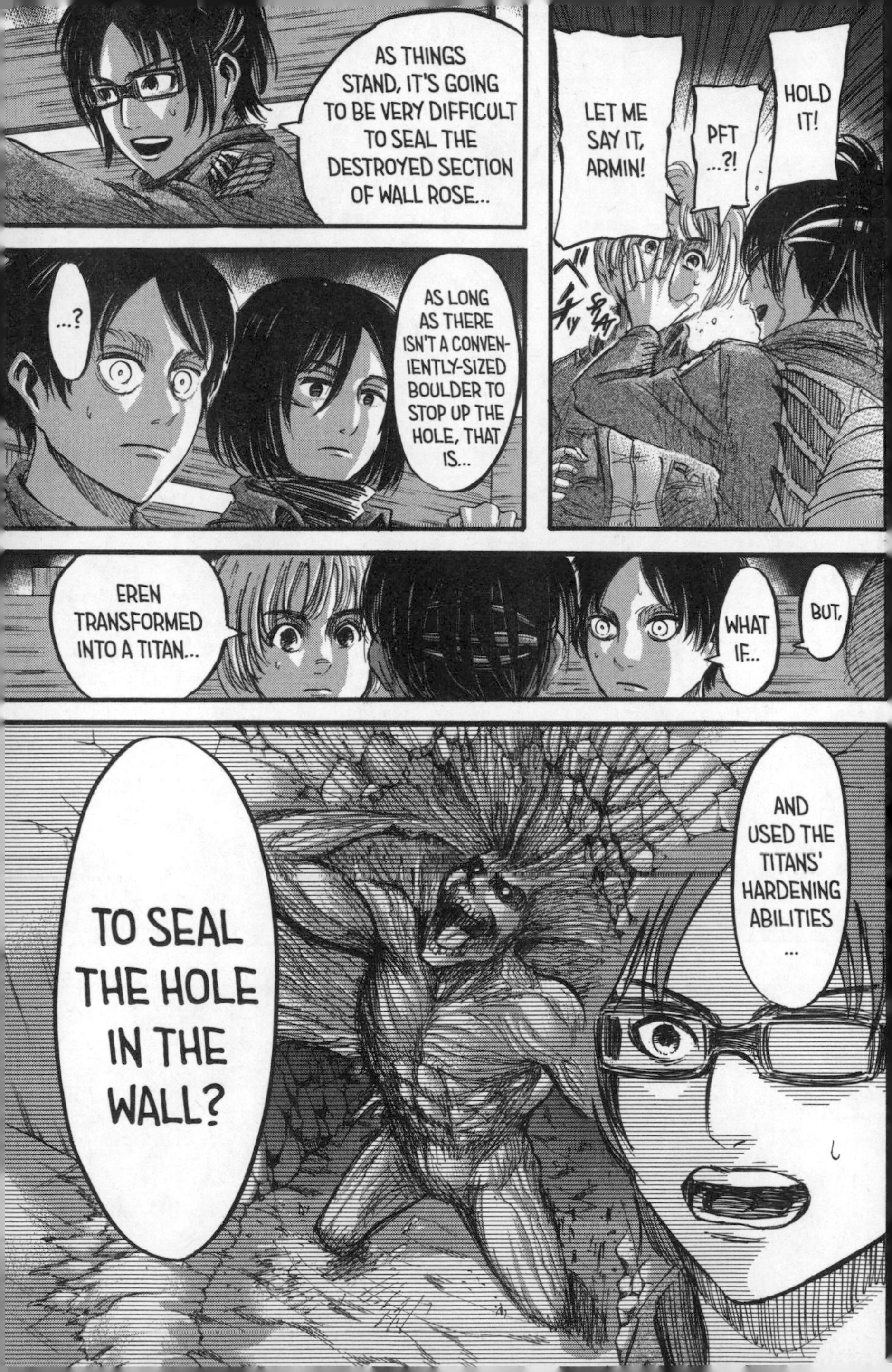
HOLD IT!
PFT ...?!
LET ME SAY IT, ARMIN!
SLAP
AS THINGS STAND, IT'S GOING TO BE VERY DIFFICULT TO SEAL THE DESTROYED SECTION OF WALL ROSE...
AS LONG AS THERE ISN'T A CONVEN-IENTLY-SIZED BOULDER TO STOP UP THE HOLE, THAT IS...
...?
BUT,
WHAT IF...
EREN TRANSFORMED INTO A TITAN...
AND USED THE TITANS' HARDENING ABILITIES ...
TO SEAL THE HOLE IN THE WALL?

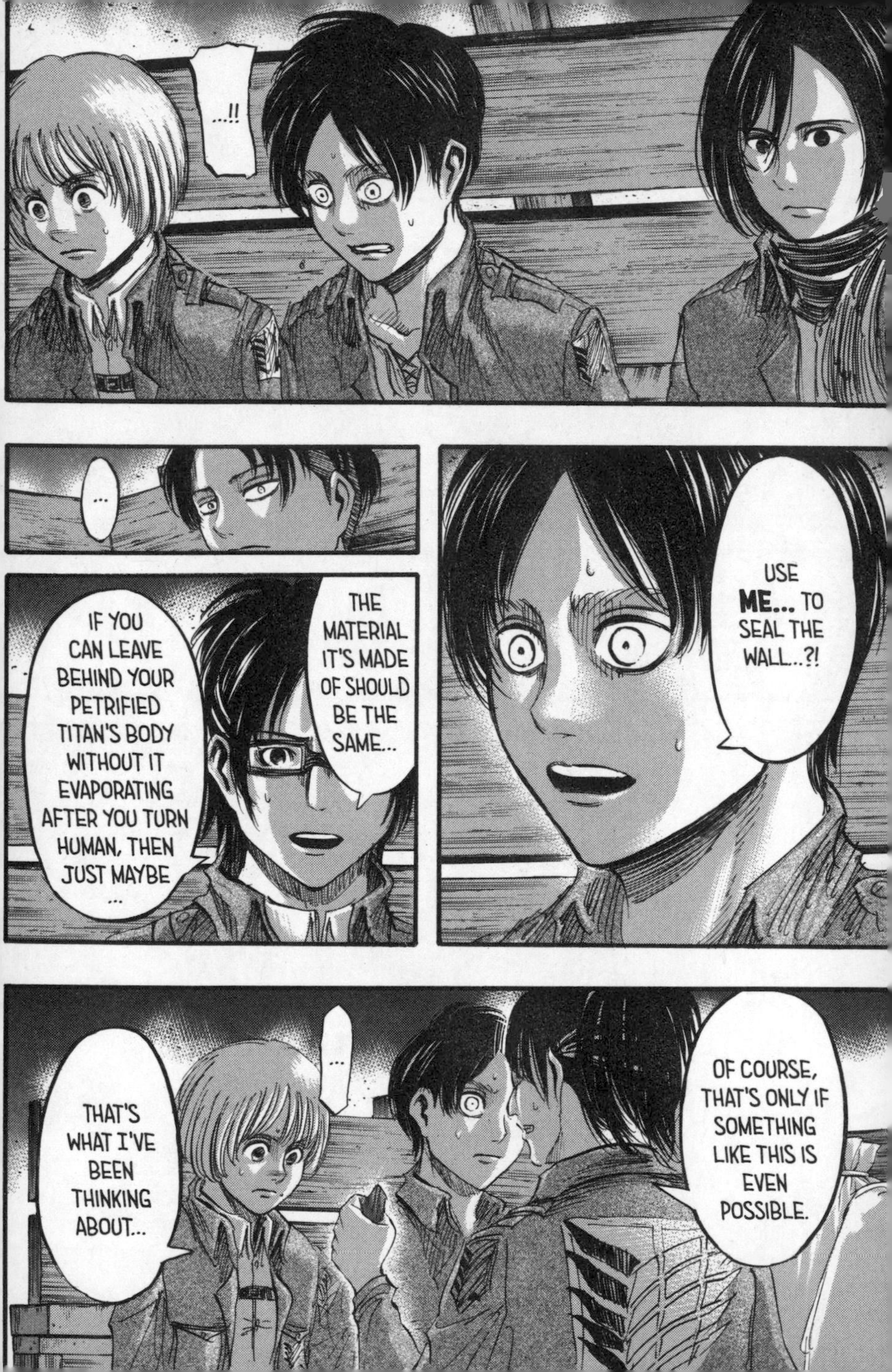
...!!
USE ME... TO SEAL THE WALL...?!
...
THE MATERIAL IT'S MADE OF SHOULD BE THE SAME...
IF YOU CAN LEAVE BEHIND YOUR PETRIFIED TITAN'S BODY WITHOUT IT EVAPORATING AFTER YOU TURN HUMAN, THEN JUST MAYBE ...
OF COURSE, THAT'S ONLY IF SOMETHING LIKE THIS IS EVEN POSSIBLE.
...
THAT'S WHAT I'VE BEEN THINKING ABOUT...

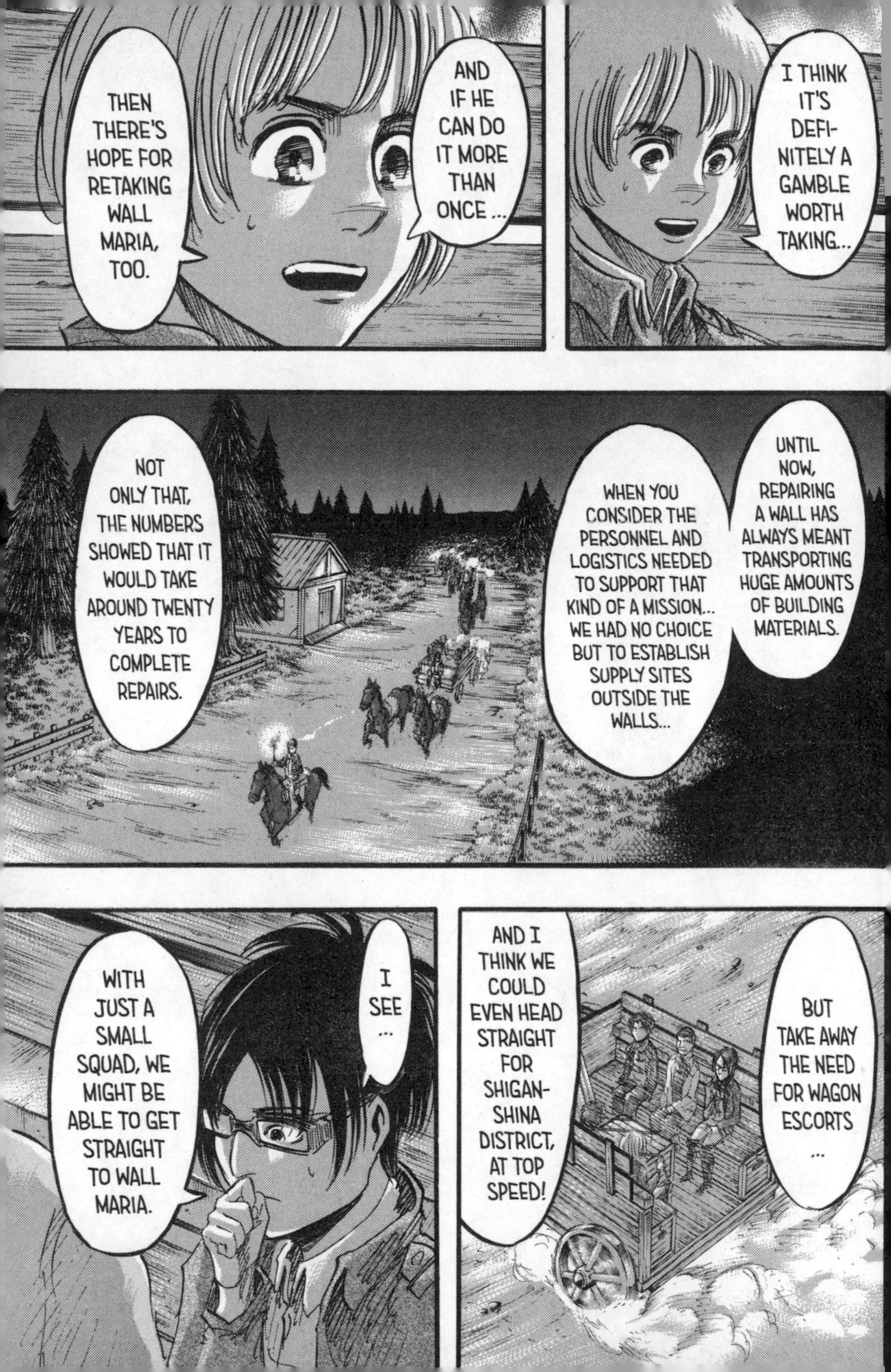
I THINK IT'S DEFINITELY A GAMBLE WORTH TAKING...
AND IF HE CAN DO IT MORE THAN ONCE ...
THEN THERE'S HOPE FOR RETAKING WALL MARIA, TOO.
UNTIL NOW, REPAIRING A WALL HAS ALWAYS MEANT TRANSPORTING HUGE AMOUNTS OF BUILDING MATERIALS.
WHEN YOU CONSIDER THE PERSONNEL AND LOGISTICS NEEDED TO SUPPORT THAT KIND OF A MISSION... WE HAD NO CHOICE BUT TO ESTABLISH SUPPLY SITES OUTSIDE THE WALLS...
NOT ONLY THAT, THE NUMBERS SHOWED THAT IT WOULD TAKE AROUND TWENTY YEARS TO COMPLETE REPAIRS.
BUT TAKE AWAY THE NEED FOR WAGON ESCORTS ...
AND I THINK WE COULD EVEN HEAD STRAIGHT FOR SHIGAN-SHINA DISTRICT, AT TOP SPEED!
I SEE ...
WITH JUST A SMALL SQUAD, WE MIGHT BE ABLE TO GET STRAIGHT TO WALL MARIA.

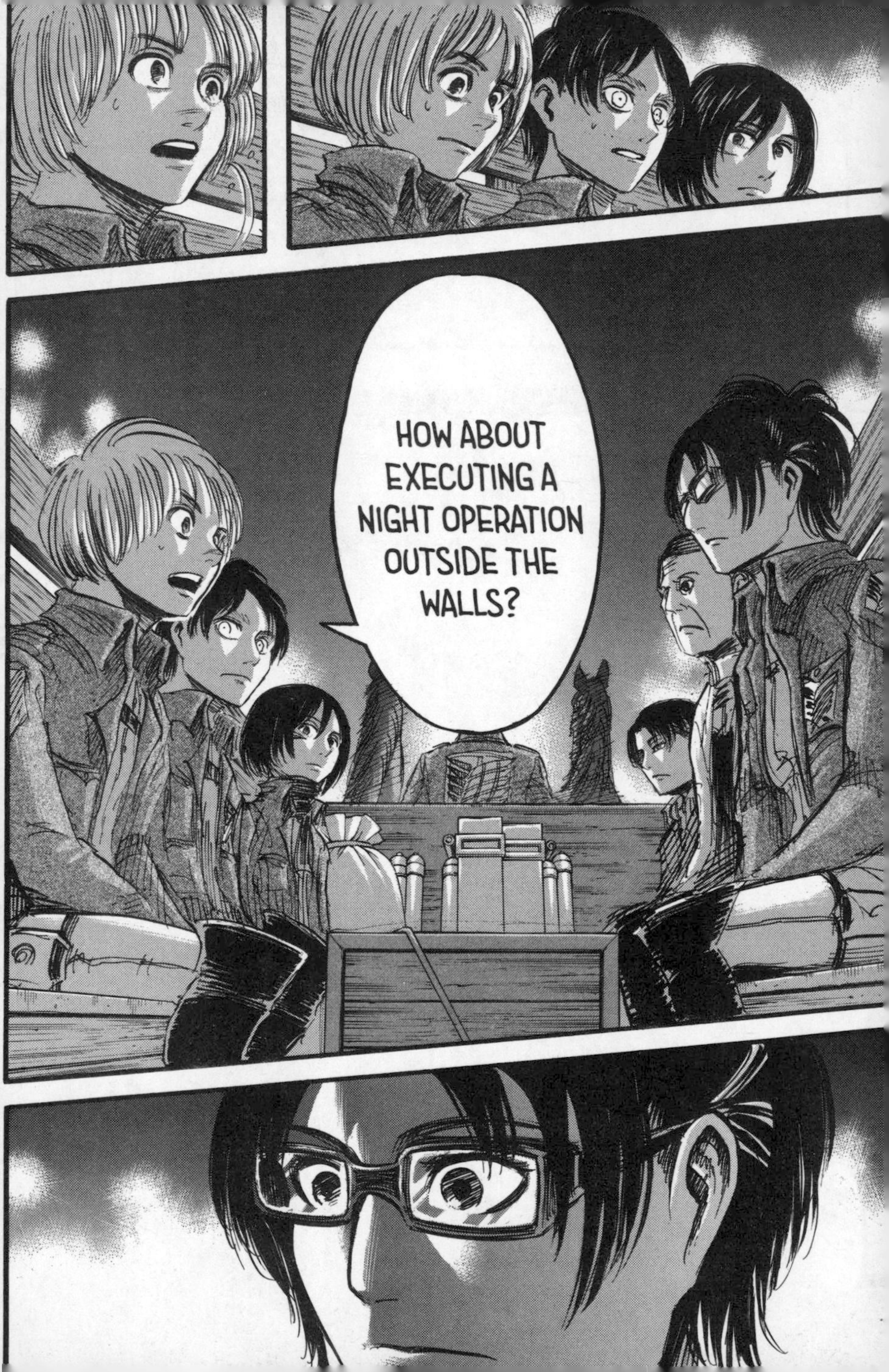
HOW ABOUT EXECUTING A NIGHT OPERATION OUTSIDE THE WALLS?

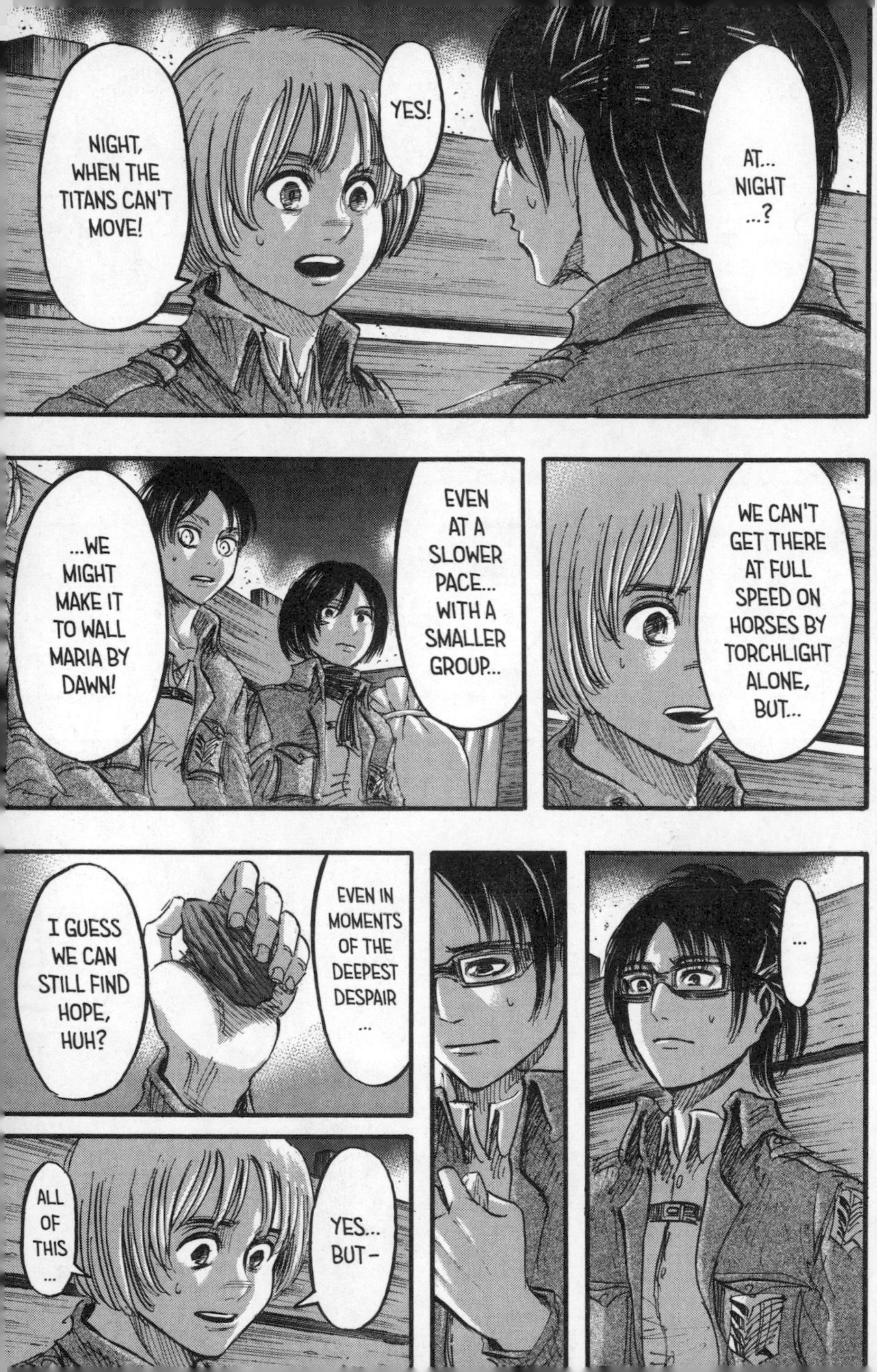
AT... NIGHT ...?
YES!
NIGHT, WHEN THE TITANS CAN'T MOVE!
WE CAN'T GET THERE AT FULL SPEED ON HORSES BY TORCHLIGHT ALONE, BUT...
EVEN AT A SLOWER PACE... WITH A SMALLER GROUP...
...WE MIGHT MAKE IT TO WALL MARIA BY DAWN!
...
EVEN IN MOMENTS OF THE DEEPEST DESPAIR ...
I GUESS WE CAN STILL FIND HOPE, HUH?
YES... BUT -
ALL OF THIS ...

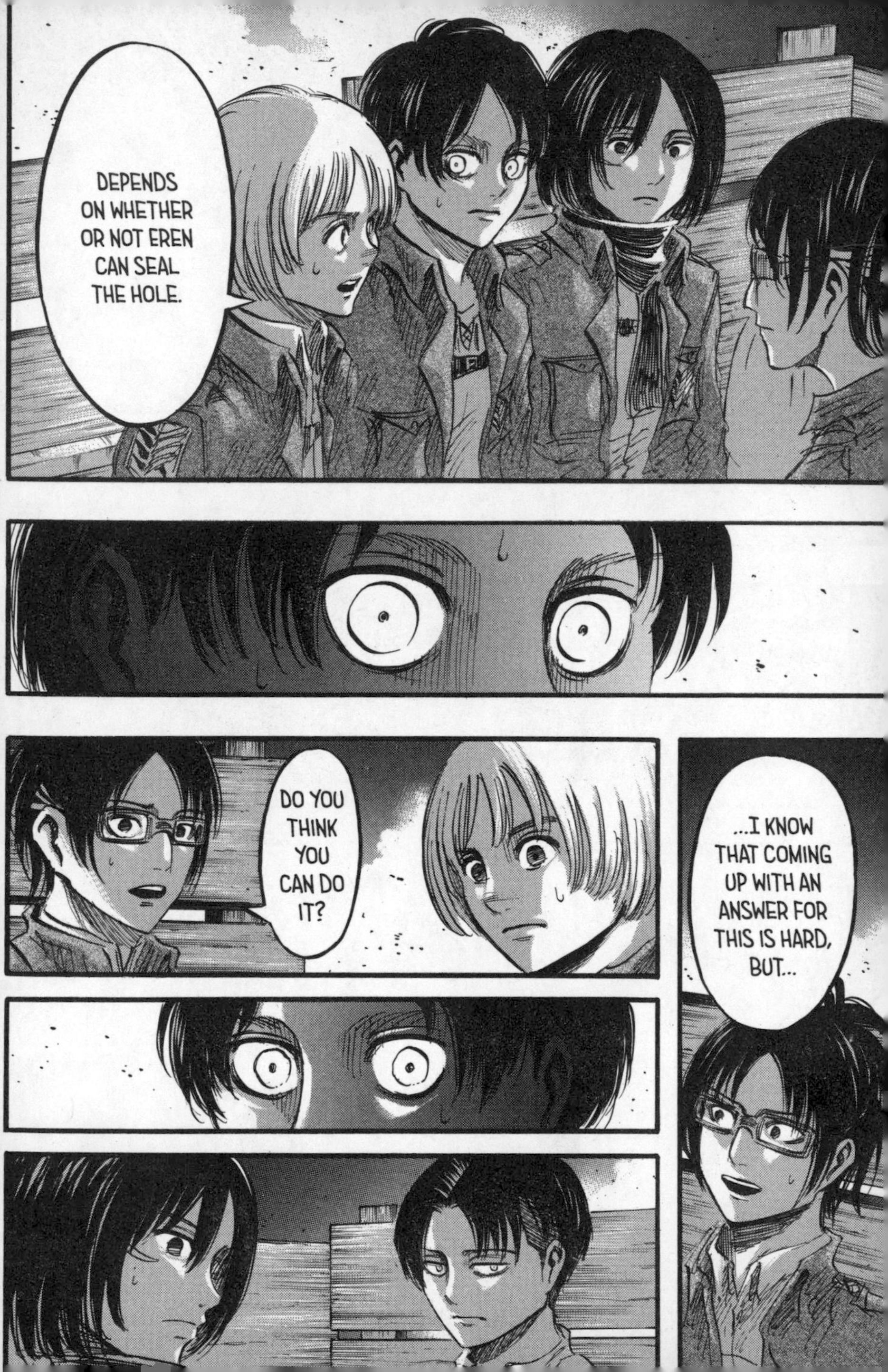
DEPENDS ON WHETHER OR NOT EREN CAN SEAL THE HOLE.
...I KNOW THAT COMING UP WITH AN ANSWER FOR THIS IS HARD, BUT...
DO YOU THINK YOU CAN DO IT?

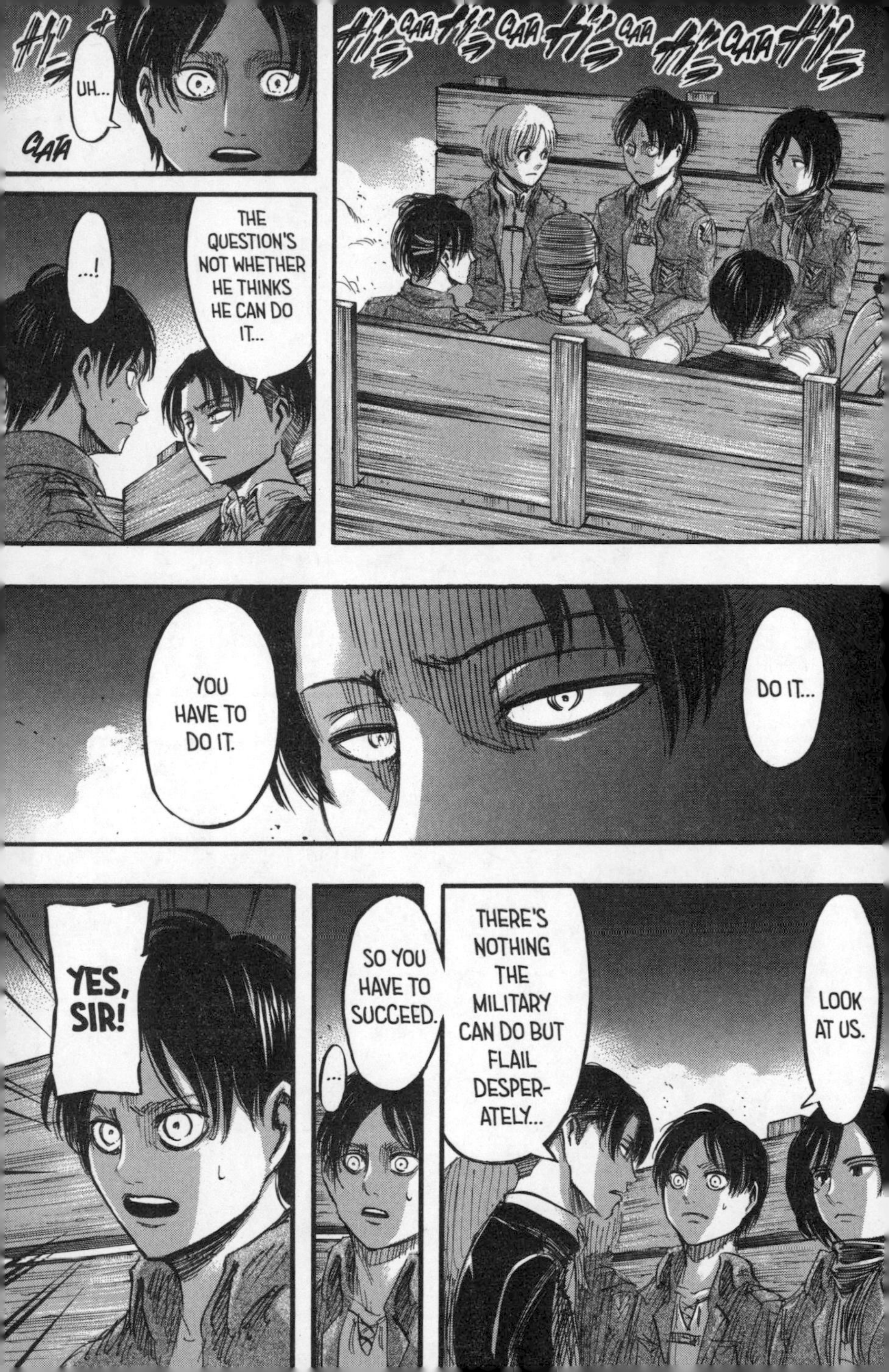
CLATA
CLATA
CLATA
CLATA
UH...
CLATA
...!
THE QUESTION'S NOT WHETHER HE THINKS HE CAN DO IT...
DO IT...
YOU HAVE TO DO IT.
LOOK AT US.
THERE'S NOTHING THE MILITARY CAN DO BUT FLAIL DESPER-ATELY...
SO YOU HAVE TO SUCCEED.
...
YES, SIR!

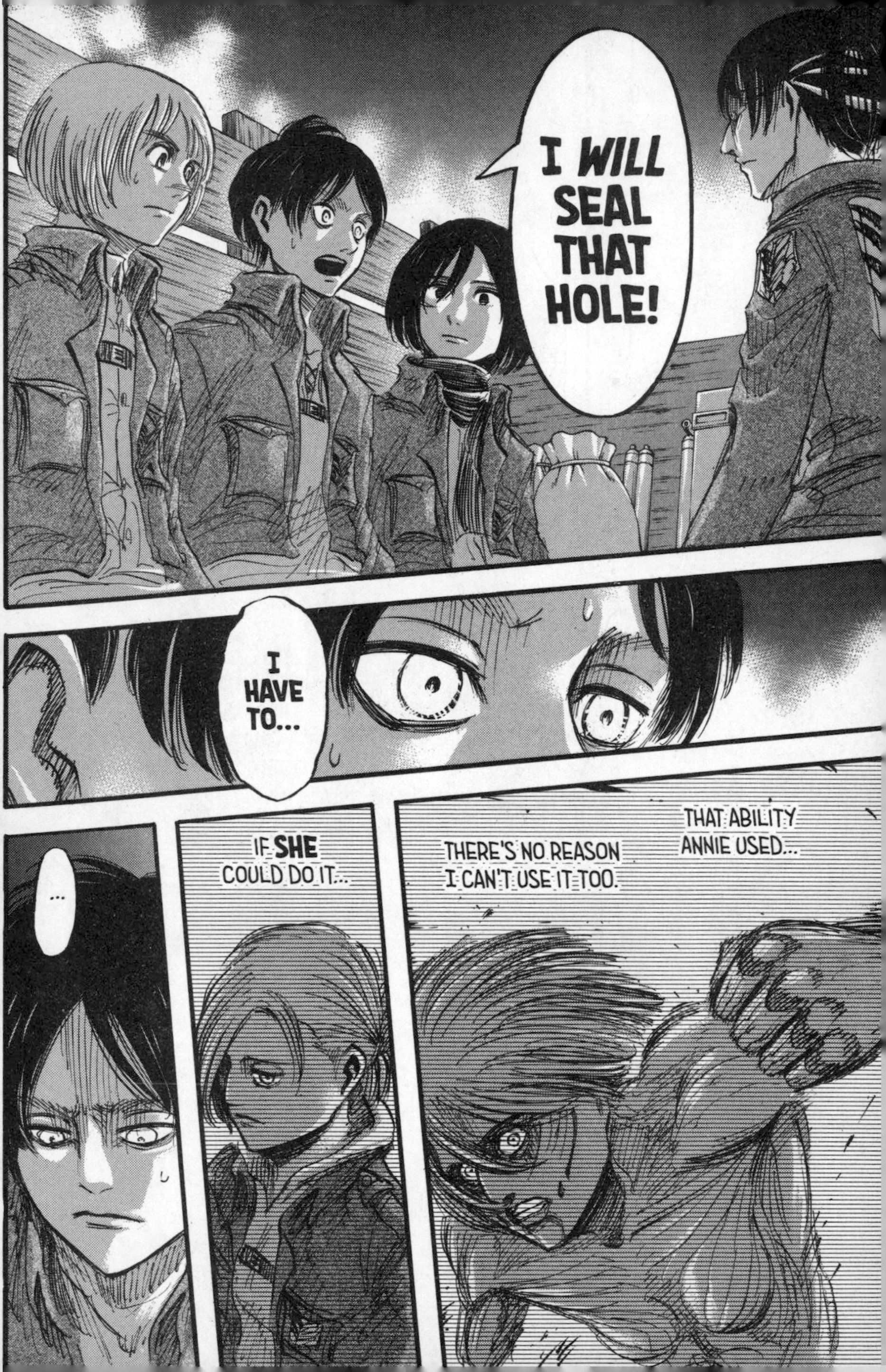
I WILL SEAL THAT HOLE!
I HAVE TO...
THAT ABILITY ANNIE USED...
THERE'S NO REASON I CAN'T USE IT TOO.
IF SHE COULD DO IT...
...

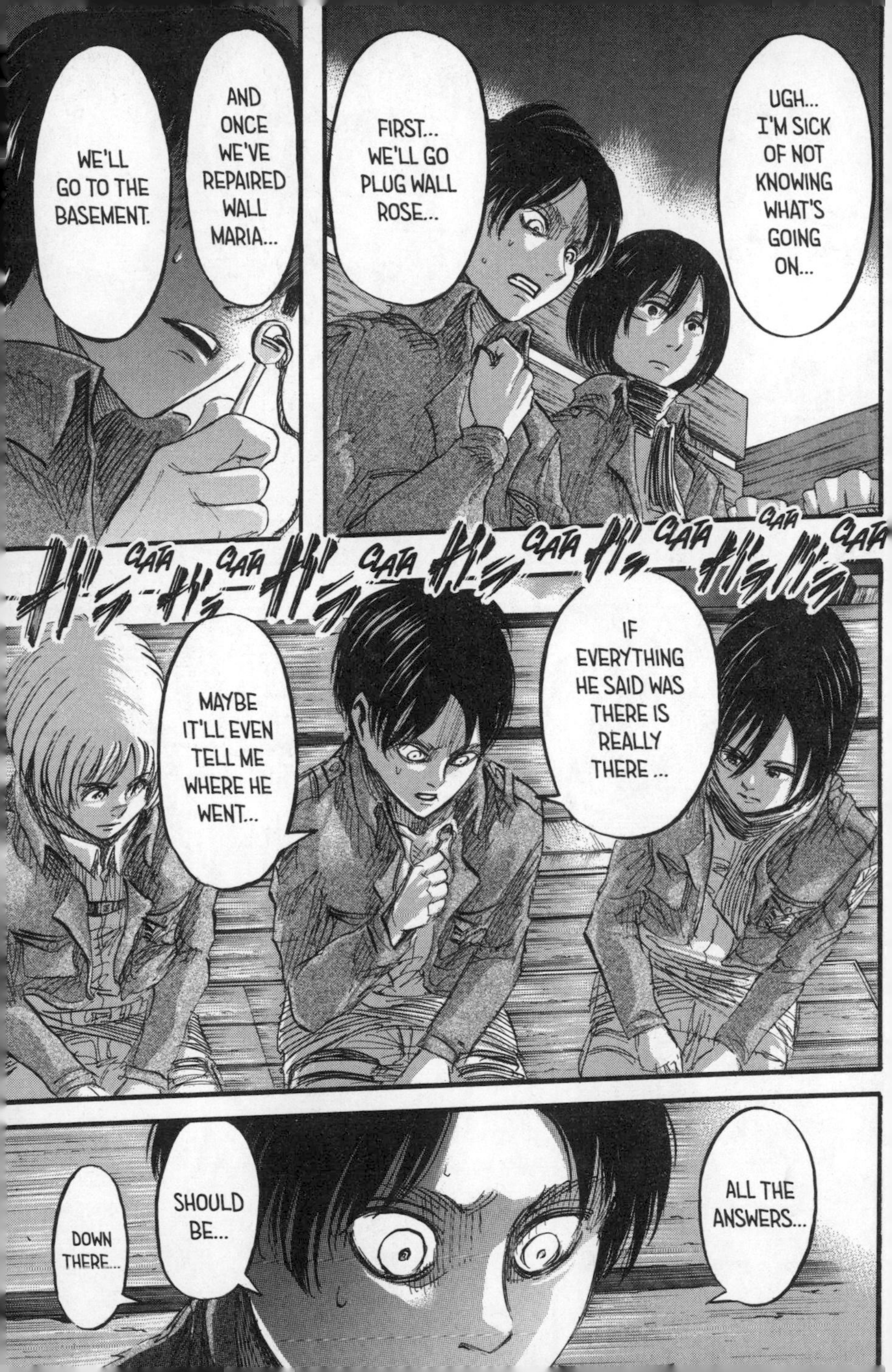
UGH... I'M SICK OF NOT KNOWING WHAT'S GOING ON...
FIRST... WE'LL GO PLUG WALL ROSE...
AND ONCE WE'VE REPAIRED WALL MARIA...
WE'LL GO TO THE BASEMENT.
CLATA CLATA CLATA CLATA CLATA CLATA CLATA
IF EVERYTHING HE SAID WAS THERE IS REALLY THERE ...
MAYBE IT'LL EVEN TELL ME WHERE HE WENT...
ALL THE ANSWERS...
SHOULD BE...
DOWN THERE...

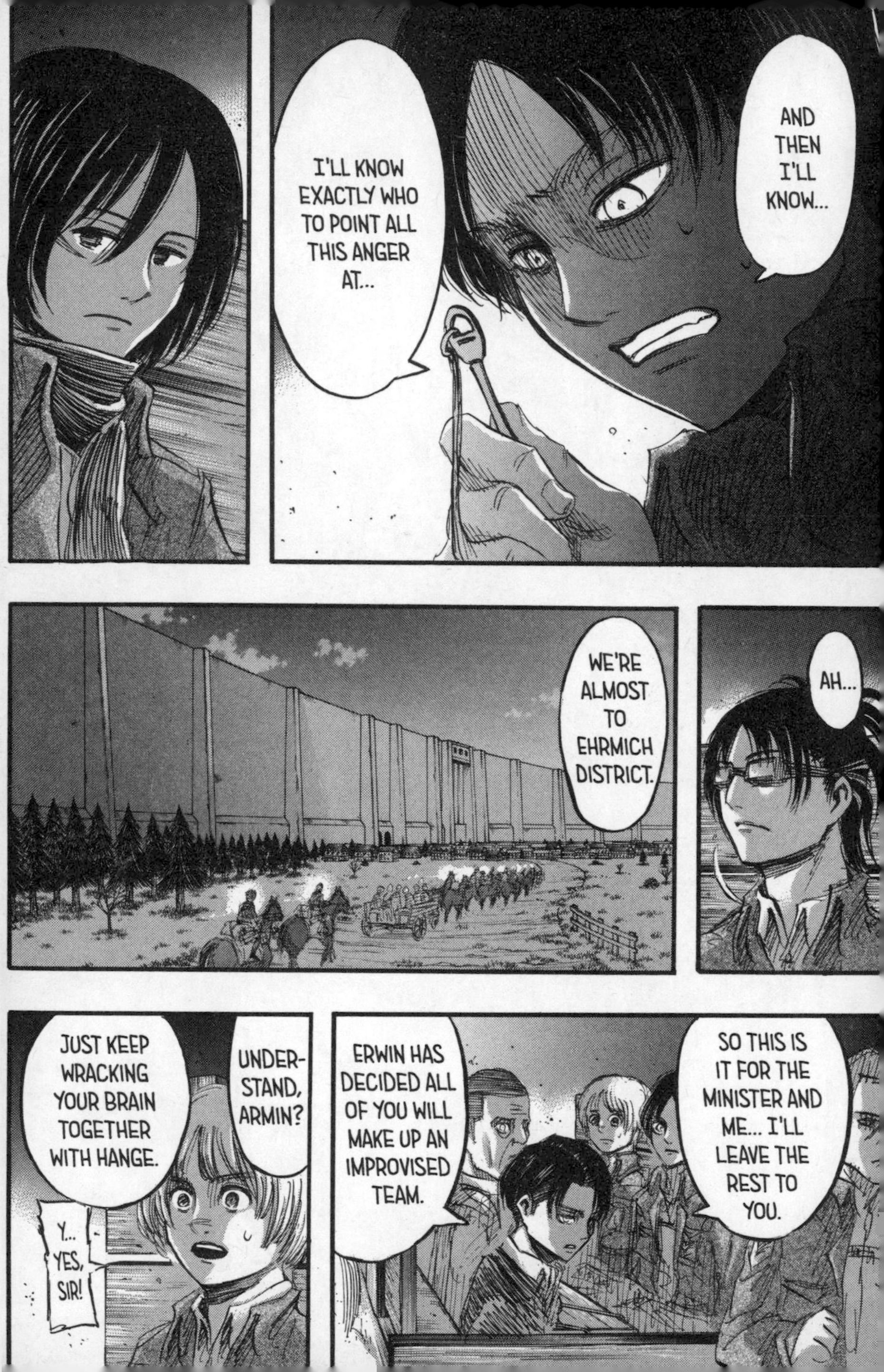
AND THEN I'LL KNOW...
I'LL KNOW EXACTLY WHO TO POINT ALL THIS ANGER AT...
AH...
WE'RE ALMOST TO EHRMICH DISTRICT.
SO THIS IS IT FOR THE MINISTER AND ME... I'LL LEAVE THE REST TO YOU.
ERWIN HAS DECIDED ALL OF YOU WILL MAKE UP AN IMPROVISED TEAM.
UNDER-STAND, ARMIN?
JUST KEEP WRACKING YOUR BRAIN TOGETHER WITH HANGE.
Y... YES, SIR!

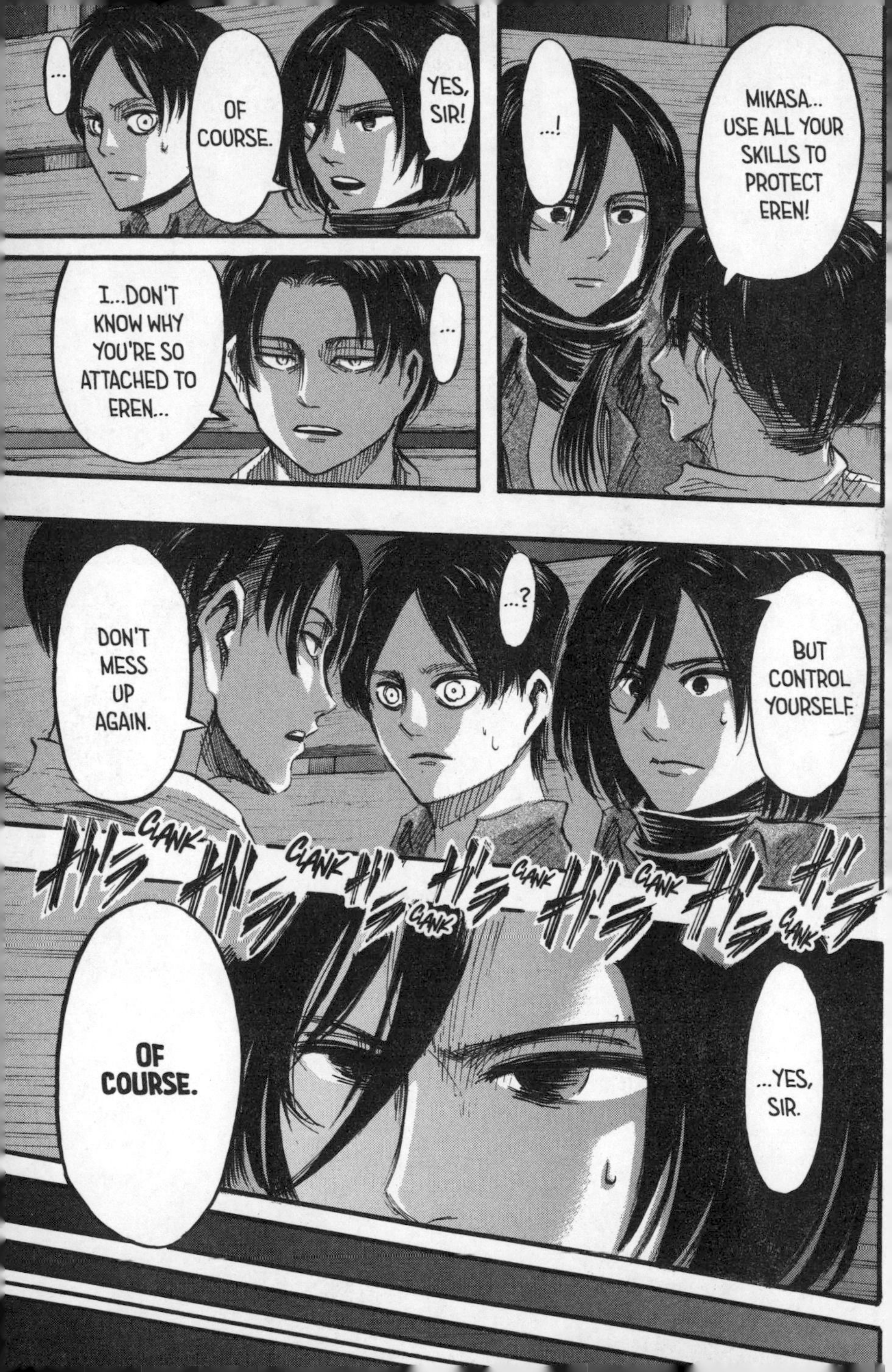
MIKASA... USE ALL YOUR SKILLS TO PROTECT EREN!
...!
YES, SIR!
OF COURSE.
...
...
I...DON'T KNOW WHY YOU'RE SO ATTACHED TO EREN...
BUT CONTROL YOURSELF.
...?
DON'T MESS UP AGAIN.
CLANK CLANK CLANK CLANK CLANK CLANK
...YES, SIR.
OF COURSE.

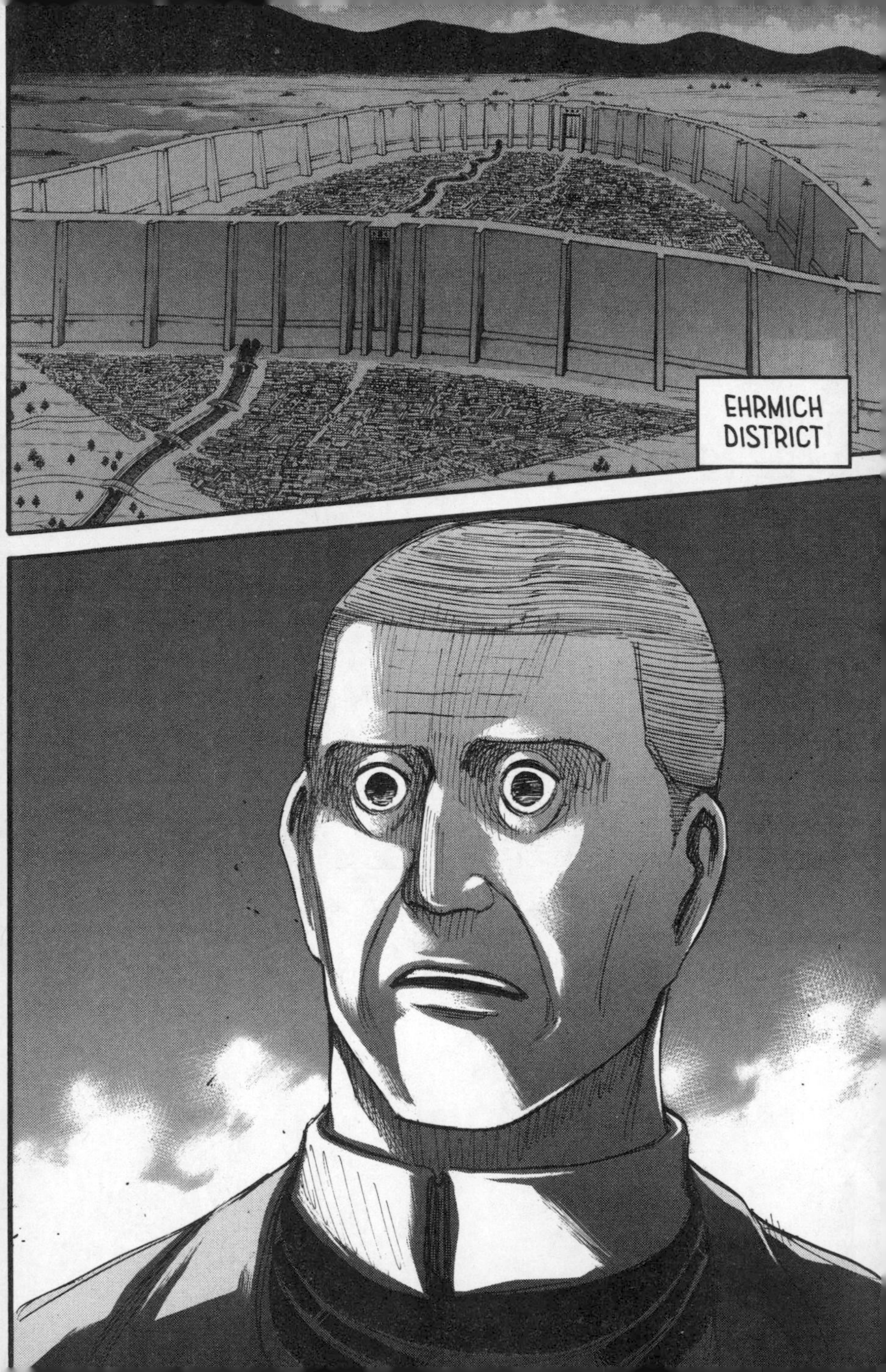
EHRMICH
DISTRICT

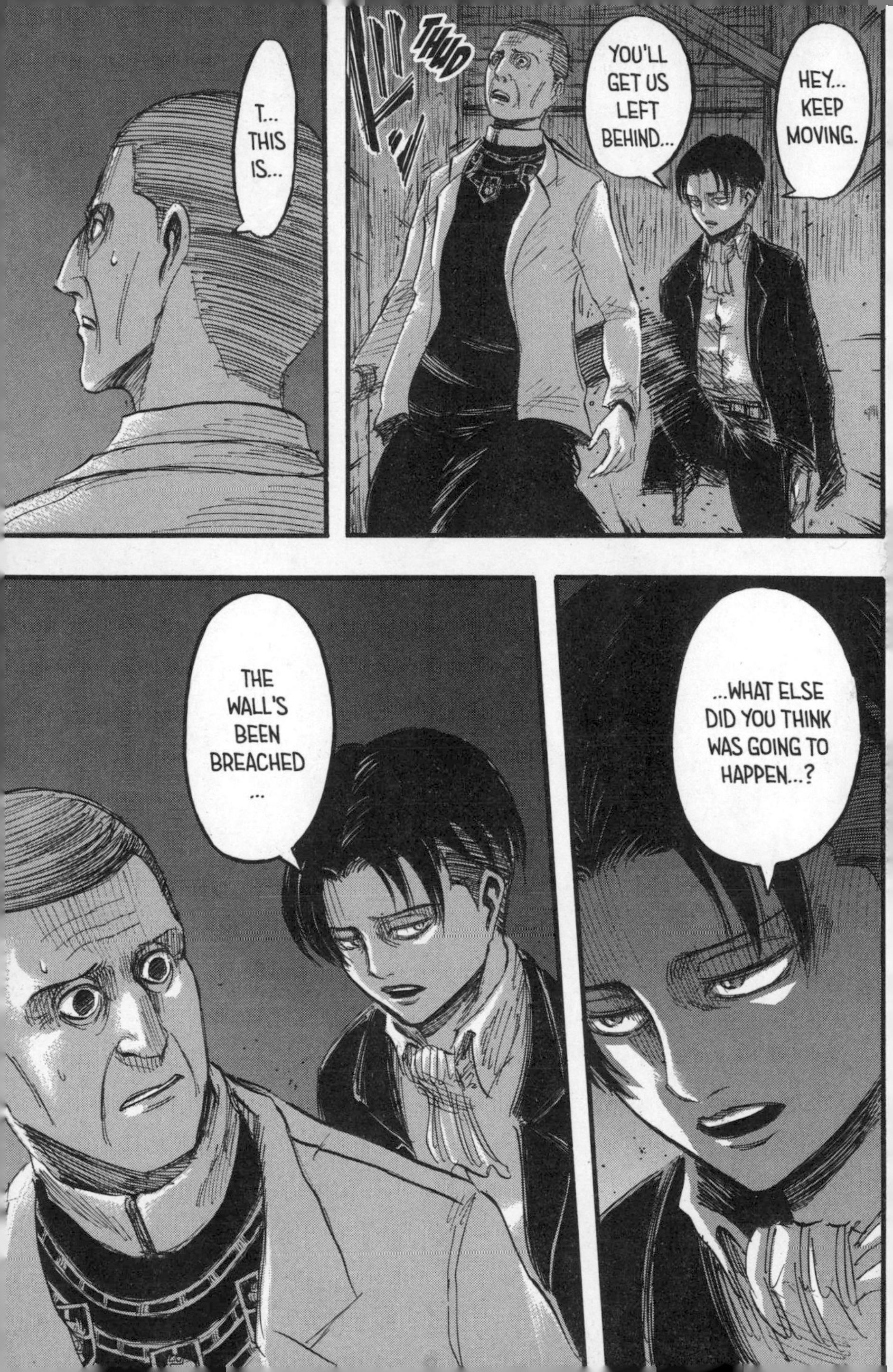
HEY... KEEP MOVING.
YOU'LL GET US LEFT BEHIND...
THUD
T... THIS IS...
...WHAT ELSE DID YOU THINK WAS GOING TO HAPPEN...?
THE WALL'S BEEN BREACHED ...

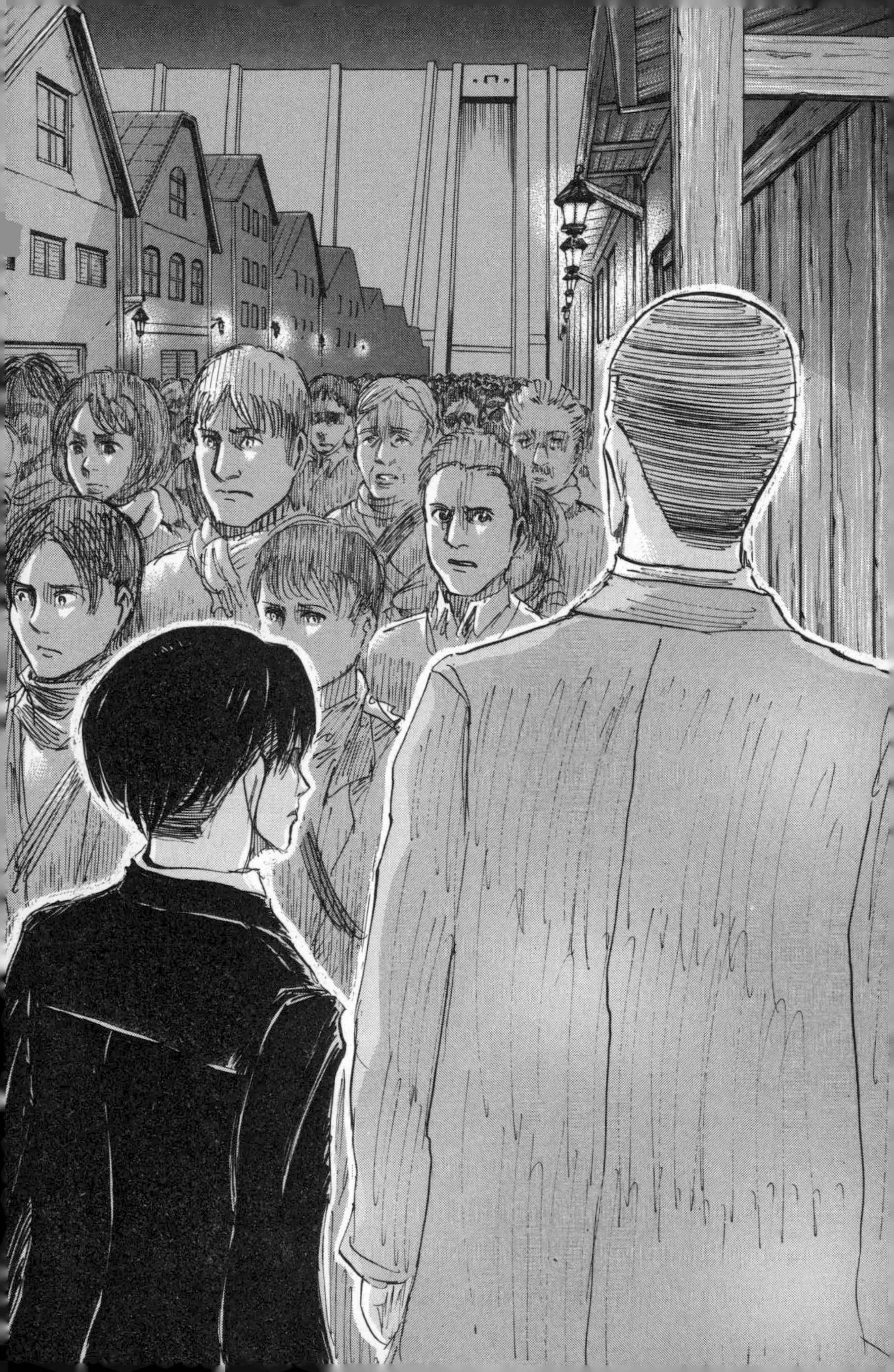

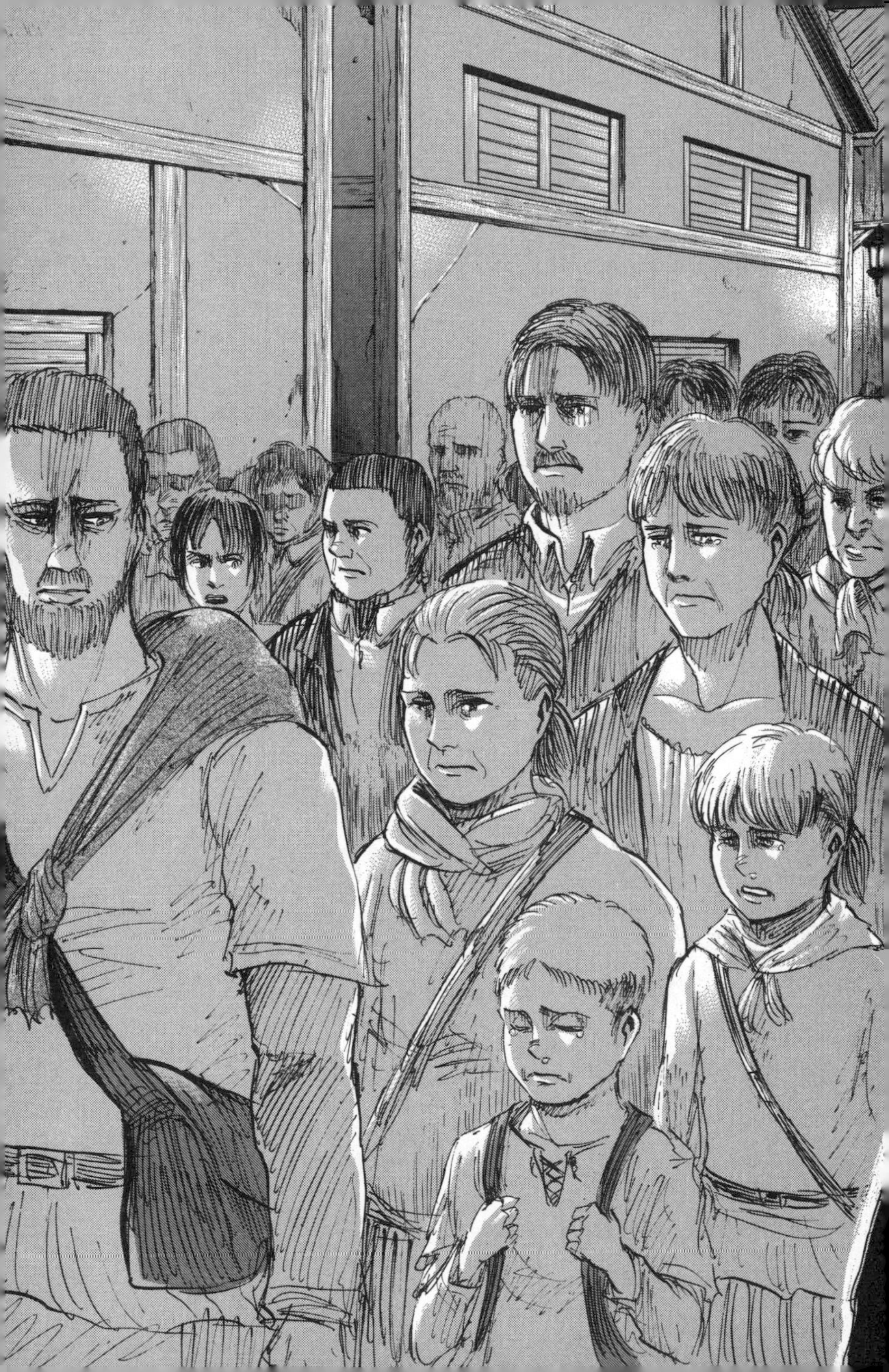

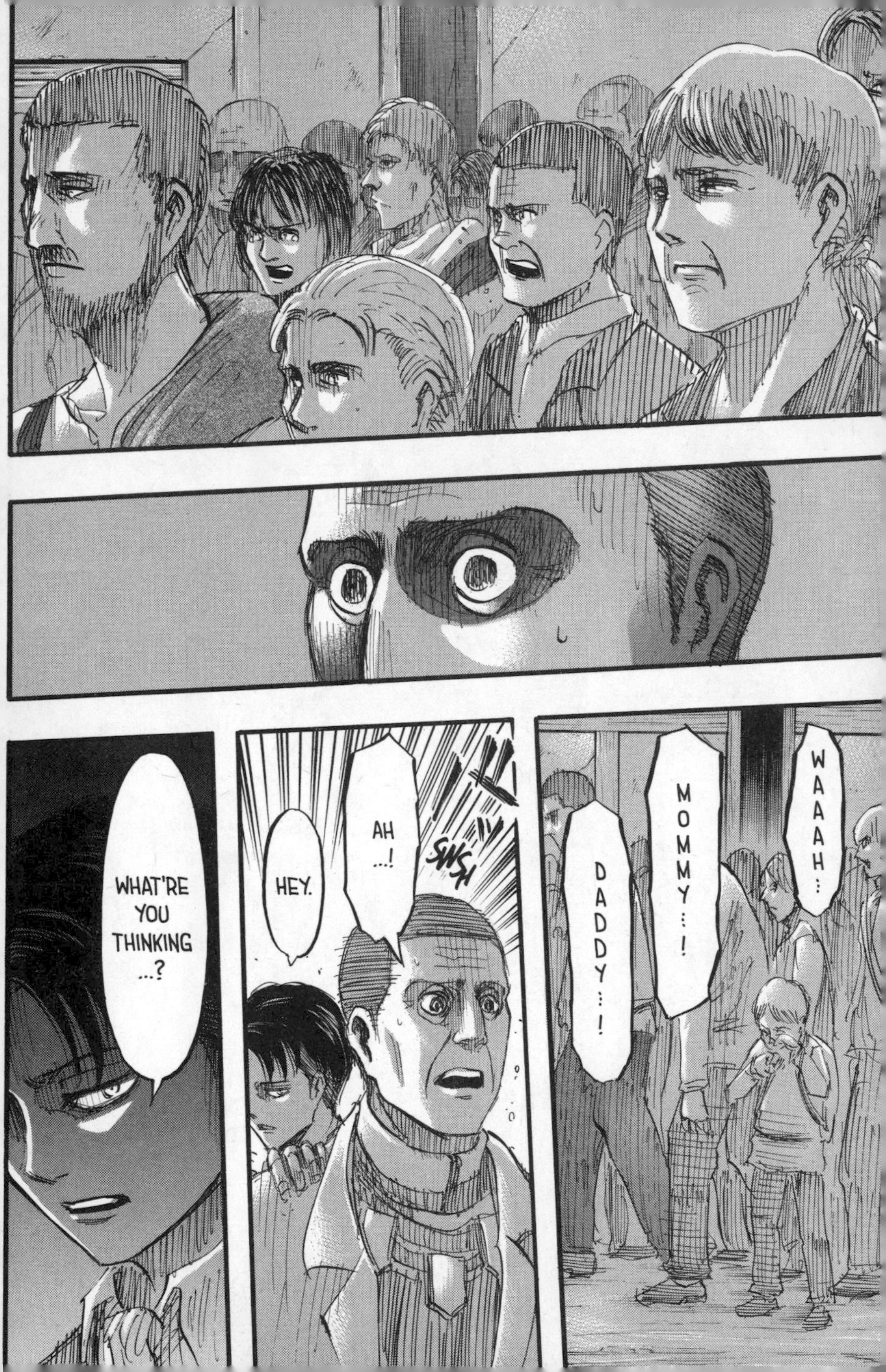
WAAAH...
MOMMY...!
DADDY...!
AH ...!
SWSH
HEY.
WHAT'RE YOU THINKING ...?

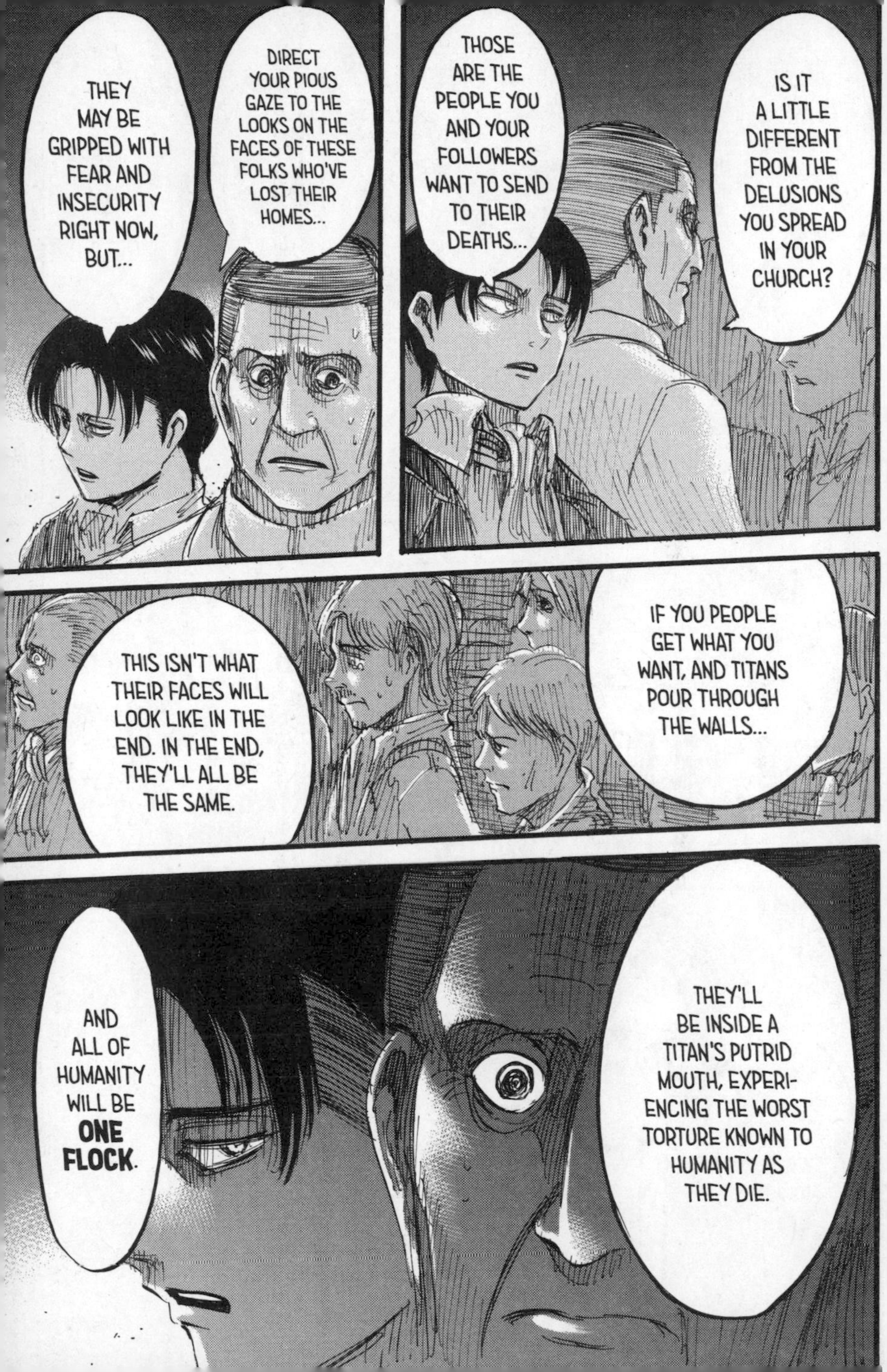
IS IT A LITTLE DIFFERENT FROM THE DELUSIONS YOU SPREAD IN YOUR CHURCH?
THOSE ARE THE PEOPLE YOU AND YOUR FOLLOWERS WANT TO SEND TO THEIR DEATHS...
DIRECT YOUR PIOUS GAZE TO THE LOOKS ON THE FACES OF THESE FOLKS WHO'VE LOST THEIR HOMES...
THEY MAY BE GRIPPED WITH FEAR AND INSECURITY RIGHT NOW, BUT...
IF YOU PEOPLE GET WHAT YOU WANT, AND TITANS POUR THROUGH THE WALLS...
THIS ISN'T WHAT THEIR FACES WILL LOOK LIKE IN THE END. IN THE END, THEY'LL ALL BE THE SAME.
THEY'LL BE INSIDE A TITAN'S PUTRID MOUTH, EXPERI-ENCING THE WORST TORTURE KNOWN TO HUMANITY AS THEY DIE.
AND ALL OF HUMANITY WILL BE **ONE FLOCK**.

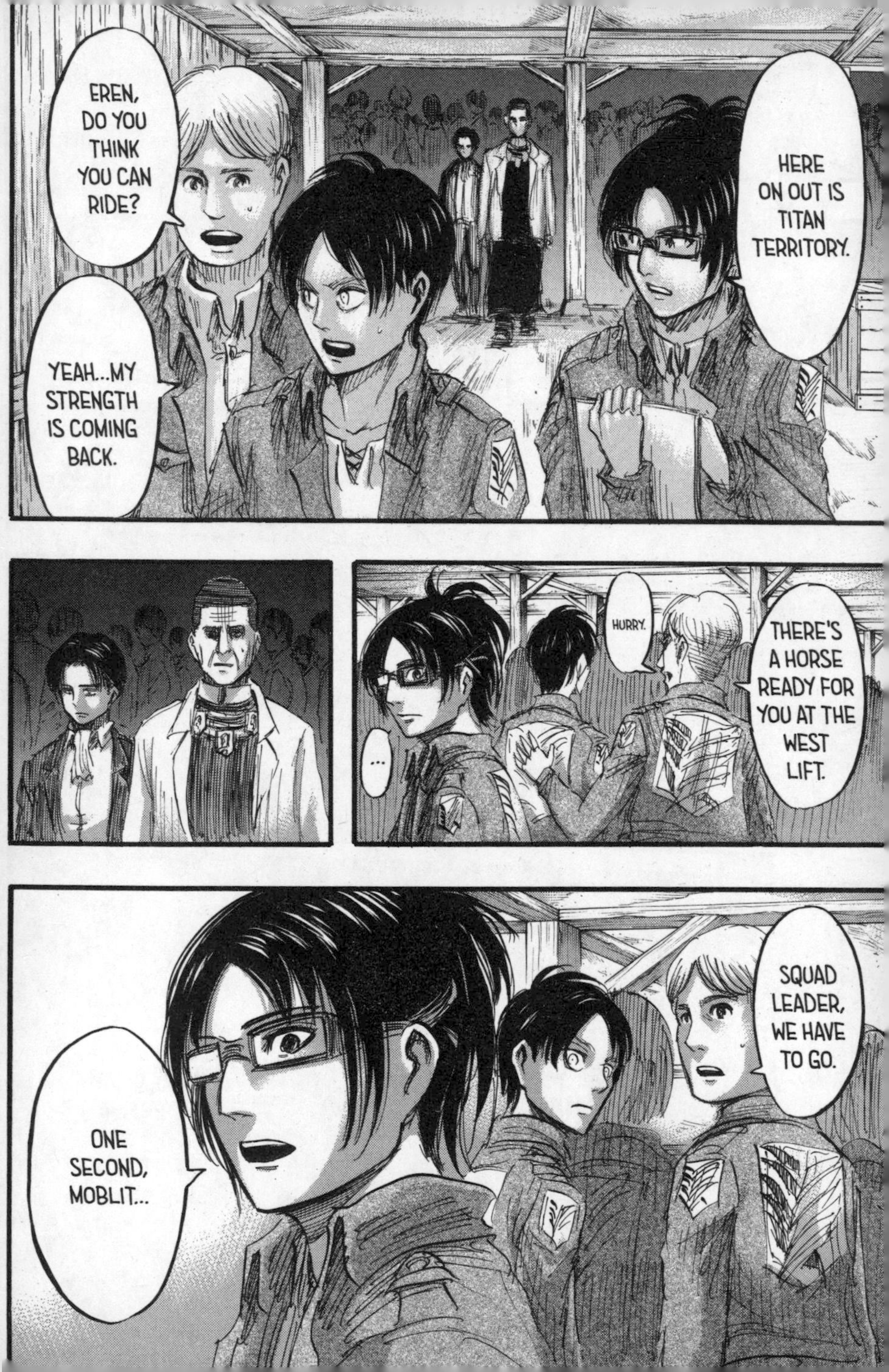
HERE ON OUT IS TITAN TERRITORY.
EREN, DO YOU THINK YOU CAN RIDE?
YEAH...MY STRENGTH IS COMING BACK.
THERE'S A HORSE READY FOR YOU AT THE WEST LIFT.
HURRY.
...
SQUAD LEADER, WE HAVE TO GO.
ONE SECOND, MOBLIT...

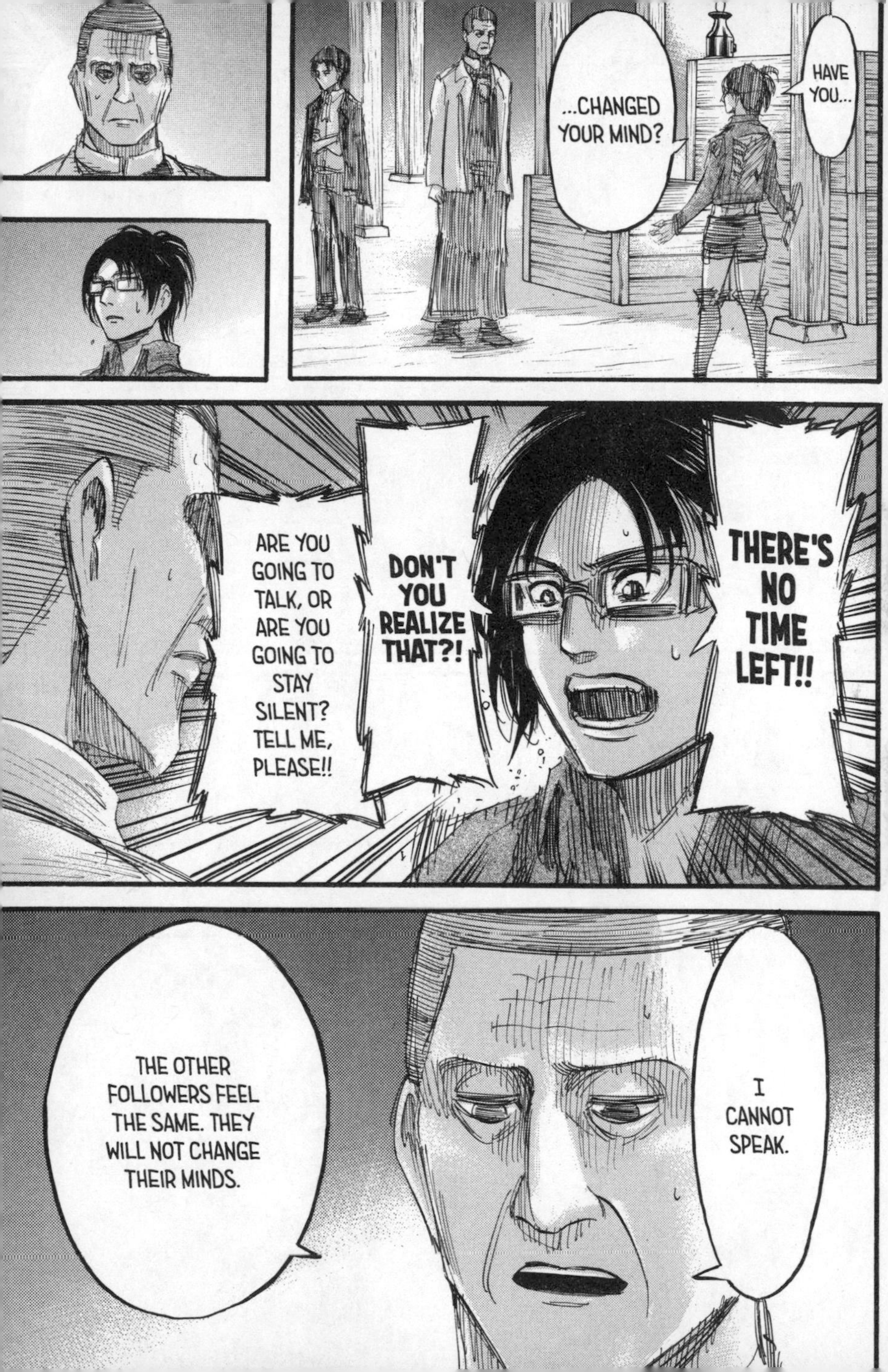
HAVE YOU...
...CHANGED YOUR MIND?
THERE'S NO TIME LEFT!!
DON'T YOU REALIZE THAT?!
ARE YOU GOING TO TALK, OR ARE YOU GOING TO STAY SILENT? TELL ME, PLEASE!!
I CANNOT SPEAK.
THE OTHER FOLLOWERS FEEL THE SAME. THEY WILL NOT CHANGE THEIR MINDS.

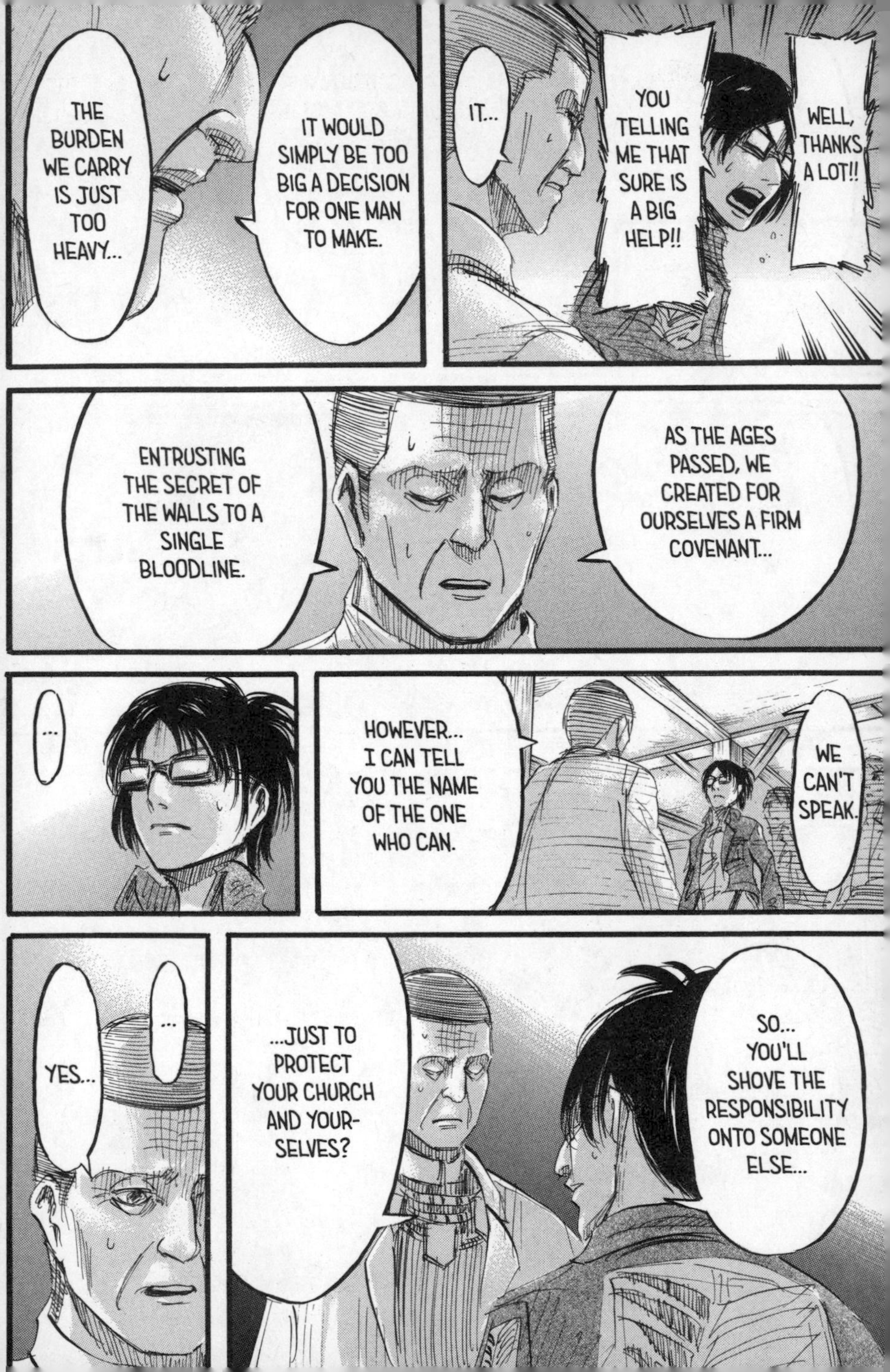
WELL, THANKS A LOT!!
YOU TELLING ME THAT SURE IS A BIG HELP!!
IT...
IT WOULD SIMPLY BE TOO BIG A DECISION FOR ONE MAN TO MAKE.
THE BURDEN WE CARRY IS JUST TOO HEAVY...
AS THE AGES PASSED, WE CREATED FOR OURSELVES A FIRM COVENANT...
ENTRUSTING THE SECRET OF THE WALLS TO A SINGLE BLOODLINE.
WE CAN'T SPEAK.
HOWEVER... I CAN TELL YOU THE NAME OF THE ONE WHO CAN.
...
SO... YOU'LL SHOVE THE RESPONSIBILITY ONTO SOMEONE ELSE...
...JUST TO PROTECT YOUR CHURCH AND YOUR-SELVES?
...
YES...

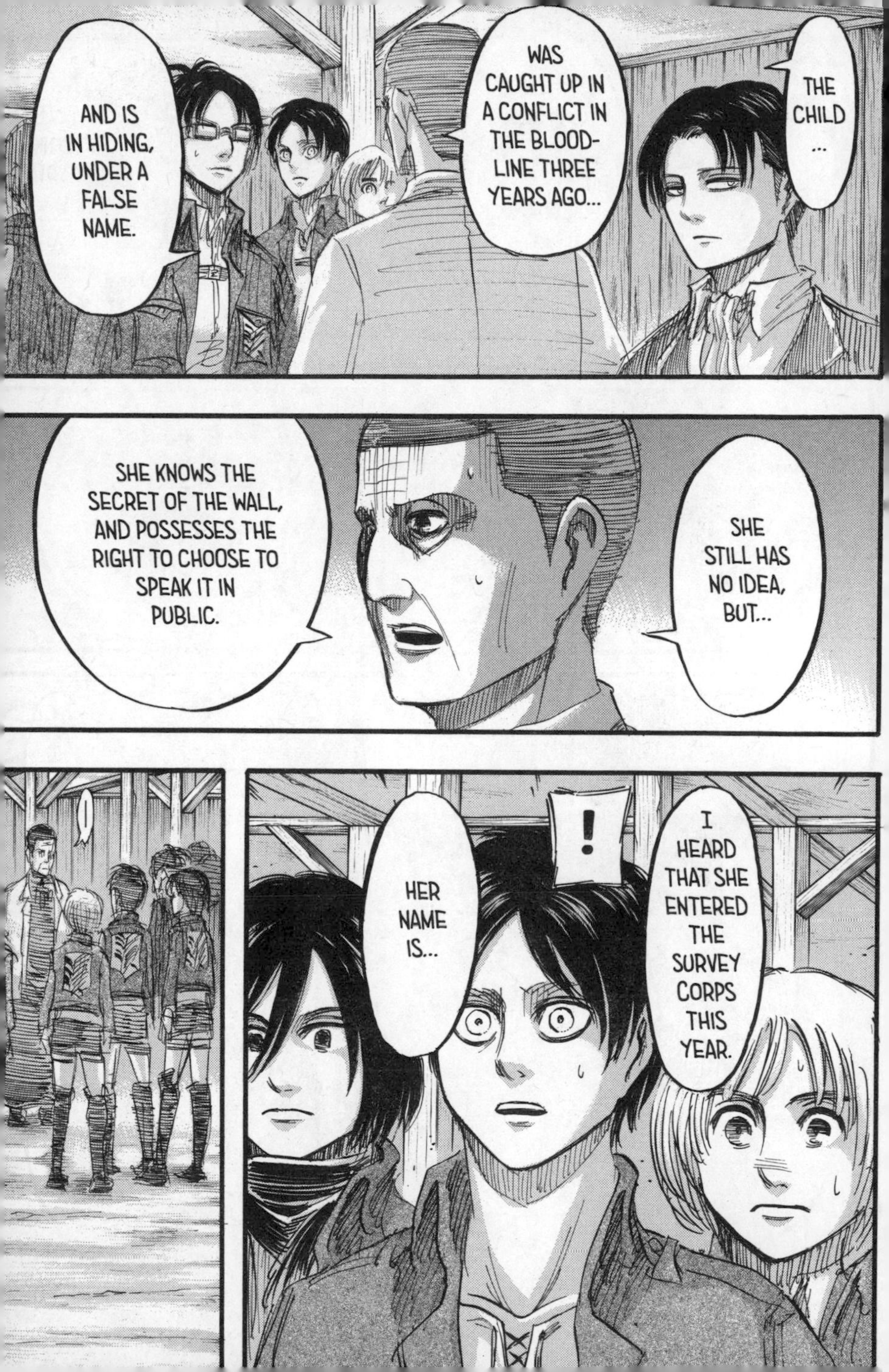
THE CHILD ...
WAS CAUGHT UP IN A CONFLICT IN THE BLOOD-LINE THREE YEARS AGO...
AND IS IN HIDING, UNDER A FALSE NAME.
SHE STILL HAS NO IDEA, BUT...
SHE KNOWS THE SECRET OF THE WALL, AND POSSESSES THE RIGHT TO CHOOSE TO SPEAK IT IN PUBLIC.
I HEARD THAT SHE ENTERED THE SURVEY CORPS THIS YEAR.
!
HER NAME IS...
!

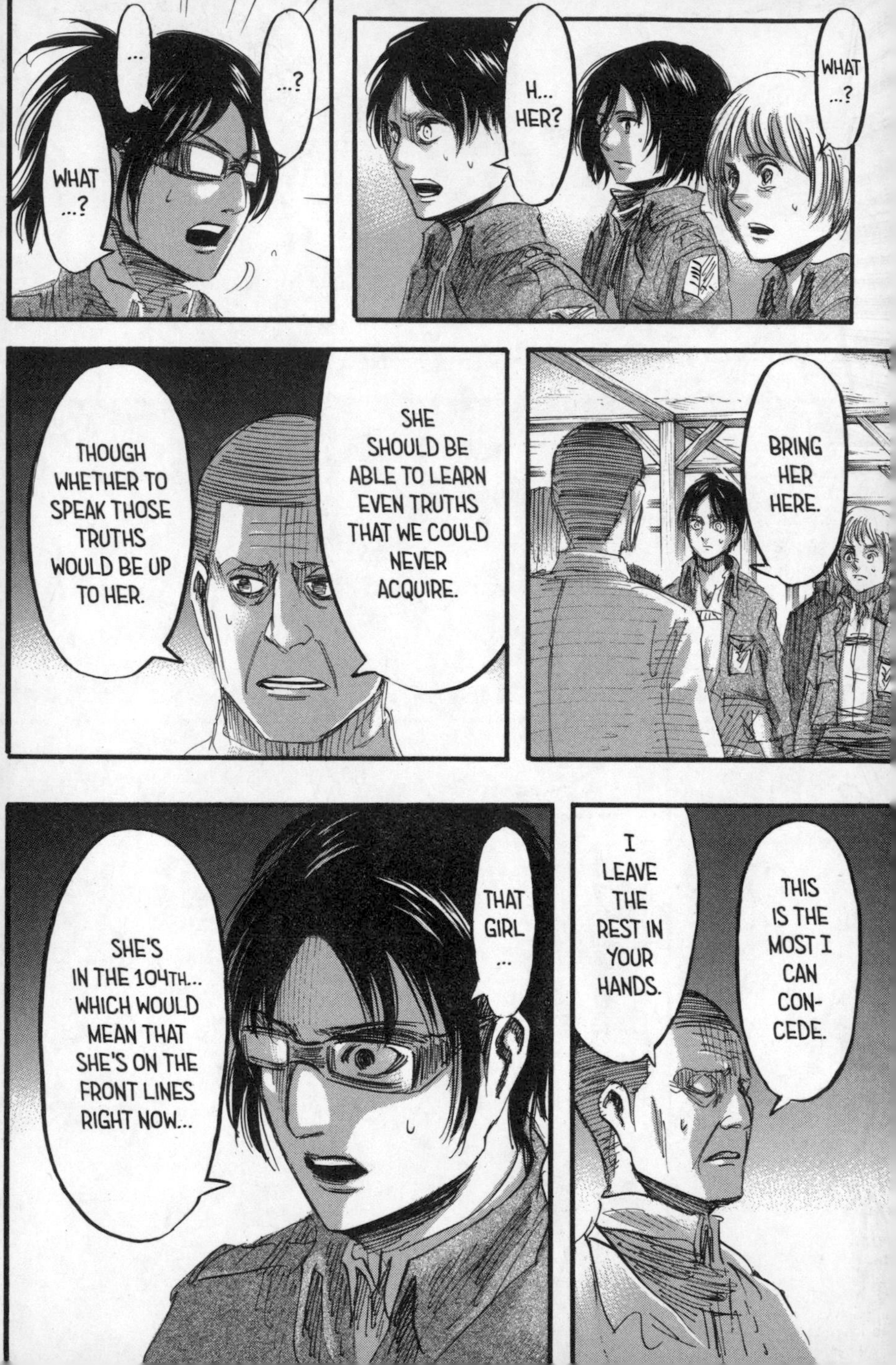
WHAT ...?
H... HER?
...?
...
WHAT ...?
BRING HER HERE.
SHE SHOULD BE ABLE TO LEARN EVEN TRUTHS THAT WE COULD NEVER ACQUIRE.
THOUGH WHETHER TO SPEAK THOSE TRUTHS WOULD BE UP TO HER.
THIS IS THE MOST I CAN CON-CEDE.
I LEAVE THE REST IN YOUR HANDS.
THAT GIRL ...
SHE'S IN THE 104TH... WHICH WOULD MEAN THAT SHE'S ON THE FRONT LINES RIGHT NOW...

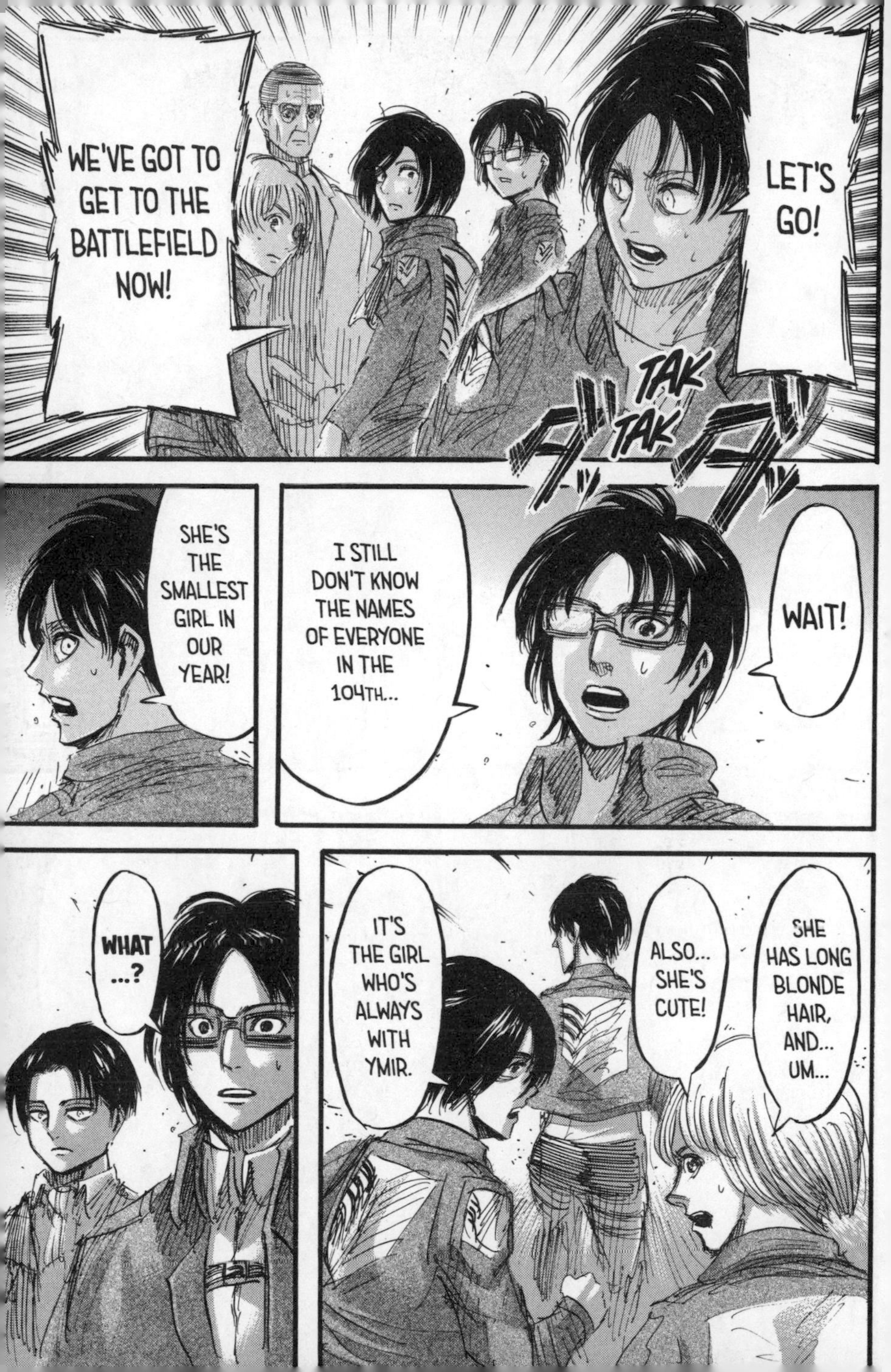
LET'S GO!
WE'VE GOT TO GET TO THE BATTLEFIELD NOW!
TAK TAK
WAIT!
I STILL DON'T KNOW THE NAMES OF EVERYONE IN THE 104TH...
SHE'S THE SMALLEST GIRL IN OUR YEAR!
SHE HAS LONG BLONDE HAIR, AND... UM...
ALSO... SHE'S CUTE!
IT'S THE GIRL WHO'S ALWAYS WITH YMIR.
WHAT ...?

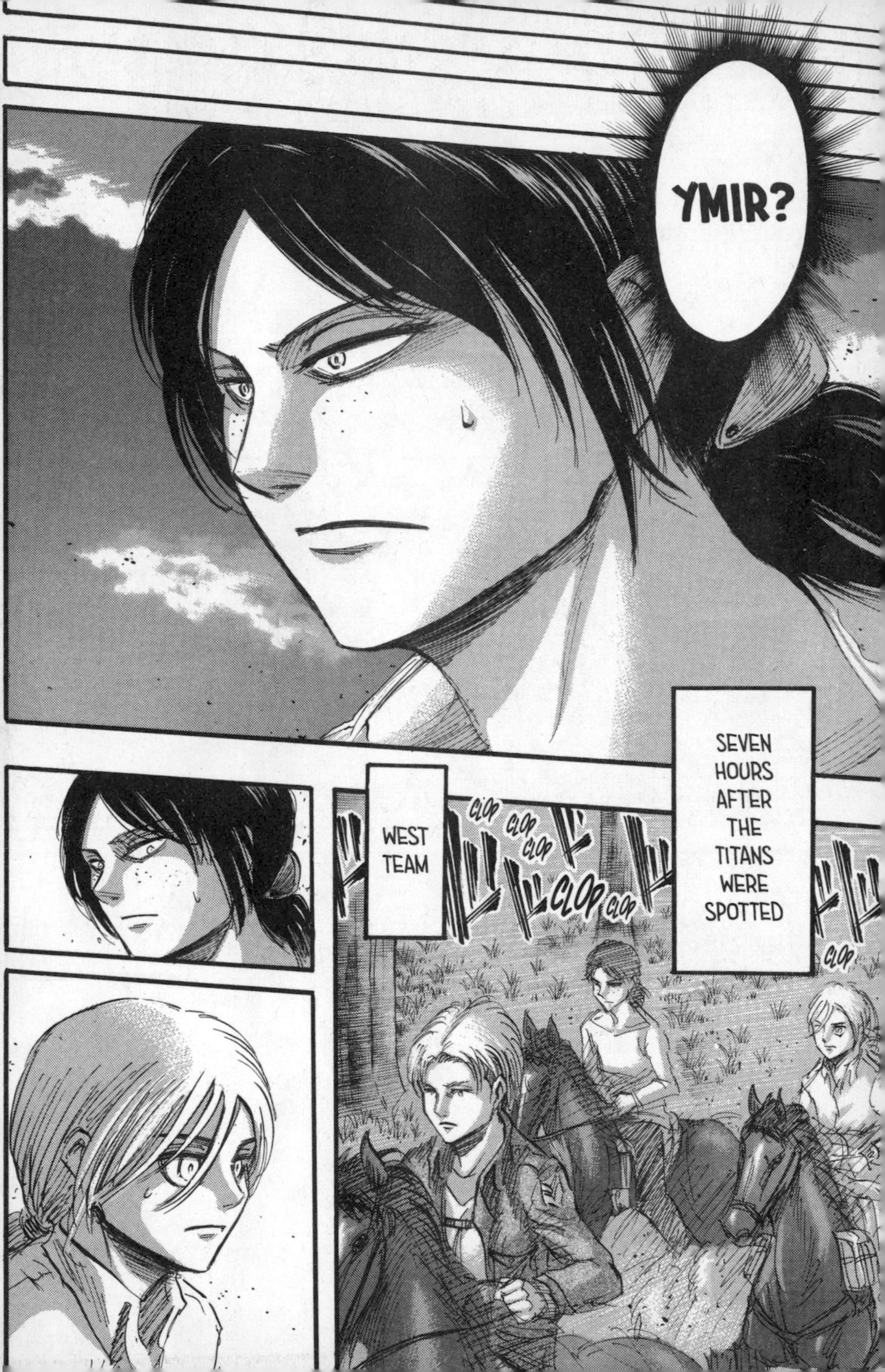
YMIR?
SEVEN HOURS AFTER THE TITANS WERE SPOTTED
CLOP
WEST TEAM
CLOP
CLOP
CLOP
CLOP
CLOP

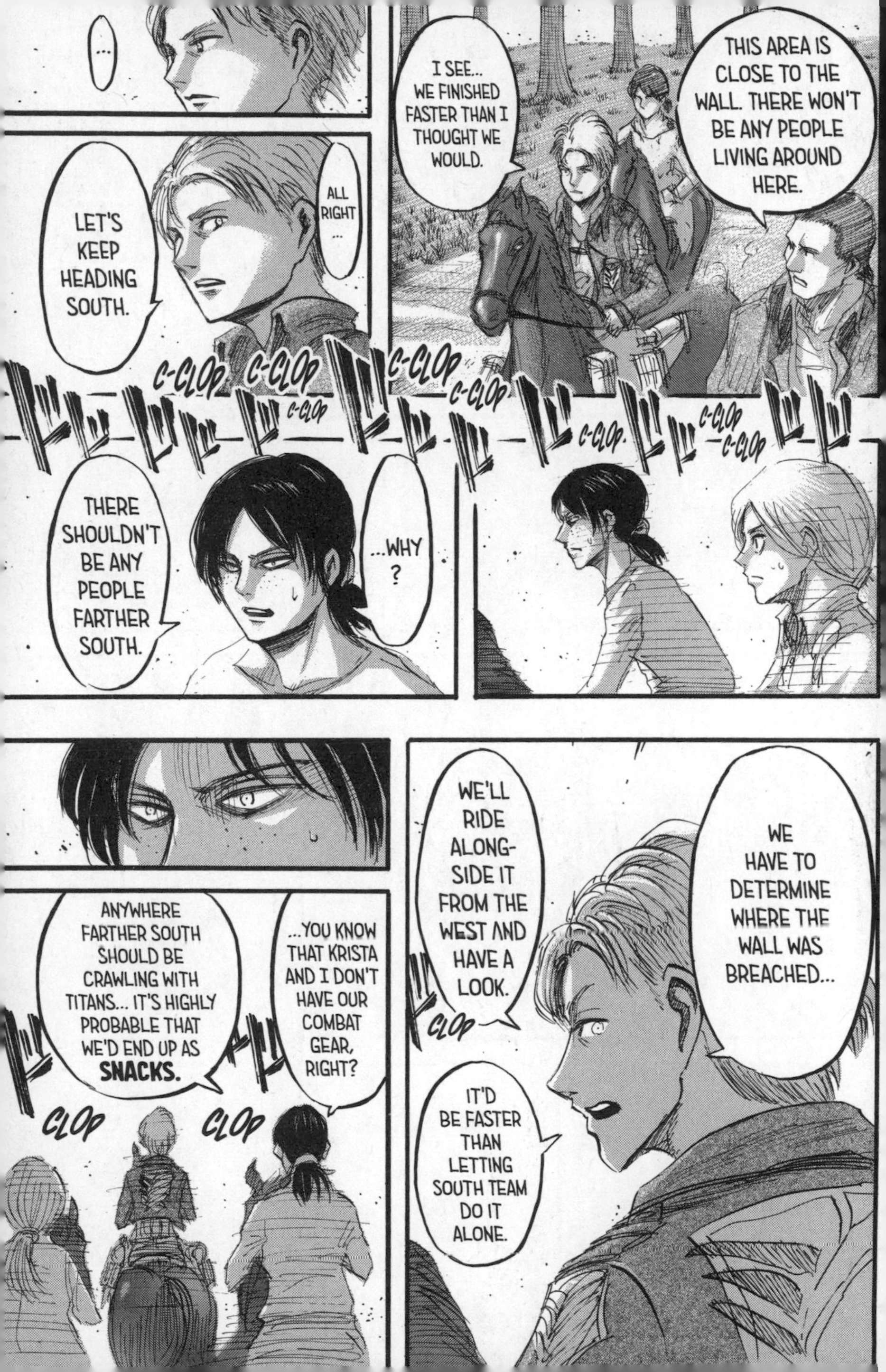
THIS AREA IS CLOSE TO THE WALL. THERE WON'T BE ANY PEOPLE LIVING AROUND HERE.
I SEE... WE FINISHED FASTER THAN I THOUGHT WE WOULD.
...
ALL RIGHT ...
LET'S KEEP HEADING SOUTH.
C-CLOP C-CLOP C-CLOP C-CLOP C-CLOP C-CLOP C-CLOP C-CLOP C-CLOP
...WHY ?
THERE SHOULDN'T BE ANY PEOPLE FARTHER SOUTH.
WE HAVE TO DETERMINE WHERE THE WALL WAS BREACHED...
WE'LL RIDE ALONG-SIDE IT FROM THE WEST AND HAVE A LOOK.
CLOP
IT'D BE FASTER THAN LETTING SOUTH TEAM DO IT ALONE.
...YOU KNOW THAT KRISTA AND I DON'T HAVE OUR COMBAT GEAR, RIGHT?
ANYWHERE FARTHER SOUTH SHOULD BE CRAWLING WITH TITANS... IT'S HIGHLY PROBABLE THAT WE'D END UP AS **SNACKS.**
CLOP
CLOP

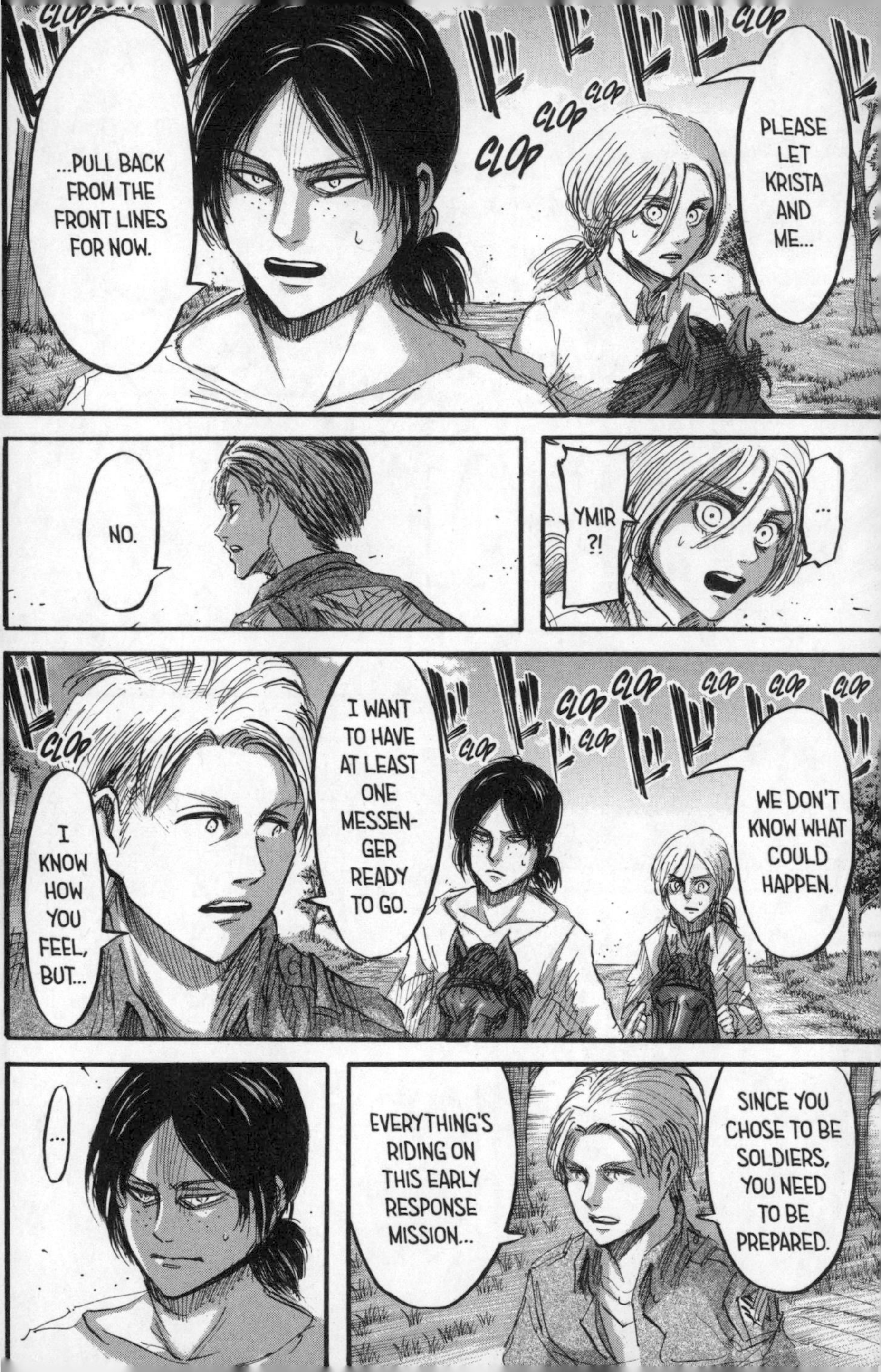
CLOP
CLOP
CLOP CLOP
CLOP
PLEASE LET KRISTA AND ME...
CLOP
...PULL BACK FROM THE FRONT LINES FOR NOW.
YMIR ?!
...
NO.
CLOP CLOP CLOP CLOP
WE DON'T KNOW WHAT COULD HAPPEN.
CLOP CLOP CLOP
I WANT TO HAVE AT LEAST ONE MESSEN-GER READY TO GO.
CLOP
I KNOW HOW YOU FEEL, BUT...
SINCE YOU CHOSE TO BE SOLDIERS, YOU NEED TO BE PREPARED.
EVERYTHING'S RIDING ON THIS EARLY RESPONSE MISSION...
...

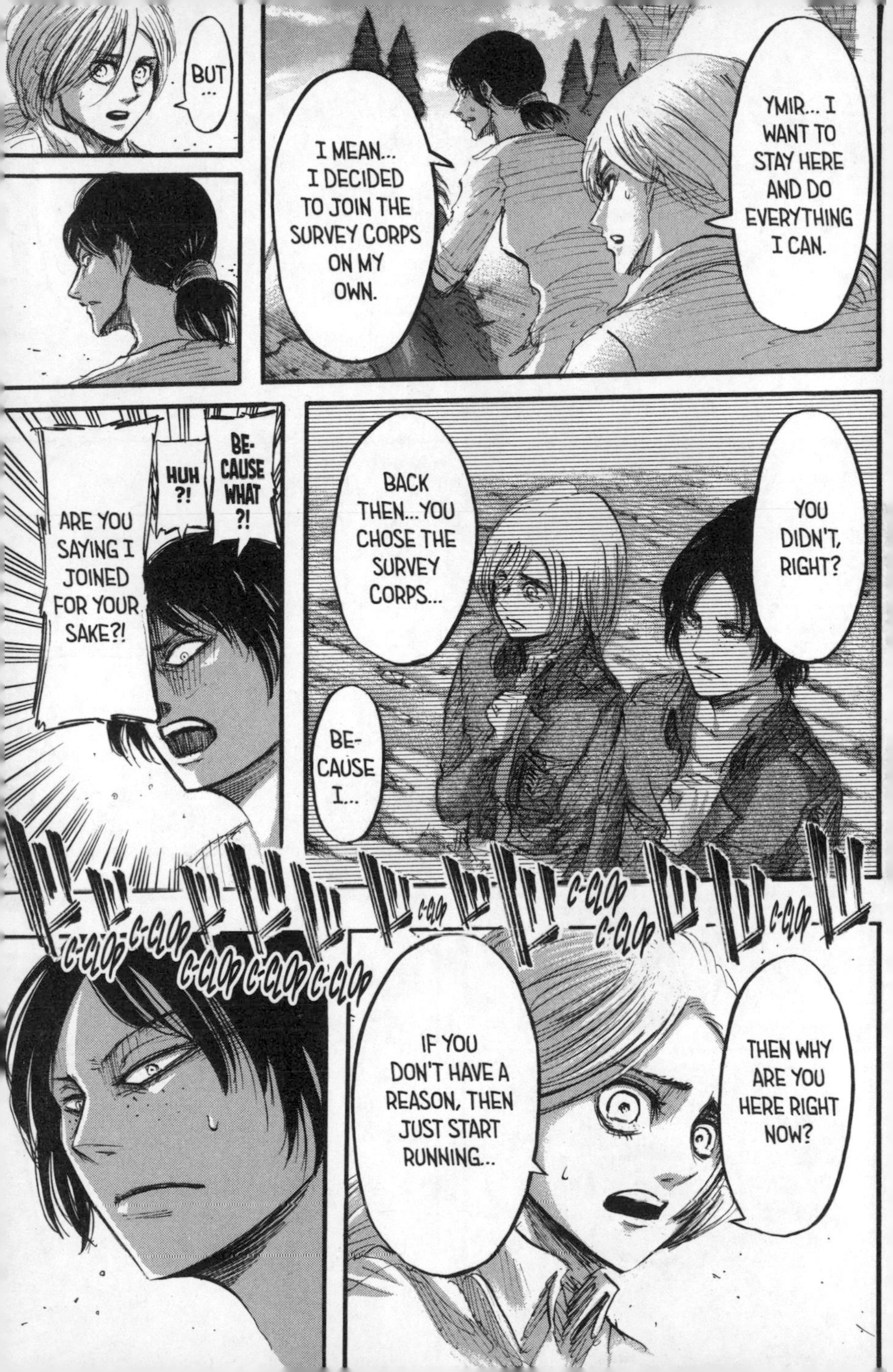
YMIR... I WANT TO STAY HERE AND DO EVERYTHING I CAN.
I MEAN... I DECIDED TO JOIN THE SURVEY CORPS ON MY OWN.
BUT ...
YOU DIDN'T, RIGHT?
BACK THEN...YOU CHOSE THE SURVEY CORPS...
BE-CAUSE I...
BE-CAUSE WHAT ?!
HUH ?!
ARE YOU SAYING I JOINED FOR YOUR SAKE?!
C-CLOP
C-CLOP
C-CLOP
C-CLOP
C-CLOP
C-CLOP
C-CLOP
C-CLOP
C-CLOP
C-CLOP
THEN WHY ARE YOU HERE RIGHT NOW?
IF YOU DON'T HAVE A REASON, THEN JUST START RUNNING...

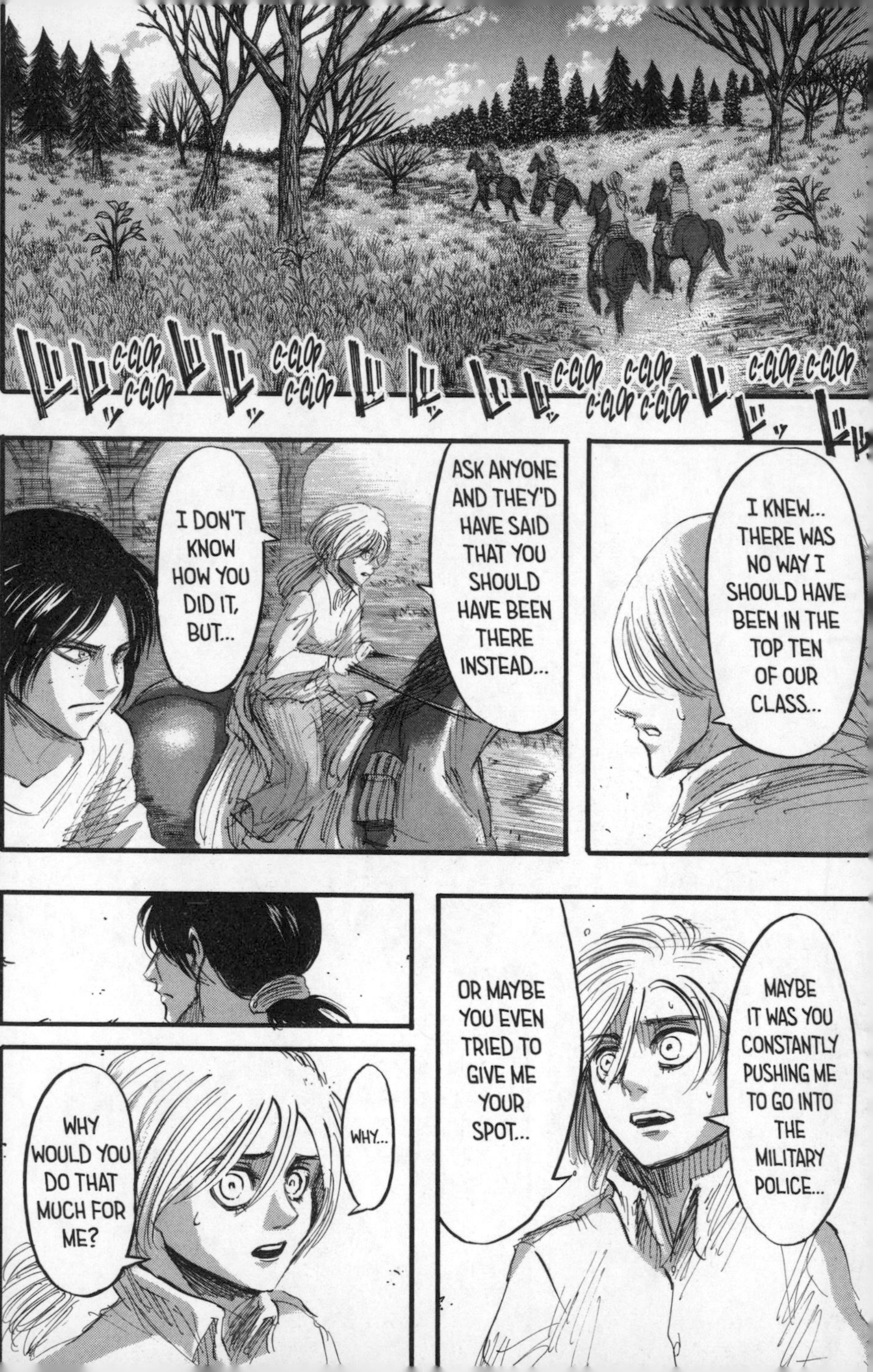
C-CLOP C-CLOP
C-CLOP C-CLOP
C-CLOP C-CLOP
C-CLOP C-CLOP
C-CLOP C-CLOP
C-CLOP C-CLOP
I KNEW... THERE WAS NO WAY I SHOULD HAVE BEEN IN THE TOP TEN OF OUR CLASS...
ASK ANYONE AND THEY'D HAVE SAID THAT YOU SHOULD HAVE BEEN THERE INSTEAD...
I DON'T KNOW HOW YOU DID IT, BUT...
MAYBE IT WAS YOU CONSTANTLY PUSHING ME TO GO INTO THE MILITARY POLICE...
OR MAYBE YOU EVEN TRIED TO GIVE ME YOUR SPOT...
WHY...
WHY WOULD YOU DO THAT MUCH FOR ME?

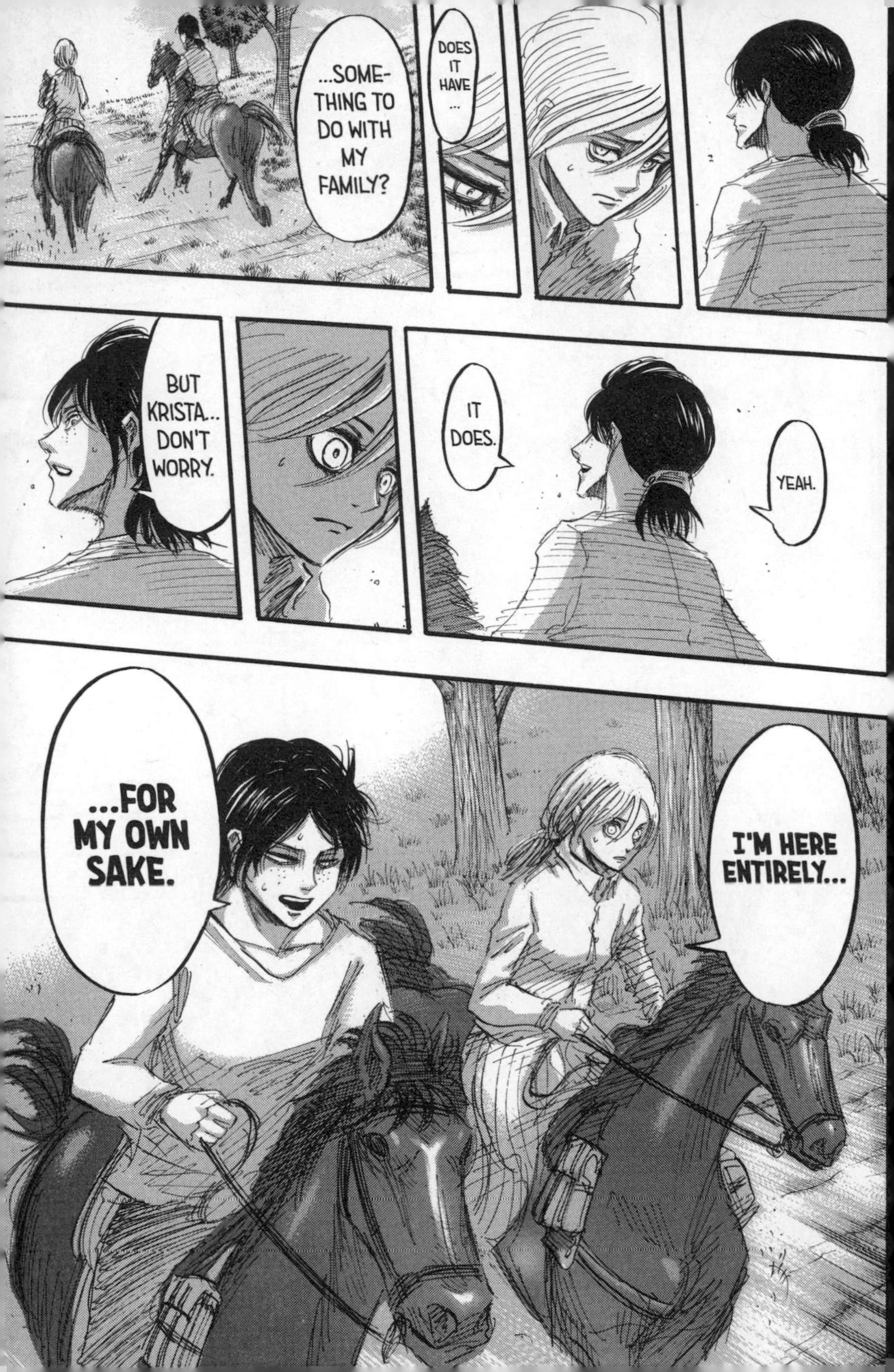
DOES IT HAVE...
...SOME-THING TO DO WITH MY FAMILY?
YEAH.
IT DOES.
BUT KRISTA... DON'T WORRY.
I'M HERE ENTIRELY...
...FOR MY OWN SAKE.

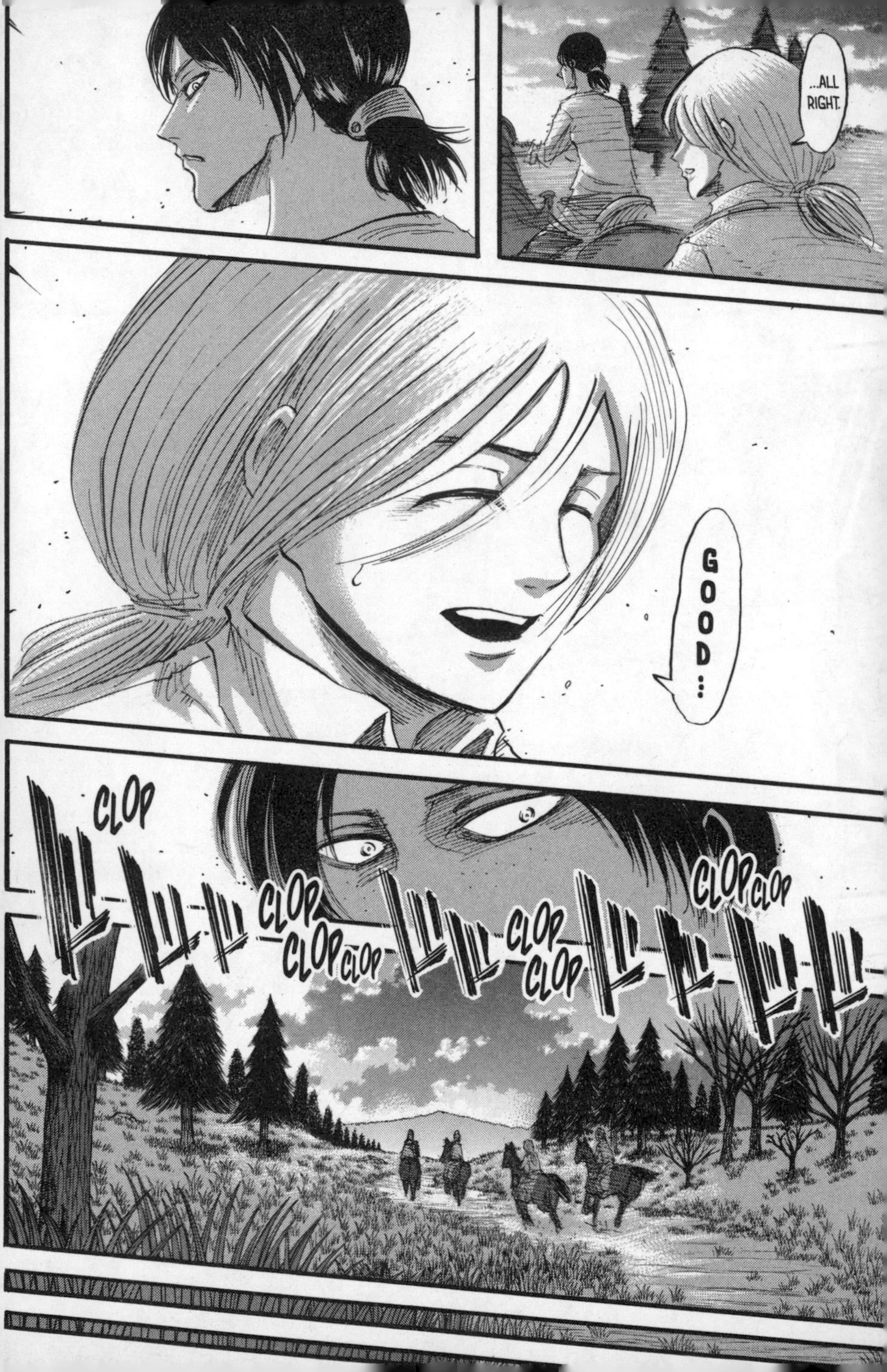
...ALL RIGHT.
GOOD...
CLOP CLOP
CLOP CLOP
CLOP CLOP CLOP
CLOP

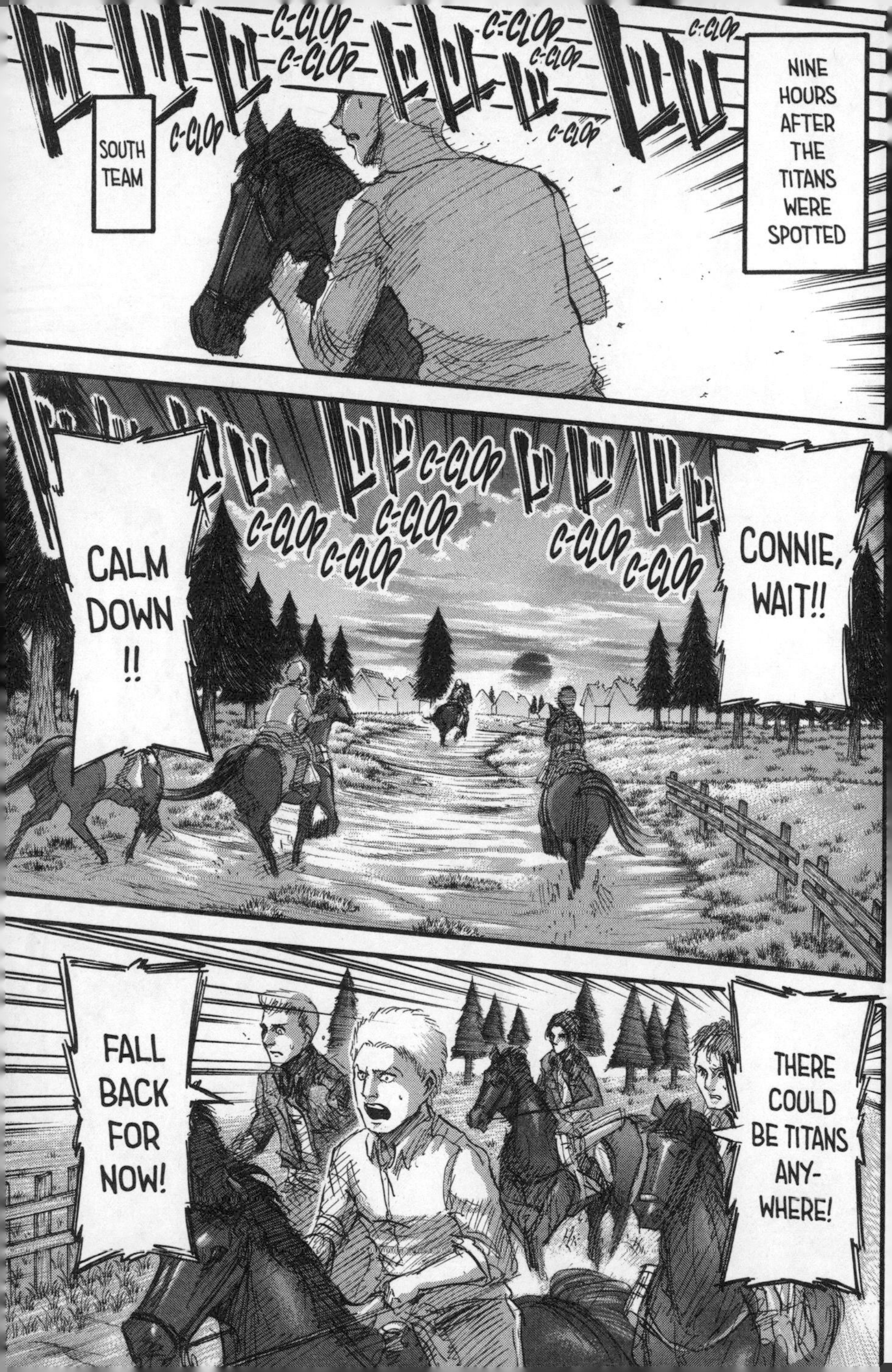
NINE HOURS AFTER THE TITANS WERE SPOTTED
C-CLOP
C-CLOP
C-CLOP
C-CLOP
C-CLOP
C-CLOP
SOUTH TEAM
C-CLOP
CONNIE, WAIT!!
C-CLOP
C-CLOP
C-CLOP
C-CLOP
C-CLOP
C-CLOP
CALM DOWN !!
THERE COULD BE TITANS ANY-WHERE!
FALL BACK FOR NOW!

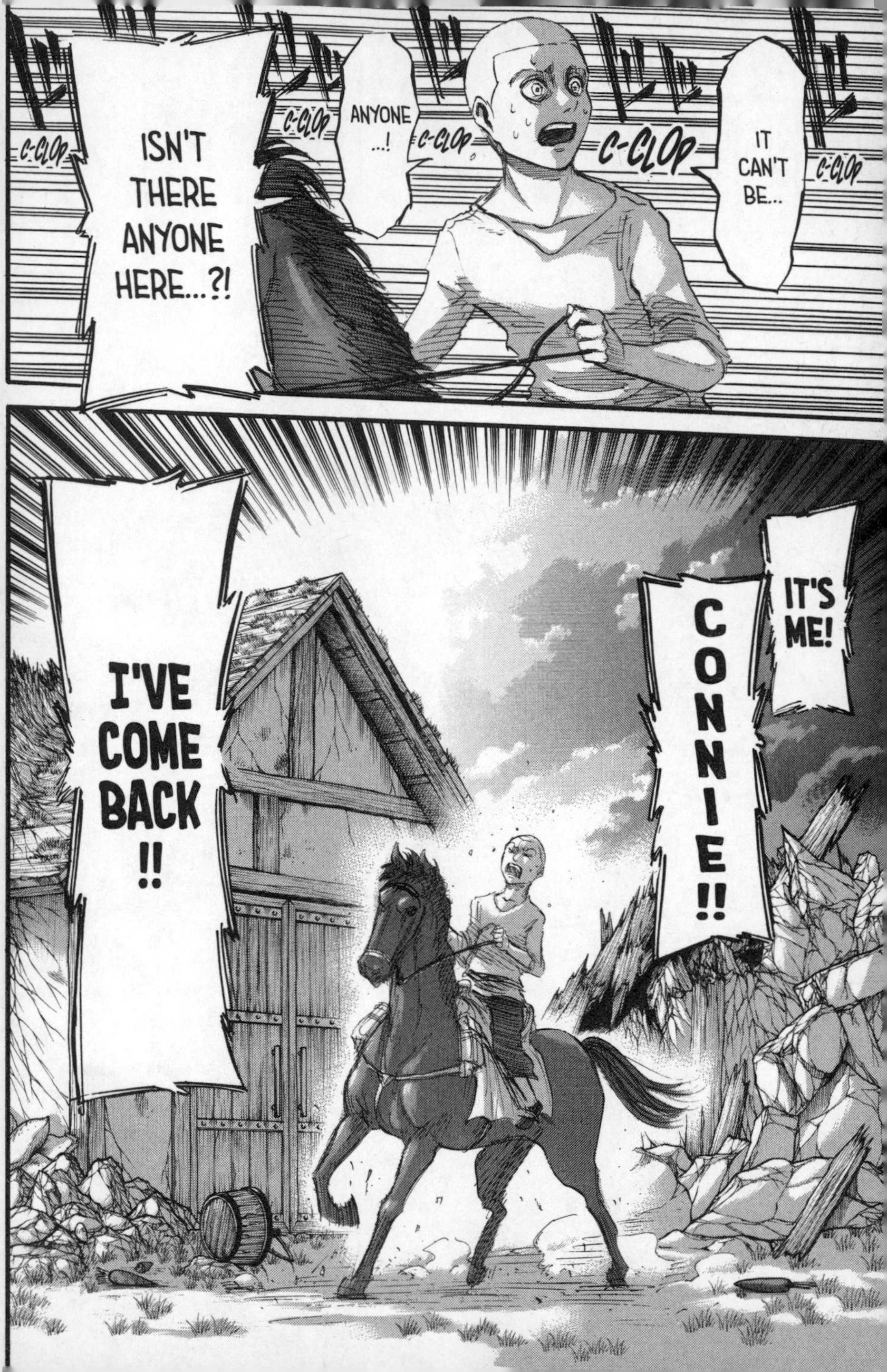
C-CLOP
IT CAN'T BE...
C-CLOP
C-CLOP
ANYONE ...!
C-CLOP
ISN'T THERE ANYONE HERE...?!
C-CLOP
IT'S ME!
CONNIE!!
I'VE COME BACK!!

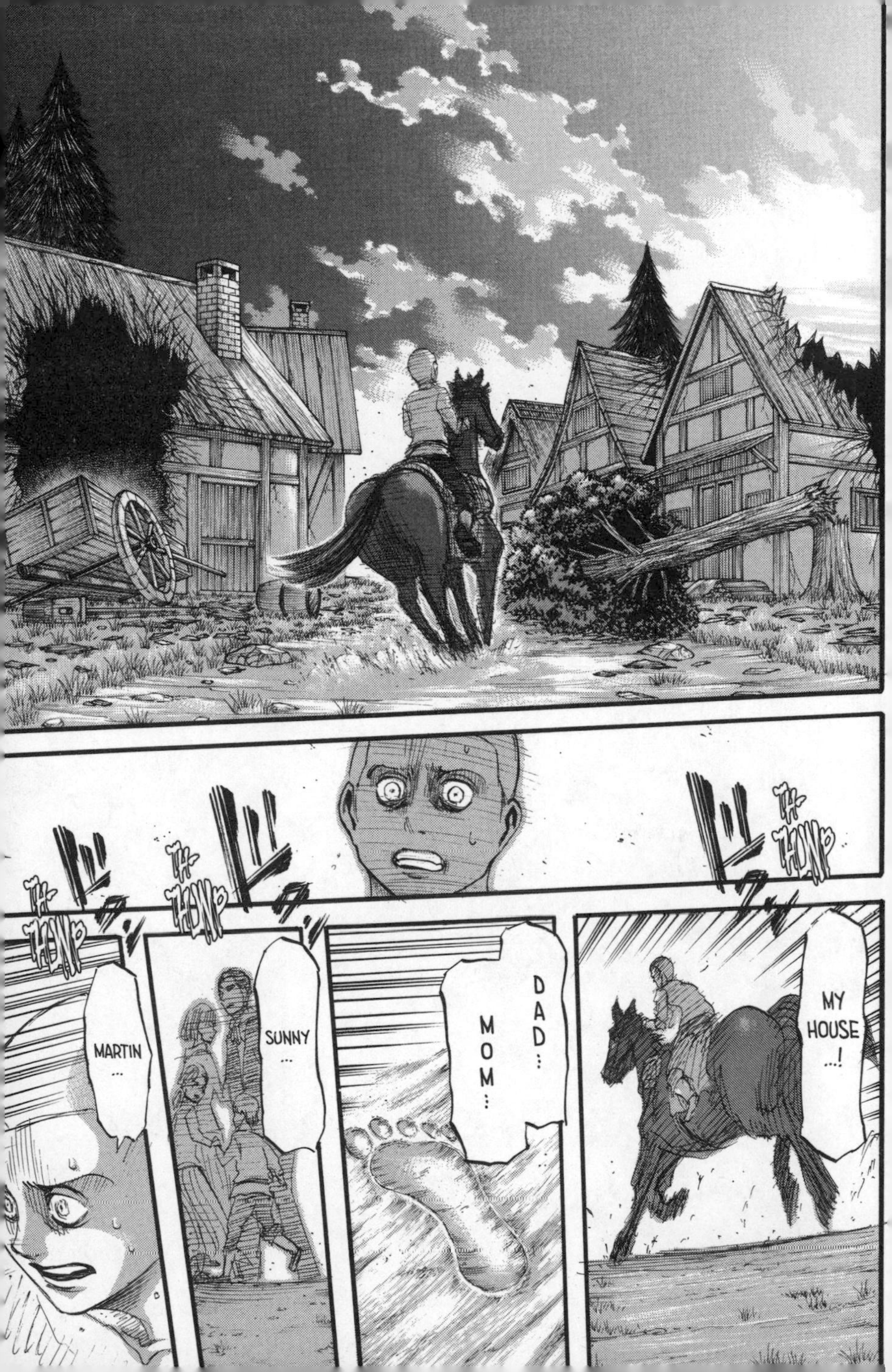
THA THUMP
THA THUMP
THA THUMP
MY HOUSE ...!
DAD... MOM...
SUNNY ...
MARTIN ...

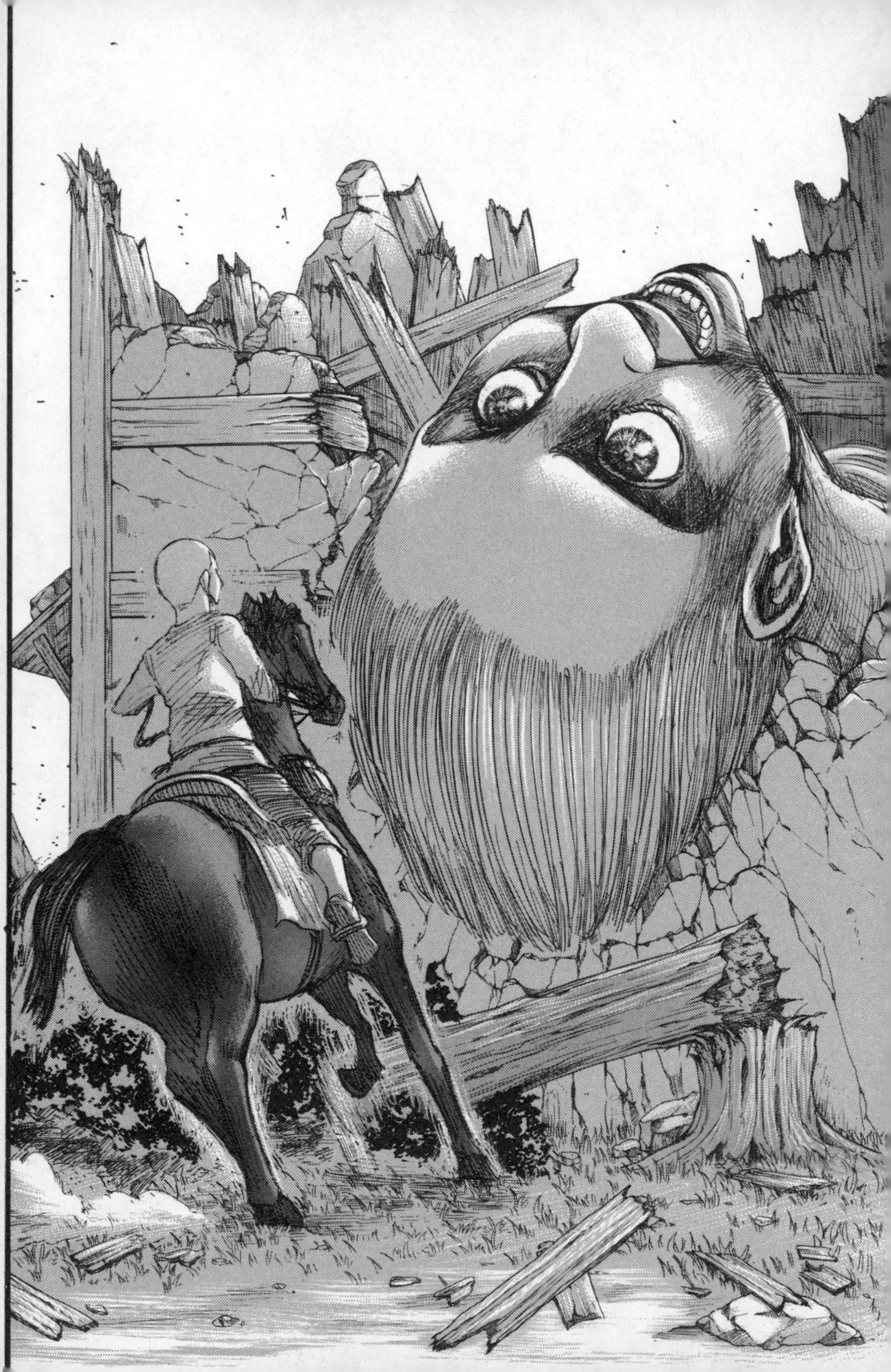

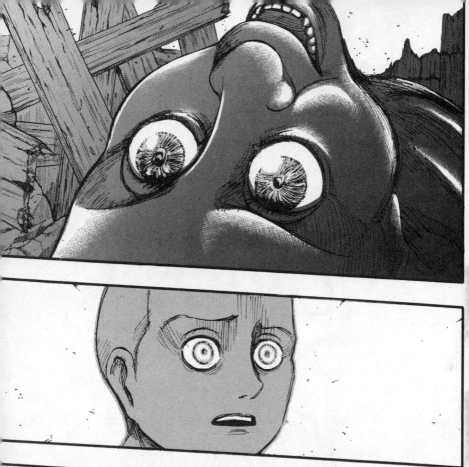

MY...

I...
IT'S...
MY
HOUSE
...

HH GRASP

CONNIE! FALL
BACK!!

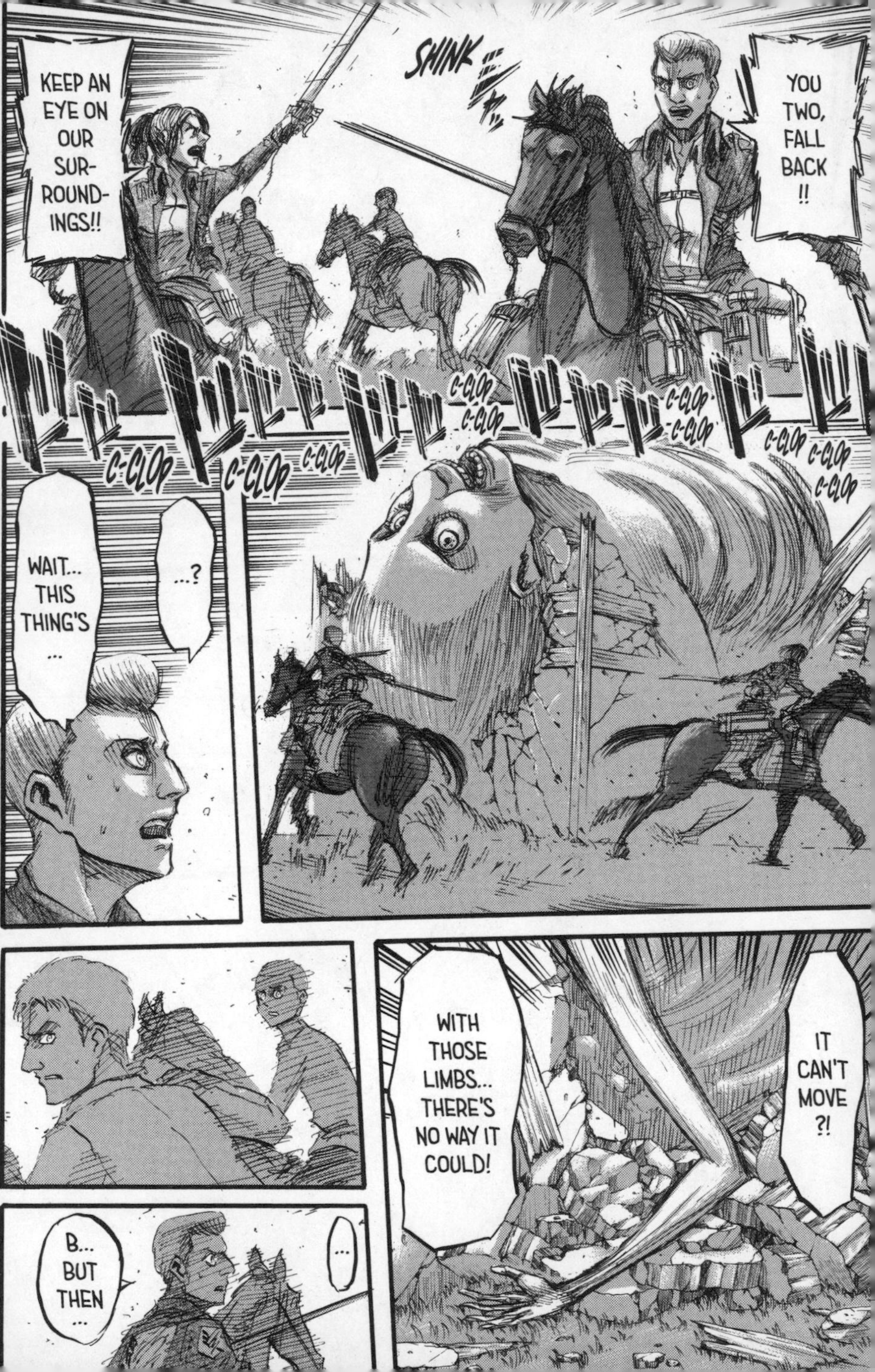
YOU TWO, FALL BACK!!
SHINK
KEEP AN EYE ON OUR SUR-ROUNDINGS!!
C-CLOP C-CLOP
C-CLOP C-CLOP
C-CLOP C-CLOP C-CLOP
C-CLOP
C-CLOP
C-CLOP
...?
WAIT... THIS THING'S ...
IT CAN'T MOVE?!
WITH THOSE LIMBS... THERE'S NO WAY IT COULD!
...
B... BUT THEN ...

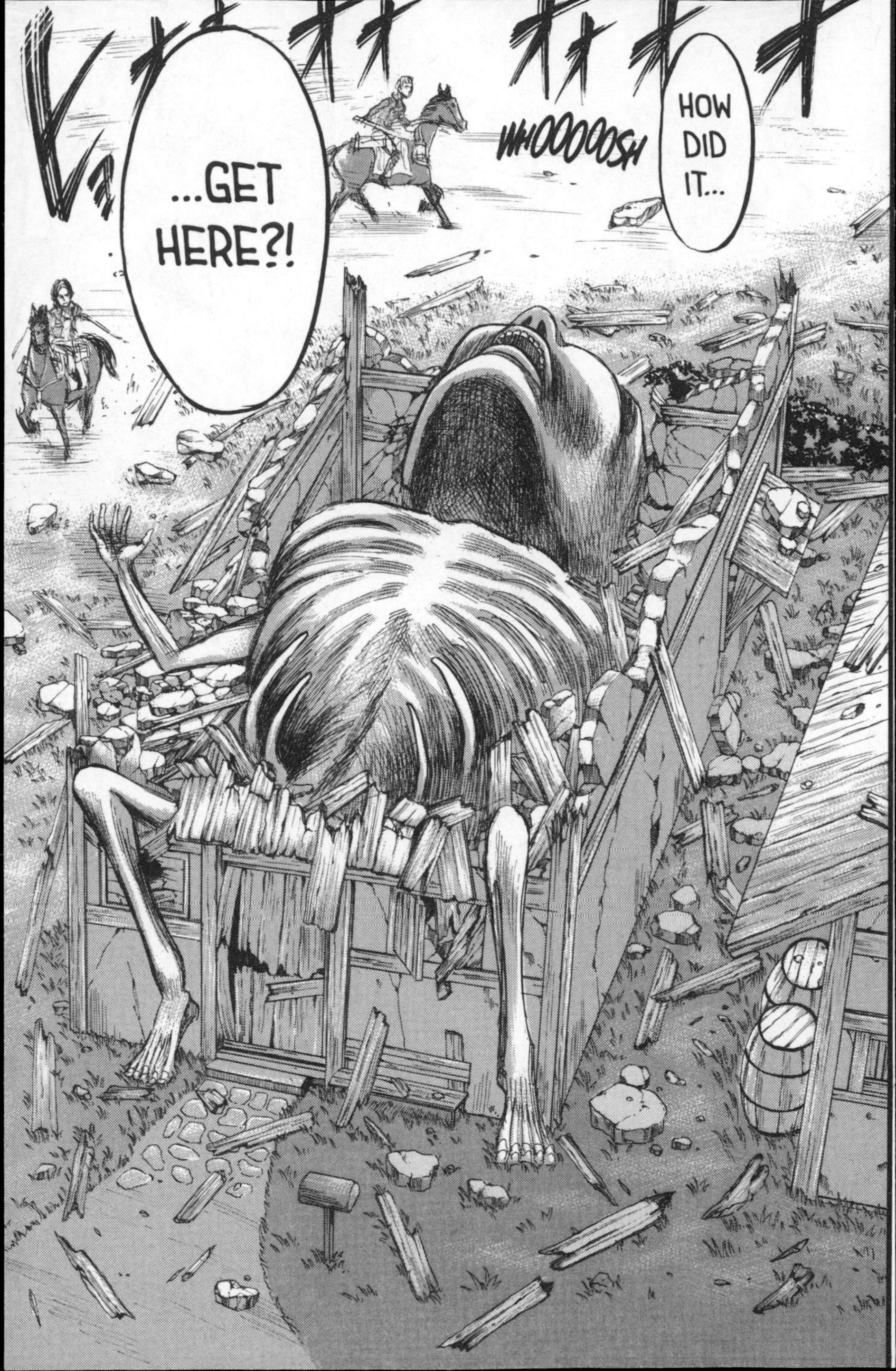
HOW DID IT...
WHOOOOOOSH
...GET HERE?!

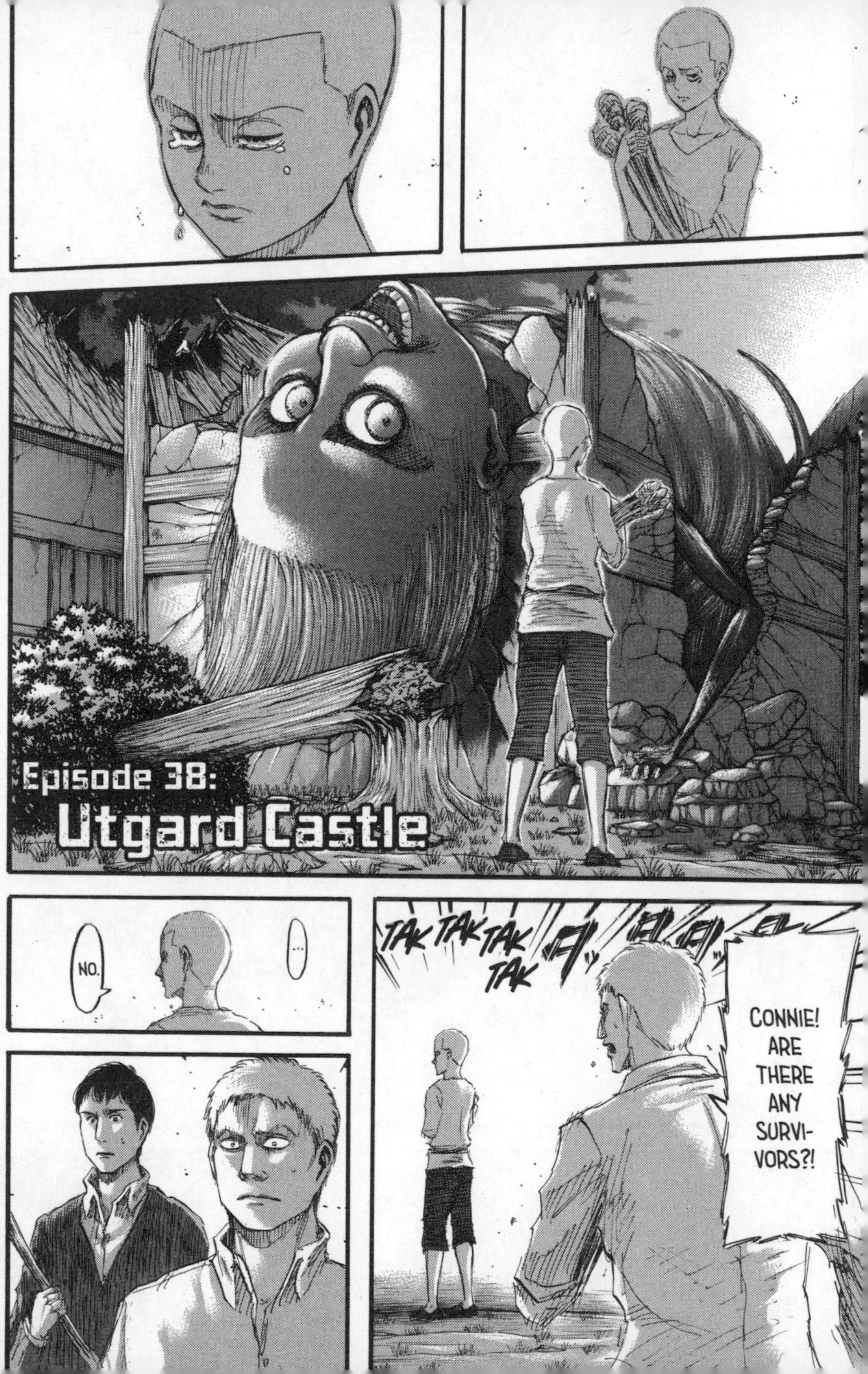
Episode 38:
Utgard Castle
TAK TAK TAK TAK TAK
CONNIE! ARE THERE ANY SURVIVORS?!
...
NO.

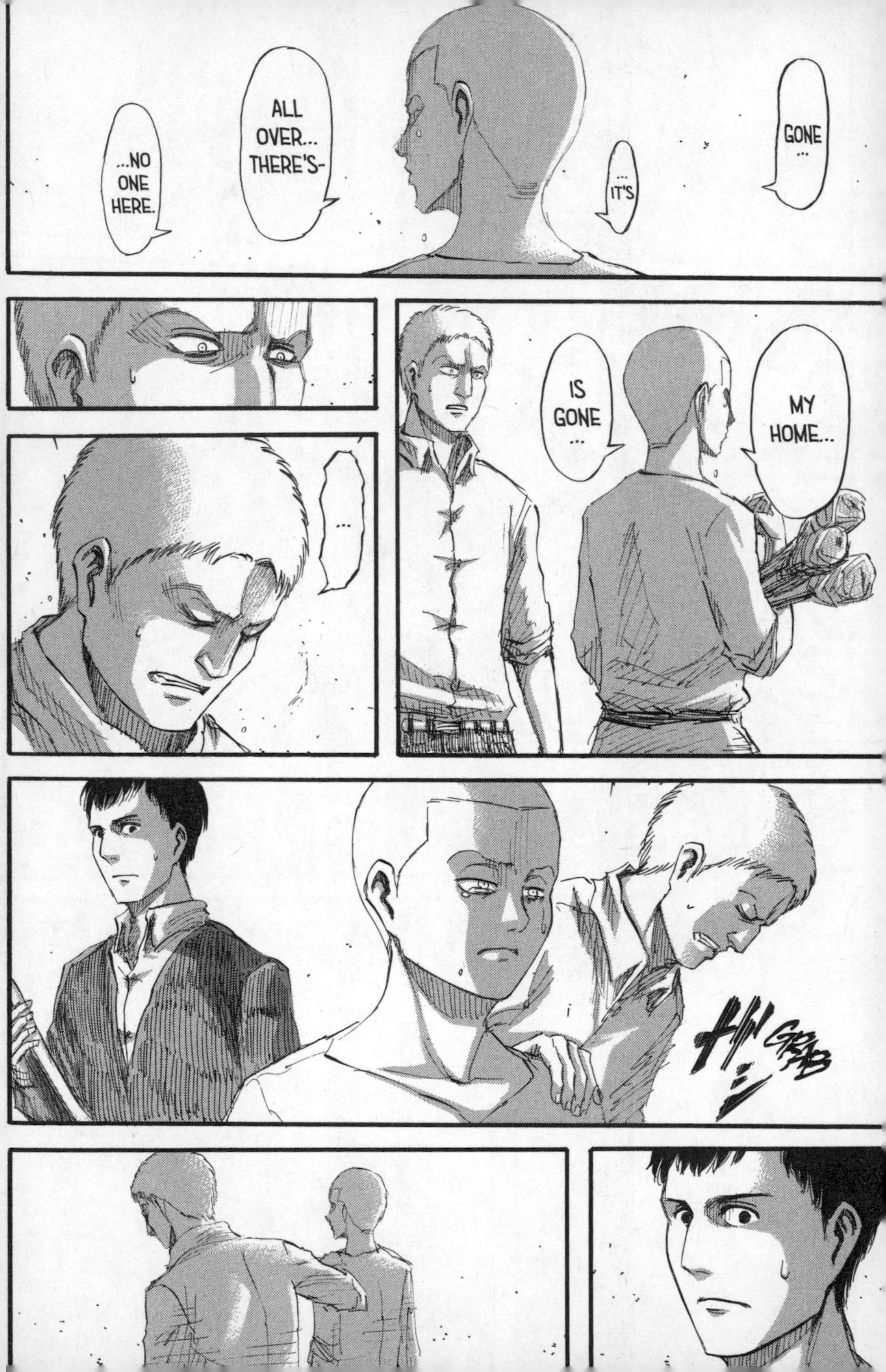
GONE...
...IT'S
ALL OVER... THERE'S-
...NO ONE HERE.
MY HOME...
IS GONE...
...
GRAB

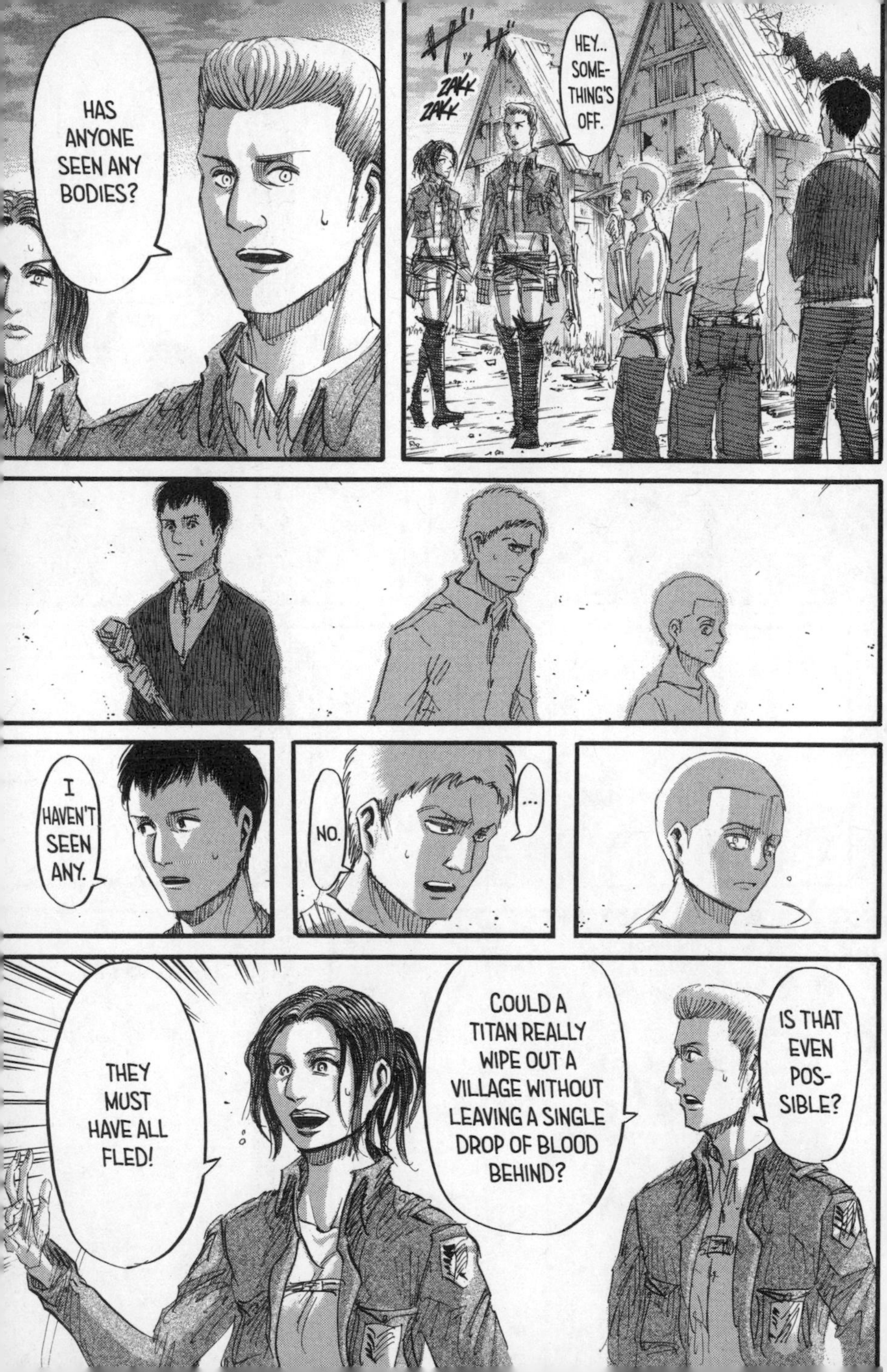
HEY... SOME-THING'S OFF.
ZAKK ZAKK
HAS ANYONE SEEN ANY BODIES?
...
NO.
I HAVEN'T SEEN ANY.
IS THAT EVEN POS-SIBLE?
COULD A TITAN REALLY WIPE OUT A VILLAGE WITHOUT LEAVING A SINGLE DROP OF BLOOD BEHIND?
THEY MUST HAVE ALL FLED!

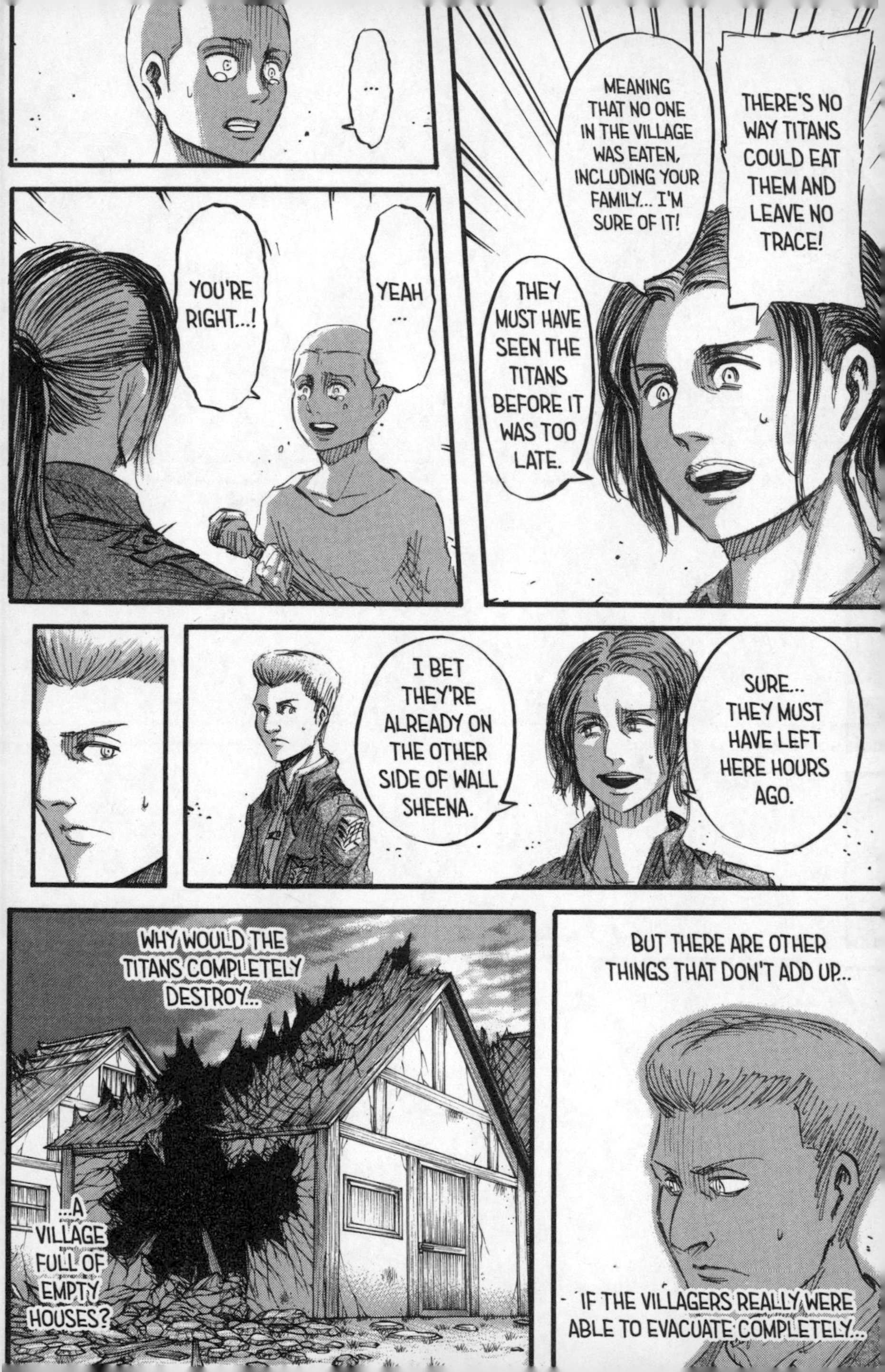
THERE'S NO WAY TITANS COULD EAT THEM AND LEAVE NO TRACE!
MEANING THAT NO ONE IN THE VILLAGE WAS EATEN, INCLUDING YOUR FAMILY... I'M SURE OF IT!
THEY MUST HAVE SEEN THE TITANS BEFORE IT WAS TOO LATE.
...
YEAH ...
YOU'RE RIGHT...!
SURE... THEY MUST HAVE LEFT HERE HOURS AGO.
I BET THEY'RE ALREADY ON THE OTHER SIDE OF WALL SHEENA.
BUT THERE ARE OTHER THINGS THAT DON'T ADD UP...
IF THE VILLAGERS REALLY WERE ABLE TO EVACUATE COMPLETELY...
WHY WOULD THE TITANS COMPLETELY DESTROY...
...A VILLAGE FULL OF EMPTY HOUSES?

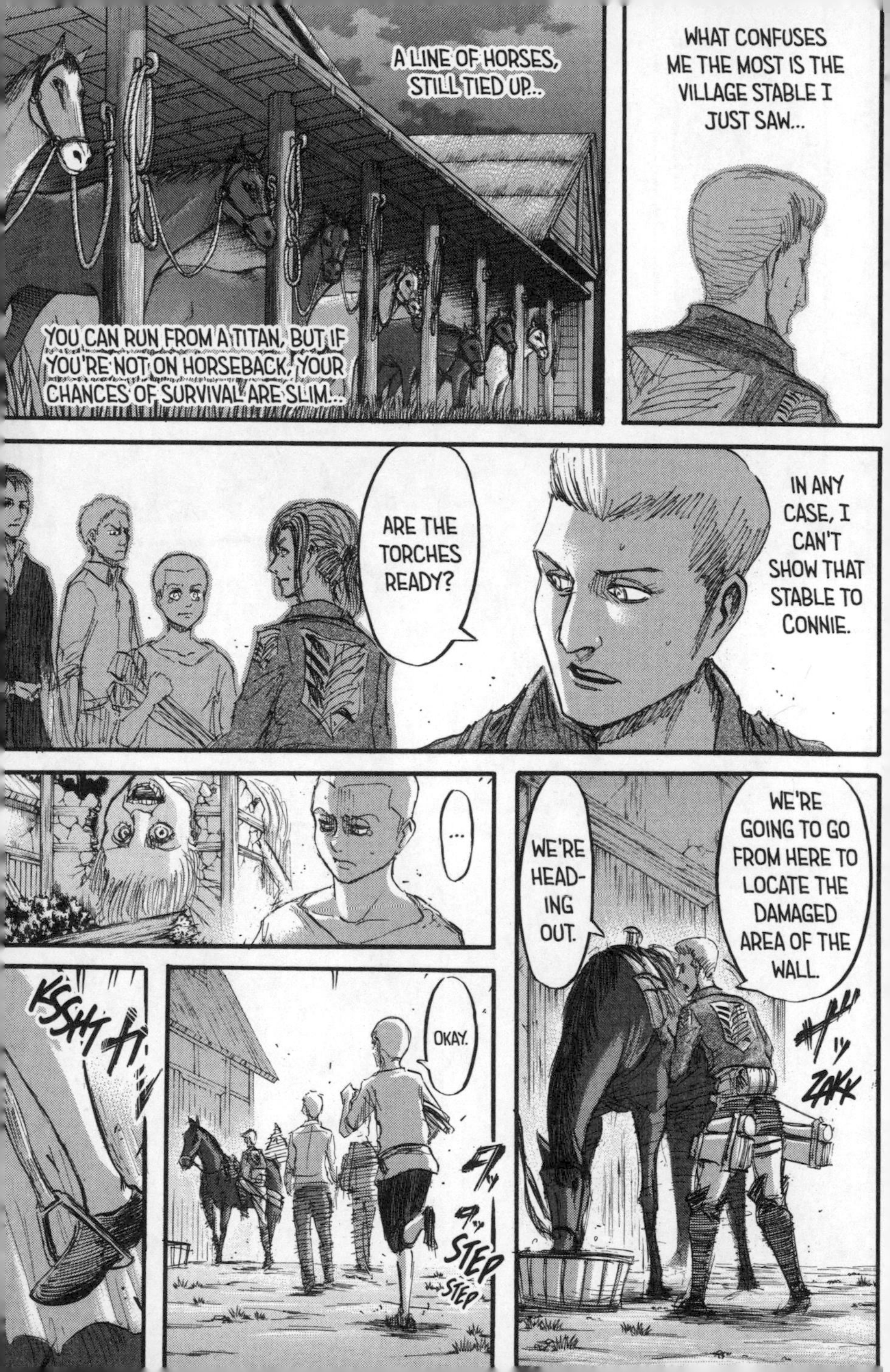
WHAT CONFUSES ME THE MOST IS THE VILLAGE STABLE I JUST SAW...
A LINE OF HORSES, STILL TIED UP...
YOU CAN RUN FROM A TITAN, BUT IF YOU'RE NOT ON HORSEBACK, YOUR CHANCES OF SURVIVAL ARE SLIM...
IN ANY CASE, I CAN'T SHOW THAT STABLE TO CONNIE.
ARE THE TORCHES READY?
WE'RE GOING TO GO FROM HERE TO LOCATE THE DAMAGED AREA OF THE WALL.
WE'RE HEAD-ING OUT.
ZAKK
...
OKAY.
STEP
STEP
KSSHH

WELC...
OME...
HOME...

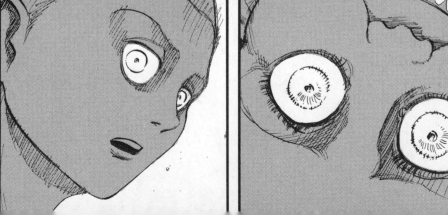

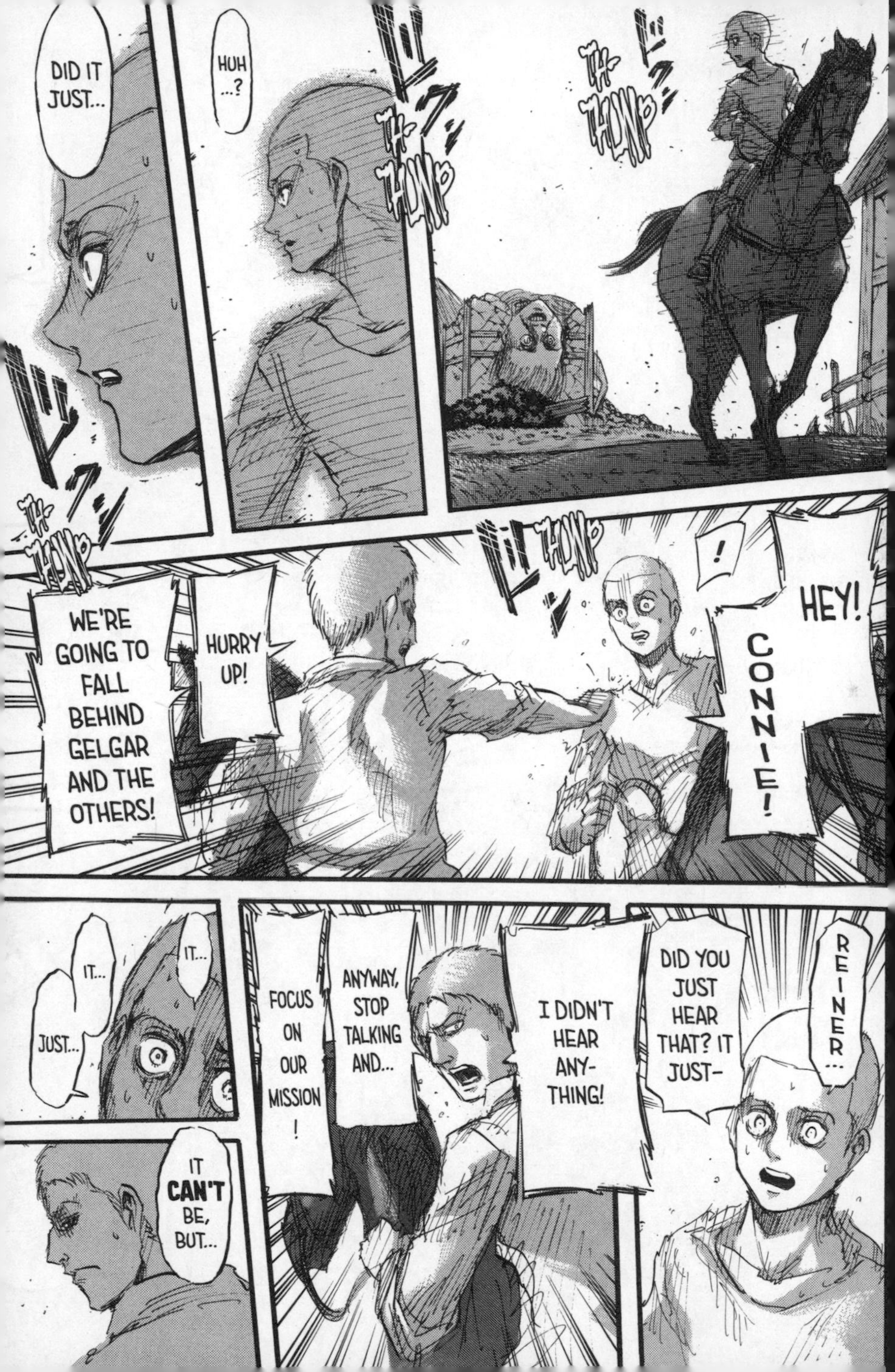

THA THUMP
HUH ...?
THA THUMP
DID IT JUST...
THA THUMP
HEY!
CONNIE!
!
THUMP
HURRY UP!
WE'RE GOING TO FALL BEHIND GELGAR AND THE OTHERS!
REINER...
DID YOU JUST HEAR THAT? IT JUST-
I DIDN'T HEAR ANY-THING!
ANYWAY, STOP TALKING AND...
FOCUS ON OUR MISSION!
IT...
IT...
JUST...
IT CAN'T BE, BUT...

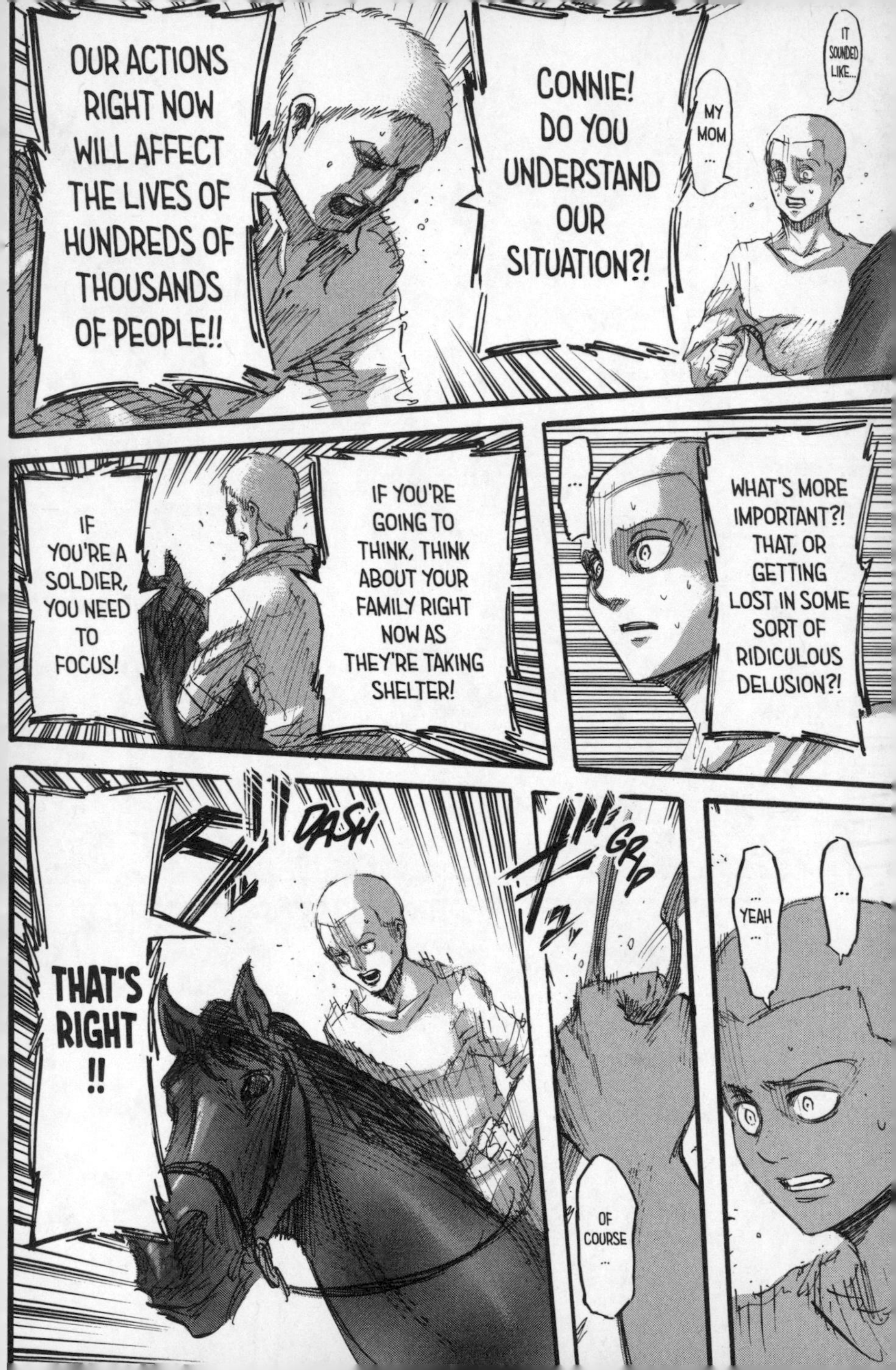
IT SOUNDED LIKE...
MY MOM ...
CONNIE! DO YOU UNDERSTAND OUR SITUATION?!
OUR ACTIONS RIGHT NOW WILL AFFECT THE LIVES OF HUNDREDS OF THOUSANDS OF PEOPLE!!
WHAT'S MORE IMPORTANT?! THAT, OR GETTING LOST IN SOME SORT OF RIDICULOUS DELUSION?!
...
IF YOU'RE GOING TO THINK, THINK ABOUT YOUR FAMILY RIGHT NOW AS THEY'RE TAKING SHELTER!
IF YOU'RE A SOLDIER, YOU NEED TO FOCUS!
...
... YEAH ...
OF COURSE ...
GRIP
DASH
THAT'S RIGHT !!

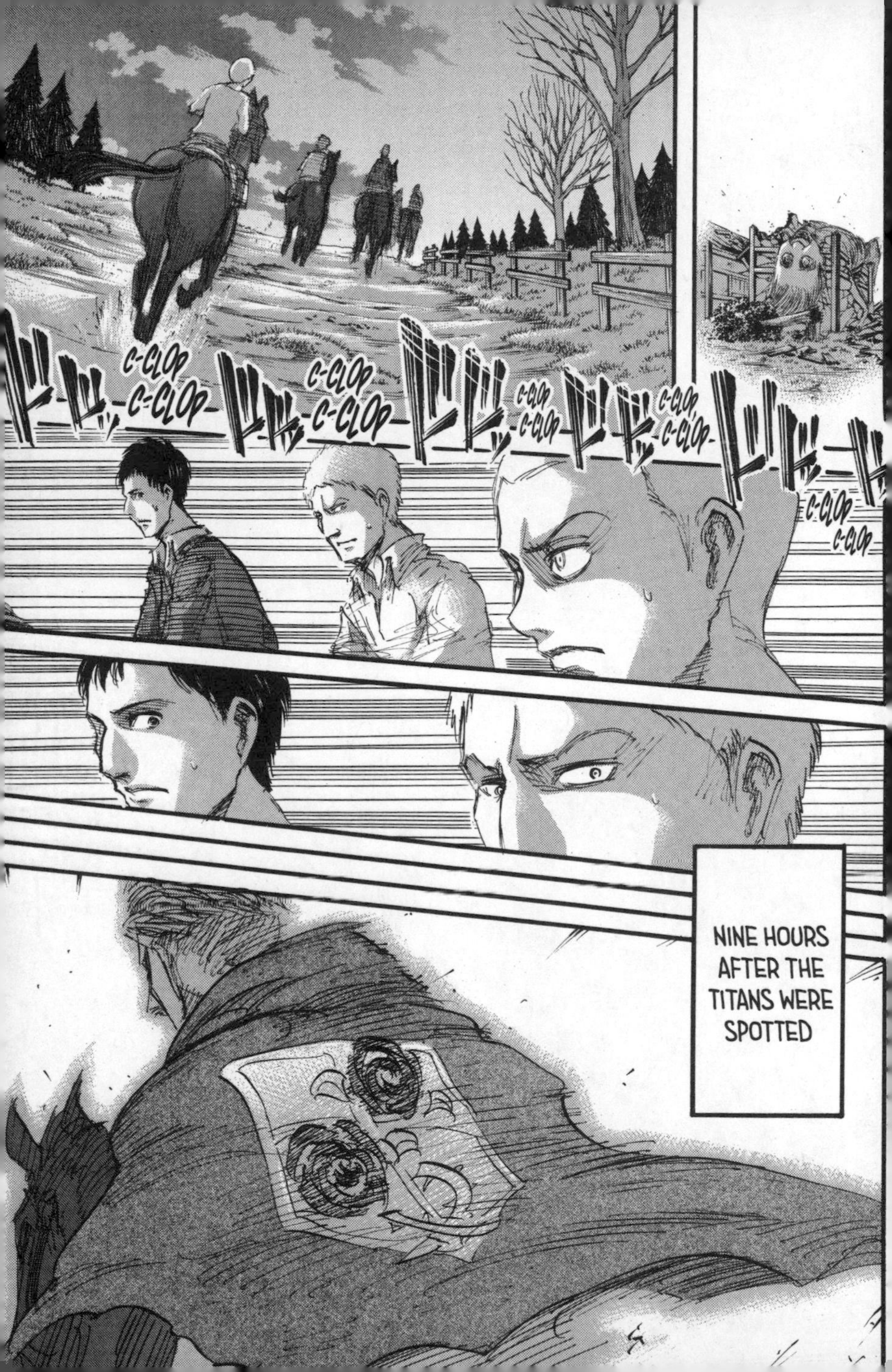
C-CLOP C-CLOP
C-CLOP C-CLOP
C-CLOP C-CLOP
C-CLOP C-CLOP
C-CLOP C-CLOP
NINE HOURS AFTER THE TITANS WERE SPOTTED

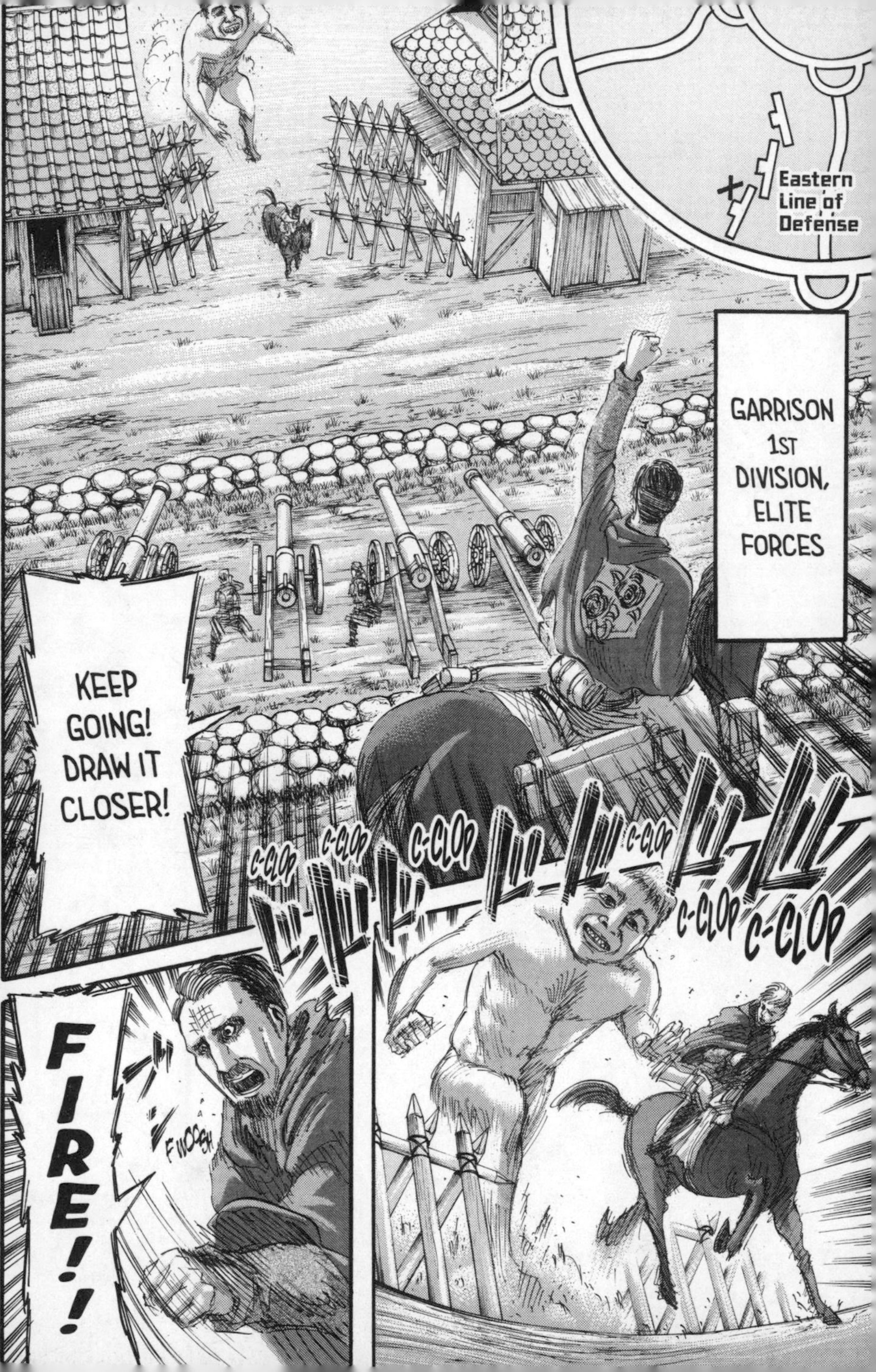
Eastern Line of Defense
GARRISON 1ST DIVISION, ELITE FORCES
KEEP GOING! DRAW IT CLOSER!
C-CLOP
C-CLOP
C-CLOP
C-CLOP
C-CLOP
C-CLOP
FIRE!!
FWOOSH

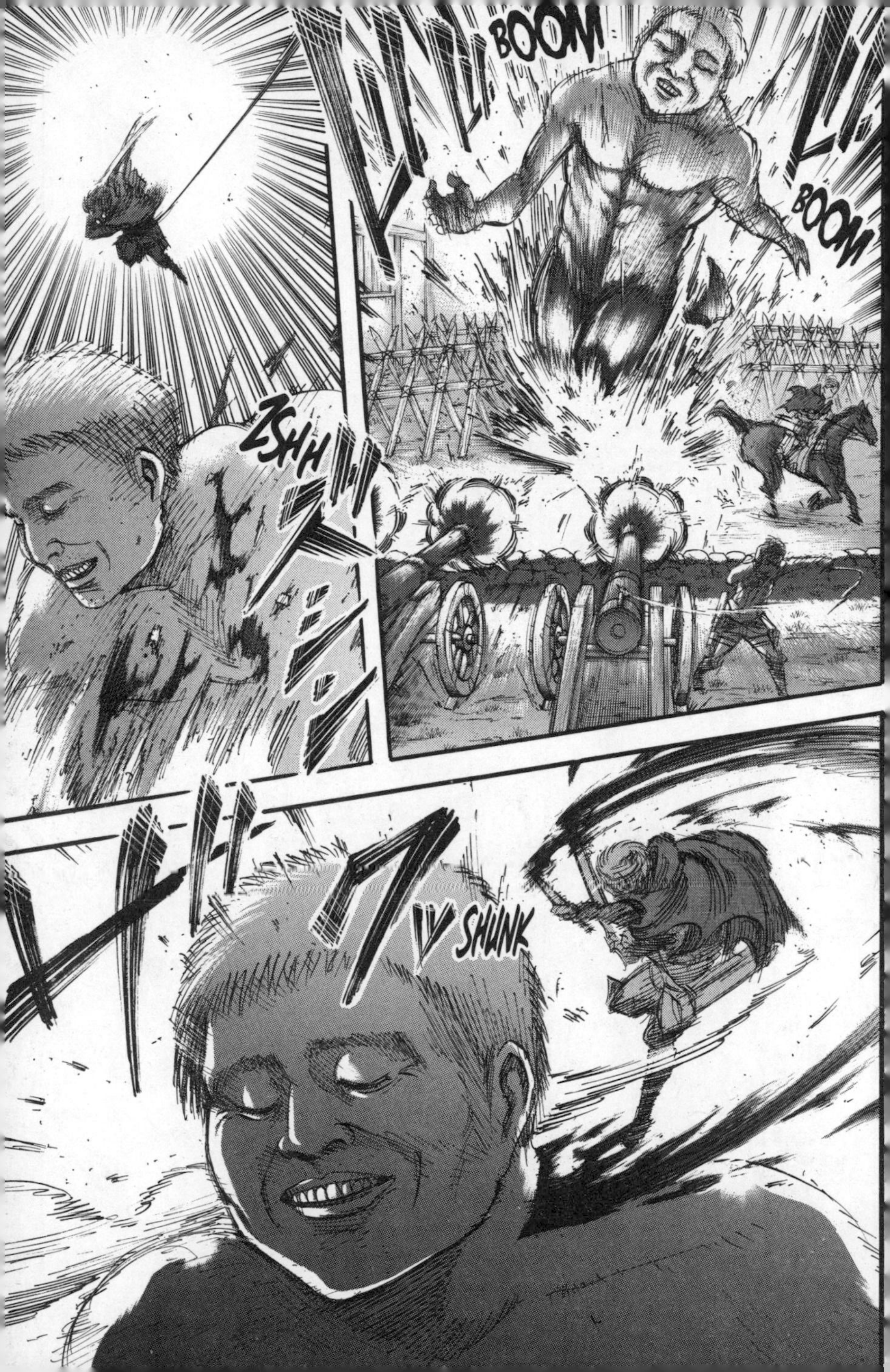
BOOM
BOOM
ZSHH
SHUNK

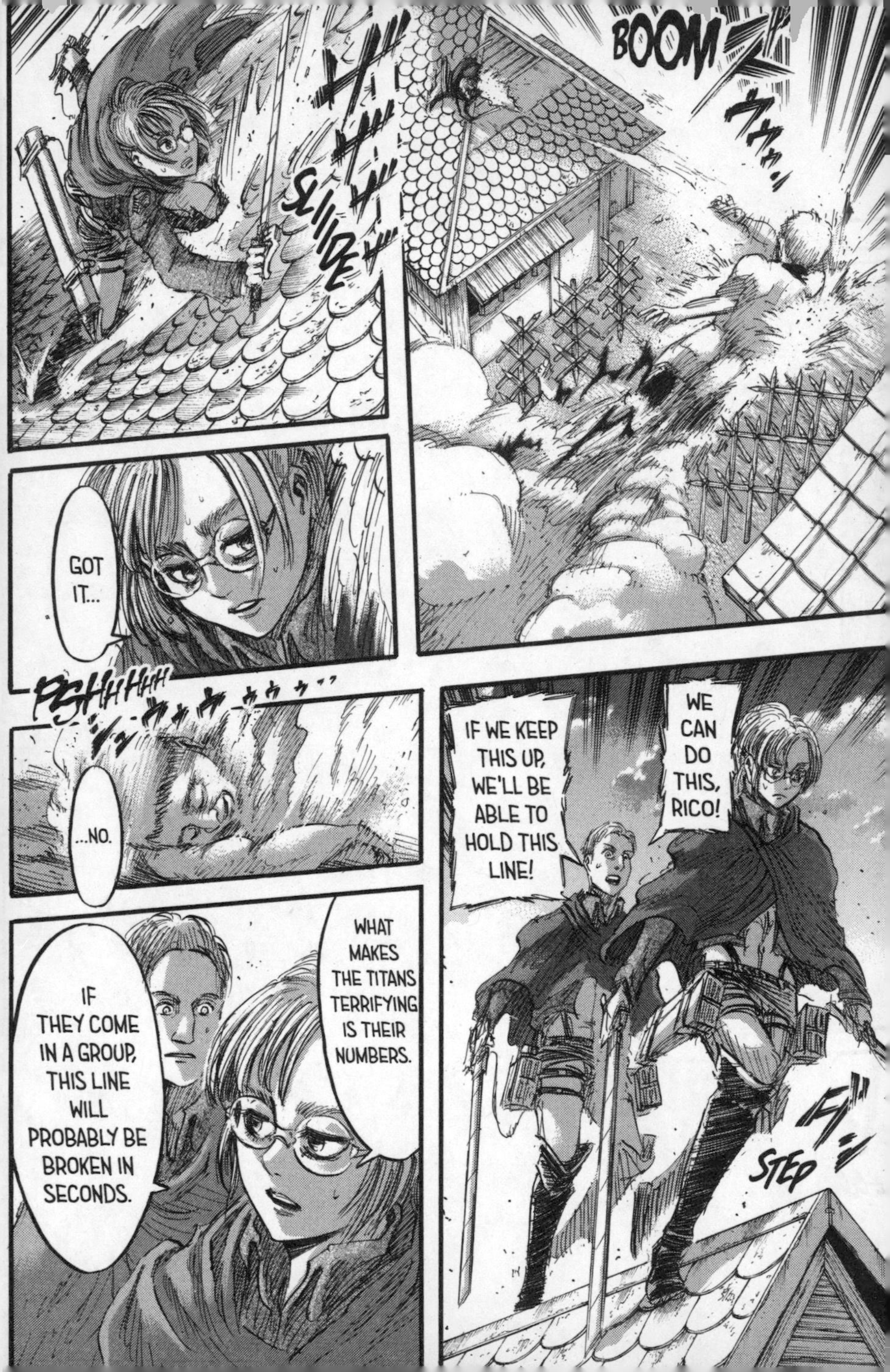
BOOM
SLIIIDE
GOT IT...
WE CAN DO THIS, RICO!
IF WE KEEP THIS UP, WE'LL BE ABLE TO HOLD THIS LINE!
STEP
PSHHHHH
...NO.
WHAT MAKES THE TITANS TERRIFYING IS THEIR NUMBERS.
IF THEY COME IN A GROUP, THIS LINE WILL PROBABLY BE BROKEN IN SECONDS.

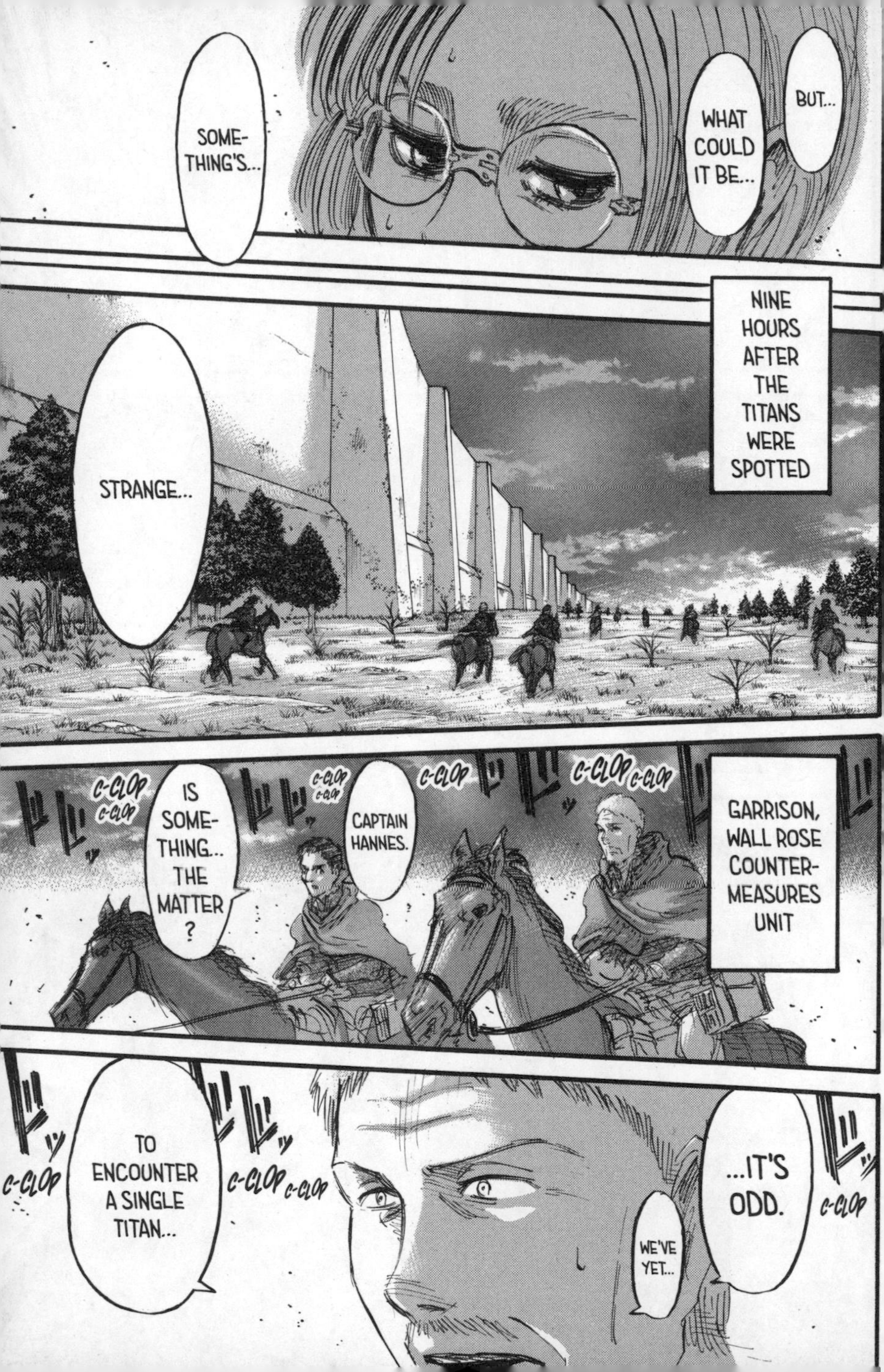
BUT...
WHAT COULD IT BE...
SOME-THING'S...
NINE HOURS AFTER THE TITANS WERE SPOTTED
STRANGE...
GARRISON, WALL ROSE COUNTER-MEASURES UNIT
C-CLOP C-CLOP
C-CLOP
CAPTAIN HANNES.
C-CLOP C-CLOP
IS SOME-THING... THE MATTER?
C-CLOP C-CLOP
C-CLOP
...IT'S ODD.
WE'VE YET...
TO ENCOUNTER A SINGLE TITAN...
C-CLOP C-CLOP
C-CLOP

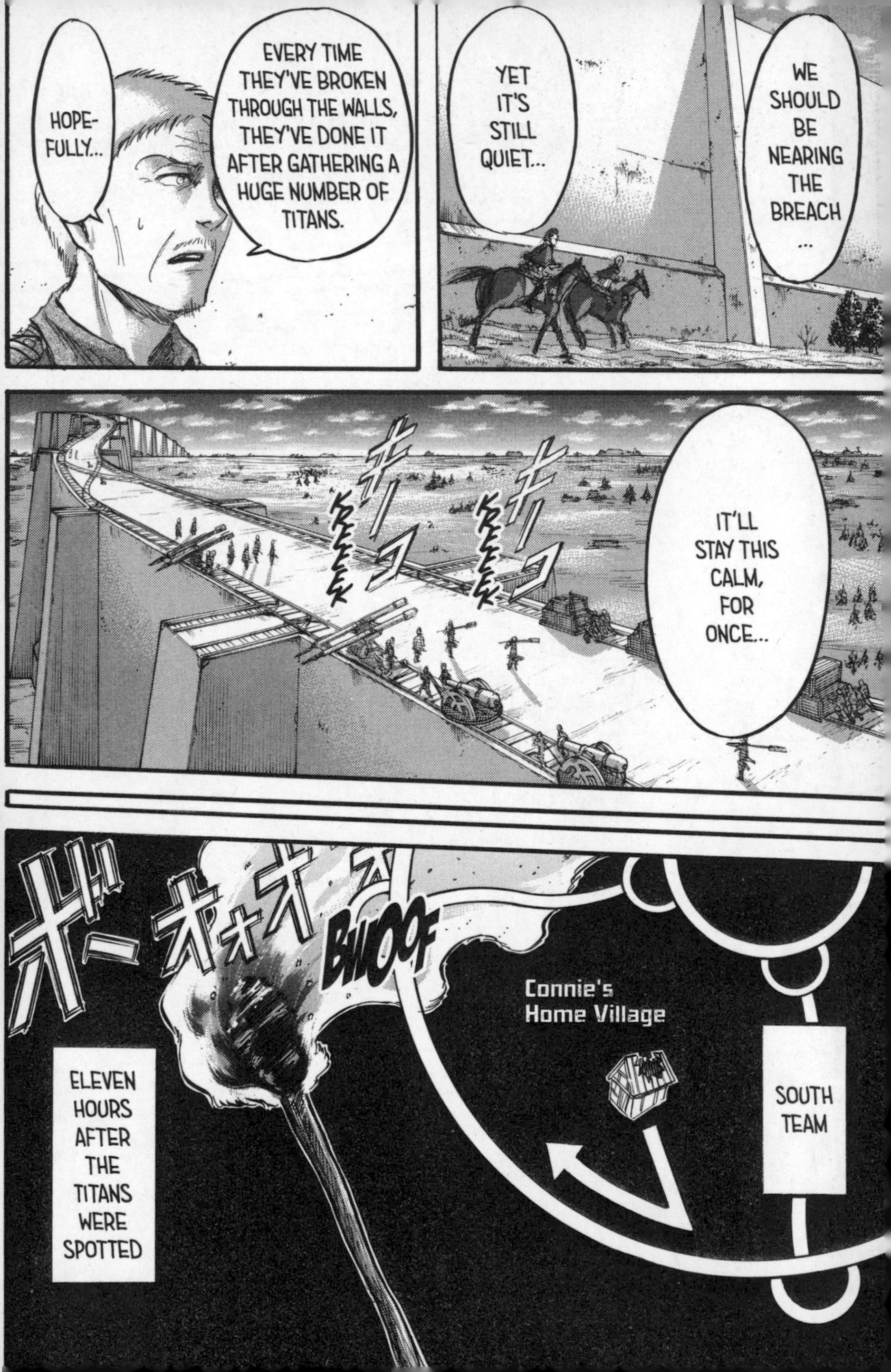
WE SHOULD BE NEARING THE BREACH...
YET IT'S STILL QUIET...
EVERY TIME THEY'VE BROKEN THROUGH THE WALLS, THEY'VE DONE IT AFTER GATHERING A HUGE NUMBER OF TITANS.
HOPE-FULLY...
IT'LL STAY THIS CALM, FOR ONCE...
KREEEK
KREEEK
BWOOF
SOUTH TEAM
Connie's Home Village
ELEVEN HOURS AFTER THE TITANS WERE SPOTTED

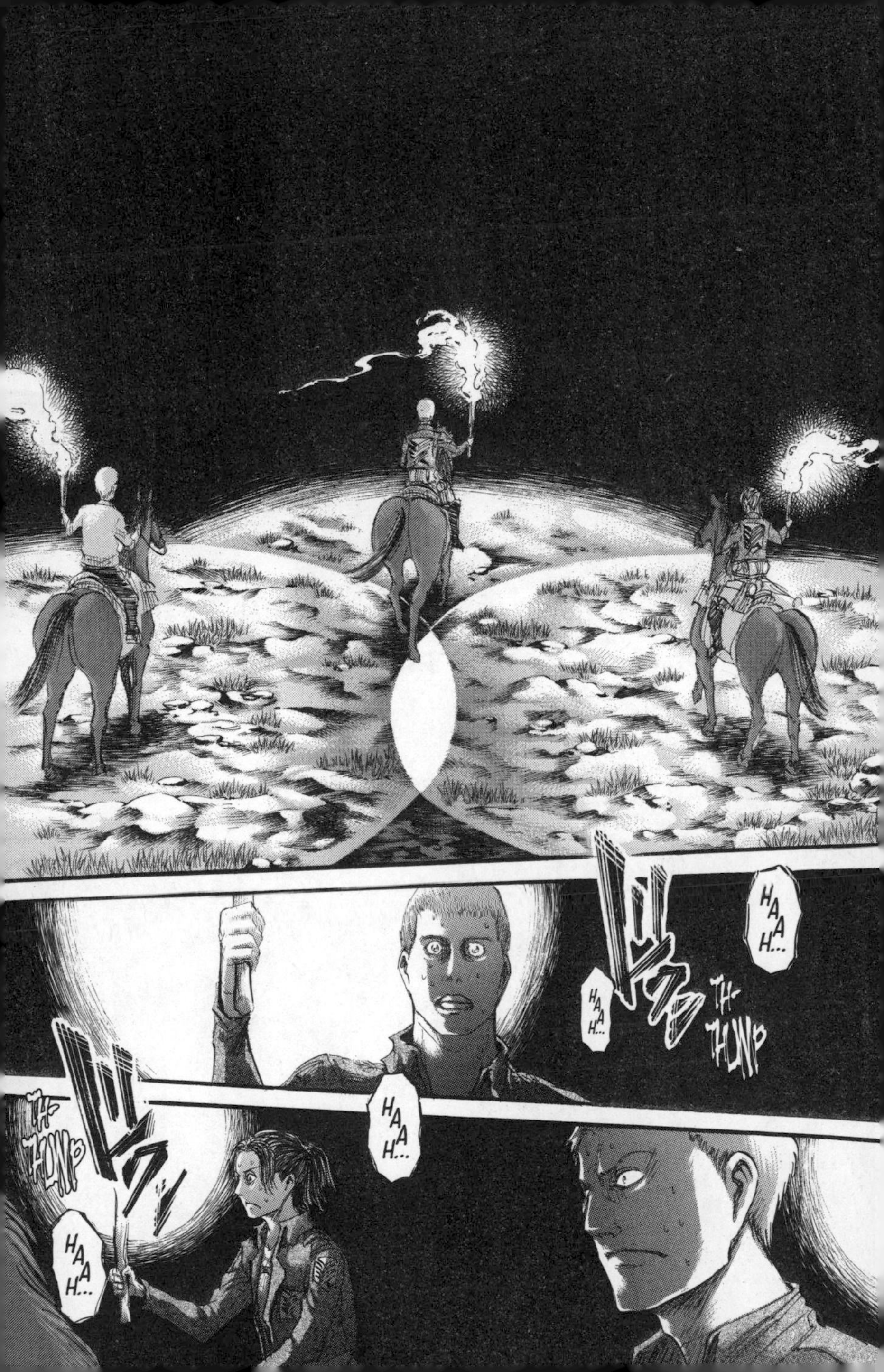
HAAAH...
HAAAH...
TH-THUMP
HAAAH...
TH-THUMP
HAAAH...

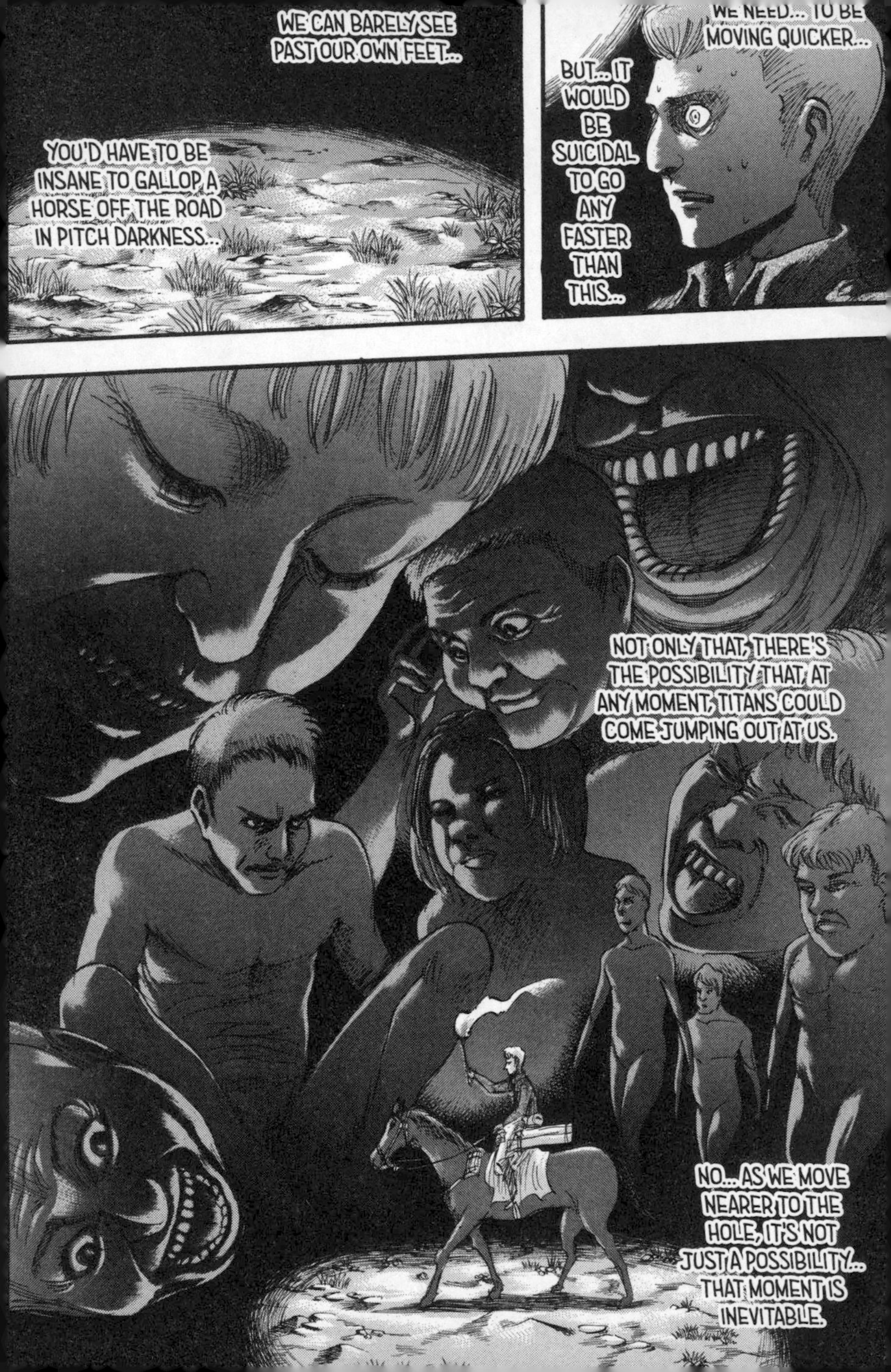
WE NEED... TO BE MOVING QUICKER...
BUT... IT WOULD BE SUICIDAL TO GO ANY FASTER THAN THIS...
WE CAN BARELY SEE PAST OUR OWN FEET...
YOU'D HAVE TO BE INSANE TO GALLOP A HORSE OFF THE ROAD IN PITCH DARKNESS...
NOT ONLY THAT, THERE'S THE POSSIBILITY THAT, AT ANY MOMENT, TITANS COULD COME JUMPING OUT AT US.
NO... AS WE MOVE NEARER TO THE HOLE, IT'S NOT JUST A POSSIBILITY... THAT MOMENT IS INEVITABLE.

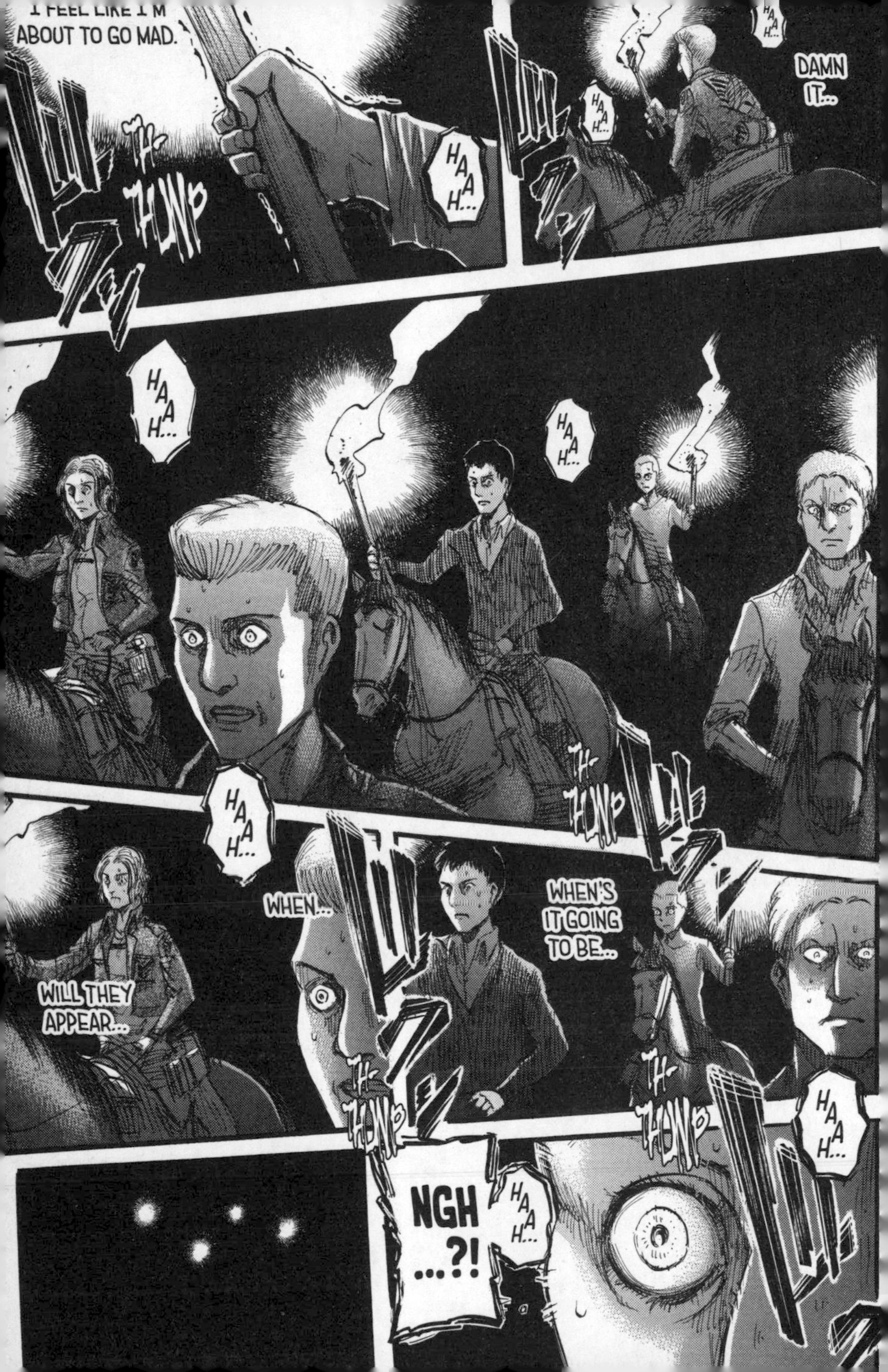

HAAH...
DAMN IT...
HAAH...
I FEEL LIKE I'M ABOUT TO GO MAD.
HAAH...
TH-THUMP
HAAH...
HAAH...
TH-THUMP
HAAH...
WHEN'S IT GOING TO BE...
TH-THUMP
WHEN...
TH-THUMP
WILL THEY APPEAR...
HAAH...
HAAH...
NGH ...?!

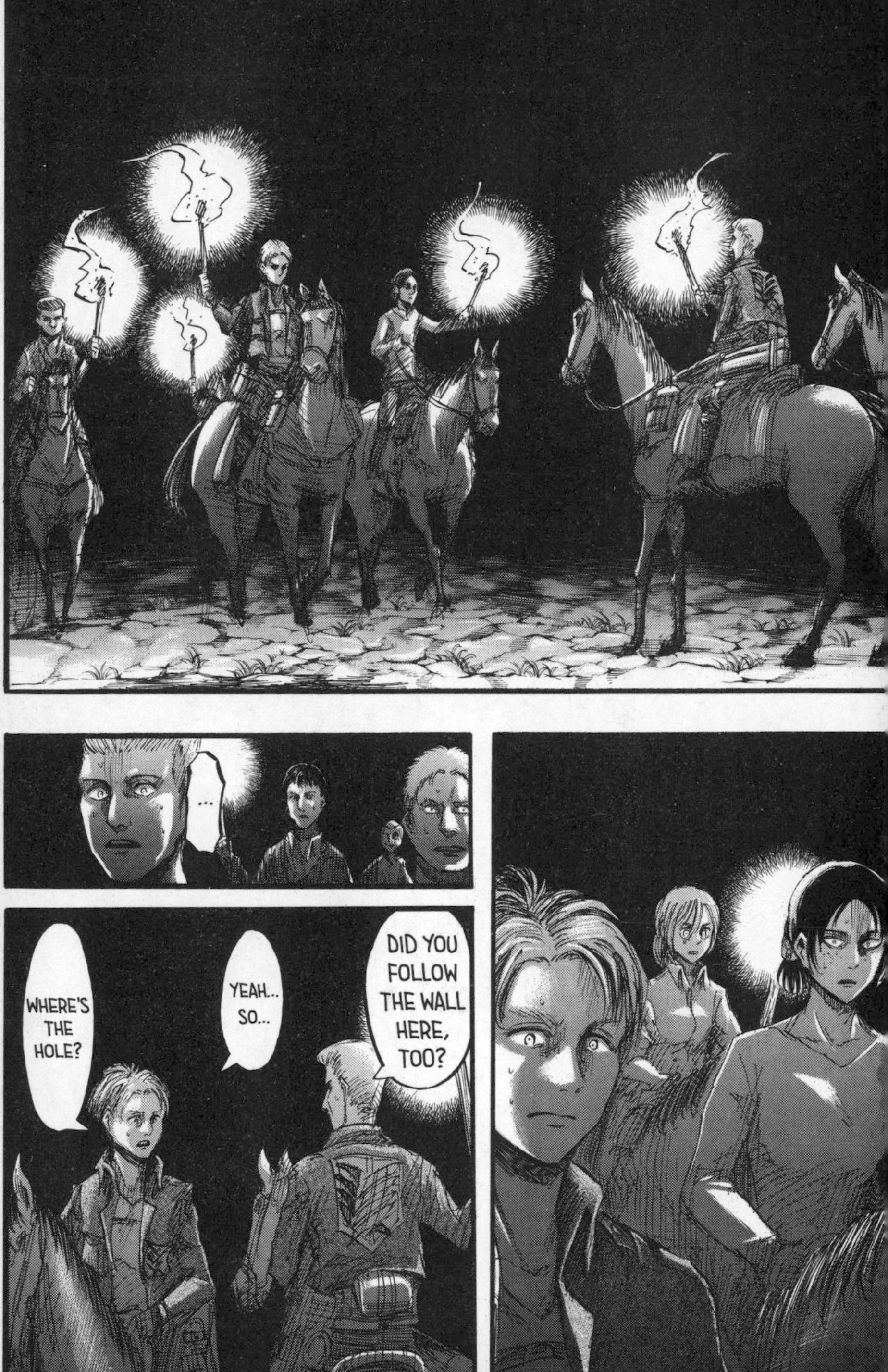
...
DID YOU FOLLOW THE WALL HERE, TOO?
YEAH... SO...
WHERE'S THE HOLE?

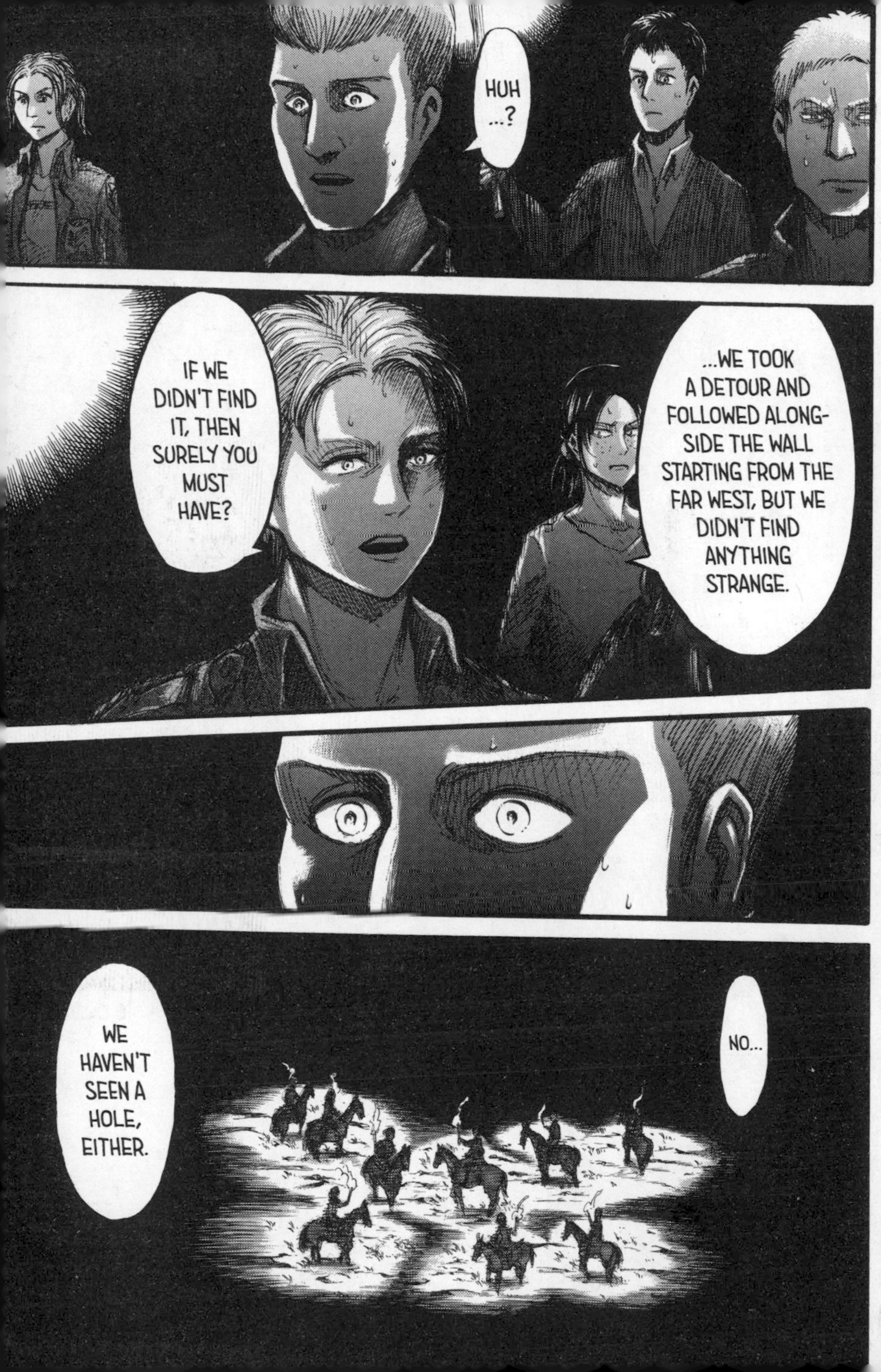
HUH ...?
...WE TOOK A DETOUR AND FOLLOWED ALONG-SIDE THE WALL STARTING FROM THE FAR WEST, BUT WE DIDN'T FIND ANYTHING STRANGE.
IF WE DIDN'T FIND IT, THEN SURELY YOU MUST HAVE?
NO...
WE HAVEN'T SEEN A HOLE, EITHER.

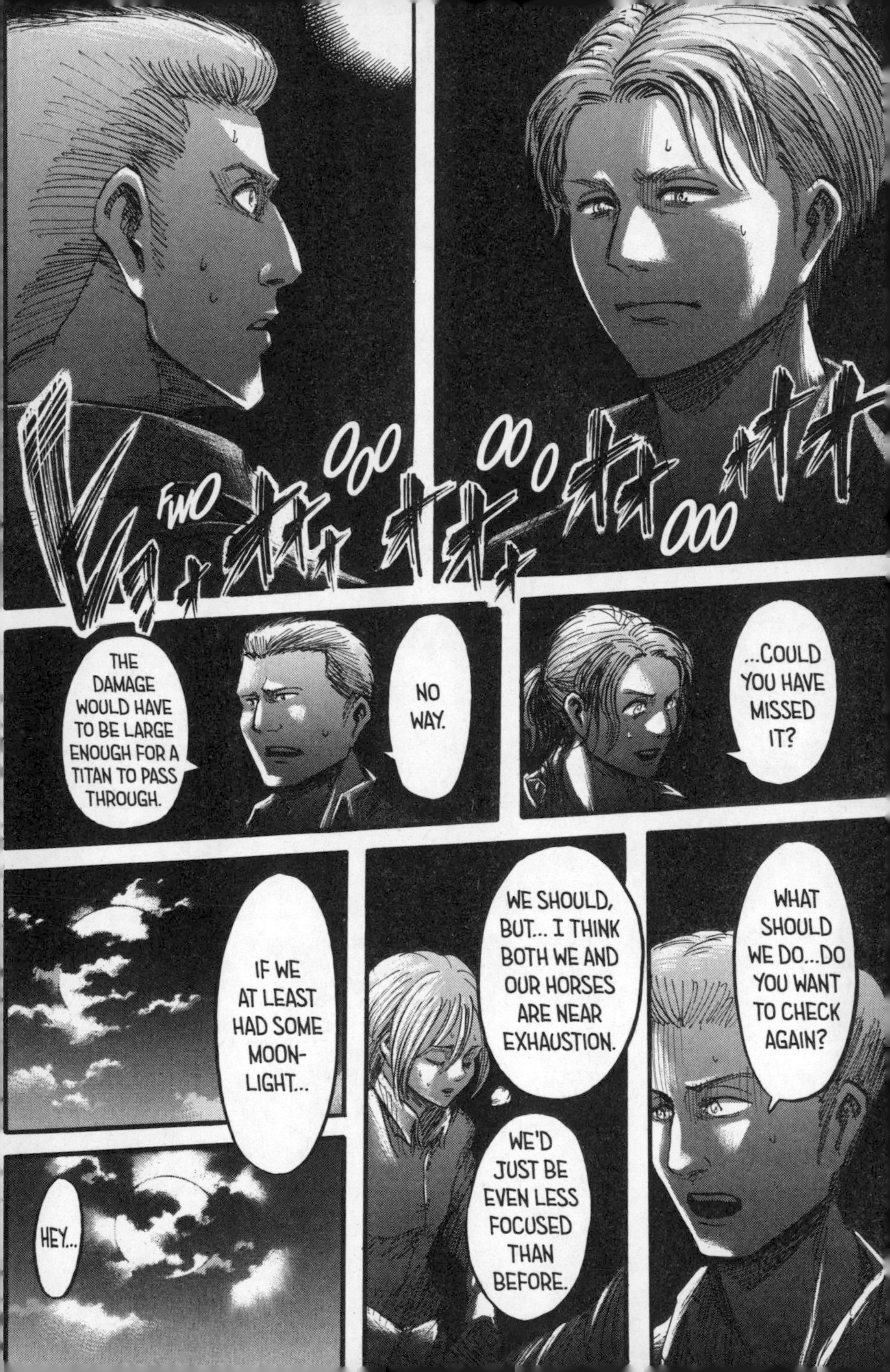
FWOOOOOOOOOO
...COULD YOU HAVE MISSED IT?
NO WAY.
THE DAMAGE WOULD HAVE TO BE LARGE ENOUGH FOR A TITAN TO PASS THROUGH.
WHAT SHOULD WE DO...DO YOU WANT TO CHECK AGAIN?
WE SHOULD, BUT... I THINK BOTH WE AND OUR HORSES ARE NEAR EXHAUSTION.
WE'D JUST BE EVEN LESS FOCUSED THAN BEFORE.
IF WE AT LEAST HAD SOME MOON-LIGHT...
HEY...

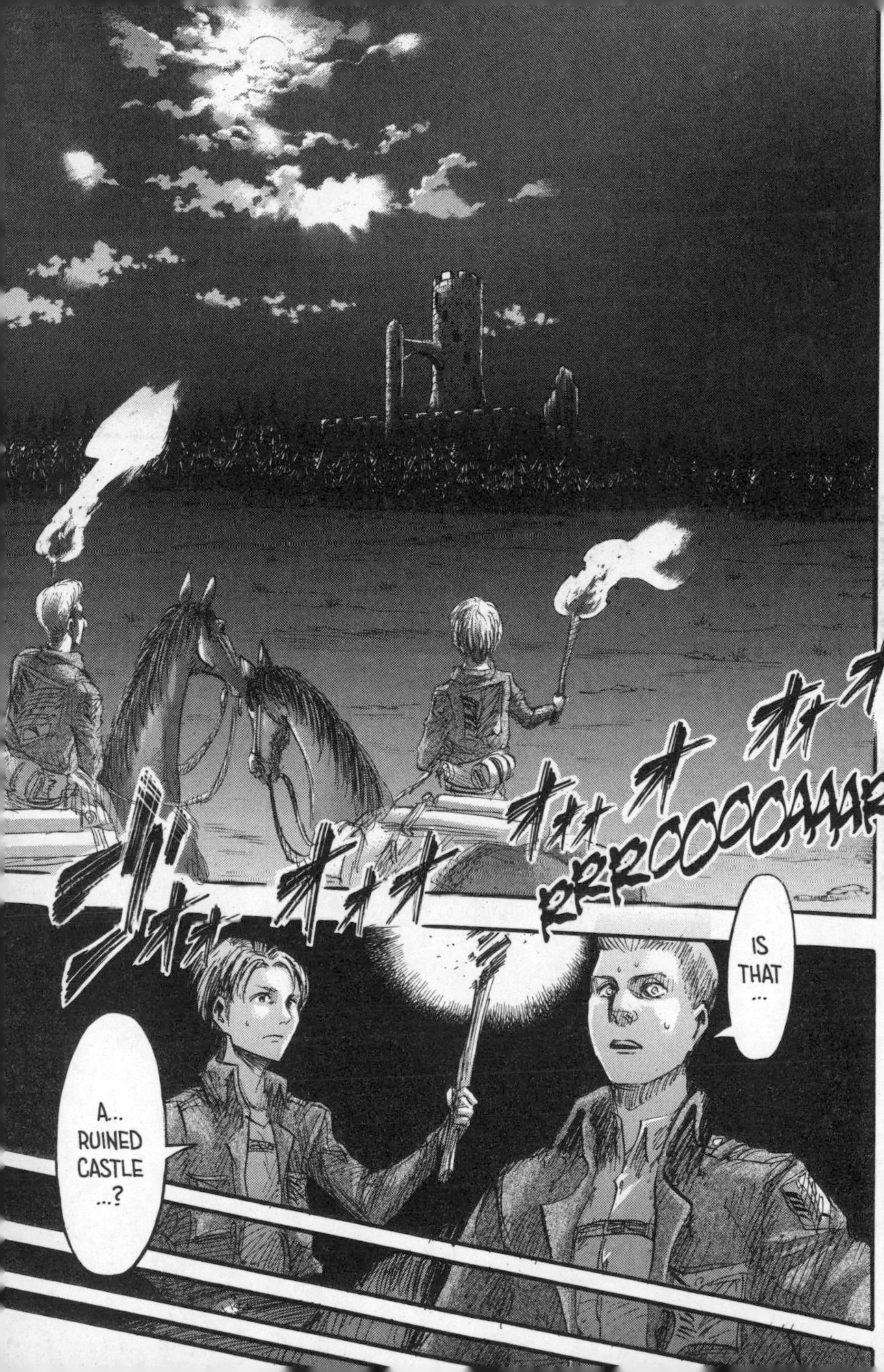
RRROOOOAAAR
IS THAT ...
A... RUINED CASTLE ...?

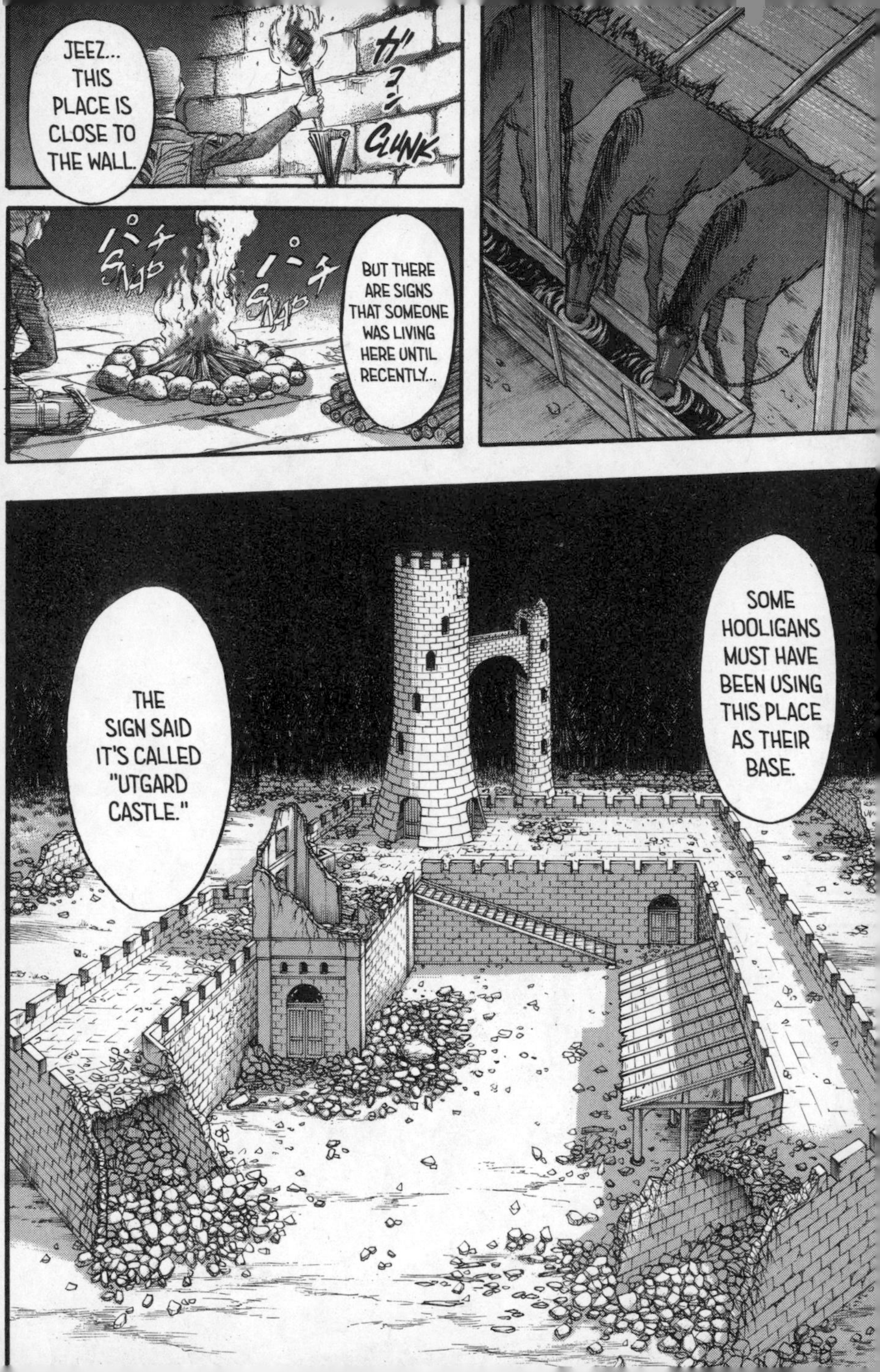
JEEZ... THIS PLACE IS CLOSE TO THE WALL.
ガコン
CLUNK
パチ
パチ
BUT THERE ARE SIGNS THAT SOMEONE WAS LIVING HERE UNTIL RECENTLY...
SOME HOOLIGANS MUST HAVE BEEN USING THIS PLACE AS THEIR BASE.
THE SIGN SAID IT'S CALLED "UTGARD CASTLE."

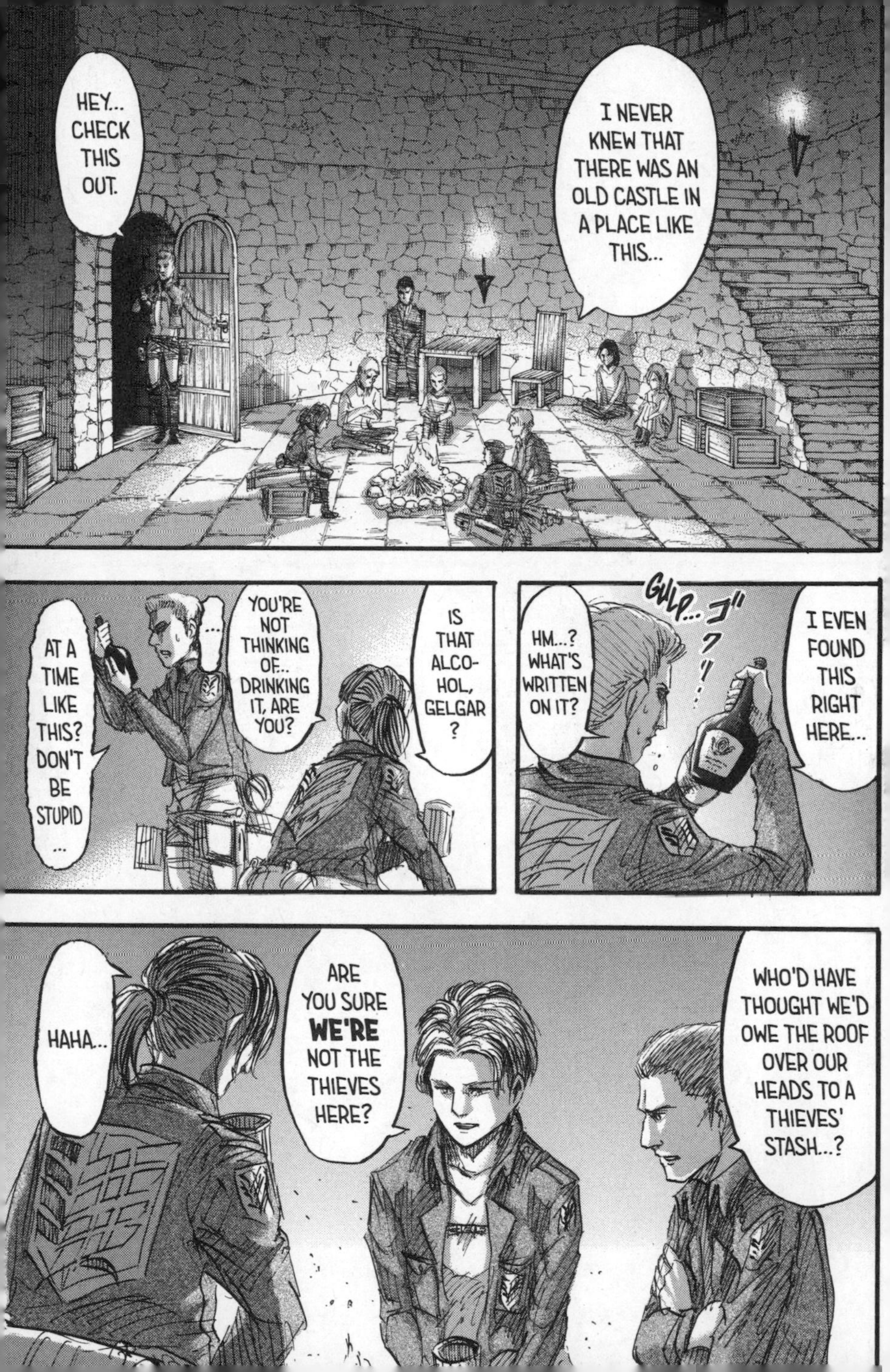

I NEVER KNEW THAT THERE WAS AN OLD CASTLE IN A PLACE LIKE THIS...
HEY... CHECK THIS OUT.
I EVEN FOUND THIS RIGHT HERE...
GULP...
ゴクリ...
HM...? WHAT'S WRITTEN ON IT?
IS THAT ALCOHOL, GELGAR?
YOU'RE NOT THINKING OF... DRINKING IT, ARE YOU?
...
AT A TIME LIKE THIS? DON'T BE STUPID...
WHO'D HAVE THOUGHT WE'D OWE THE ROOF OVER OUR HEADS TO A THIEVES' STASH...?
ARE YOU SURE **WE'RE** NOT THE THIEVES HERE?
HAHA...

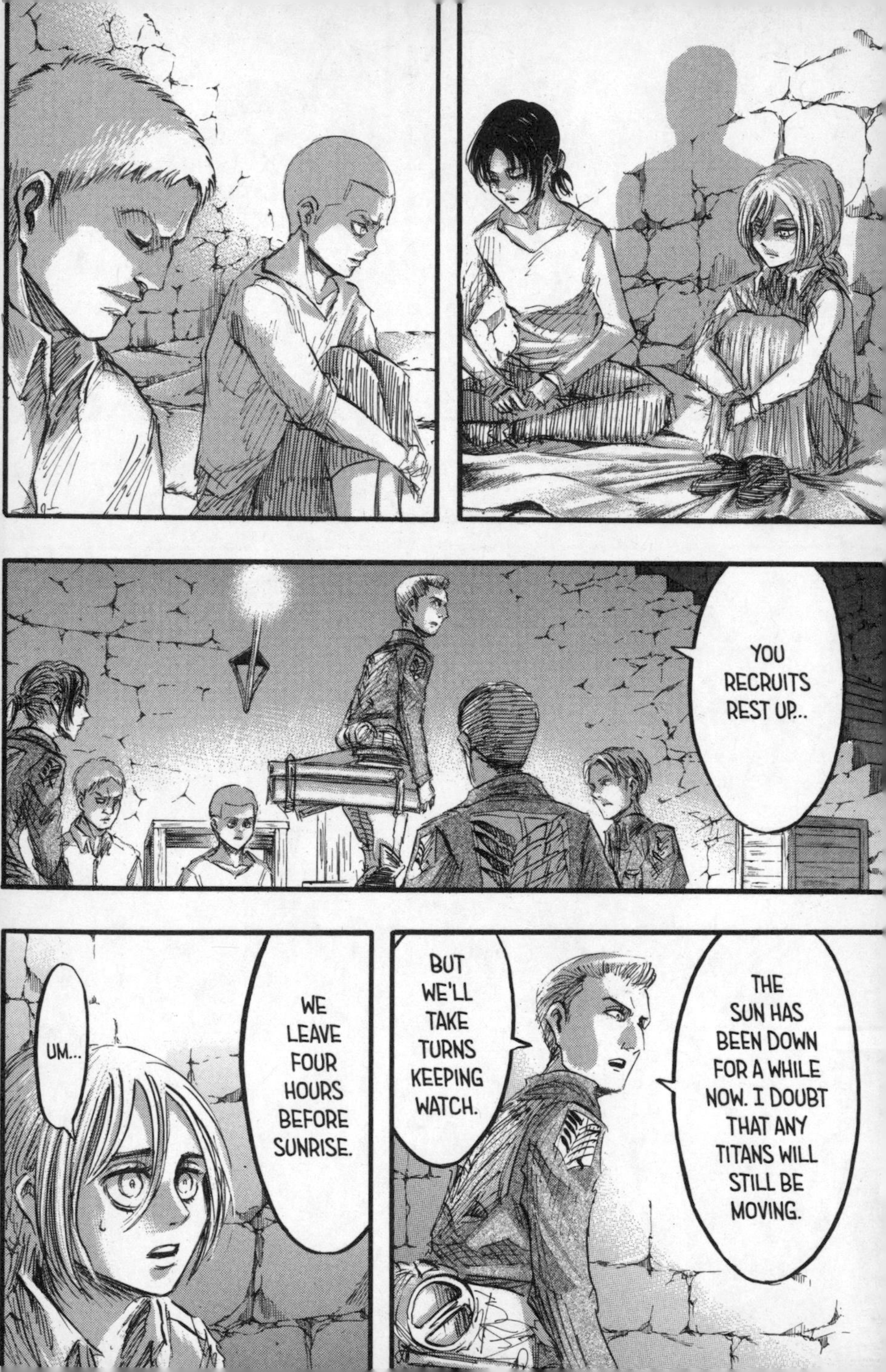
YOU RECRUITS REST UP...
THE SUN HAS BEEN DOWN FOR A WHILE NOW. I DOUBT THAT ANY TITANS WILL STILL BE MOVING.
BUT WE'LL TAKE TURNS KEEPING WATCH.
WE LEAVE FOUR HOURS BEFORE SUNRISE.
UM...

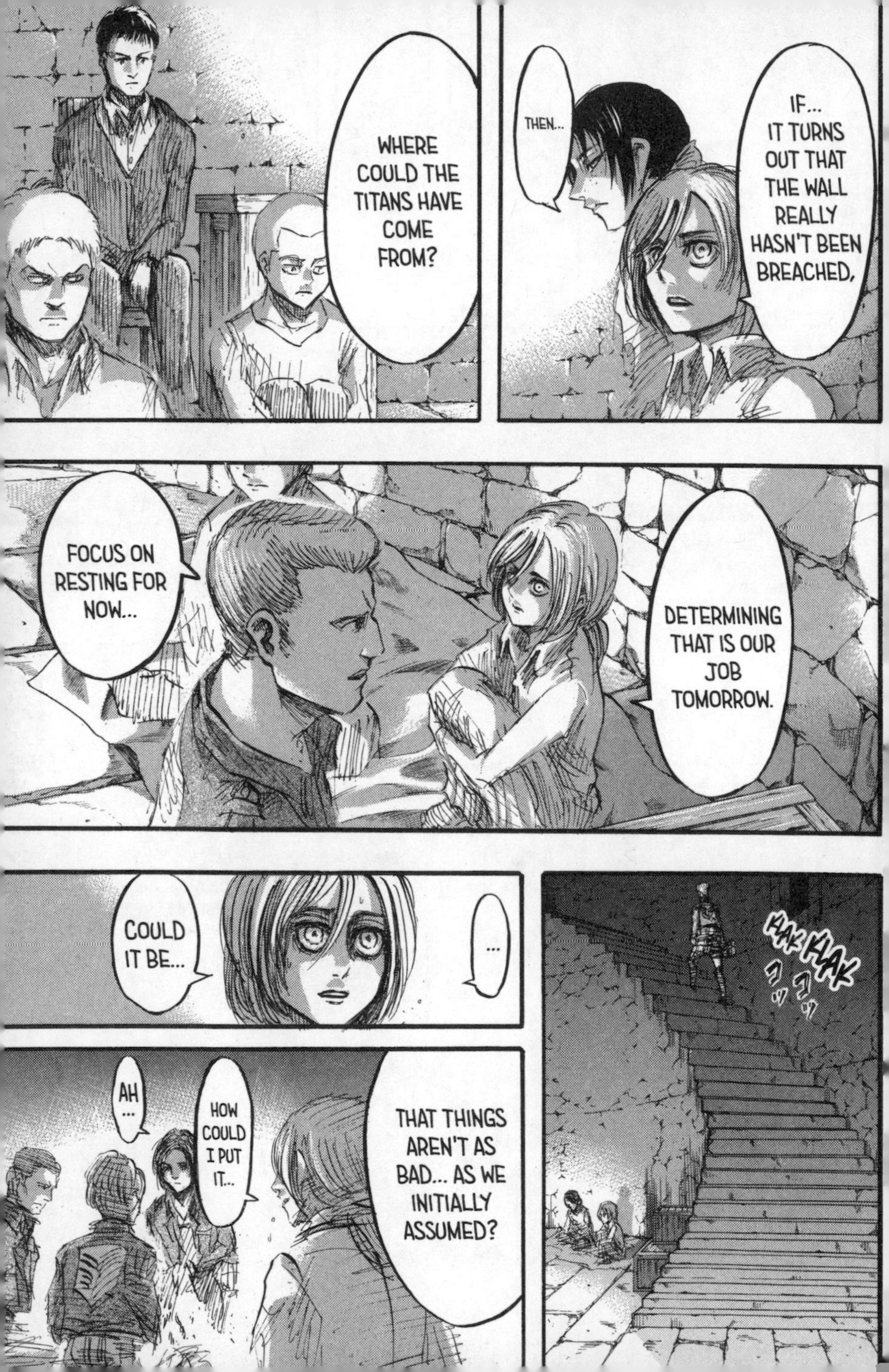

IF... IT TURNS OUT THAT THE WALL REALLY HASN'T BEEN BREACHED,
THEN...
WHERE COULD THE TITANS HAVE COME FROM?
DETERMINING THAT IS OUR JOB TOMORROW.
FOCUS ON RESTING FOR NOW...
KLAK KLAK
コッ コッ
...
COULD IT BE...
THAT THINGS AREN'T AS BAD... AS WE INITIALLY ASSUMED?
HOW COULD I PUT IT...
AH...

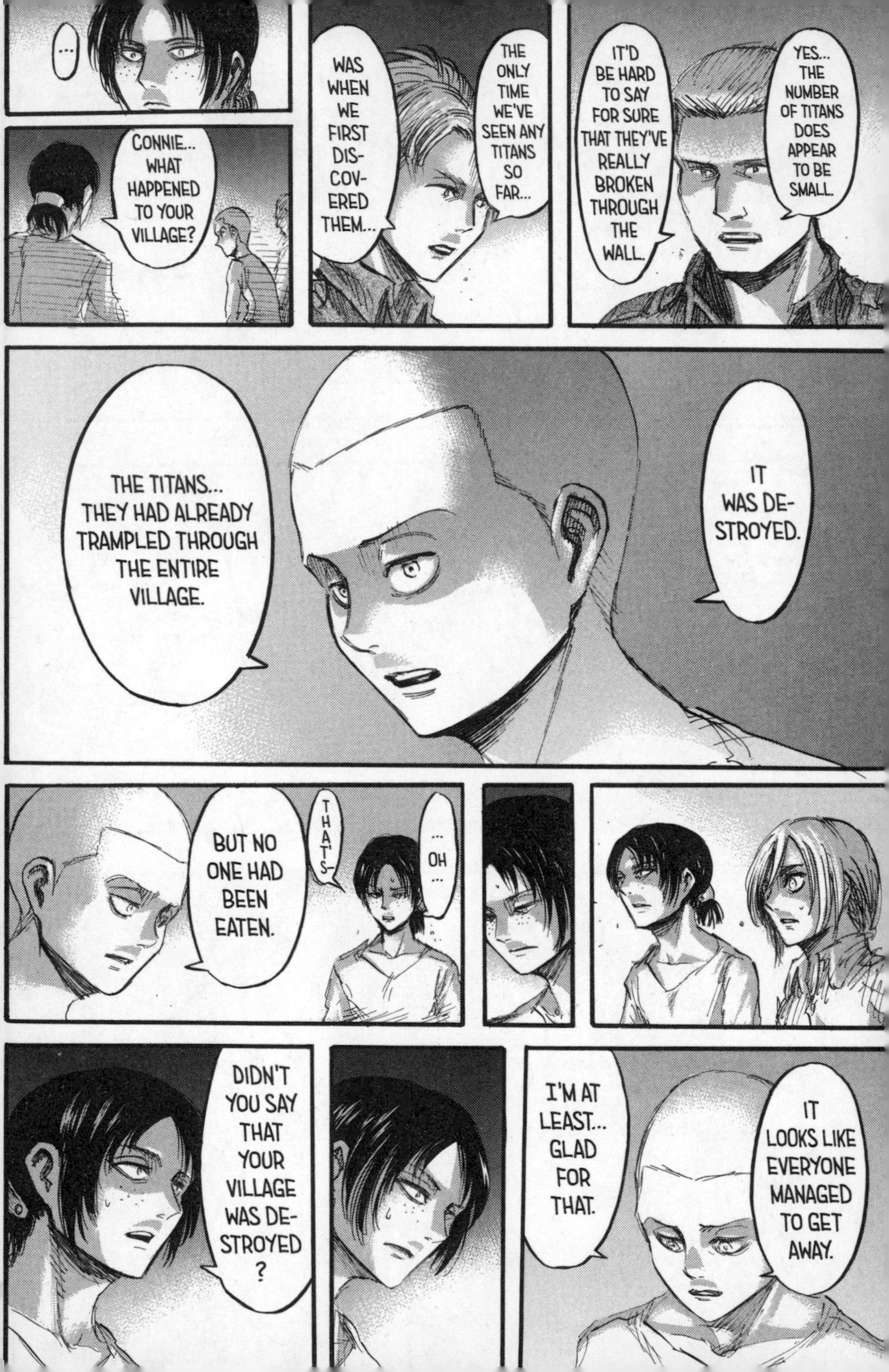
YES... THE NUMBER OF TITANS DOES APPEAR TO BE SMALL.
IT'D BE HARD TO SAY FOR SURE THAT THEY'VE REALLY BROKEN THROUGH THE WALL.
THE ONLY TIME WE'VE SEEN ANY TITANS SO FAR...
WAS WHEN WE FIRST DISCOVERED THEM...
...
CONNIE... WHAT HAPPENED TO YOUR VILLAGE?
IT WAS DESTROYED.
THE TITANS... THEY HAD ALREADY TRAMPLED THROUGH THE ENTIRE VILLAGE.
...OH...
THAT'S-
BUT NO ONE HAD BEEN EATEN.
IT LOOKS LIKE EVERYONE MANAGED TO GET AWAY.
I'M AT LEAST... GLAD FOR THAT.
DIDN'T YOU SAY THAT YOUR VILLAGE WAS DESTROYED?

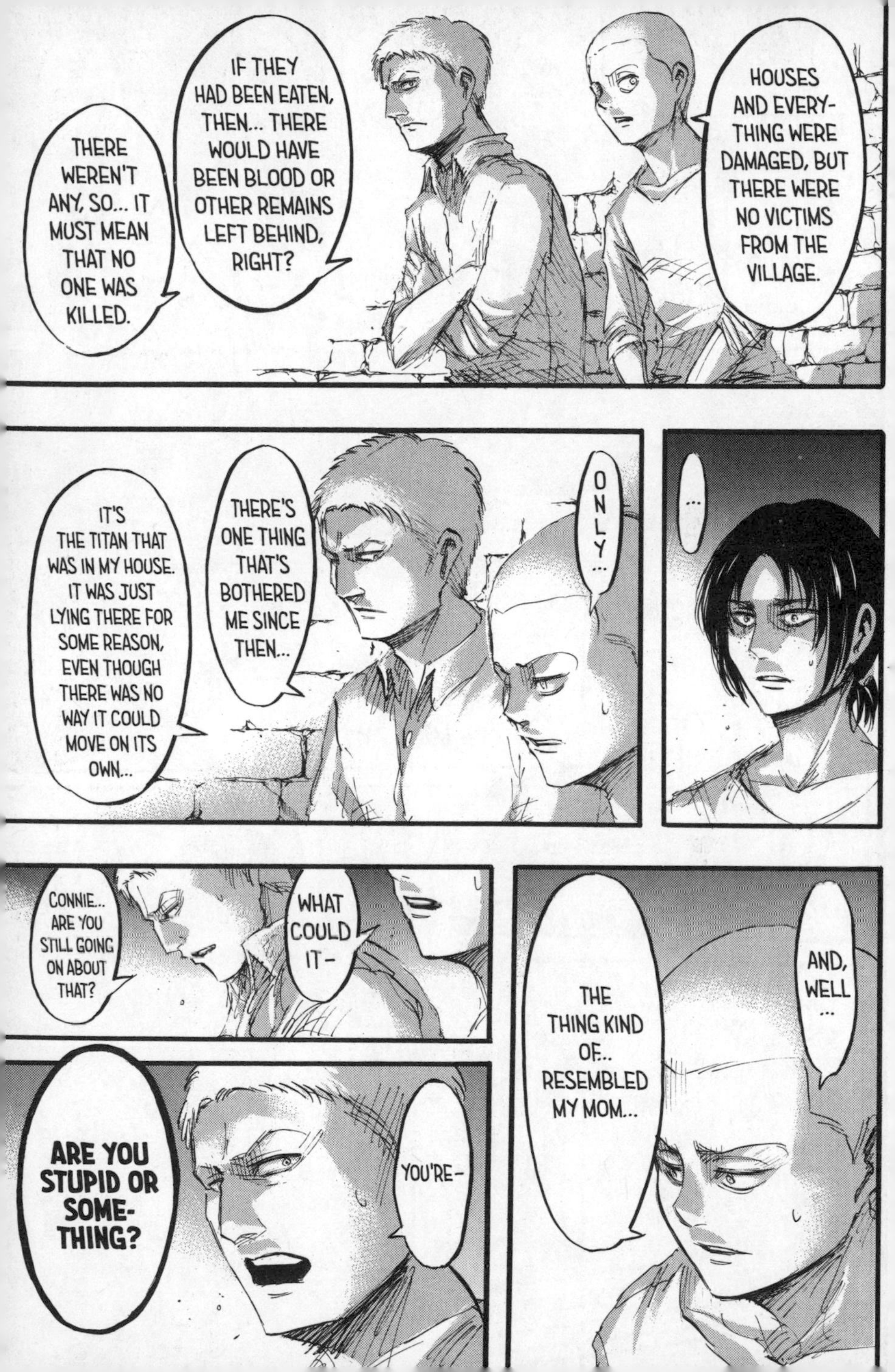
HOUSES AND EVERY-THING WERE DAMAGED, BUT THERE WERE NO VICTIMS FROM THE VILLAGE.
IF THEY HAD BEEN EATEN, THEN... THERE WOULD HAVE BEEN BLOOD OR OTHER REMAINS LEFT BEHIND, RIGHT?
THERE WEREN'T ANY, SO... IT MUST MEAN THAT NO ONE WAS KILLED.
...
ONLY...
THERE'S ONE THING THAT'S BOTHERED ME SINCE THEN...
IT'S THE TITAN THAT WAS IN MY HOUSE. IT WAS JUST LYING THERE FOR SOME REASON, EVEN THOUGH THERE WAS NO WAY IT COULD MOVE ON ITS OWN...
AND, WELL...
THE THING KIND OF... RESEMBLED MY MOM...
WHAT COULD IT-
CONNIE... ARE YOU STILL GOING ON ABOUT THAT?
YOU'RE-
ARE YOU STUPID OR SOME-THING?

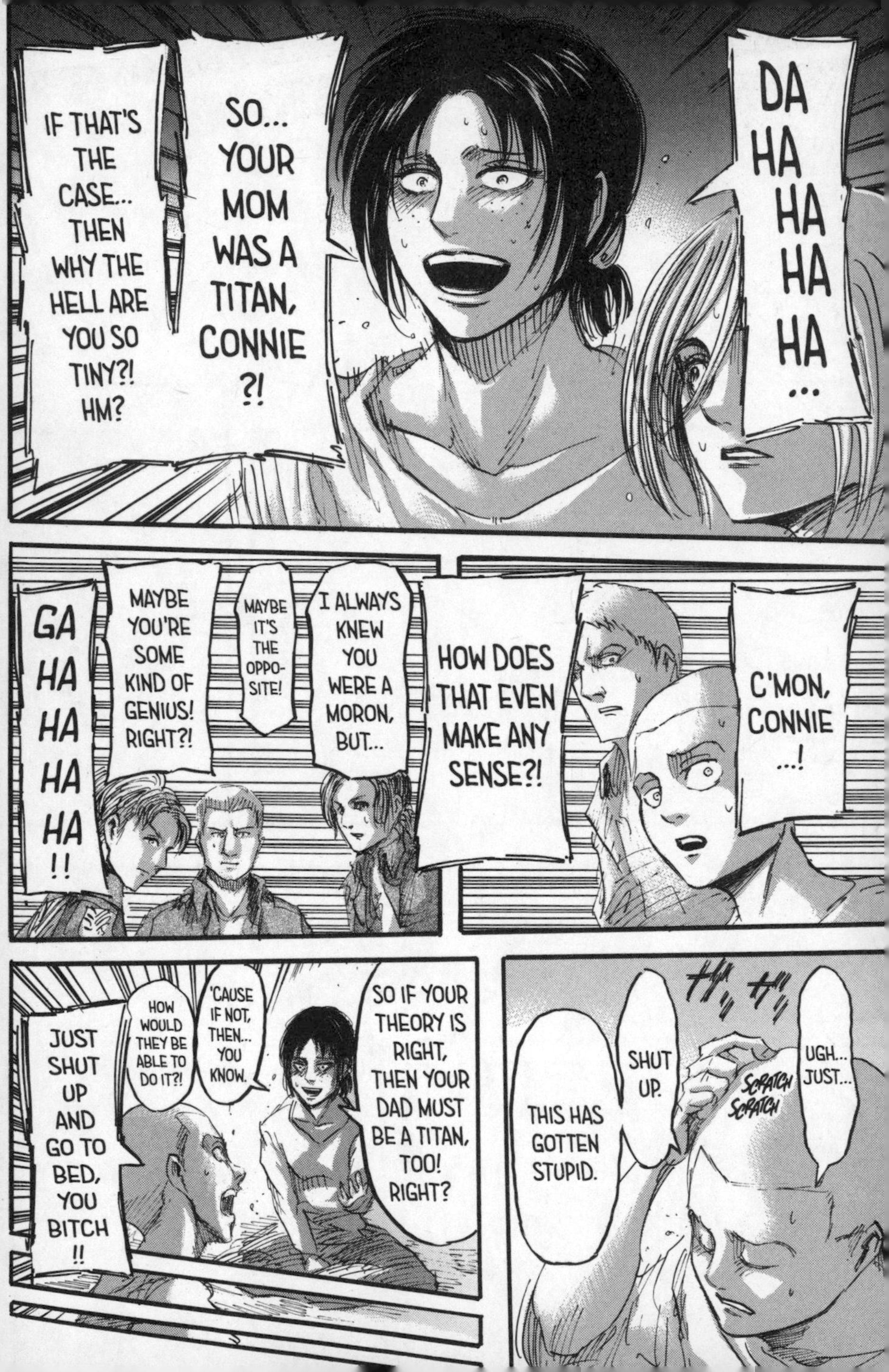
DA HA HA HA HA HA...
SO... YOUR MOM WAS A TITAN, CONNIE?!
IF THAT'S THE CASE... THEN WHY THE HELL ARE YOU SO TINY?! HM?
C'MON, CONNIE...!
HOW DOES THAT EVEN MAKE ANY SENSE?!
I ALWAYS KNEW YOU WERE A MORON, BUT...
MAYBE IT'S THE OPPOSITE!
MAYBE YOU'RE SOME KIND OF GENIUS! RIGHT?!
GA HA HA HA HA HA!!
UGH... JUST...
SCRATCH SCRATCH
SHUT UP.
THIS HAS GOTTEN STUPID.
SO IF YOUR THEORY IS RIGHT, THEN YOUR DAD MUST BE A TITAN, TOO! RIGHT?
'CAUSE IF NOT, THEN... YOU KNOW.
HOW WOULD THEY BE ABLE TO DO IT?!
JUST SHUT UP AND GO TO BED, YOU BITCH!!

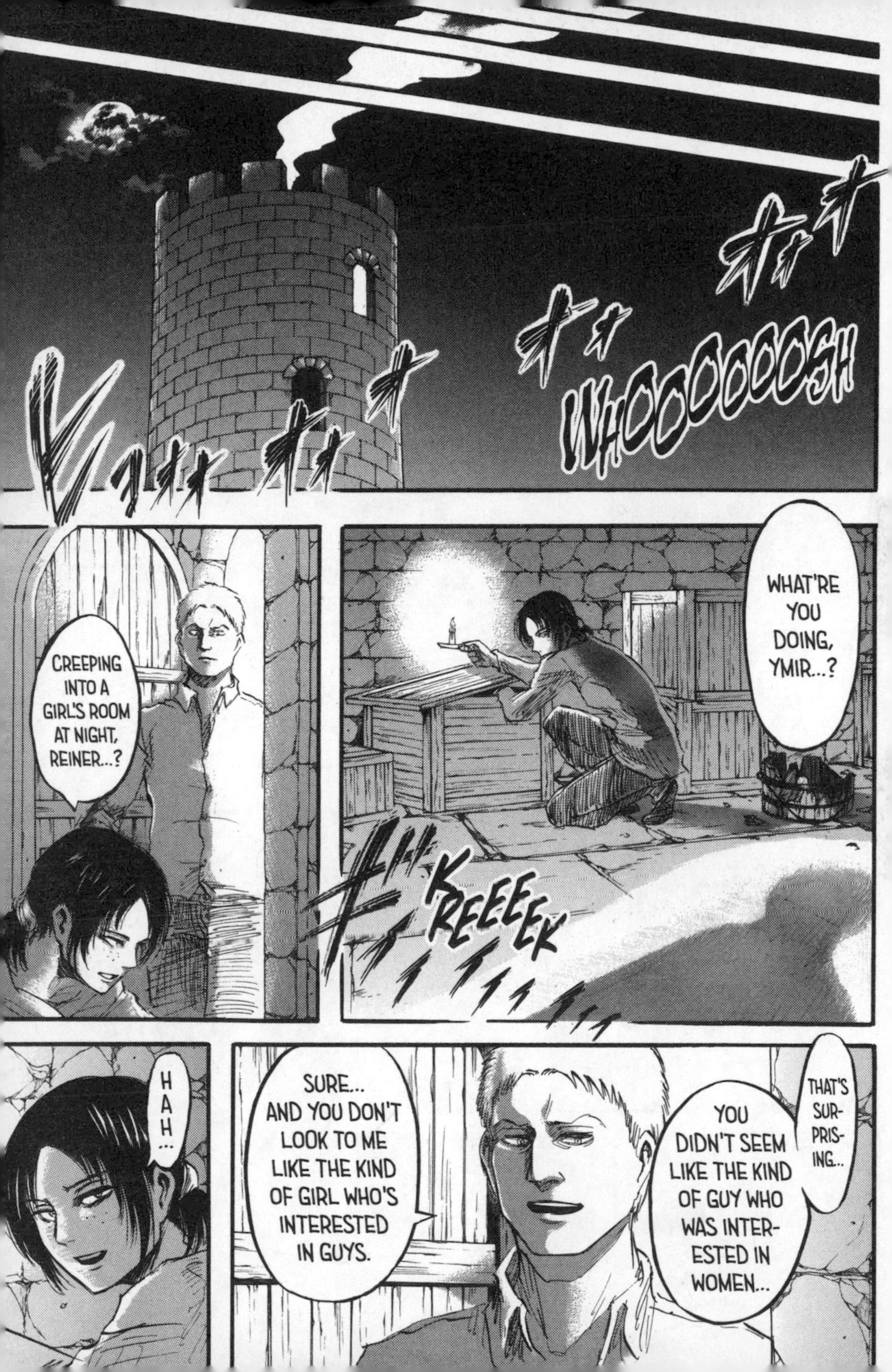
WHOOOOOOOSH
WHAT'RE YOU DOING, YMIR...?
KREEEEK
CREEPING INTO A GIRL'S ROOM AT NIGHT, REINER...?
THAT'S SURPRISING...
YOU DIDN'T SEEM LIKE THE KIND OF GUY WHO WAS INTERESTED IN WOMEN...
SURE... AND YOU DON'T LOOK TO ME LIKE THE KIND OF GIRL WHO'S INTERESTED IN GUYS.
HAH...

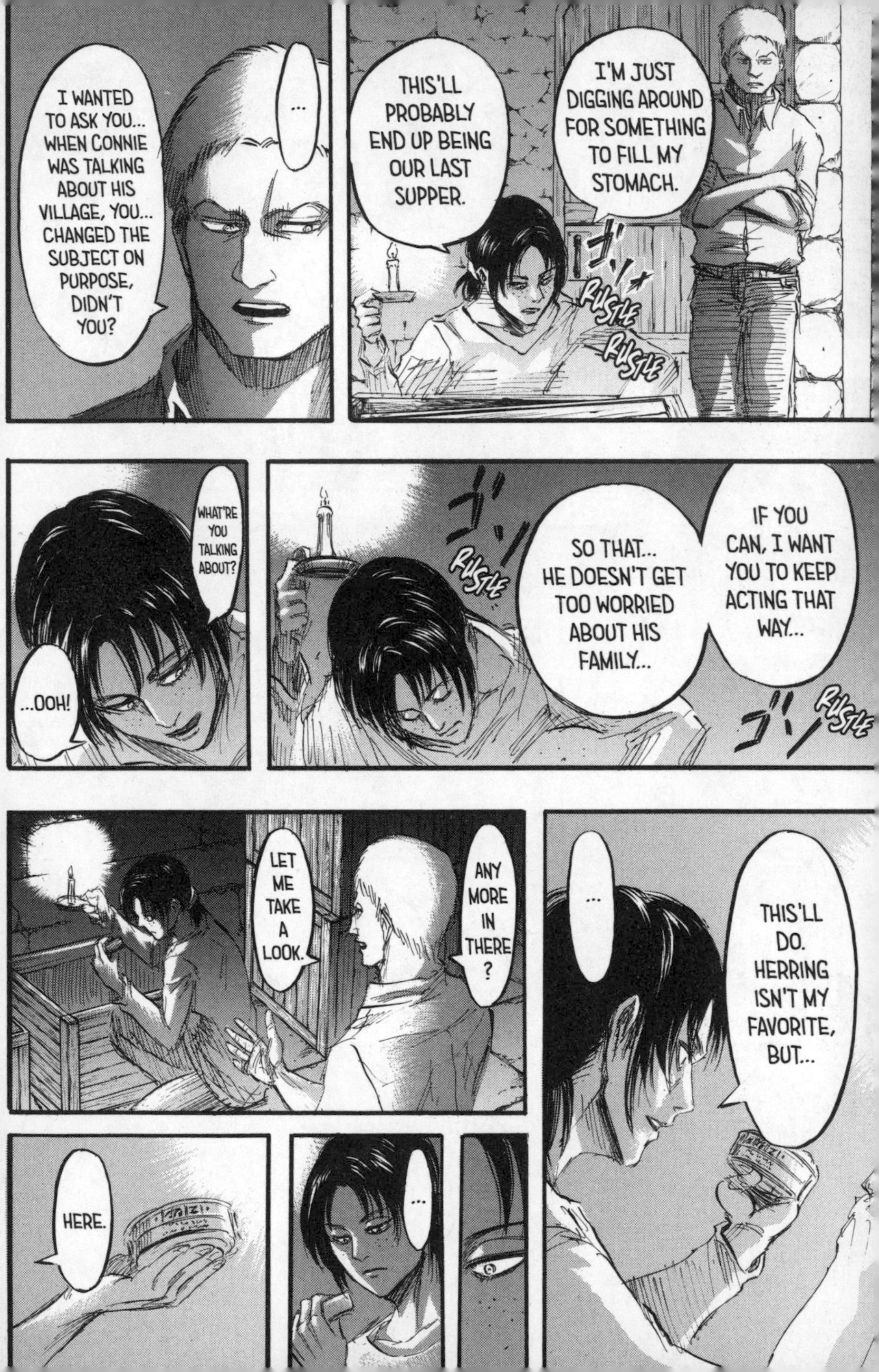
I'M JUST DIGGING AROUND FOR SOMETHING TO FILL MY STOMACH.
THIS'LL PROBABLY END UP BEING OUR LAST SUPPER.
RUSTLE
RUSTLE
...
I WANTED TO ASK YOU... WHEN CONNIE WAS TALKING ABOUT HIS VILLAGE, YOU... CHANGED THE SUBJECT ON PURPOSE, DIDN'T YOU?
IF YOU CAN, I WANT YOU TO KEEP ACTING THAT WAY...
SO THAT... HE DOESN'T GET TOO WORRIED ABOUT HIS FAMILY...
RUSTLE
RUSTLE
WHAT'RE YOU TALKING ABOUT?
...OOH!
THIS'LL DO. HERRING ISN'T MY FAVORITE, BUT...
...
ANY MORE IN THERE?
LET ME TAKE A LOOK.
...
HERE.

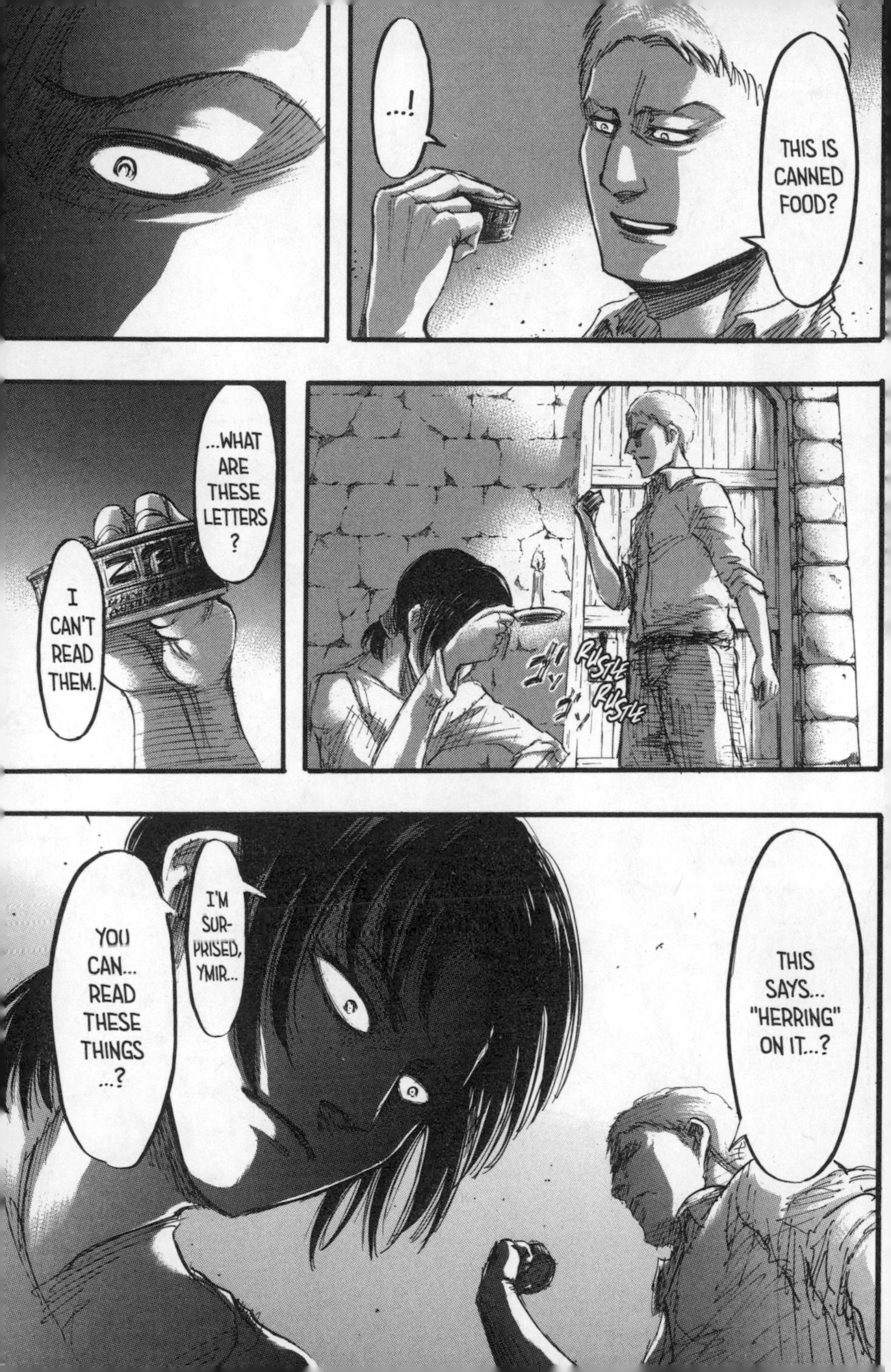
THIS IS CANNED FOOD?
...!
RUSTLE RUSTLE
...WHAT ARE THESE LETTERS?
I CAN'T READ THEM.
THIS SAYS... "HERRING" ON IT...?
I'M SUR-PRISED, YMIR...
YOU CAN... READ THESE THINGS ...?

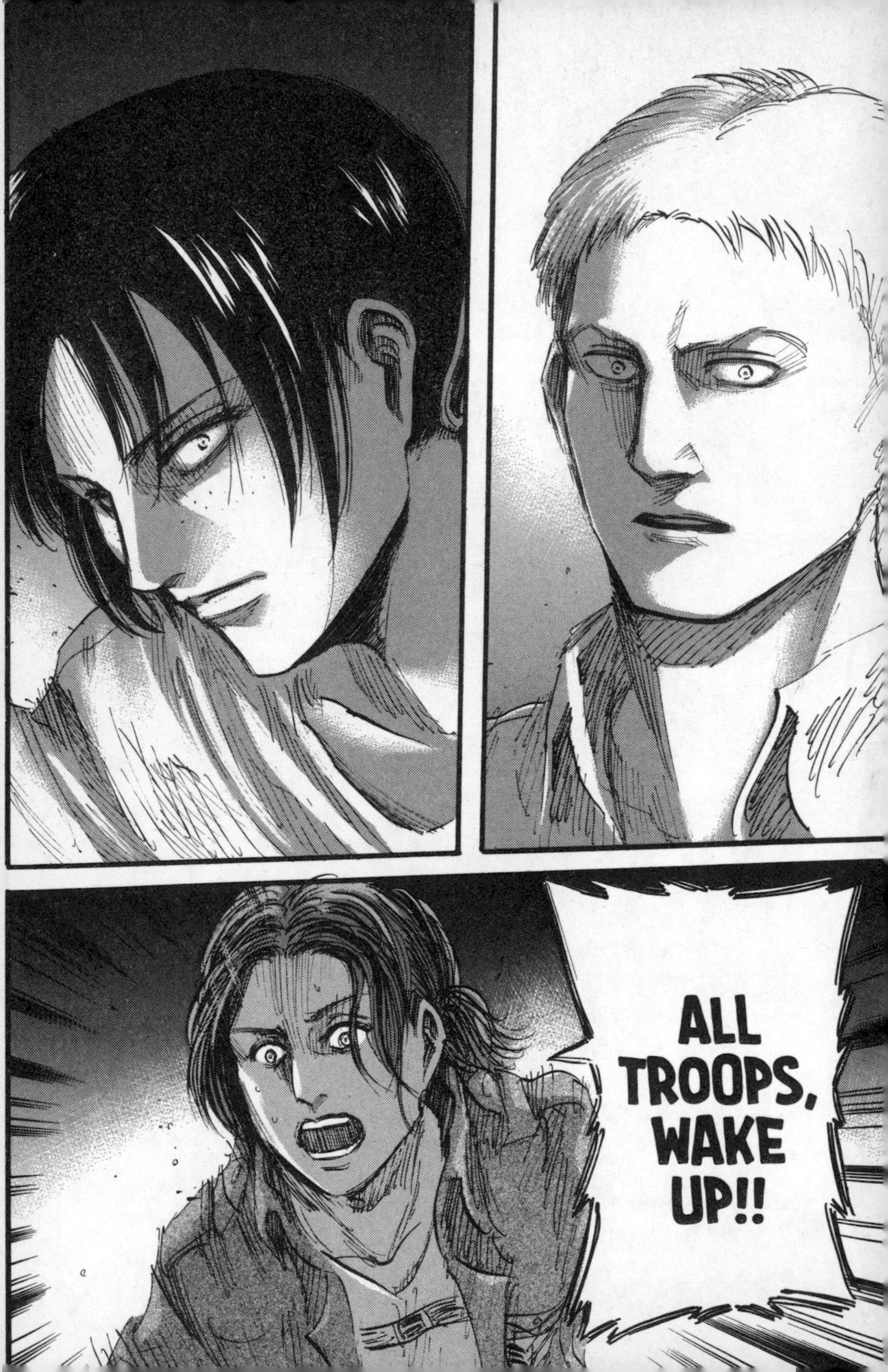
ALL TROOPS, WAKE UP!!

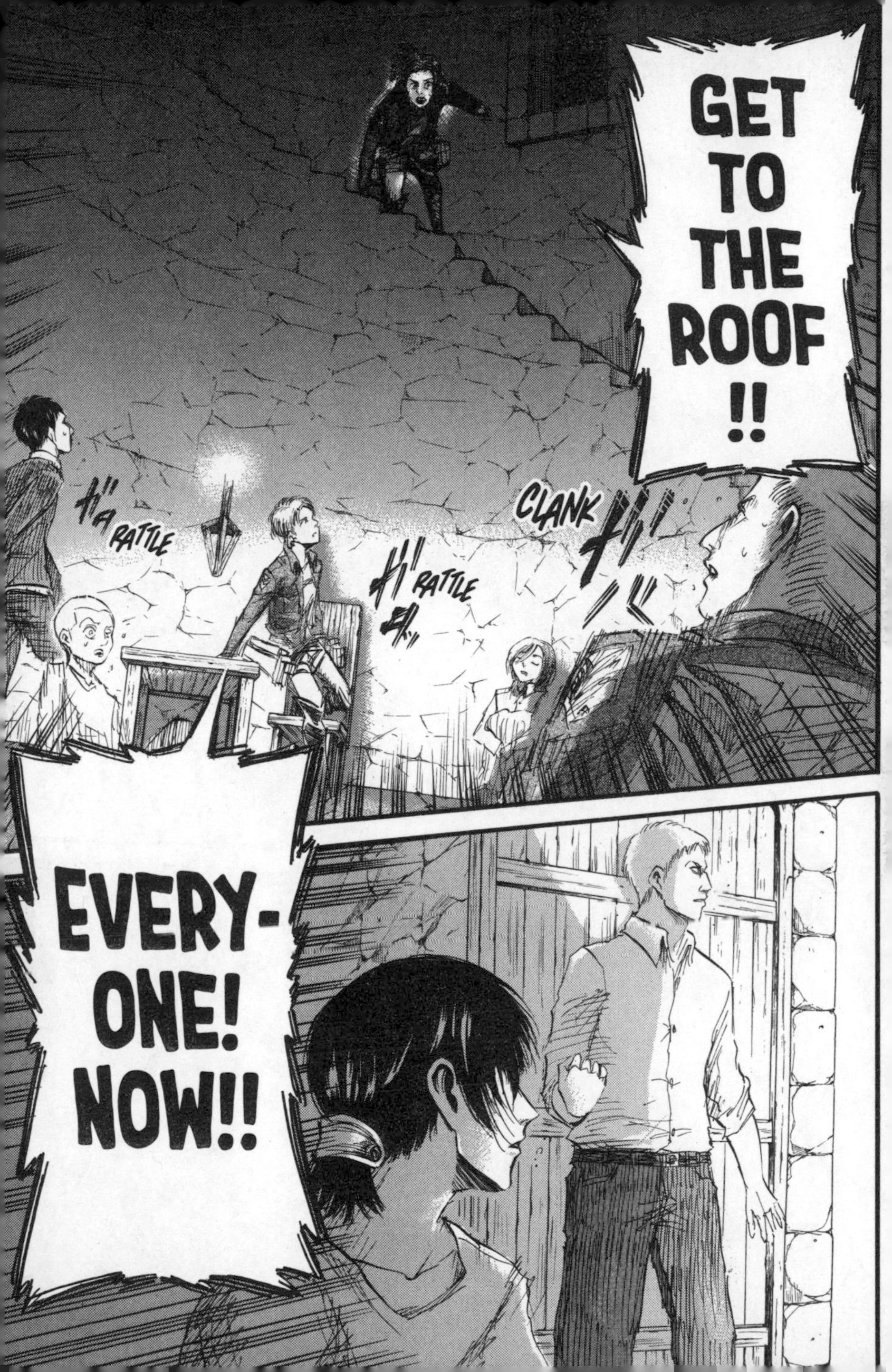
GET TO THE ROOF!!
CLANK
RATTLE
RATTLE
EVERY-ONE! NOW!!

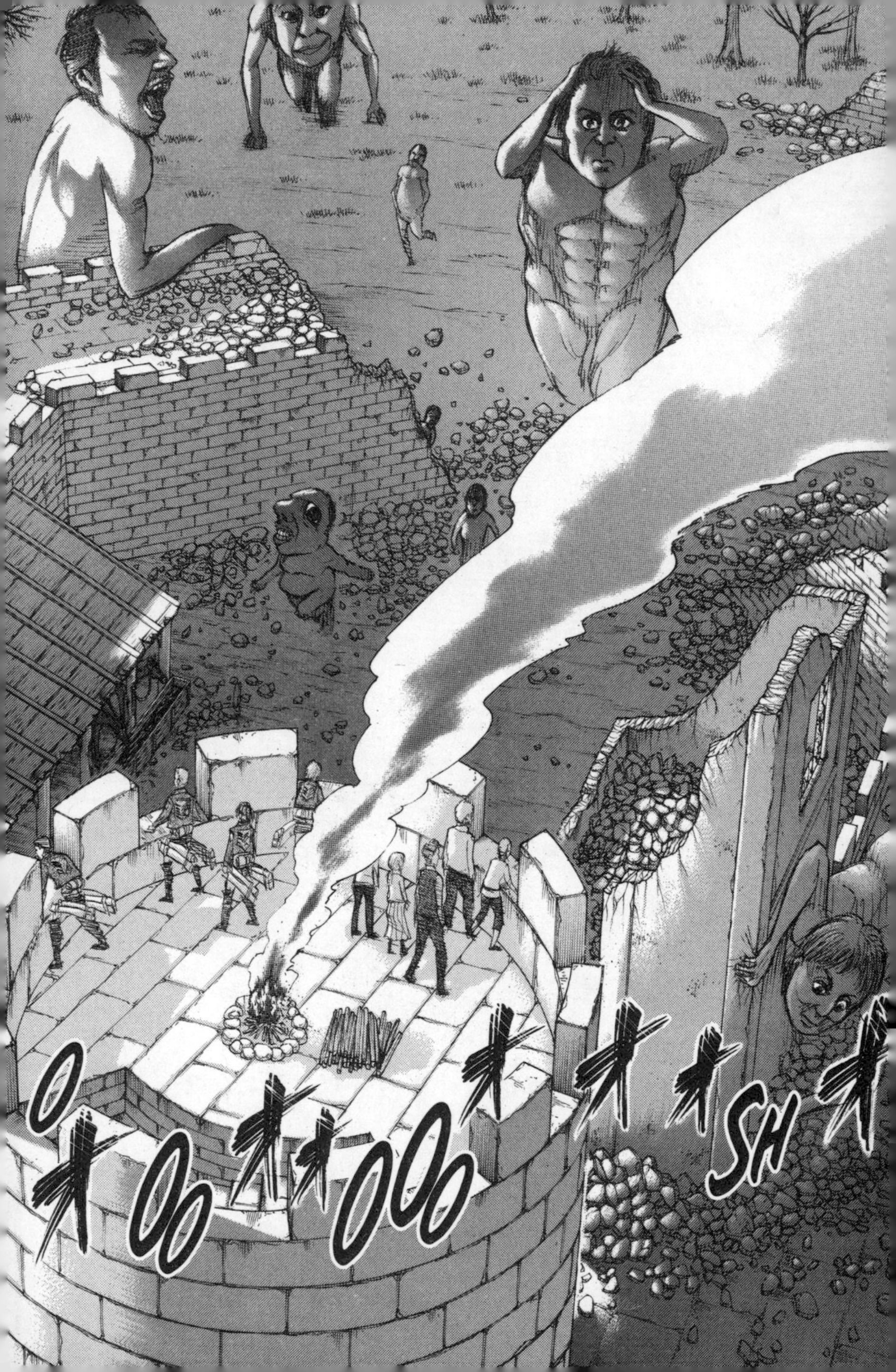
OOOOOOSH

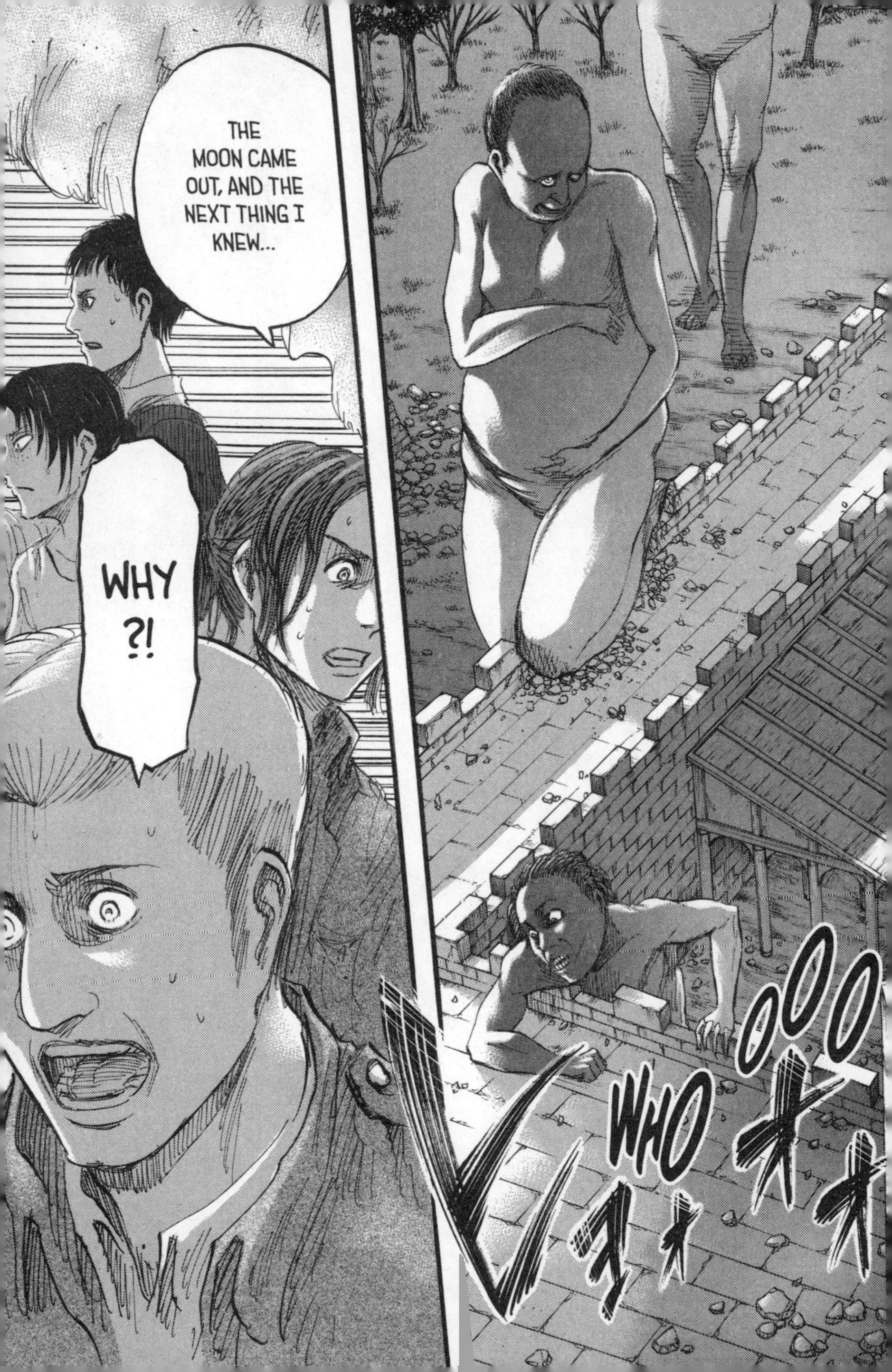
WHOOOO
THE MOON CAME OUT, AND THE NEXT THING I KNEW...
WHY ?!

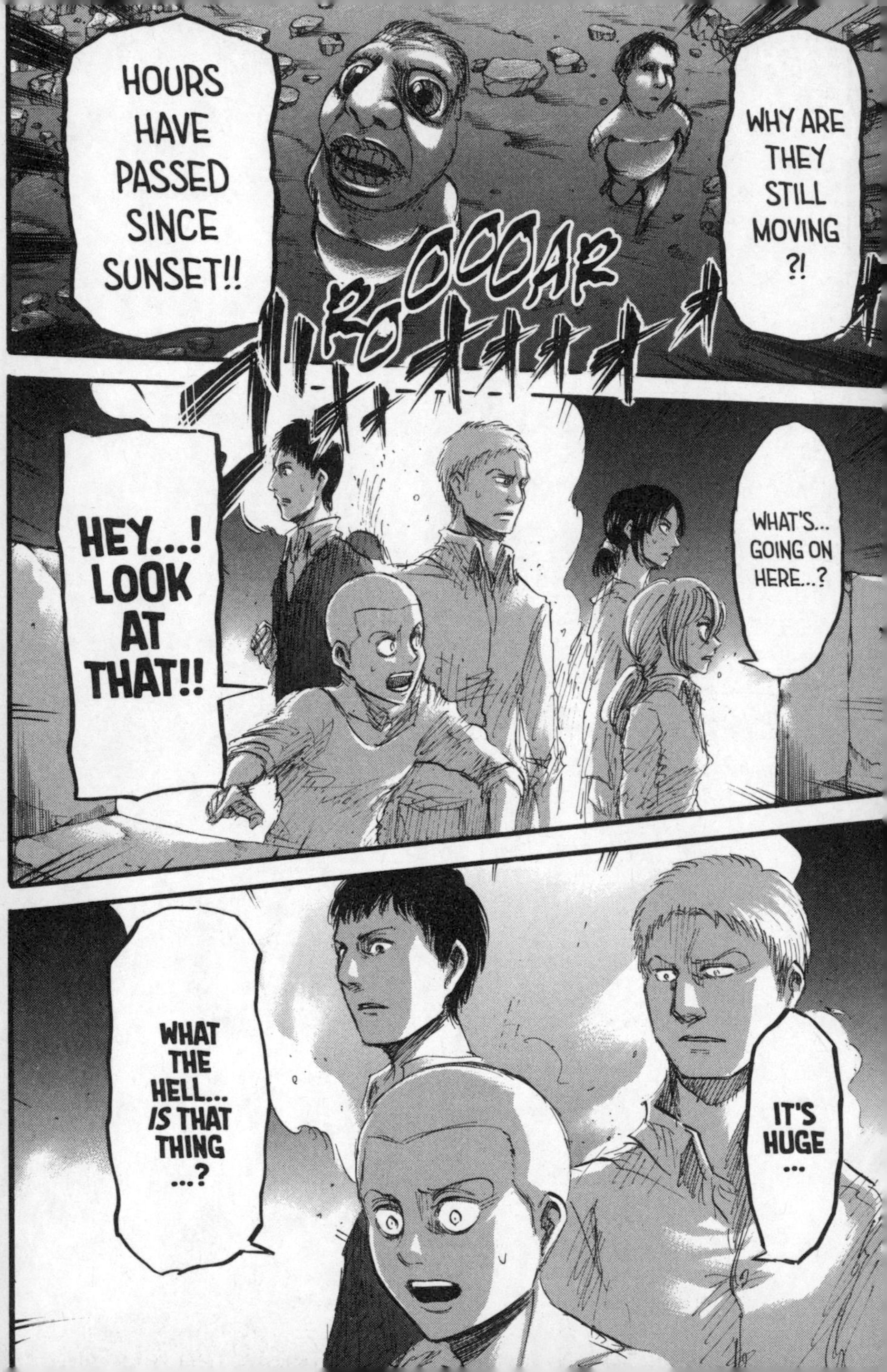
WHY ARE THEY STILL MOVING ?!
HOURS HAVE PASSED SINCE SUNSET!!
ROOOOAR
WHAT'S... GOING ON HERE...?
HEY...! LOOK AT THAT!!
IT'S HUGE ...
WHAT THE HELL... *IS* THAT THING ...?

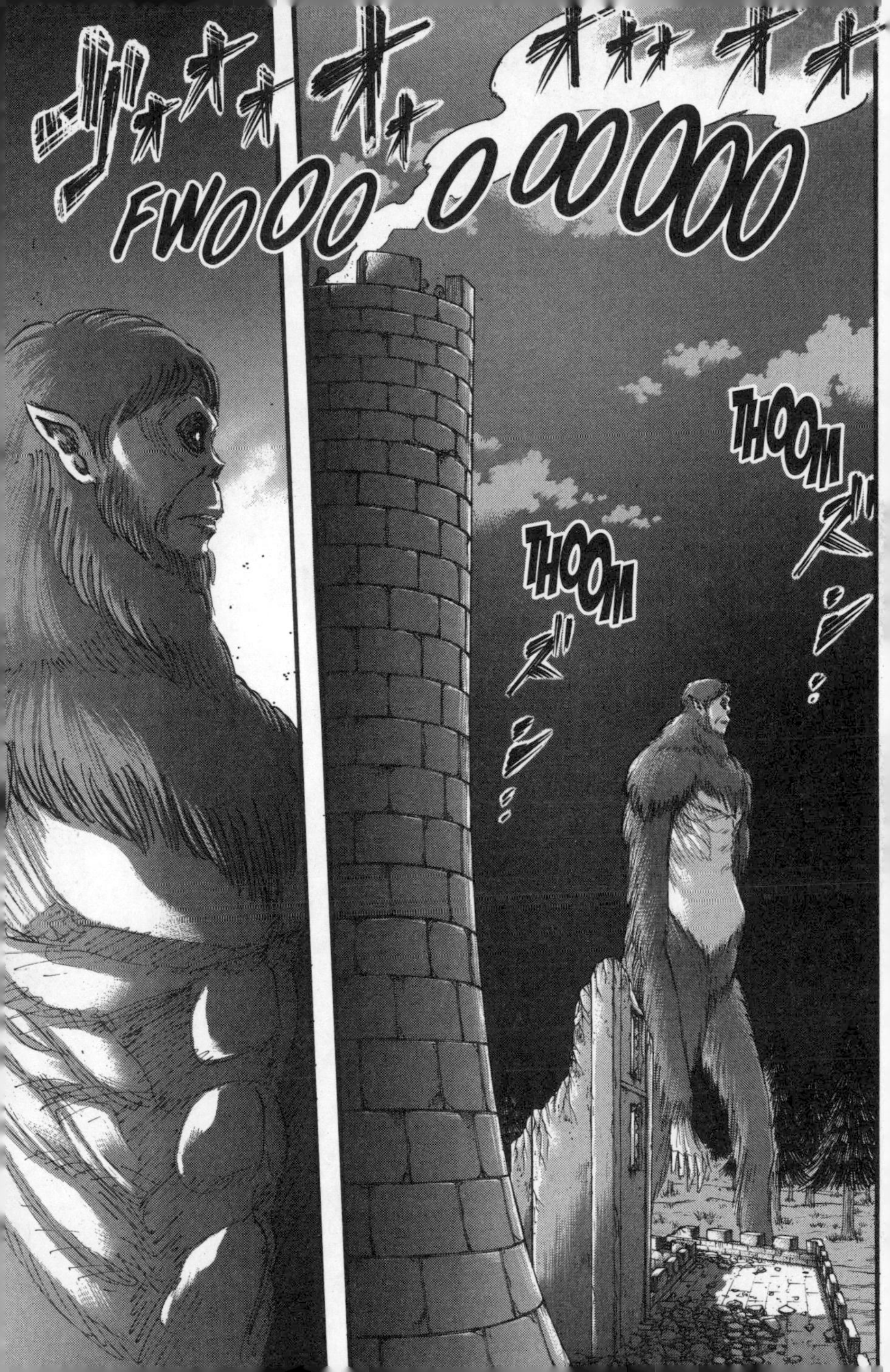
FWOOOOOOOOOOO
THOOM
THOOM

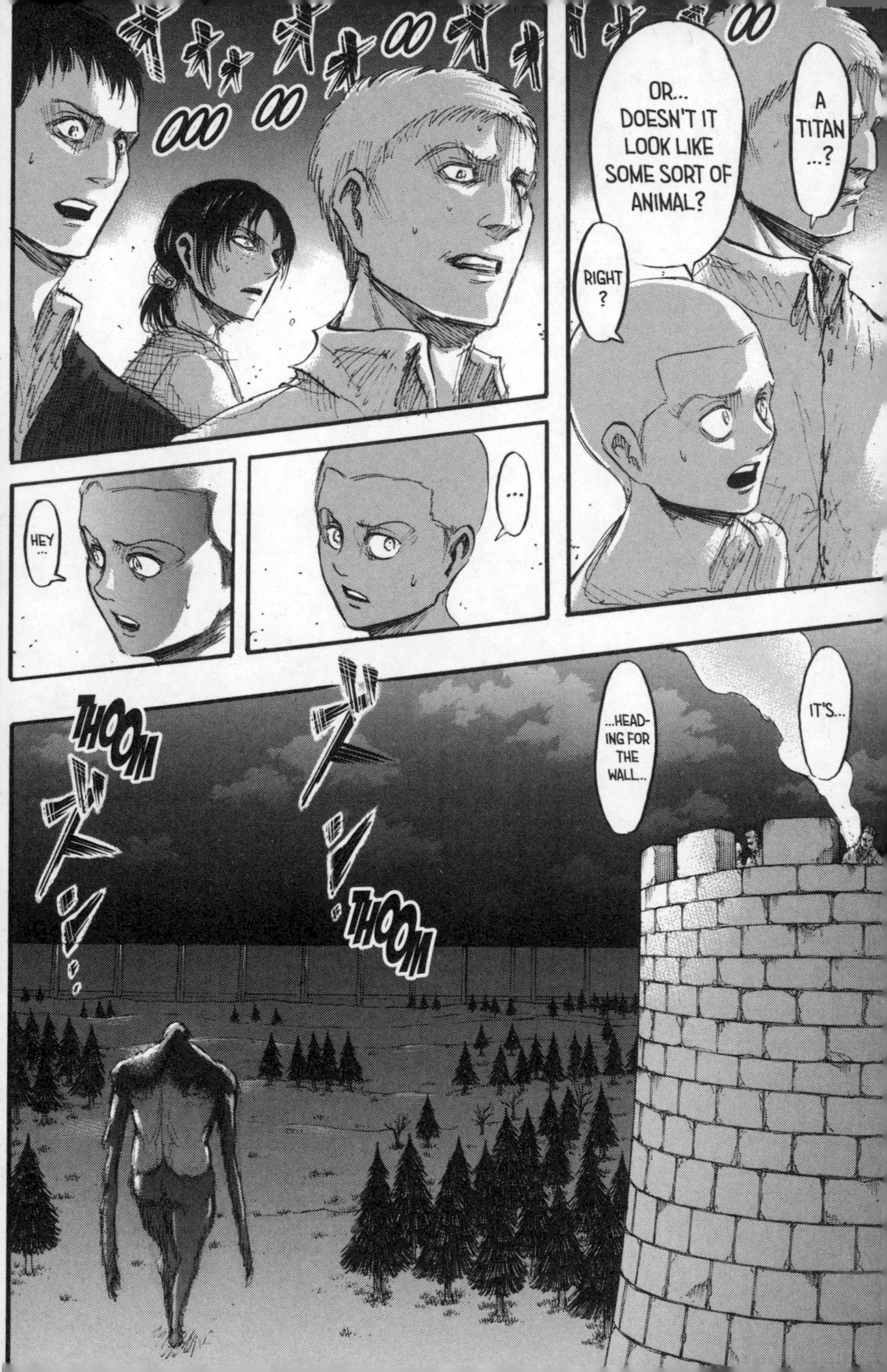
A TITAN ...?
OR... DOESN'T IT LOOK LIKE SOME SORT OF ANIMAL?
RIGHT ?
...
HEY ...
IT'S...
...HEAD-ING FOR THE WALL..
THOOM
THOOM

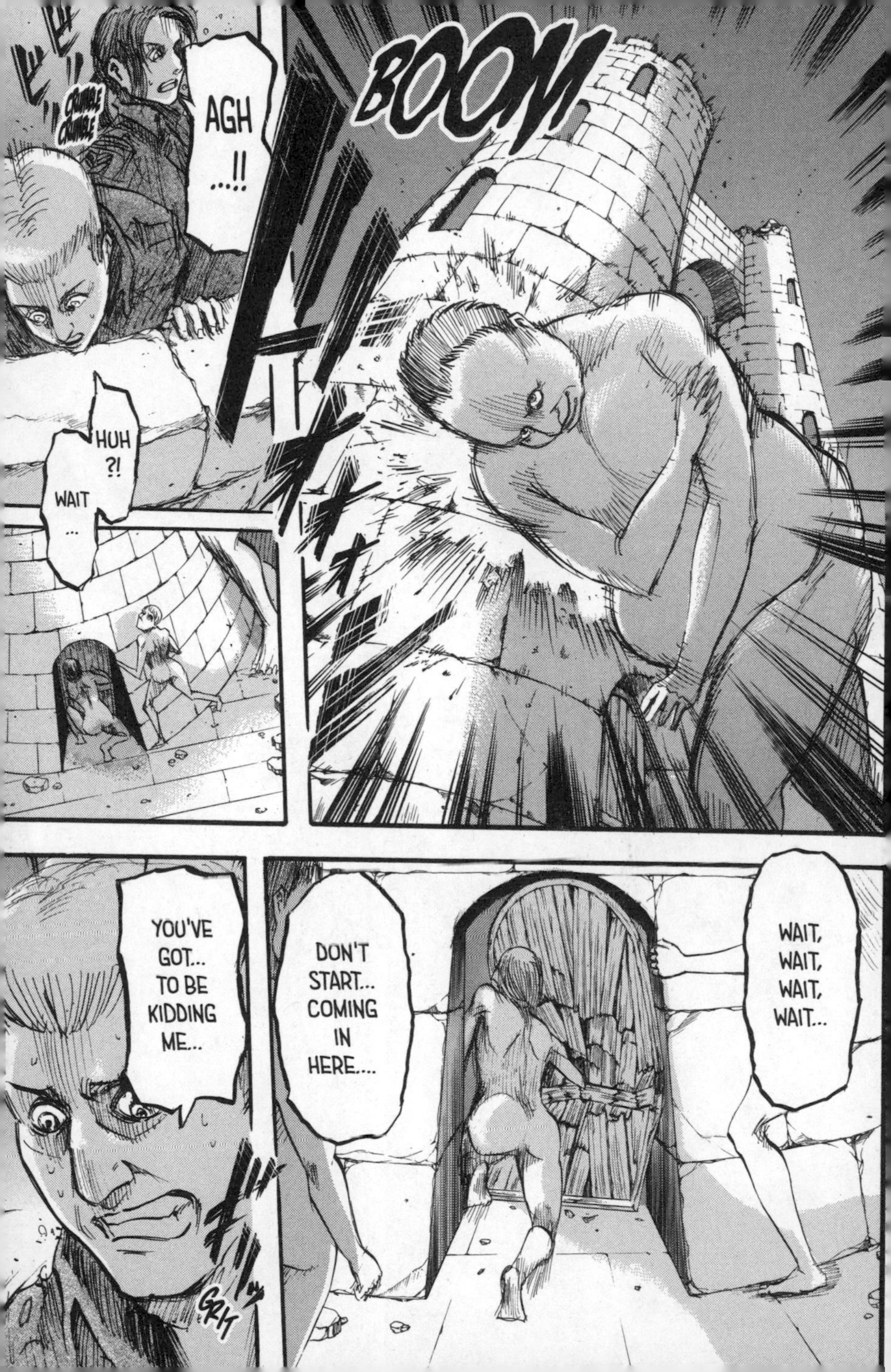
BOOM
CRUMBLE CRUMBLE
AGH ...!!
HUH?!
WAIT ...
WAIT, WAIT, WAIT, WAIT...
DON'T START... COMING IN HERE....
YOU'VE GOT... TO BE KIDDING ME...
GRK

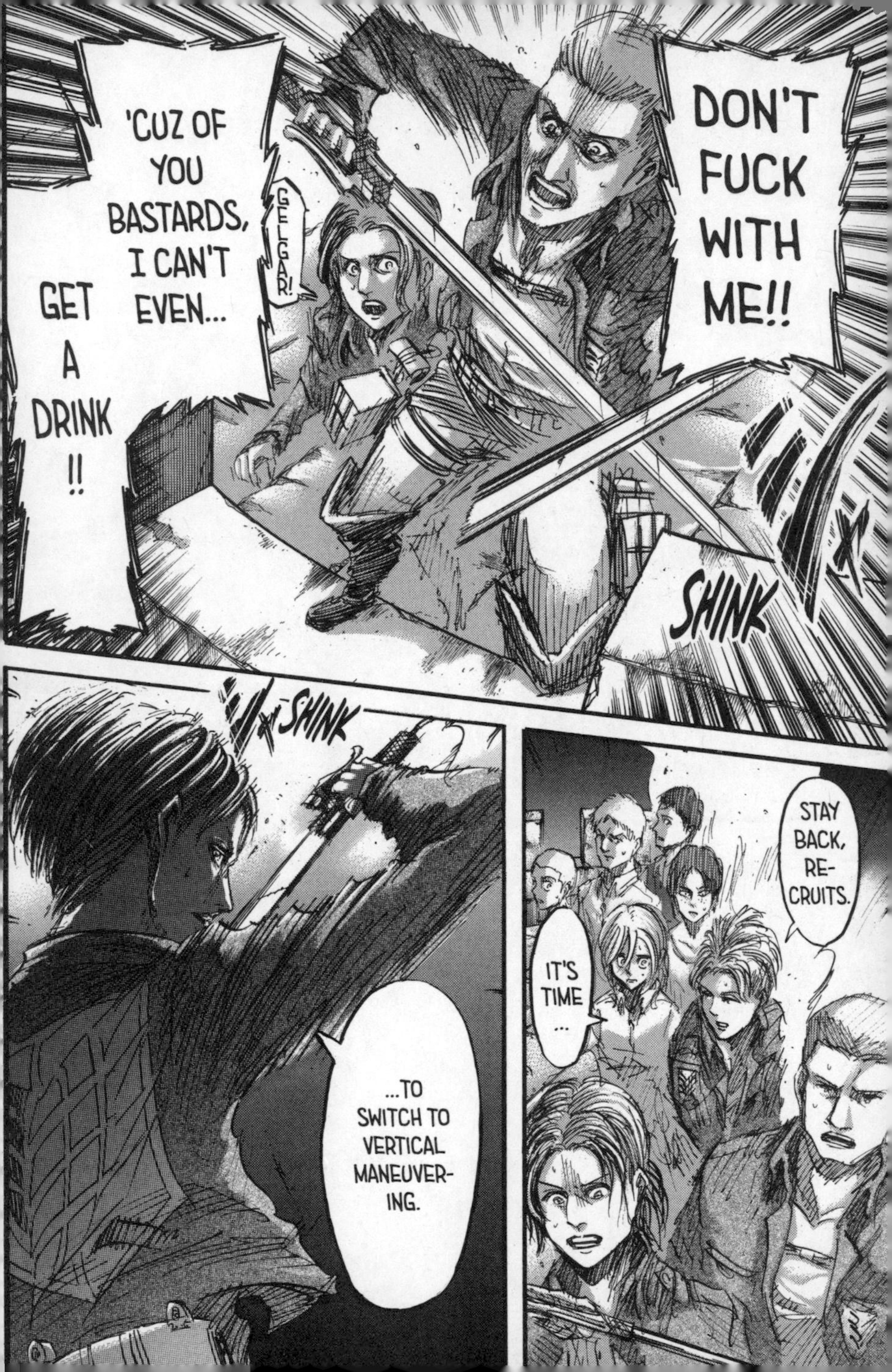
DON'T FUCK WITH ME!!
GELGAR!
'CUZ OF YOU BASTARDS, I CAN'T EVEN... GET A DRINK!!
SHINK
STAY BACK, RE-CRUITS.
IT'S TIME...
SHINK
...TO SWITCH TO VERTICAL MANEUVER-ING.

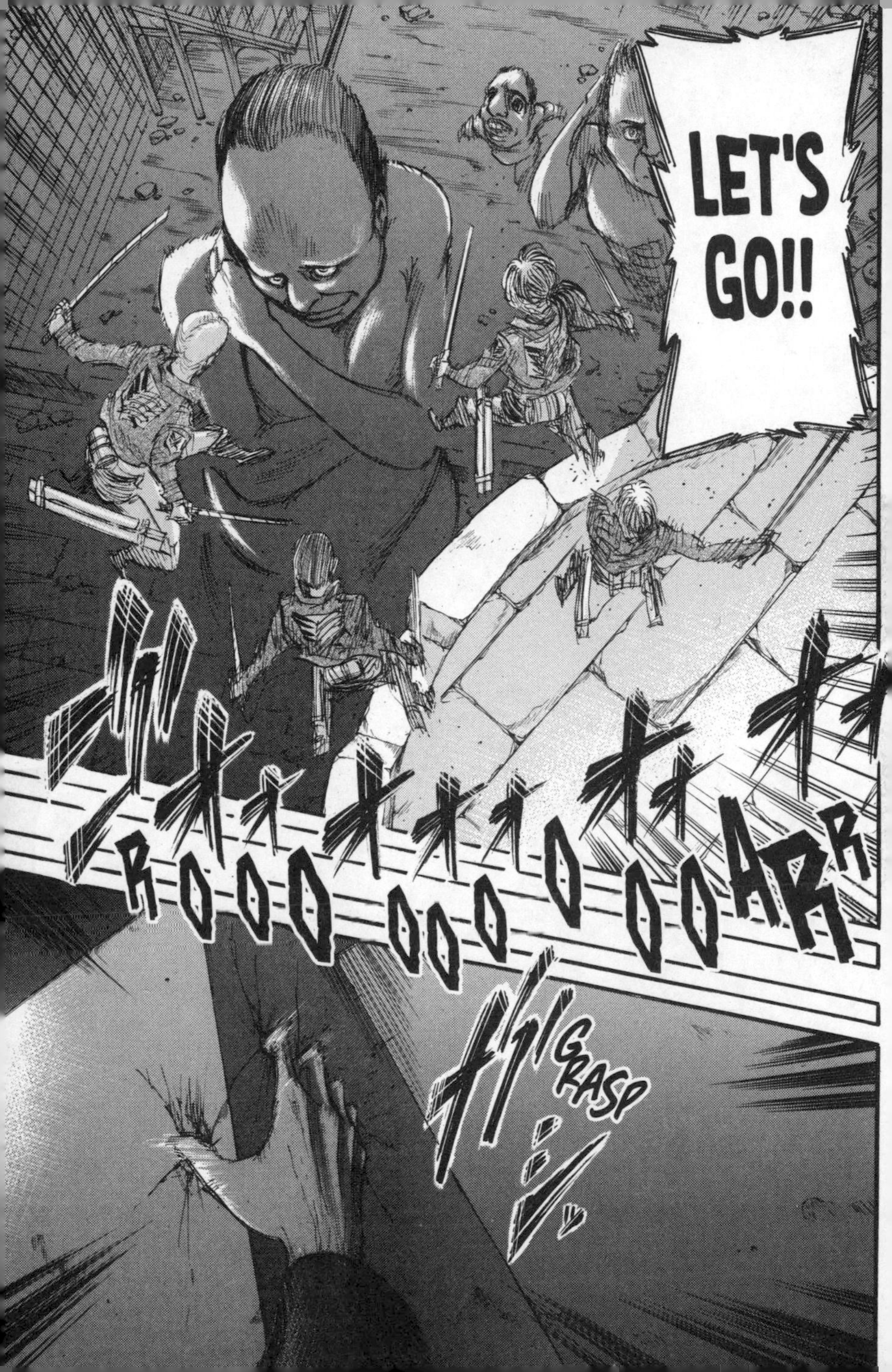
LET'S GO!!
ROOOOOOOOOARR
GRASP

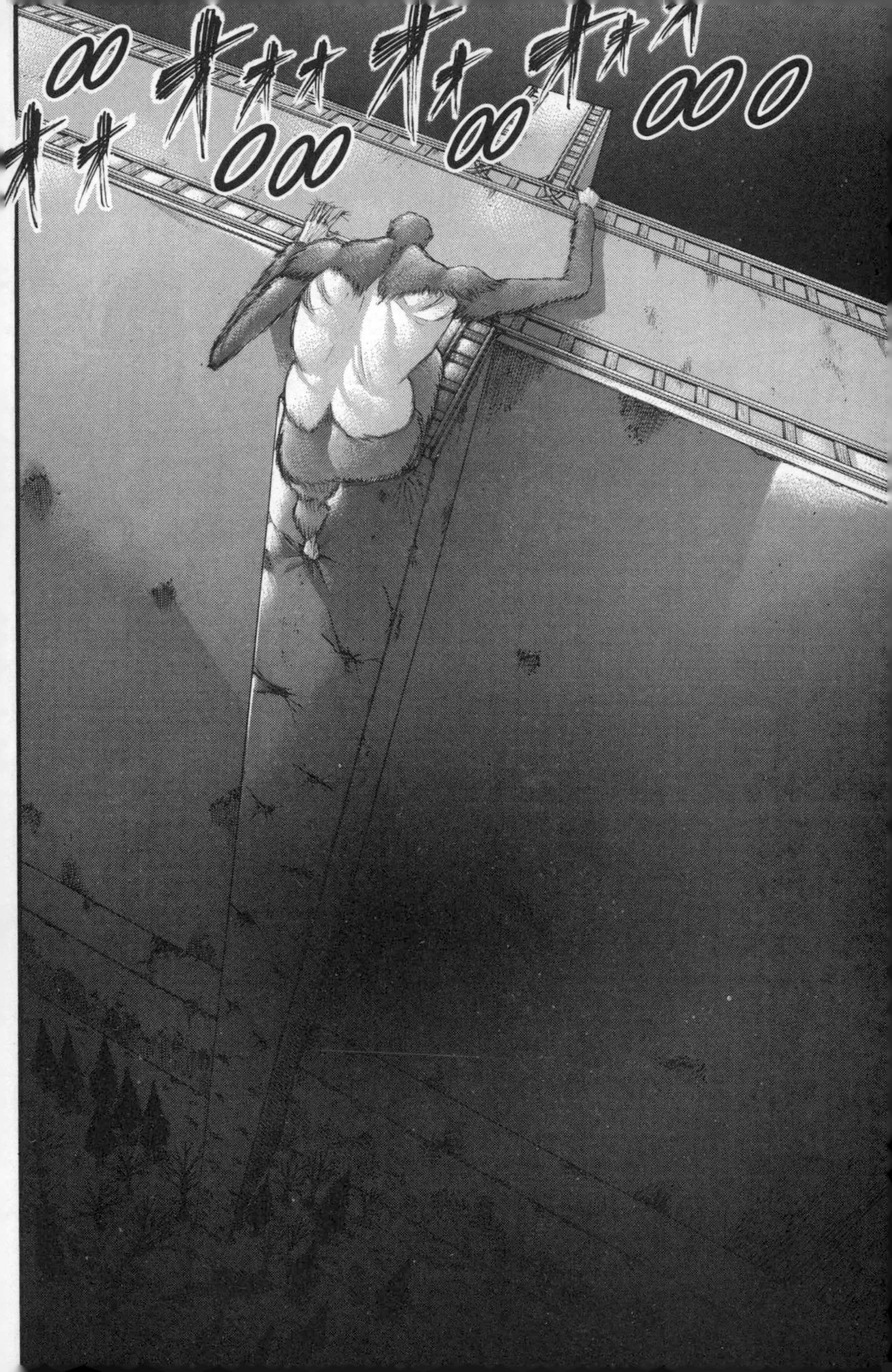
oo オオ オオオ ooo オオ oo オオヘ ooo o

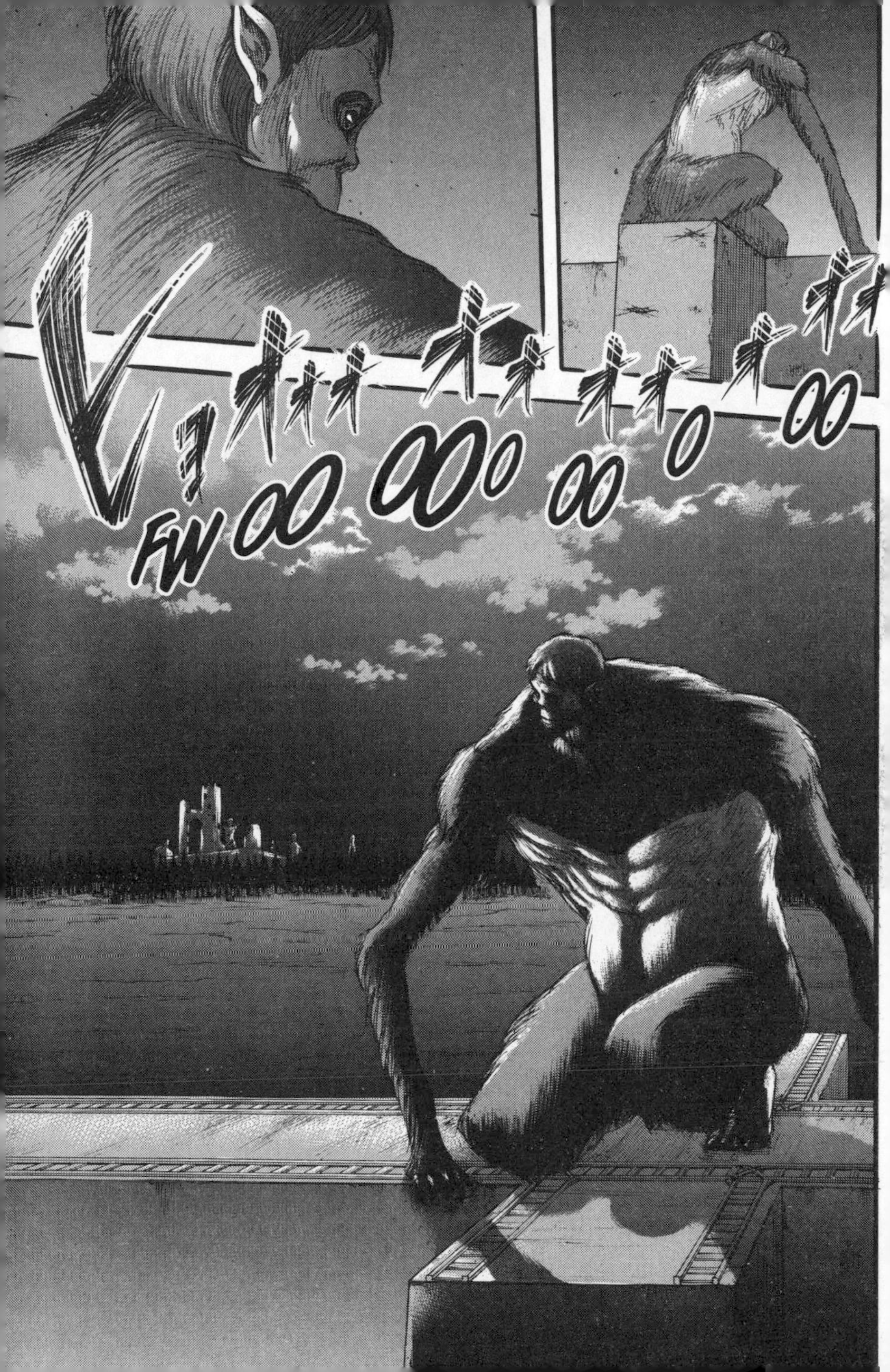
FWOOOOOOOOOO

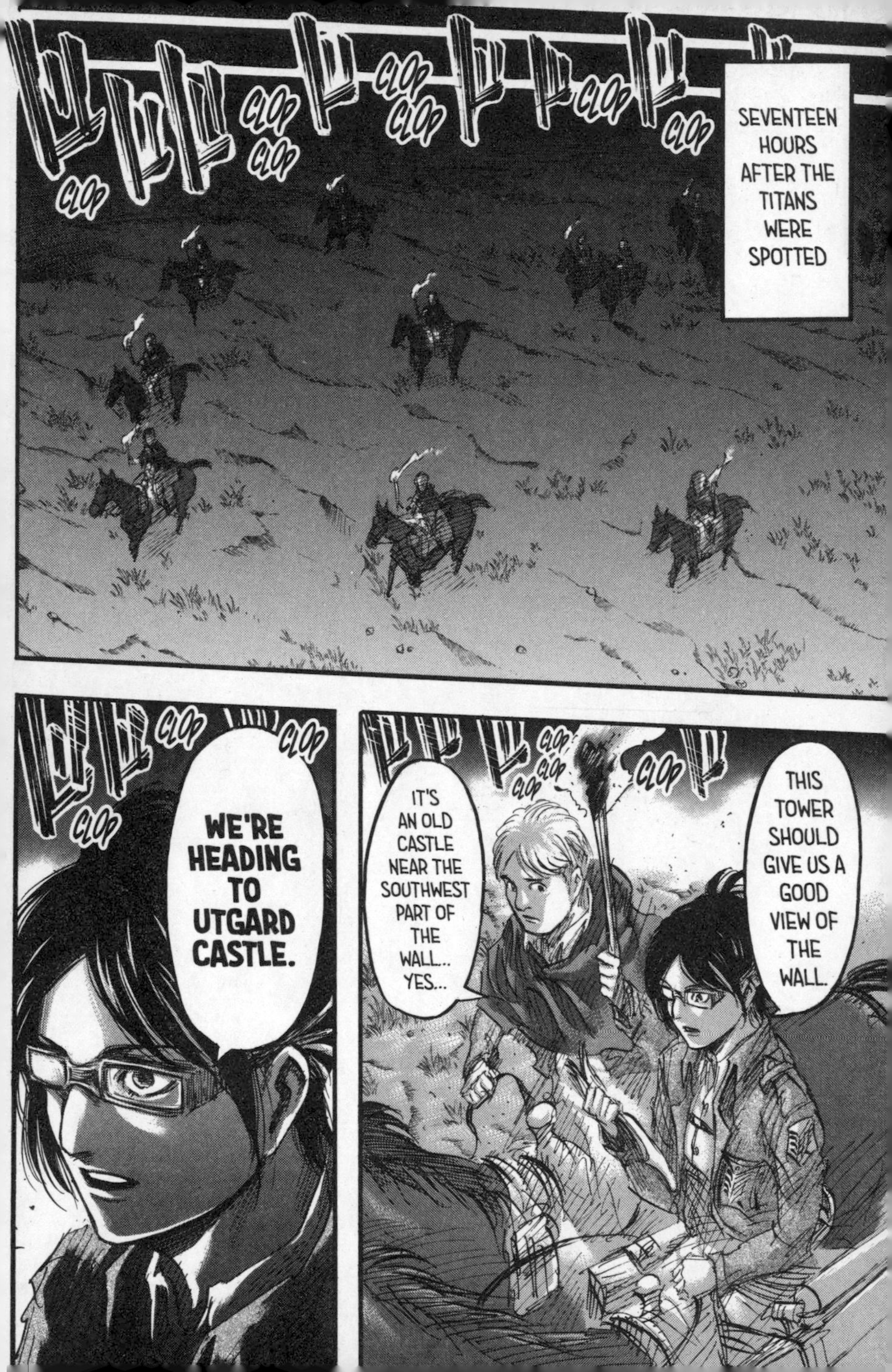
SEVENTEEN HOURS AFTER THE TITANS WERE SPOTTED
CLOP
CLOP
CLOP
CLOP
CLOP
CLOP
CLOP
CLOP
CLOP
CLOP
CLOP
CLOP
THIS TOWER SHOULD GIVE US A GOOD VIEW OF THE WALL.
IT'S AN OLD CASTLE NEAR THE SOUTHWEST PART OF THE WALL... YES...
CLOP
CLOP
CLOP
CLOP
WE'RE HEADING TO UTGARD CASTLE.

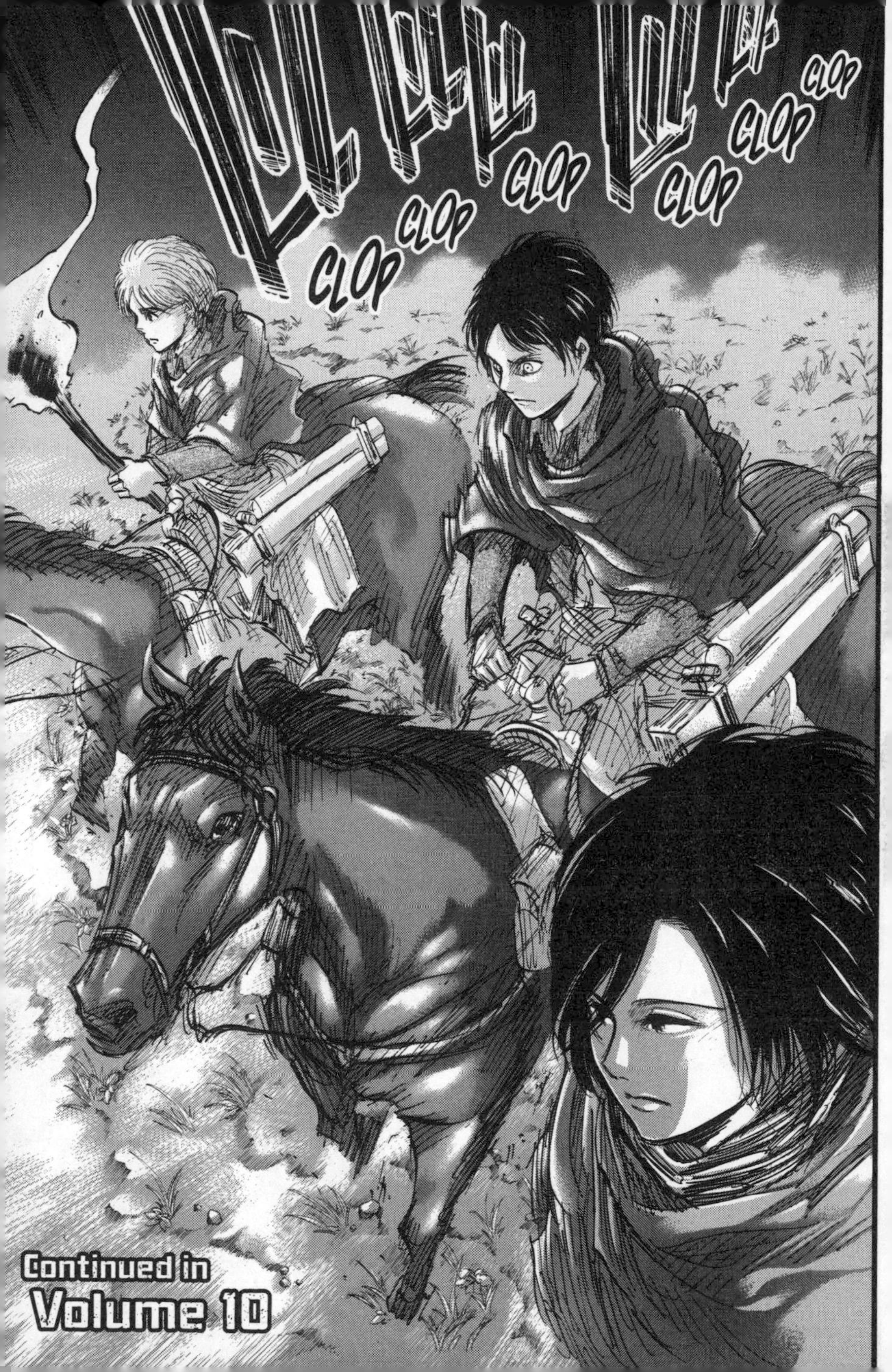
CLOP
CLOP
CLOP
CLOP
CLOP
CLOP
CLOP
Continued in
Volume 10

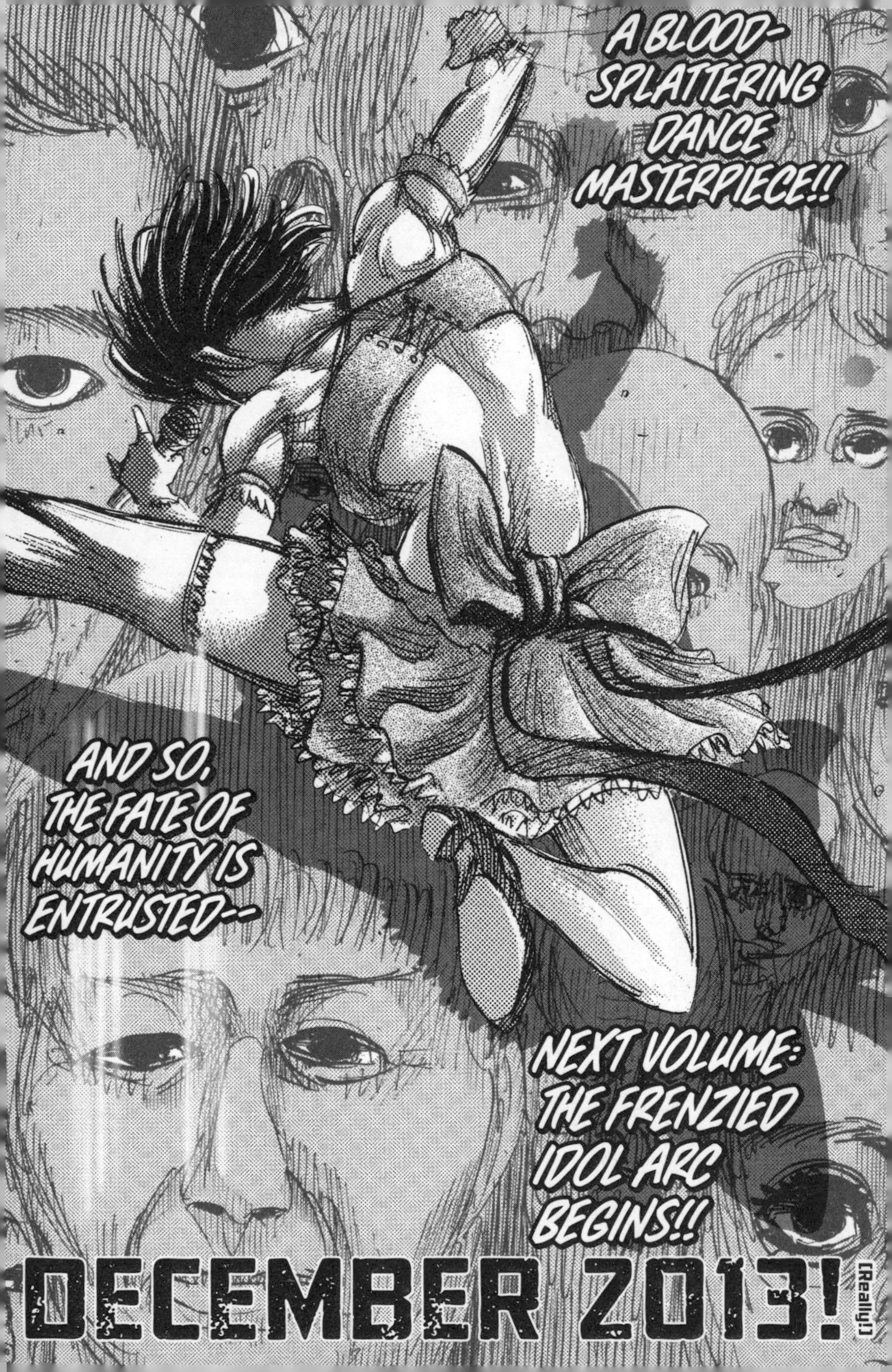
A BLOOD-SPLATTERING DANCE MASTERPIECE!!
AND SO, THE FATE OF HUMANITY IS ENTRUSTED--
NEXT VOLUME: THE FRENZIED IDOL ARC BEGINS!!
DECEMBER 2013!
[Really!]

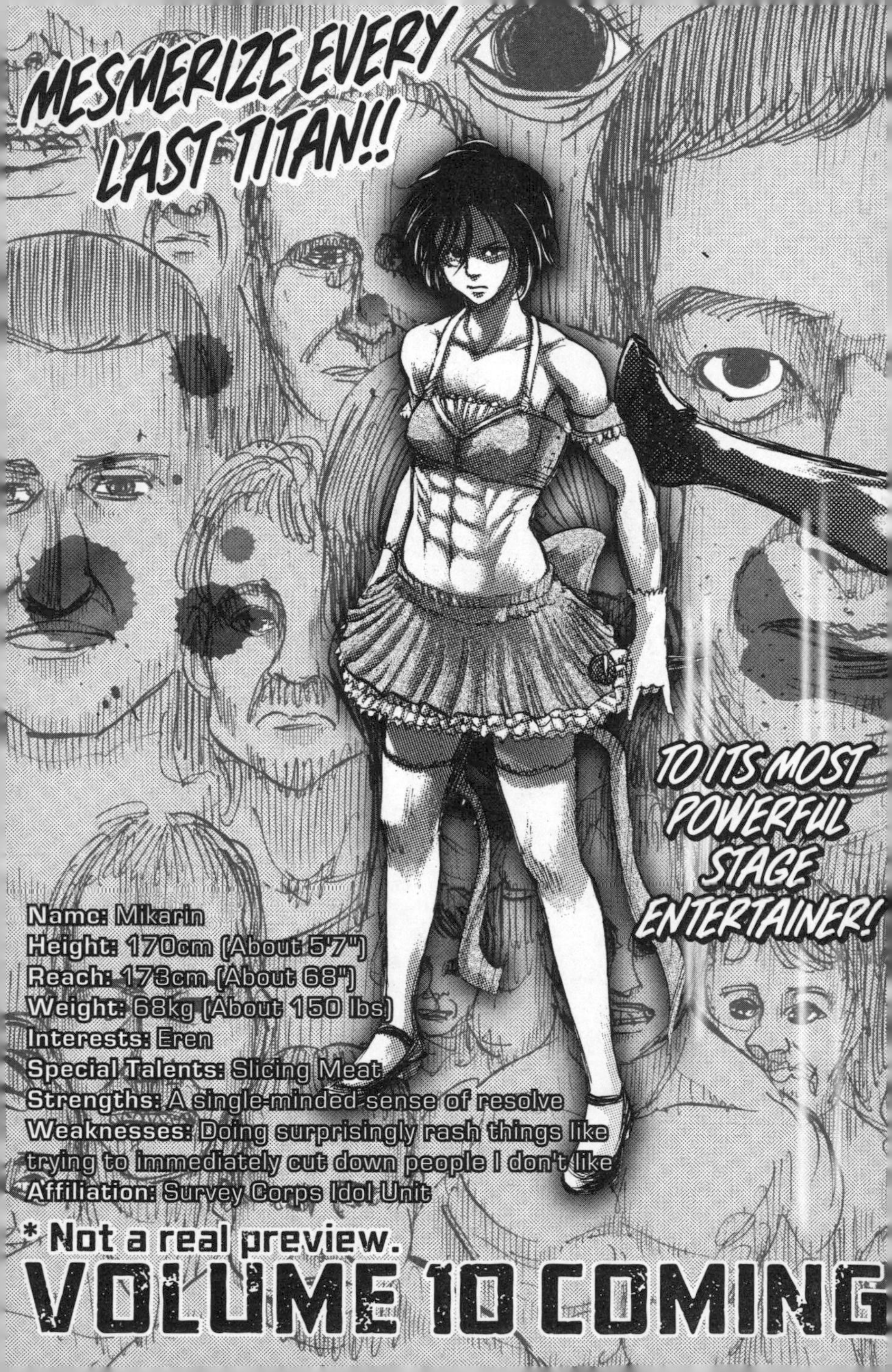
MESMERIZE EVERY LAST TITAN!!
TO ITS MOST POWERFUL STAGE ENTERTAINER!
Name: Mikarin
Height: 170cm (About 5'7")
Reach: 173cm (About 68")
Weight: 68kg (About 150 lbs)
Interests: Eren
Special Talents: Slicing Meat
Strengths: A single-minded sense of resolve
Weaknesses: Doing surprisingly rash things like trying to immediately cut down people I don't like
Affiliation: Survey Corps Idol Unit
* Not a real preview.
VOLUME 10 COMING

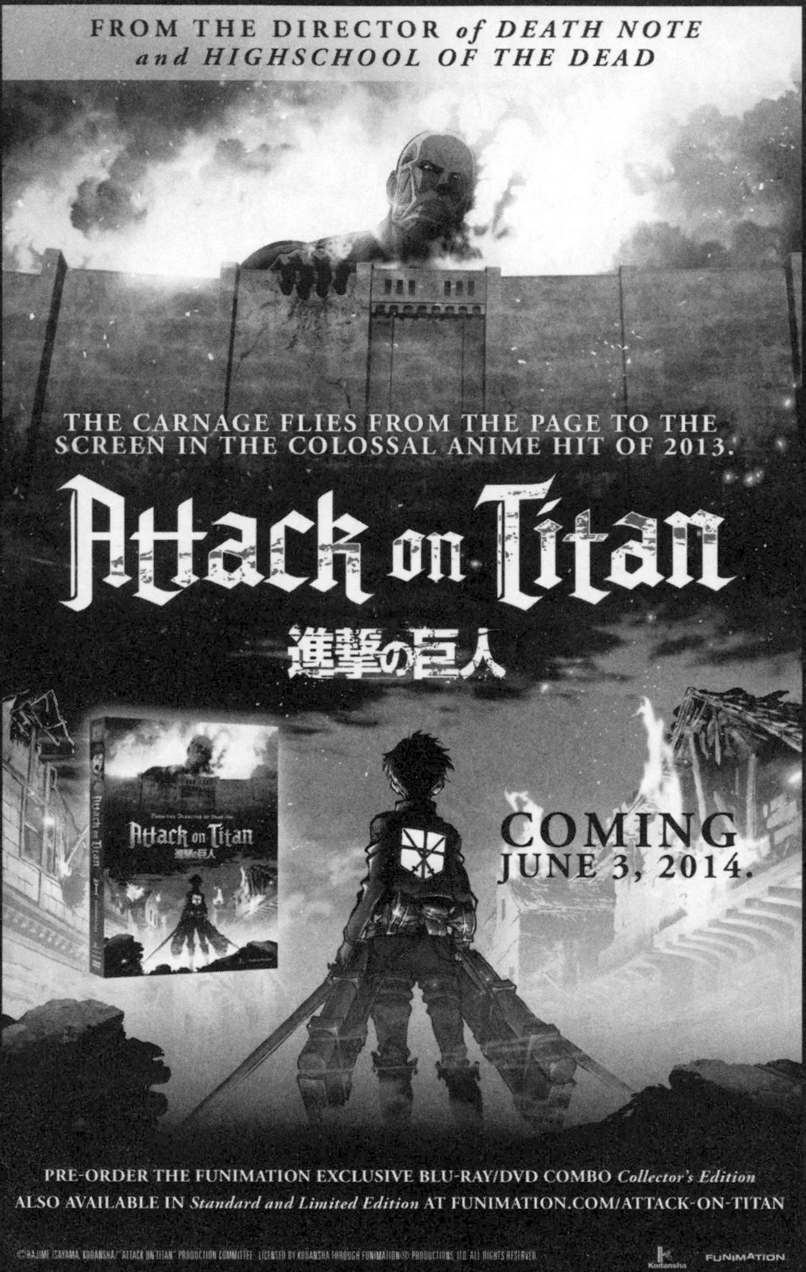
FROM THE DIRECTOR of DEATH NOTE
and HIGHSCHOOL OF THE DEAD
THE CARNAGE FLIES FROM THE PAGE TO THE SCREEN IN THE COLOSSAL ANIME HIT OF 2013.
Attack on Titan
進撃の巨人
Attack on Titan
進撃の巨人
COMING
JUNE 3, 2014.
PRE-ORDER THE FUNIMATION EXCLUSIVE BLU-RAY/DVD COMBO Collector's Edition
ALSO AVAILABLE IN Standard and Limited Edition AT FUNIMATION.COM/ATTACK-ON-TITAN
©HAJIME ISAYAMA, KODANSHA/"ATTACK ON TITAN" PRODUCTION COMMITTEE. LICENSED BY KODANSHA THROUGH FUNIMATION® PRODUCTIONS, LTD. ALL RIGHTS RESERVED.
Kodansha
FUNIMATION